BEYOND
THE
KHYBER
PASS

BEYOND
THE
KHYBER
PASS

The Road to British Disaster
in the First Afghan War

JOHN H. WALLER

RANDOM HOUSE NEW YORK

Library of Congress Cataloging-in-Publication Data
Waller, John H.
Beyond the Khyber Pass: the road to British disaster
in the First Afghan War/by John H. Waller.
p. cm.
Includes bibliographical references.
ISBN 0-394-56934-2
1. Afghan Wars. I. Title.
DS363.W35 1990 958.104'3—dc20 89-43431

Manufactured in the United States of America
Book design by J. K. Lambert
2 4 6 8 9 7 5 3
First Edition

For Greg

PREFACE

THERE IS AN OLD PERSIAN PROVERB: "HISTORY IS A MIRROR OF THE PAST/ And a lesson for the present." Afghans may ask their historical mirror on the wall, "Who is the fairest of them all?" and feel slighted when not named. But for all their shortcomings as a modern nation, they have learned how to resist the fatal embraces of unwanted violators. Their mirror has told them that independence from foreign aggressors has been preserved by their own determination to remain free whatever the cost, their inhospitable terrain and their knack for playing one covetous power against another.

This is the story of the British failure to have and to hold Afghanistan in the early 1840s as they competed with Czarist Russia for strategic advantage and while the two empires collided in Central Asia. The story is an eerie precurser of events today in which Soviet Russia rather than Great Britain pays the price for an ill-advised invasion of Afghanistan.

If the USSR consulted history before embarking on its adventure in Afghanistan in 1979, it did not listen to the lesson it told. It told how the British, concerned with protecting their Indian empire, saw a client Afghanistan as a buffer against Russian advances but learned too late that their actions only put India in greater jeopardy. The Soviet decision to invade Afghanistan in 1979 was similarly justified as a need to create a controlled buffer state on its important Central Asian border for strategic reasons—and also to preserve a beholden Communist regime as required by the Brezhnev Doctrine. The Soviet adversary was the United States, whose problems with Iran, Moscow feared, would lead to a compensatory military and political buildup in Pakistan and the Persian Gulf, if not ultimately in Afghanistan itself.

The Soviet Union in the late twentieth century and Britain in the nineteenth made the same fatal mistake of exaggerating their adversaries' intentions and the threats they posed, thus allowing themselves to be provoked into taking unwise action. Great Britain and Russia played the "Great Game," as Kipling so well described their rivalry in the nineteenth century, while the USSR became engaged in a Middle East "Cold War" with the United States in the latter part of the twentieth century— different labels for essentially the same kind of conflict. But the British and Russians both broke the rules by escalating the contest and resorting to armed intervention in Afghanistan. As a result, each in its own day reaped a whirlwind of Afghan opposition. The xenophobic and devoutly religious tribes, whose way of life was intertribal guerrilla warfare and whose God and Prophet stood staunchly behind each of them, momentarily abandoned their own blood feuds to declare Holy War against the infidel *ferangi,* the unbelieving foreigner who invaded them. In the mid-nineteenth century, Persia's claim on Herat and the Sikhs' claim on Peshawar lent a regional note to complicate the great-power rivalry between Great Britain and Russia. Today two million Afghan refugees in Iran and three million in Pakistan loom as regional problems that will persist to plague both countries.

In this story we shall see that the British invaded Afghanistan in 1839 confident of their military superiority over the primitive Afghan tribesmen. Their confidence was misplaced; homemade Afghan *jazails,* those long-barreled, smooth-bore muzzle loaders, could shoot farther and truer than British muskets. British artillery and cavalry were next to useless in the steep Afghan passes where much of the fighting took place. Today United States–made Stinger missiles fired from the shoulder by the tribal Mujahidin guerrillas—latter-day *jazails*—negate the effectiveness of Soviet-provided gunships, and the vaunted Soviet tanks are no more useful off the road in the mountains than British cavalry had been against the Afghans perched high above them in the rocks 150 years ago. Two foreign armies, modern for their time, somehow could not find a practical way to overcome the simple Afghan tribesman who resented the intrusions.

Both Great Britain and the Soviet Union suffered terrible losses for their missteps in Afghanistan. In 1842 the British estimated their casualties as being about fifteen thousand, and the Russian casualties were approximately the same. Political casualties are more difficult to estimate. British loss of face sustained in the First Afghan War contributed to two Sikh wars and the catastrophic mutiny of 1857 in the Indian Army. The full effects of the recent Soviet withdrawal of its army from Afghanistan in 1989 are yet to be known, but surely they will have an impact on Moscow's internal politics as well as its foreign relations.

Comparisons between historical events should never be taken too far; certainly there were many differences between the British experience in 1839–42 and the Soviet experience today. Yet the story of the First Afghan War, sometimes described as the worst military disaster suffered by the British until the fall of Singapore to the Japanese in World War II, as seen in the mirror of history has lessons for today—and tomorrow.

ACKNOWLEDGMENTS

I WOULD LIKE TO EXPRESS MY APPRECIATION AND GREAT RESPECT FOR THE several institutions whose resources I used in doing research for this book, particularly the United States Library of Congress; The British Library, including the India Office Library and Records; the National Portrait Gallery; The Tate Gallery; and the National Army Museum in London.

I am grateful to the Oriental Club of London for permitting me to use a photocopy of its fine portrait of Major General Sir William Nott as an illustration. I would also like to acknowledge the kindness of Mr. George Pottinger, author of *The Afghan Connection* and his publisher, Scottish Academic Press Ltd., in permitting me to reproduce the portrait of Eldred Pottinger. I owe thanks to Miss Pamela Magrath of London for being most helpful in enabling me to locate a collection of letters written by her great-grandfather, Captain Beauchamp Magrath, who served in the First Afghan War. Miss Helena Lawrence of London also deserves my deep gratitude for all she has done to assist me.

I thank Mr. Samuel Halpern for his assistance. My wife, Bobby, as usual graciously gave of her time and talent in helping to prepare my manuscript and has my thanks.

I admire and am grateful for the skill and patience of my editor, Mr. Robert Loomis, and appreciate the contributions of all the others who helped in the editing and production of this book.

CONTENTS

PROLOGUE

CAPTAIN ARTHUR CONOLLY OF THE BENGAL CAVALRY IS GENERALLY CRED-
ited with being the first to describe the nineteenth-century jousting between Imperial Russia and Great Britain in Central Asia as "the Great
Game," even though it was Rudyard Kipling who popularized this jolly-
sounding reference to intrigue and derring-do in his Victorian romances
of empire. The Game, in reality, was one of deadly serious political maneuver, espionage, long-range reconnaissance and, when things got out of
hand, bloody combat. The euphemism Great Game also captured the
devil-may-care adventurousness of many of the young players who sought
glory in the service of empire. They were latter-day crusaders who often
found the contest, and sometimes their careers, more compelling than the
cause.

The British played the Game to protect India, brightest jewel of the
empire, while for czars the object of the Game was to keep the British from
interfering with Russia's "Eastern Destiny." Both empires were determined to stake out buffer zones, or spheres of strategic influence and
commercial advantage. Trouble arose when the imperial ambition of one
interfered with that of the other, or when the natives resented their
homelands becoming the playgrounds for competition between foreign
infidels—impartially disparaged.

The playing fields of the Great Game, from the Caucasus to farthest
Central Asia, were the borderlands where the expanding Eastern empires
of Russia and Great Britain veered toward collision. Lending piquancy to
the rivalry, the areas in contention were virtually unknown to either side.
The players were all the more remarkable for braving impossible terrain
and inhospitable peoples, often with no more than a modest escort, or even
quite alone as agents in native disguise. A quick wit, bluff and charm were

their weapons. Decisions were often their own, guided by instinct and only the vaguest of instructions. Perhaps most remarkable of all was the youthfulness of such paladins, who in many cases found high adventure in the service of empire while still in their twenties and early thirties. Sadly, all too few saw old age; it was a deadly game. The deserts, plains and mountains of Central Asia were the stages for many bloody tableaux, the stuff of barrack-room legend.

The Great Game was uninhibited by rules. Kipling's Kim, that precocious orphan of Lahore, said matter-of-factly with the insight of a boy wise for his years, "When everyone is dead the Great Game is finished, not before." Kim can be forgiven his pessimism; the Great Game seemed endless in his day—a Central Asian Hundred Years' War. But there was one implied rule: the British and Russian armies must not meet in direct combat—the battlefields of Europe were reserved for that. As for the simple soldiers, who rarely shared in the glory of the Game but had to bear the horrors of fighting the natives, Kipling sent chills down the spines of his readers when he wrote all too vividly:

> *When you're wounded and left on Afghanistan's plains*
> *And the women come out to cut up what remains*
> *Jest roll to your rifle and blow out your brains*
> *An' go to your Gawd like a soldier.*

Plots were more ornate than Persian carpets, intrigue flourished in the labyrinths of citadels and seraglios, and danger lurked in every mountain pass.

Most extraordinarily, the soldiers who fought and died in the service of the East India Company defending British rule were for the most part native sepoys. Despite religious taboos against venturing beyond the Indus River and the oceans bounding India, and sometimes a rigorous climate they were unused to that killed as surely as bullets, the sepoys would also distinguish themselves in foreign campaigns far from home in behalf of their foreign masters.

The Great Game lasted for most of the nineteenth century, spreading eastward from Persia and Afghanistan to Tibet, not ending until 1907 when the Anglo-Russian agreement delineating boundaries and spheres of interest was concluded. This story, however, is confined to the first part of the nineteenth century and principally concerns Afghanistan, the fulcrum of competition between Imperial Russia and Great Britain. It is a cautionary tale in which the British, unduly obsessed with what they considered an immediate Russian threat to India, allowed themselves to become involved in an ill-considered, disastrous Afghanistan adventure.

The games of nations, traditional diplomacy or more Machiavellian political machinations, may be useful in carrying out foreign policy provided the objectives are realistic and the specific means used to achieve them are skillfully devised. But as seen in this tragic account of British efforts to defend India, the objectives were not realistic and the means used were inept. The story is all the more melancholy for the many brave men who lost their lives because of the folly of a few.

The arena where this story takes place begins in the west with Persia,* since antiquity a land-bridge between the Near East—the holy lands of the Mediterranean littoral—and Central Asia stretching toward the Orient. The high plateau of Persia is wedged as a keystone between the Arab world of Mesopotamia to the west and the mountains of Afghanistan to the east. To the south the Persian Gulf—or Arabian Gulf, depending upon the point of view—serves as a moat separating the ancient Indo-European culture of Persia from the Semitic culture of the Arabian Peninsula, and the predominantly Shia sect of Islam in Persia from the Sunni sect of Arabia.

The Caucasus Mountains, spanning the isthmus between the Black and Caspian seas, is a bridge between Persia and Russia to the north, generally separating Islam from Christendom. In the nineteenth century Persia posed a tempting target for the Russians, thrusting southward through the Caucasus. But just as Russia, a land power, encroached on Persia from the north, Great Britain, a sea power, exerted pressure on the shah's realm from the Persian Gulf in the south. Control of the Gulf was vital to the security of India and for the protection of British maritime commerce. Persia was strategically important to India as a land-bridge, both to the Arab lands stretching westward to Egypt, coveted by Napoleon since the end of the eighteenth century, and to the Russian empire, expanding inexorably downward through the Caucasus at the expense of Persian suzerainty in the region.

Closer to India, and thus even more immediately important to the subcontinent's security, was Afghanistan, whose passes—piercing the Hindu Kush Mountains running like a spine through the center of the country—had since ancient times admitted a succession of invaders who poured onto the plains of India. The northern slopes of the Hindu

*The term *Persis,* or *Persia,* used by the ancient Greeks, was probably derived from the Persian word *Fars,* (or *Pars*), which today applies only to the southern province of Iran, whose capital is Shiraz. *Iran,* from more ancient times, was what Persians called their country, and this term was revived as the official name by the Pahlavi dynasty in recent times.

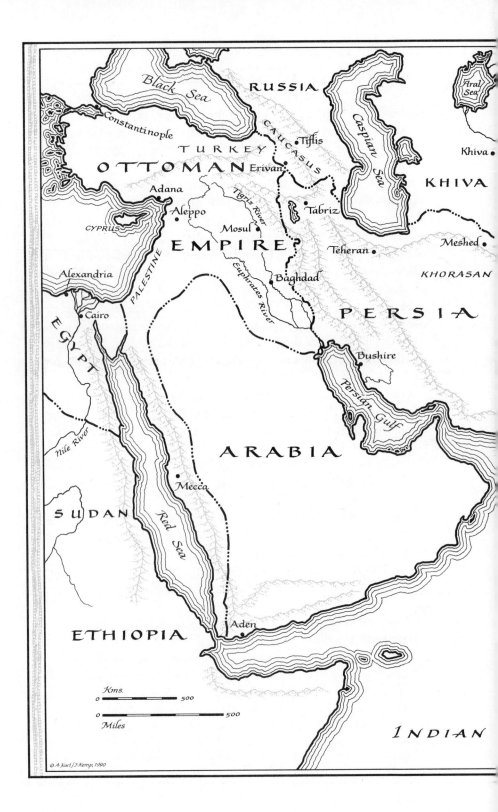

Black Sea

RUSSIA

Aral Sea

Constantinople

CAUCASUS

Tiflis

Caspian Sea

Khiva

TURKEY

KHIVA

OTTOMAN

Erivan

Adana

Tigris River

Tabriz

Aleppo

Mosul

Meshed

CYPRUS

EMPIRE

Téheran

KHORASAN

Alexandria

PALESTINE

Euphrates River

Baghdad

PERSIA

Cairo

EGYPT

Bushire

Nile River

Persian Gulf

ARABIA

SUDAN

Mecca

Red Sea

ETHIOPIA

Aden

Kms.

0   500

0   500

Miles

INDIAN

© A·Karl/J·Kemp, 1990

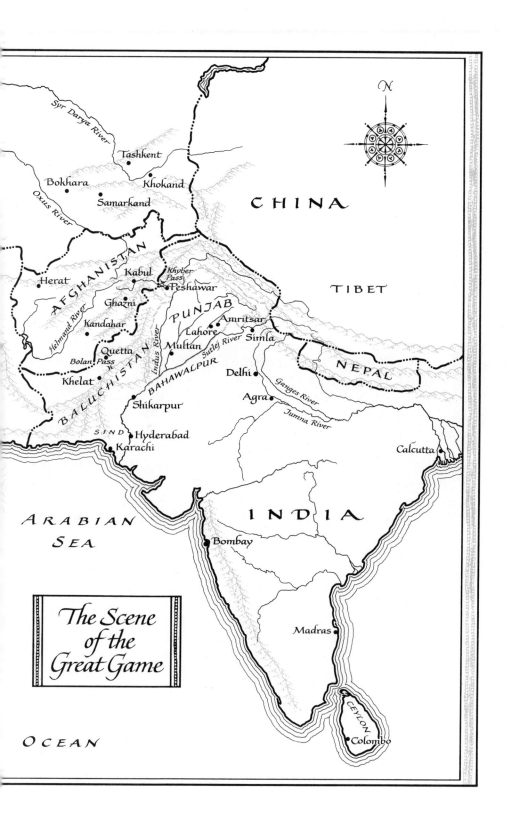

The Scene
of the
Great Game

Kush subside in the Turkestan plains east of the Caspian Sea, long the homeland of Turkish-Mongol predators, while the mighty range's eastern terminus collides with the lofty Pamir and Karakorum ranges to form a jumbled knot of some of the world's highest mountains, often called "the roof of the world." Here Afghanistan meets the western end of China and the northernmost point in the Indian subcontinent.

Frequent Afghan sorties into the Punjab, the "Land of the Five Rivers" on Moghul India's northwestern borders, had worried the East India Company, whose strategic interests and commercial ambitions demanded the protection of Delhi and unfettered access to the rivers of the Indus Valley. Then, early in the nineteenth century, British India found itself facing a new threat—rising Sikh power closer to home in the Punjab. Just as Russia had viewed the neighboring Persian empire as an antagonist in the Caucasus, the British now became apprehensive about a remarkable leader named Ranjit Singh, who had for the first time unified the Sikhs. Ranjit Singh, whose religion, an offshoot of Hinduism originally dedicated to peace but now militant in its preachings, aspired to the Delhi throne of the enfeebled Moghul emperor. If this ambition were realized it would bring the Sikhs into conflict with the British, yet the Punjab could instead prove a useful barrier against invasion if the Company played its hand skillfully with Ranjit Singh.

The defense of India was inseparable from the wider spectrum of European politics. While Napoleon Bonaparte's occupation of Egypt in 1798— an exotic extension of the continental wars—sounded alarms in Calcutta and London, the great British Admiral Horatio Nelson's decisive defeat of the French fleet at Abukir Bay off Alexandria and the French withdrawal from Egypt in 1801 removed the French threat from that quarter. But the Treaty of Tilsit in 1807 revived British fears of the French, even more formidable as allies of the Russians. When Napoleon was rowed to a raft moored in the middle of the River Niemen near Tilsit to embrace Czar Alexander I, it was a signal that both rulers had found common cause against the British in Europe—and perhaps in the East as well.

The Treaty of Tilsit did not specifically mention India, but at the East India Company's seat of government in Calcutta it was easy to imagine the worst. Napoleon, it appeared, was now free to march through Persia and Afghanistan in the footsteps of Alexander the Great, and with Russian acquiescence or assistance claim the prize of India. Napoleon, in fact, raised with Czar Alexander the possibility of an Indian campaign, and rumors of this had reached the East India Company by early 1808. But even if more sober reasoning rejected such alarming ideas, there seemed at the time cause enough to worry about the French, who for years had been troublesome rivals of the British in south India and had now become diplomatically aggressive in Persia.

Russia too had long cast covetous eyes toward India. As early as the eighteenth century, Catherine the Great considered an expedition against the subcontinent, and, more recently in January 1801, her son, Czar Paul, dispatched an army of twenty thousand Cossacks to invade India. That the force met with disaster crossing the Volga River did not discourage Paul from proposing to Napoleon a joint Franco-Russian army to march on India through Afghan passes. Napoleon, having more respect than Paul for the rigors of the Afghan mountains and the marksmanship of Afghan tribesmen, was not interested; the ambitious idea died with the czar when one of his officers strangled him.

The British were understandably apprehensive about the new Franco-Russian alliance, not only on the Continent but also as it affected the Near and Middle East, with Turkey and Persia at immediate risk and India in potential jeopardy. Must the British now consider India's first line of defense to be the Caucasus Mountains, a natural barrier between Russia and Persia? If so, the British relationship with the shah of Persia had to be strengthened. Or should the line be drawn more conservatively farther east at Herat, the western entrance to Afghanistan from Persia—gateway to the traditional military high road to India? And certainly the sudden rise of a unified Sikh nation had created a new situation even closer to India. The Sikh leader, Ranjit Singh, one-eyed "Lion of the Punjab," could be a force for either good or mischief.

But how had it come about that an English trading company in India had become the cutting edge of British imperial progress; how did the Honorable East India Company, from its inception dedicated to turning a profit for its shareholders, find itself a player in the greater game of nations driven by the exigencies of intercontinental high politics? Writers on India have had a tendency to refer interchangeably to "the British" and "the Company." In fact, a strange kind of dyarchy had evolved by the nineteenth century, making it difficult to differentiate between the two. British historian Thomas Macaulay at the time aptly described this anomaly as "the strangest of all governments designed for the strangest of all empires."

The creation of the Honorable East India Company by stalwarts with ledger book in one hand and sword in the other was a monument to capitalist enterprise, an example of England's devotion to trade, its life-blood. Founded for the purpose of gaining direct access to the spices of the East without paying the exorbitant prices charged by already entrenched Dutch and Portuguese East Indies traders, the Company was chartered at the dawn of the seventeenth century by Queen Elizabeth. Despite its pretentious name, "The Governor and Company of Merchants of London Trading into the East Indies," it was not formed by merchant princes. It was a company of shopkeepers. There were Ralph Hamer, tailor; James Deane, draper; and some two hundred others like them willing to gamble their modest savings. No more humble assemblage has set in motion so grand a destiny.

The metamorphosis of the East India Company from such modest beginnings to the greatest empire the world has known was truly astonishing. The first Companyman to reach India was Captain William Hawkins, whose ship, *Hector,* dropped anchor at the mouth of the Tapti River on India's west coast in 1608. He narrowly escaped assassination by the Portuguese in the nearby port of Surat before making his way to the court of Moghul Emperor Jehangir in Agra. Thus began a tenuous existence as the Company clung to coastal toeholds, trading stations or "factories," which managed to collect cargoes for company ships despite harassment by capricious Moghul rulers and hostile Portuguese rivals. Major regional trading centers were eventually established in Bombay, Madras and Calcutta, where the Company gradually acquired a degree of autonomy as it outgunned the rival Portuguese and Dutch fleets in the Indian Ocean and extracted progressively more concessions from Indian native rulers.

Native watchmen employed to guard Company factories were replaced by trained soldiers capable of doing battle in defense of the Company. There were predatory Indians, pirates, Dutch raiders, even English freebooters to be kept at bay. But the greatest challenge was posed by the French, who had established themselves in Pondicherry just south of Madras on India's southeast coast. The two rivals fought hard and long for preeminence in India in an exotic extension of the European War of Austrian Succession from 1740 to 1748, then again in 1750. Further Company conflicts arising from the Seven Years' War in Europe eliminated the French as serious competitors when a rising young Company star, Robert Clive, defeated the French-backed Nawab of Bengal in the Battle of Plassey near Calcutta in 1757. This was a watershed; no longer would Englishmen be intimidated by the French or be suppliants of the Moghuls. Inexorably the Company was achieving dominion over India, not as a result of planned empire-building, but more "in a fit of absent mind," as one commentator put it. Some one thousand or so Company administrators would soon find themselves ruling nearly a fifth of the world's population, commanding a powerful army—second only in size to that of Russia—conducting its own foreign affairs with much of Asia, and governing a land teeming with exotic peoples as different from each other as they were from the English.

In recognition of its growing national stake in this enterprise, the British government finally recognized its own need to oversee the East India Company and devise a formula with which to do so. The Crown and Parliament would henceforth have their say in the Company's expanding raj as a result of new legislation. In 1773 a Regulating Act banned the excesses of many Company officials, the "nabobs," who had become scandalously rich by trading for their own personal account. More significantly, in the India Act of 1784 Parliament imposed on the Company a Board of Control. This six-person body, which included two ministers of the Crown, did not govern but closely monitored the Company and now had a powerful influence on how the Company's Court of Directors in London guided Indian affairs. Policy was somehow arrived at by consensus reached between the chairman of the Court of Directors representing the stockholders and the government's president of the Board of Control. A Secret Committee of the Court of Directors served as an executive committee that issued orders to the Company's governor general in Calcutta. The eighteenth-century statesman Edmund Burke summed it up: "The East India Company did not seem to be merely a company formed for the extension of British commerce, but in reality was a delegation of the whole power and sovereignty of this kingdom sent into the East."

The governor general, who governed from his seat in Calcutta as head of the government of Bengal, or the Bengal Presidency, as it was known, had authority over the governors of the other two regional presidencies, Madras and Bombay. Similarly, the commander in chief of the Bengal Army had authority over the armies of the other two presidencies. The British-officered native troops of the Indian armies, 250,000-strong by the Victorian period of the nineteenth century, were augmented by a few royal regiments sent from England—Queen's regiments—made up of purely British units temporarily posted to India. Career officers of the Indian Army and those of the queen's army often did not get along. Each had a different professional culture. Moreover, the Indian Army paid better wages, which of course caused jealousy on the part of the queen's officers.

If Robert Clive had launched the Company into an imperial adventure by his victory at Plassey, Lord Wellesley gave it new impetus during his tenure as governor general from 1798 to 1805. Devoted to the idea of total British hegemony over the entire subcontinent, he set about eliminating pockets of Indian rule and remaining vestiges of French influence. By crushing Tipu Sultan, ruler of Mysore state in the south, at the Battle of Seringapatam, he eliminated a source of intrigue fomented by the French and cleared the way for Company annexation of much of south India. He also depleted the Company treasury in the process. For this the Company recalled Wellesely and imperial momentum was briefly arrested by the merchant-minded directors. The spirit of the shopkeeper was still alive in London, if not among the more adventurous Companymen in India.

While it was inevitable that the British government would exercise closer control of the Company, whose imperial aggrandizement had become costly and its international implications complex, a greater involvement in Indian affairs had its drawbacks as far as Companymen in India were concerned. The soldiers and civil administrators were still an independent breed. Without the leavening influence of wives and families, traditionally discouraged from coming to India, the old Companymen had been a roistering lot who incurred terrible personal debt, drank too much, gamboled with Indian mistresses and played hard at manly sports, particularly those involving horses and hunting. Even the shocking incidence of early death from disease, battle or simple overindulgence had not dampened their spirits. They assumed that life in India was a fragile thing and one should live it to the hilt; riches to be made and the glory to be earned made it seem worthwhile. Now the stultifying burdens of bureaucracy were creeping in, and missionaries, arriving in ever-increasing numbers, stood disapprovingly on watch. By establishing "British principles," imposing British institutions and preaching a faith alien to the natives, it was hoped that they could be uplifted. In fact, all this only drove a wedge between the British and the Indian people on whom they depended. The earlier swashbuckling merchants left to their own devices may have been guilty of shocking excesses, but they at least had been closer to the natives and had fostered a mutual trust essential to effective government.

By the nineteenth century the Company gained its profits more from internal revenues than from foreign trade. India was now an imperial appendage, not simply a bountiful market and source of raw materials. It was a costly responsibility that had to be supported by taxes levied in the land and gathered, Moghul-style, by collectors. Wars of pacification had been particularly expensive; three wars against the militantly nationalistic Hindus of central India, the Marathas, had drained the treasury. Now the imperial ambitions of Russia and France seemed to pose still another threat to India and promise even more crushing defense costs.

In 1807, as the century got under way, the Company prepared to receive a new governor general: Gilbert Elliot, better remembered as Lord Minto, who had a reputation for being concerned with matters of budget, not empire. Minto did not favor a "forward policy." He thought as William Pitt (the younger) had when the great statesman promulgated the India

Act of 1784, declaiming that territorial expansion in the subcontinent was "Repugnant to the wish, the honour of this nation." Minto wanted only to balance the Company's budget and restore fiscal responsibility, so lacking under his predecessor, Lord Wellesley.

Events, however, not wants, hopes or predilections, would determine policy, and in September 1807 London instructed Lord Minto to cultivate his neighbors, who might prove useful as allies in the event of an overland advance toward India by Napoleon. Lord Minto had independently become alarmed by rumors of French activity in Persia and had already planned to send envoys to adjacent territories in the northwest and Persia as well to establish links of friendship. The Great Game was beginning, with the French for the moment cast in the role of adversary.

In the cooler light of history it had been unrealistic for the British to have thought that Bonaparte's legions could brave the barren plains of Persia and the rugged mountains of Afghanistan to attack India. Yet countries astride the routes to India were undeniably important. The East India Company's mercantile empire had prospered because Britannia ruled the waves, but the subcontinent had to be defended by securing its land approaches as well.

London's instructions to Minto in 1807 were to seek the cooperation of the countries "eastward of the Indus," meaning Afghanistan, the Punjab and the lands of the Indus River delta to the south ruled by the emirs of Sind. The British also recognized the potential Russian threat and asked Lord Minto to "cultivate the Tartar tribes Eastward of the Caspian"—the Turkomans and Uzbeks who roamed the deserts north of Afghanistan. But it was the French in Persia who seemed to pose the most immediate threat and Minto was instructed to leave that problem to the British Crown. Relations with Persia had long been the delegated responsibility of the East India Company, but because of ominous French initiatives in Persia, the full, undiluted force of His Majesty's government would be brought directly to bear on the shah; the British government would send an envoy to Tehran rather than content itself with a governor general's representative sent from India.

The East India Company's connection with Persia was rooted in a long-standing trade relationship. Company trading posts had existed in the Persian Gulf since the early seventeenth century, but there had been little continuity in diplomatic relations between the two countries until the nineteenth century. The East India Company had customarily dealt with Persia through a "resident" in the Persian Gulf port of Bushire in southern Persia who reported to the governor of Bombay. Only remotely and circuitously was the British government's authority felt.

The Company in 1801 had made John Malcolm the Persian Gulf resident charged with negotiating a political and commercial treaty with Persia. Fath Ali Shah, Persia's King of Kings, agreed never to make common cause with the Afghans and to respect British sovereignty in India. In return, the British promised arms. But Russia's seizure of Persia's largest tributary in the Caucasus, the kingdom of Georgia, in 1801 had given the shah second thoughts and persuaded him that he needed French friendship more than British to contain the czar's ambition. This had led to the Franco-Persian Treaty of Finkenstein, in which the shah welcomed a French military mission under General Gardanne in response to the Russian threat and, more seriously, offered to join with the French in invading Afghanistan and India.

Malcolm's efforts to reassert the British position were rebuffed by the shah, who refused even to meet with him. These developments, placing the French in the dominant role in Persia, provoked a frustrated Malcolm to recommend that the British use force to seize the Persian island of Kharack (now called Kharg) at the head of the Persian Gulf. But before such Draconian measures would be carried out, the Crown envoy, Sir Harford Jones, "Baghdad Jones" as he was known because of service in Mesopotamia, arrived to try again through diplomacy, where Malcolm had failed, to keep the shah from embracing the French.

Jones and his deputy, James Morier, reached Bushire "to throw the aegis of the British Crown over the imperiled destiny of India."* To the Company's surprise, Persia's Fath Ali Shah was now suddenly receptive to London's initiative and welcomed Jones with as much spirit as he had rejected Malcolm. The fickle shah, it seems, had concluded that the French had been extravagant in their promises and in light of the Franco-Russian accord reached at Tilsit could not be counted on to recover Georgia for him. Revealing that traditional Persian agility in playing one power against another, Fath Ali Shah now turned to the British.

Costume and dress were important in Eastern courts, but Jones insisted on wearing English knee britches rather than Persian robes as required by court protocol. His deputy, James Morier, better remembered today as author of the classic *The Adventures of Hajji Baba of Ispahan,* captured the scene in this novelized essence of Persia published in 1824. "The King was seated on his throne of gold dressed with a magnificence that dazzled the eyes," recounted Morier's hero, Hajji, while the English ambassador and his entourage, "with their unhidden legs, their coats cut to the quick, their unbearded chins and unwhiskered lips, looked like birds moulting."

*Sir Percy Sykes, *A History of Persia,* Vol. II, 1951 edition, p. 307.

on of India had become academic even before his mission reached Pesha-
ar. Napoleon was by now fully engaged with the war in Spain where his
mies faced the Duke of Wellington, whom the French emperor had
sparagingly referred to as "that sepoy general" when he had fought
ench officers during the Maratha wars in India. There was now no
ossibility that Napoleon would lead a campaign against India, if indeed
ch a possibility ever existed.

Elphinstone was cautioned against committing the British to anything
sembling a promise to protect Shah Shuja from Persian attack. He was
confine himself simply to warning the Afghan leader against both
rench and Russian designs involving the Persians. Of course, there were
e usual protestations of friendship and the pious promise that "the veil
f separation shall be lifted."

Only days after Elphinstone had left Peshawar, news reached him that
hah Shuja had been defeated and forced to flee to the mountains. The
ompany's envoy had made a friend of Shah Shuja and had secured a
eaty, only to find that these were empty achievements as power in
Afghanistan once again changed hands. But, if Elphinstone had failed to
in a political prize, he had at least returned with the first good intelli-
ence on Afghanistan. A door to a long-closed room now stood ajar to
aunt the British and tempt them to enter and venture a fatal step farther
more than two decades later.

These initiatives with India's neighbors in the first decade of the century
ad little lasting effect, except in the case of the Punjab, where the
Company gained Ranjit Singh as an ally and more or less stabilized the
egion. Motivated by unreasonable fears of French aggression, the British
ad sought friends among India's northwest neighbors for the wrong
reasons; it soon became apparent that Russia, not France, was the problem. By 1812 the Russians had decisively defeated the Persians in the
Battle of Aslanduz and forced upon them the Treaty of Gulistan in 1813.
By this humiliating agreement Persia was forced to give up important
Caucasus cities. Then, in 1827, the Russians inflicted another crushing
defeat on the Persians in Tabriz, enabling the czar to annex Yerevan,
Nakhichevan and Lenkoran by the terms of the 1828 Treaty of Turkmanchai. By pushing their border southward in the Caucasus to the Arras
(Araks) River, the Russians had put the Persians at a strategic disadvantage. Perhaps more important, this landmark treaty gave Russia extrater-
ritorial rights in Persia; the shah was no longer unquestioned master of his
realm.

The Treaty of Turkmanchai changed the situation for the British as
well. The great bear was nearer, frighteningly nearer, as it reared up in

During the negotiations, Jones had ruffled the feathers of the aging
vizier by calling him an idiot and knocking him against the wall. But
despite such behavior on the part of the British envoy, the shah agreed to
an alliance in consideration of a £120,000 annual subvention to be paid
him so long as Great Britain was in a state of hostilities with Russia. The
British would also send a military training mission to Persia to replace
Gardanne's French mission.

While London busied itself with Persia in 1808, Lord Minto addressed
the problems of the Punjab and the Punjab's southern neighbor, Sind,
closer at hand. The East India Company watched uneasily as a unified Sikh
nation on the northwest edge of its Indian dominions grew stronger under
the precocious leadership of the young Sikh warrior, Ranjit Singh.

The Punjab, that triangular wedge perched atop the subcontinent separating India from the Afghan highlands, is a study of contrasts. On its
north side is Kashmir, whose mountains and lush valleys rise in stark
contrast with the flat, dry plains that characterize much of the Punjab. The
western side of the triangle is the great Indus River, beginning its long
journey from the frozen skirts of Mount Kailas in western Tibet. The
Indus races in a northwesterly direction through tortuous gorges along the
far slopes of the Himalayas in search of a break in the mighty range
through which it can reverse direction and flow southward until it empties
into the Arabian Sea. On the southeastern side of the triangle is Delhi,
then seat of the atrophying Moghul Empire. North of Delhi five rivers—
the Sutlej, Beas, Ravi, Chenab and Jhelum—rise in the Himalayas and
flow southwestward to drain the Punjab and contribute their waters to the
Indus. The land between the rivers are known as *doabs,* "beggars' mantles
fringed with gold." Thanks to these riverine fringes worth much more than
gold to its inhabitants, the arid Punjab has been able to sustain life, but
most fertile of all is the Cis-Sutlej, that part of the Punjab nearest Delhi.

The Punjab was no longer a mere collection of small feudal communities
quarreling among themselves. Under Ranjit Singh it had become a nation,
already boasting a formidable army. It behooved the Company to win the
Sikhs as allies so that they could provide a useful buffer against aggression.
Ranjit Singh had his own ambitions, however, and aspired to absorbing the
entire Punjab, including the rich area between Delhi and the Sutlej River,
the Cis-Sutlej, where independent chiefs enjoyed the protection of the
British.

It would not have been prudent of the British to allow Ranjit Singh to
extend his rule to the very gates of Delhi. The Sikh leader might next try
to seat himself on the now-tottering Moghul throne and impose his own
raj on India. Certainly, there was no more powerful contender for control

in northern India than the British themselves. Yet, the Company needed the friendship of Ranjit Singh, whose realm bordering Afghanistan was critical to the defense of India. If treaties with Persia and the Afghans were important to British strategy, a similar understanding with Ranjit Singh's Sikh kingdom of Lahore was no less vital. But when the maharajah with his army crossed the Sutlej in 1807 and advanced toward Delhi, threatening British preeminence in the Cis-Sutlej, Calcutta found itself faced with a dilemma: how to reconcile the Company's strategic need to defend Delhi with its need to have good relations with Ranjit Singh in the event of any new Afghan adventure or a French invasion launched from Persia through Afghanistan. It was this diplomatic challenge that was entrusted to a twenty-three-year-old Company officer of promise named Charles Theophilus Metcalfe, whom Lord Minto instructed to halt "that infernal villain, Buonaparte."

Shortly before Metcalfe left on his mission to Ranjit Singh in 1808, Captain David Seton of the Bombay government met with the emirs of Sind in Hyderabad near the mouth of the Indus. Strategically placed, commanding the Indus delta between the Punjab and the Arabian Sea, Sind was another important gateway to India. (It is today the southern province of Pakistan, whose capital is Karachi, near Hyderabad.) Nominally tributary to Kabul but under the influence of Ranjit Singh, the emirs of Sind warranted special attention by the Company to assure their cooperation in the event of an attack against India by way of Persia and to prevent interference with hoped-for British trade along the Indus waterway.

Trying desperately to outbid the Persians, who were intriguing with the emirs, Seton exceeded his instructions and signed a treaty draft committing the Indian government to defend Sind against Afghanistan, an affront to the Afghan king, Shah Shuja-ol-Mulk (hereafter referred to more simply as Shah Shuja), whose friendship Minto sought. Moreover, a mutual-assistance clause agreeing that neither country would protect the enemies of the other was sure to excite Ranjit Singh's suspicions as to British intentions toward his southern flank, thereby compromising Metcalfe's mission to Lahore. Seton, having made a muddle of things, was recalled in some disgrace and replaced by a new envoy, Nicholas Hankey Smith, who disavowed the unauthorized treaty and put things back on track by refusing to commit the Company to any act unfriendly to Kabul or the Punjab. The emirs agreed to a meaningless treaty of friendship promising quaintly never to allow "the tribe of the French" to settle in their country.

The British interest in Sind and Afghanistan was nonetheless worrisome to Ranjit Singh as he began his talks with Metcalfe. The Sikh leader was not impressed with the alleged French threat and considered it only a British pretense for their new frontier initiatives and a spurious rationale

for expanding British power in the Punjab and beyond at negotiations that followed in the course of the next few exercise in frustration. It was a tribute to Metcalfe that and threat in just the right proportions to arrive finally agreement.

Ranjit Singh was too unsure of Sikh victory to risk his of arms and concluded that it would be preferable to s rather than lose it all to the British. After a Company a position to advance on the Punjab, Ranjit Singh agreed to and signed the Treaty of Lahore, in which both sides ple to "perpetual friendship" and the British retained prote over the Cis-Sutlej states. No agreement is perpetual, b alliance lasted the lifetime of Ranjit Singh, who proved t The relationship would, however, seriously complicate with the Afghans.

Looming as thunderclouds to the north was the incre situation in Afghanistan troubling the British and Sikhs a pressure on Persia increased. Lord Minto entrusted th Mountstuart Elphinstone, a young officer whom he sent as Shuja, unsteady king of the Afghans.

As Elphinstone entered Peshawar, the Afghan king's wi 1808—the third prong of Minto's border initiatives—the cr tors was so dense that the Royal Mounted Bodyguard, led Pathan known as "Rasul the Mad," had to lash out with the way clear. Except for an English mercenary who died in with Emperor Aurangzeb's army in the seventeenth century was the first Englishman to enter Afghan territory. The Afg their visitor out of curiosity as he entered town, but there wa his mission was a harbinger of conquest. It was said by a traveled to India and were wise in the ways of the *ferangis*, that the British were "very designing" people.

Shah Shuja had been busy rushing from one crisis to anothe his realm to stanch hemorrhages of power as rivals and woul intrigued against him. He had looked forward to the meeting stone; in self-interest he hoped the British relationship would in his struggle to remain in power and control the unruly realm. Almost in desperation, the king grasped at the oppo sented by Elphinstone, promising that England and Afgha destined by the Creator to be united by "bonds of everlasting Unfortunately for the British, Shah Shuja's estimate of th intentions would prove wide of the mark.

Elphinstone's original purpose to secure a barrier against F

Persia. The treaty had not only reduced Persia to a state of subservience but had forced the British to modify their own treaty with the shah. Despite an auspicious preamble in which the British agreement of 1814 referred to the pages in its text as "happy leaves, a nosegay plucked from the thornless garden of concord," some sharp Russian thorns had undeniably appeared. Persia was now in no position to serve as a British-dominated buffer between India and Russia.

In Calcutta the mood was apprehensive. London was worried as well. Lord Ellenborough, who had become president of the Board of Control overseeing Indian policy in the Duke of Wellington's government, was concerned that Russian influence in Tehran "would practically place the resources of Persia at the disposal of the Court of St. Petersburg."

If the Russians had outscored the British in northern Persia, it was even more important for the Company to concentrate on its immediately adjacent neighbors, the Punjab and Sind. These were the real anterooms of India. Moreover, if Ellenborough was right in predicting a trade battle with Russia for Central Asian markets, the Indus River would be of utmost importance as the most economical way to move British goods toward the north. It was time for the British to survey the great river and solidify its alliance with Ranjit Singh.

Governor General Minto chose a twenty-five-year-old East India Company fledgling named Alexander Burnes for this important task. This would be the beginning of a decade-long odyssey of high adventure, fame and failure for Burnes, ending violently in the streets of Kabul. It would also begin a decade of British involvement in Afghanistan ending in disaster.

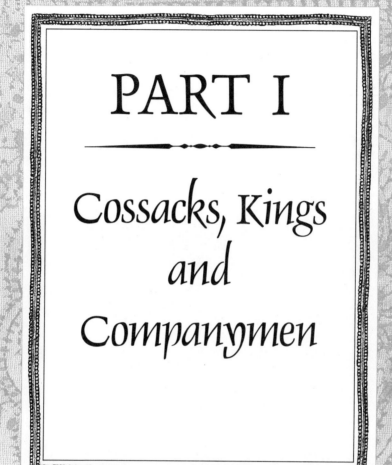

PART I

Cossacks, Kings and Companymen

Chapter I

ALEXANDER BURNES,
IMPERIAL OUTRIDER

ALEXANDER BURNES WATCHED WITH DISMAY AS HIS SMALL FLEET OF native coasters tossed about in a bad storm that had blown up without warning in the Indus estuary off the coast of Sind. The gale had struck at midnight, February 14, 1831, scattering his vessels, snapping the masts of two of them. But Burnes's concern was for his cargo of five magnificent dray horses, being transported with great care all the way from England. Stationed at the remote Company political agency at Kutch on the Arabian Sea, some four hundred miles northwest of Bombay as the crow flies, Burnes had been selected by the East India Company to deliver the prize horses as gifts to Ranjit Singh, Sikh maharajah of the Punjab. This offering was meant to ensure that the one-eyed Lion of the Punjab, key to British frontier strategy, remained a friend.

It had been planned that Burnes's thousand-mile journey would take him and his party up the Indus as far as the princely state of Bahawalpur wedged between the Punjab and Sind. From there they would travel up the Chenab tributary of the Indus by boat to the ancient city of Multan before branching off on the Ravi River to get within easy marching distance of Ranjit Singh's capital, Lahore. Aside from being easier on the horses, the river journey would give Burnes an opportunity to test the navigability of the Indus and its tributaries as avenues of commerce. Since the days of Alexander the Great, and doubtless before, the Indus River network had been the key to the Punjab. It was important for the British to have free passage on the Indus for strategic reasons, but the river would be useful in cutting transport costs as well. Just as Russia could take advantage of the Volga and the Caspian Sea to bring goods cheaply to the edge of Central Asia, the British hoped to carry goods up the Indus from the Arabian Sea at competitive prices. The great Ganges waterway of northern India could also be linked with the five rivers of the Punjab for purposes of trade, with only a short overland porterage between its Jumna tributary at Delhi and the Sutlej tributary of the Indus. But the Company had to consider Ranjit Singh's wishes in this matter before it began plying the rivers of the Punjab. It was Burnes's task to gain the Sikh leader's acquiescence.

It was a tribute to Burnes that Sir John Malcolm, governor of Bombay, had chosen him for this assignment. In the ten years since Burnes first arrived in India at age sixteen—a "griffin," as the new ensigns in the East India Company Army were called—he had done well. He was born in Montrose, County Angus, on May 16, 1805, the year that Sir Walter Scott wrote *The Lay of The Last Minstrel,* and the great Scott's opening line in his introduction—"The way was long, the wind was cold"—could aptly be applied to the last few years of Burnes's ill-omened career in Afghanistan. His beginnings, in fact, were not auspicious; he had been a puny child, so fragile at birth that his family rushed to have him baptized in the fear that he would die nameless. He would always be slight of stature, a fact that bothered him as an adult. But puny or not, he came from good Scottish stock. His grandfather and that of Scotland's beloved poet Robert Burns were brothers. His father was a pillar of the community, serving first as town clerk, then as provost of Montrose, and had enough influence to get Alexander accepted for service in the East India Company.

Alexander was regarded as somewhat of a roughneck during his early school days, more interested in sports than in his studies. One schoolboy friend at Montrose Academy remembered his bad habit of running hard with untied boot laces, which frequently caused him to trip and fall. Others remembered him at school as clever and precocious, although Burnes himself later recalled, "I was very dull at school and reckoned a dolt."[1] Coming from a family of professional men and a father who had achieved local prominence may account for Burnes's overcritical view of himself, and it probably also had something to do with his lifelong drive to succeed—to prove himself.

Young Burnes loved to debate. In one school debate over whether reading or traveling was most advantageous, Burnes defended reading with a ringing opinion that seems ironic coming from a person destined to achieve fame as a traveler to exotic lands and forfeit his life in a signal disaster. He declaimed: "By reading we have it in our power to amuse ourselves with the book which contains all the disasters without the labors encountered" in experiencing them.[2]

Alexander rounded the Cape of Africa on the long voyage to Bombay aboard the sailing ship *Sarah*. With him was his brother, James, about to begin his career as a doctor in the medical department of the Bombay government. Traveling together, the two boys felt less homesick than many of the new cadets who set out on their adventures while still adolescents. The India they found and came to know so intimately was momentarily at peace as far as the British were concerned. Four years earlier the Company had finally tamed the nationalistic Maratha marauders of Central India, who resented Moghul rule and British intrusion alike, and added their lands to the Bombay Presidency. Now Lord Moira, Marquess of Hastings, as governor general concerned himself with consolidating Company holdings rather than seeking new ones.

The English in Bombay were known as "Ducks," a nickname based on their favorite dish of curried dried fish known as Bombay duck. When Burnes arrived, Bombay was considered a backwater where careers could easily stagnate. The Company directors branded it a place of "little importance to the Company," enough to discourage any young officer eager for action and rapid promotion.

New cadets like Burnes were comfortably enough housed in barracks, but the climate was beastly during much of the year, either stiflingly hot or drenchingly wet in the monsoon season beginning in June. Worst of all, there was not much to do. Burnes was determined not to stagnate and passed much of the time studying. Languages came easy to him and within a year he had mastered Hindustani. He assiduously studied the country itself; it fascinated him. In his diary Burnes wrote: "I have begun to gain as much information concerning the manners, customs, laws and religions of these people . . . for what is it that makes a man but a knowledge of men and manners?"[3]

Burnes's first regimental posting was with the 1st Battalion of the 3rd Regiment of the Bombay Infantry. He was ecstatic: "I have everything to be wished for, plenty of time to myself, a gentlemanly commanding officer

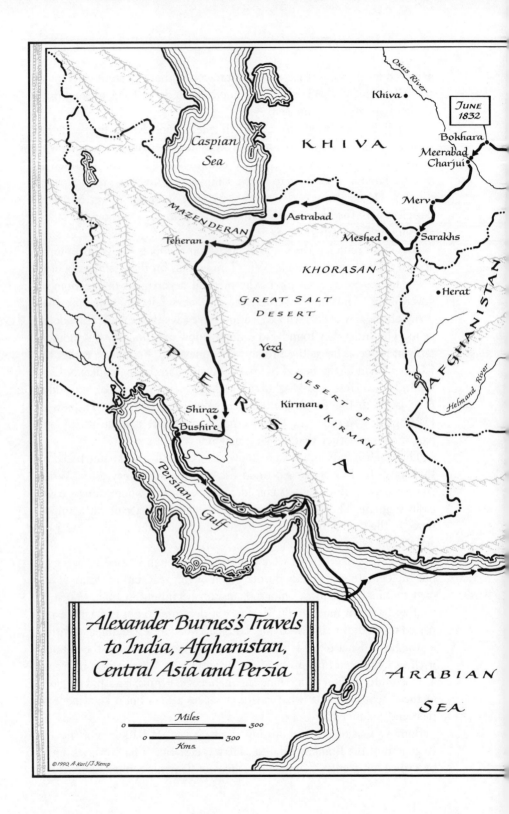

Khiva

Oxus River

JUNE
1832

Bokhara

Meerabad
Charjui

Caspian
Sea

KHIVA

Merv

MAZENDERAN

Astrabad

Sarakhs

Teheran

Meshed

KHORASAN

Herat

AFGHANISTAN

GREAT SALT
DESERT

PERSIA

Yezd

Helmand River

DESERT OF KIRMAN

Shiraz

Kirman

Bushire

Persian Gulf

Alexander Burnes's Travels
to India, Afghanistan,
Central Asia and Persia

ARABIAN

SEA

Miles

0   300

0   300

Kms.

©1990 A. Karl/J. Kemp

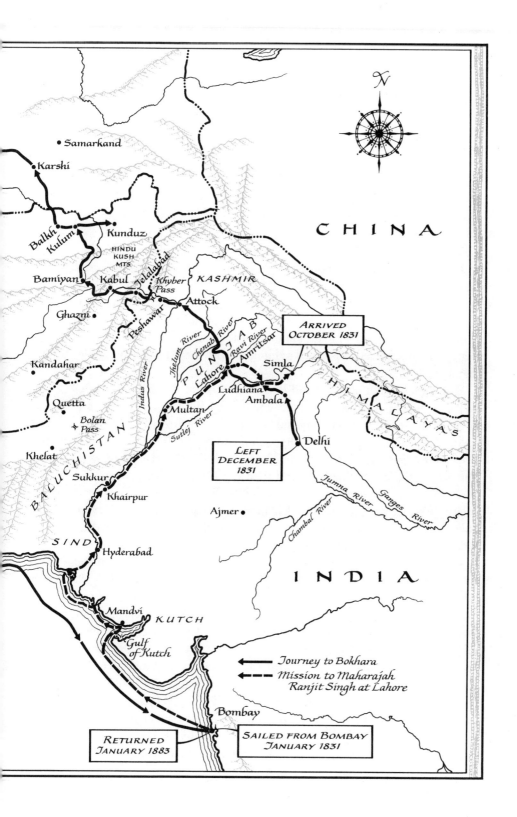

Samarkand

Karshi

Balkh
Kulum
Kunduz
HINDU KUSH MTS.

Bamiyan
Kabul
Jelalabad
Khyber Pass

KASHMIR

CHINA

N

Ghazni
Peshawar
Attock

Kandahar

Khelat

Quetta

Bolan Pass

BALUCHISTAN

Sukkur

Khairpur

SIND

Hyderabad

Mandvi

KUTCH

Gulf
of Kutch

Indus River

Jhelum River

Chenab River

PUNJAB
Lahore
Ravi River
Amritsar

Multan

Sutlej River

Simla

Ludhiana
Ambala

HIMALAYAS

Delhi

Ajmer

Jumna River

Chambal River

Ganges River

INDIA

ARRIVED
OCTOBER 1831

LEFT
DECEMBER
1831

Bombay

RETURNED
JANUARY 1883

SAILED FROM BOMBAY
JANUARY 1831

Journey to Bokhara
Mission to Maharajah
Ranjit Singh at Lahore

and several very pleasant fellow officers." But stirrings in China rang alarm bells that aroused Burnes from his idyll to crave the glory of war. He was determined to volunteer for China service if his regiment was not among those drawn from India. Combat and the opportunity it presented for glory obsessed most young officers of the Indian Army as it did those of the British Army itself, and whenever one of the numerous imperial wars of the nineteenth century broke out, red-blooded officers pulled all the strings they could to join the fray. As Burnes wrote in his diary, "if a man does not push on he will never see service, and, of course, will never be an officer worth anything." With reference to China specifically, he quipped, "What will the poor old maids of Montrose do for want of tea?"[4]

In fact, war did not then break out in China and Burnes had to satisfy himself with Poona, inland from Bombay on the Deccan Plateau. Back to reality, he now began to study Persian, court language of the Moghuls and a required language if one were ever to be assigned to Persia or the Persian Gulf, responsibility for which traditionally came under the Bombay Presidency. He was, however, assigned as interpreter to the 1st Bombay Native Infantry at Surat.

Surat, a few miles up the Tapti River just north of Bombay, had been the first trading post, or "factory," founded by the Company, and for much of the seventeenth century had been the headquarters of the Honorable East India Company. Surat slipped into obscurity after King Charles II acquired Bombay as part of the dowry of his bride, the Portuguese Infanta, Catherine of Braganza, and then granted it to the Company in 1668 for a much-needed loan. Superseded by Bombay, it had become a relatively minor post, but Burnes delighted in his new responsibilities and was elated when he soon was made adjutant of the 21st Bombay Native Infantry with a lieutenant's salary of five hundred rupees a month.

Unlike many new officers in India, Burnes did not have contempt for the native troops he commanded. While convinced that the British were ordained to rule, he understood the importance of maintaining a good relationship with the sepoys. Native noncommissioned officers handled most of the drill and troop-level administration. In time of combat one's life, of course, depended on the loyalty and steadfastness of the native troops. Discipline was stern; not until 1827 was corporal punishment for Indian troops abandoned. But the sepoys were reconciled to that so long as punishment was justly administered; they could console themselves with the thought that English troops were also flogged for their transgressions. The deterioration of discipline after flogging was later abandoned was, in fact, as upsetting to the sepoys as it was to their English officers, who could sense a lowering of morale as a result.

The chasm between British officers and British soldiers was as wide, if not wider, than between British officers and Indian troops. Nearly half the queen's soldiers were illiterate. They were brutalized in a way inconceivable in a modern army. In dread of having to be treated for wounds in an age when anesthetics were unavailable, British soldiers drank too much before going into battle, and bored by garrison life when not in combat, they caroused and consorted with the lowest kinds of Indian prostitutes.

In a moving passage in his memoirs, one British sergeant, rare for his literacy, reflected on what it meant to serve then in India. A soldier, he wrote, "is a man forced down under the brutalising machine of military life, which presses out nature from the very veins and bones of its victims, and shapes from the warm living flesh a puppet, a tool, a thing, a creature without eyes or ears or sense of will of its own—a plaything for death, a missile in the merciless hand of the state for pomp and vainglory." The author of these words, one Sergeant Pearman of the 3rd (King's Own) Light Dragoons, had little love for his officers, adding: "I have oftimes put my foot on a dead officer as we put his body under ground and said to myself, 'where is your rank now?' "[5]

The Indian sepoy, in contrast, had a kind of grace and dignity that flowed from an older, more structured civilization in which soldiering was considered a noble profession, particularly among the martial peoples of the north, and religious faith gave stability to life. It was not uncommon to find high-caste sepoys who could take pride in their status in Indian society, however lowly they may have seemed to British officers on the parade ground.

The sepoys had an understood partnership with their British officers, whom they usually respected. A sepoy could weep by the side of the newly dug grave of his beloved officer. But why were the sepoys willing to die for an alien master they little understood? The Indians had long suffered one or another alien master; the British were more just than the Turkic-Moghuls who had swept in from Central Asia, the Afghan dynasties or the Arab kings of the caliphate before that. More specifically, sepoy loyalty may have been a matter of honor and pride, or perhaps it was simply a question of good leadership, that elusive quality that determines the performance of all armies. When discipline broke down in Indian regiments it was usually because of poor leadership, but in the Great Mutiny of 1857, the sepoys of the Bengal Army rose en masse against the British because they had come to believe that "Company Bahadur," as they called the East India Company, was undermining their religions, Moslem and Hindu alike, and their time-honored way of life. This was in the future, but hints of trouble ahead could be seen at the time Burnes began his career.

The old Company army was beginning to change, particularly in the Bengal Army, where discipline was loosening. A remarkable Indian havildar (noncommissioned officer) named Sita Ram wrote his memoirs in 1873 with the help of his old commanding officer, giving rare insights into the Bengal Army of Burnes's day from the vantage point of the humble Indian soldier. Sita Ram was contemptuous of the Bengal Army disciplinary system. "The commanding officer has to ask a dozen officers before he can punish a sepoy," he wrote; and "by the time the punishment is inflicted, half of the men will have forgotten all about the case, and the effect of punishment will have been lost."[6]

Burnes, however, had his sights on adventure beyond the parade ground and the problems of the troops. If because of blessed peace he was denied the excitement of regimental combat, he was determined to find it elsewhere. And, indeed, there was another path to glory for an ambitious officer: the Political Department, where agents scouted out unknown lands beyond India's borders, established networks of native spies, or "newswriters," across the frontier and represented the Company in the courts of neighboring native rulers. Only by calculated guile and manipulation, the weapons of the "politicals," could the Company conduct its foreign affairs. Surely no army could ever be large enough to police the subcontinent and defend it from predatory neighbors by brute force alone. With his aptitude for languages and his ability to get along with the natives, Burnes was a natural political officer. His hopes rose when he was assigned to a field force assembled to campaign against the troublesome emirs of Sind, but the operation was called off for political reasons. He was promoted, however, and judged a promising officer worthy of being assigned to the quartermaster-general at GHQ Bombay.

Burnes was finally accepted in the Political Department and sent as assistant resident to the desolate area of Kutch, a feudal enclave still beyond Company direct administration. In 1829 he was granted permission to explore the little-known Great Indian Desert of Rajputana (Rajasthan) and establish contact with the Rajput princes who ruled there. This was high adventure, what Burnes liked best, so he was bitterly disappointed when he was recalled from his reconnaissance mission by no less a personage than the governor general, Lord William Bentinck.

Burnes had learned a lesson in Company politics. A faction in Calcutta opposed adventures beyond the Company frontiers. Its leader, Charles Metcalfe, whose early contacts with Ranjit Singh more than twenty years before had conditioned him to respect the Sikh leader and be solicitous of his sensibilities, strongly resisted any action that might weaken Company bonds with the Punjab. Nor did he want to see the Company do anything that might stir up the surly Sindis to the west.

Policy and politics in London, not Calcutta, however, were setting the course for India. In October 1829, a book written by Colonel de Lacy Evans entitled *The Practicability of an Invasion of British India* had appeared in England and reinforced the fear of Russia already reflected in British official thinking. Lord Ellenborough, president of the government's Board of Control for India, was so impressed that he sent a copy to Bentinck, reiterating his conviction that London needed "full information as to Cabul, Bokhara and Khiva." Pointedly he added that his requests of a year ago for such information had not produced any results. "I dare say nothing has been done,"[7] he complained.

The prime minister, the venerable Duke of Wellington, counseled caution but agreed that it was vital and urgent for information to be collected in the border areas from the Indus River to the Caspian. After an important conversation with Wellington in December 1829, Ellenborough felt the Company had a mandate to follow a more aggressive policy on the assumption that ultimately there would be confrontation with the Russians in Afghanistan, but in the meantime there would surely be a contest for commercial primacy in Central Asia. Determined to prevent the Russians from advancing "beyond their present limits," Ellenborough conveyed the official line to Calcutta in January 1830, in effect committing the Government of India to greater involvement in Sind, the Punjab and Afghanistan. This was the first step on a slippery slope.

Although the Duke of Wellington was forced from office in November 1830 and replaced as prime minister by the Whig leader, Lord Earl Grey, with Lord Palmerston (Henry John Temple Palmerston) as his foreign secretary, policy toward India as enunciated by Ellenborough remained much the same. The Court of Directors in London continued to believe that Ranjit Singh's friendship was worth keeping warm, and that now seemed an opportune time to pay court to the powerful Lion of the Punjab, on whose friendship so much depended. The excuse decided upon for an official visit to the maharajah was to assure him of British friendship, and to bear gifts in reciprocation of some priceless Kashmir shawls earlier sent by him to the king of England—not that this nice point of etiquette would fool the maharajah, who understood British motives well enough.

Ranjit Singh had a passion for women, horses, power and war. It would not be fitting to pander to the Sikh leader's lust, and certainly he should not be encouraged in his love of power or his craving for war. That left horses as the most appropriate gift to memorialize a neighborly expression of goodwill. Five (there had been six but one died at sea) huge dapple-gray dray horses especially selected in England would surely please the Punjab monarch.

Charles Metcalfe still railed against the government's forward policy and warned the Company against taking steps that might lead to conflict with Russia. Moreover, he did not want the Company to deceive his old friend, Ranjit Singh.[8] "The scheme for surveying the Indus under the pretense of sending a present to Rajah Ranjit Singh seems to be highly objectionable," he protested. "It is a trick unworthy of our government, which cannot fail when detected to excite the jealousy and indignation of the powers on whom we play it." More seriously, argued Metcalfe, "it is not impossible that it will lead to war."[9] But Metcalfe's objections fell on deaf ears.

So it was that Alexander Burnes, accompanied by Ensign J. D. Leckie, a Company surveyor named Mohammed Ali and an Indian physician to cater to their medical needs, had sailed from Bombay in January 1831 with the dapple-gray charges and an ornate carriage for the horses to draw. As an eager and linguistically accomplished young officer, Burnes had caught the eye of the Bombay governor, Sir John Malcolm, and been given the important assignment despite his youth and lack of seniority. Obviously thrilled, he wrote home about "the noble prospects which awaited him in being selected for such a delicate and hazardous journey." He knew the main chance when he saw it.

Burnes's secret instructions were to chart the Indus, "the depth of its water, the direction and breadth of the stream, its facility for steam navigation, the food supplies and fuel to be found on its banks and the conditions of the princes and people who possess the country bordering on it."[10] But first, he had to convince the Sind chieftains, scions of the Talpura clan, to permit free passage through the lower reaches of the Indus.

———— ·•·• ————

ONLY WITH DIFFICULTY HAD BURNES'S FLOTILLA REACHED HYDERABAD, principal city of Sind, after the buffeting it had suffered from the storm in the Indus estuary. It had not been an auspicious beginning. But, while nature's tantrum had finally abated, the temper of the Sind leaders had not. They were upset at the prospect of British trespassing. One venerable holy man of Sind muttered: "Alas, Sind is now gone, since the English have seen the river which is the road to conquest." These remarks were more prescient than the old xenophobe knew; his gloomy prediction would one day come to pass.

The Sindis did everything they could to block Burnes's mission. They harassed his boats from the shore, firing at them and hurling insulting epithets, and tried to prevent food from reaching the British party. Only after blunt language transmitted to the emirs by the Company resident in

Kutch, Henry Pottinger, warning that the British would invade Sind if they remained obdurate, did they acquiesce. There had been two months of painful negotiations before Burnes and his colleagues were at last allowed to proceed. This was only the curtain raiser, however; the main act would be Burnes's meeting with Ranjit Singh.

Company intelligence on Ranjit Singh and the Sikhs was not lacking. A network of newswriters, reporting to political agent Claude Martine Wade in Ludhiana, the Company's advance outpost in the Cis-Sutlej, had kept the Company well informed. Before Burnes meets the maharajah it is worth glancing back at the Punjab, its history and this charismatic leader who seemed to have sprung so suddenly from the land of the five rivers to build a new nation. Just who were the Sikhs and who was their ruler, so important to British strategy; how did he get there and what were his objectives?

Chapter 2

RANJIT SINGH, LION OF THE PUNJAB

POWER HAD ALWAYS BEEN AN EPHEMERAL THING IN THE PUNJAB, SOMEthing to be gained by two sharp weapons—the sword and intrigue—and lost the same way. This, perhaps, was to be expected of the Sikhs who dominated the Punjab; they were a warrior people whose every man considered himself a chief, a sardar. The Sikhs had loosely allied themselves in a group of twelve feudal military fraternities, each of which collected its own taxes and protected its own communities from Afghan predators. But, as the very word for these brotherhoods, *misl,* connotes, each member was "equal." Each band's leader, chosen for his superior bravery, was only first among equals.

For all the Sikhs' martial reputation, their religion began as a force for peace. A twenty-year-old Hindu named Nanak had a revelation in 1499 in which God ordained him the "Supreme Guru" and instructed him to go forth among his people and preach religious tolerance. This was meant to be an antidote to the Hindu-Moslem communal tensions that even then plagued India. "The age is like a knife—kings are butchers," Nanak said in despair as he set out on his mission.

After Nanak's death, a succession of Sikh gurus perpetuated the faith. The tenth guru, Gobind, who lived in the latter part of the seventeenth century, was responsible for endowing the religion with a martial emphasis. He established a Sikh military fraternity in which initiates were baptized with water stirred by a bloody sword. The Sikh brotherhood of warriors was known as the Khalsa, or "pure," to memorialize five of Gobind's closest lieutenants who dramatically demonstrated their willingness to die for the faith. Since then, Sikhs initiated into the Khalsa have ritually drunk water stirred by a knife, and renounced caste discrimination, wine and tobacco. Baptized Sikhs to this day also swear never to cut their hair, and promise to wear short cotton underwear, carry a comb, carry a dagger and wear an iron bangle on the wrist—all symbolic acts. They must vow never to turn their backs on an enemy—a way of saying "never retreat"— and to take the surname Singh, meaning "lion."

The Sikh *misls* in the mid-eighteenth century managed to find common cause against the frequent invasions—nine in all—launched by Ahmad Shah Abdali, the great unifier of the Afghans and founder of the Durrani royal dynasty in Afghanistan. But as the end of the century approached, unity of purpose had dissolved and the feudal bands spent their energies quarreling among themselves.

Zaman Shah, grandson of the great Ahmad Shah Abdali, revived Afghan ambitions toward the Punjab. In 1796, on the third attempt he made to invade the Punjab, Zaman Shah's army of thirty thousand Afghans came perilously close to the Sikh capital of Lahore, causing many in the Punjab to flee to the hills in panic. Only one Sikh leader was brave enough to stand and fight the invaders. This Sikh David willing to meet the Afghan Goliath was the one-eyed pock-faced young man named Ranjit Singh, whose passion for fighting had been exhibited at the early age of ten when he led loyal Sikh horsemen against a hostile band of sardars as his father lay dying, and again at age thirteen when he defended himself from a murderous assault by slicing off his assailant's head and bearing it home proudly, impaled on his lance.

In an astonishing act of leadership for one still so young, Ranjit Singh during this crisis rallied enough of the other Sikh leaders to stand against the invading Afghan army despite its overwhelming numbers. Fortunately for the Sikhs, the Afghan invaders, suddenly faced with insurrection back home, retreated toward Kabul. This gave Ranjit Singh an opportunity to harass the retiring Afghans in locations of his choosing. At a place called

Ram Nagar he decisively defeated them to become the Punjab's man of the hour.

The British too were vitally interested in events of the Punjab and apprehensive about Zaman Shah's persistent efforts to invade India. But if Ranjit Singh had checked the Afghans, what did the rise of a Sikh hero, forging a Punjabi nation for the first time, portend for British frontier security? Would Ranjit Singh prove to be a useful buffer against the Afghans or would he become a new and perhaps greater threat to British India, one closer to home than Zaman Shah and thus infinitely more dangerous?

With the defeat of the Afghans, Lahore was occupied and governed by a triumvirate of three Sikh leaders. Their stewardship was a sorry affair, however, further corrupted by appalling dissipation and gross injustice. In desperation the residents turned to their hero in battle, Ranjit Singh. After intrigue worthy of Machiavelli, Ranjit Singh accepted a secret appeal by the citizenry and, on July 7, 1799, surrounded Lahore with twenty-five thousand soldiers loyal to him. The city gates were flung open and he entered the city triumphantly. Ranjit, now only eighteen years old, was serenaded by "trumpets of happiness . . . and kettle drums of victory."[1]

To understand Ranjit Singh the man, it is necessary to know something of the boy, his traumatic upbringing and precocious clan leadership. If during his adulthood Ranjit became known for his bacchanalian revels, sexual extravaganzas and drinking binges, a glimpse of his impressionable years may help to explain this. The wonder of it all is that he became the leader he did and guided his people wisely despite his flaws.

According to a British political agent[2] in the Punjab at the time, the sins of the father had been visited on his son. As the story goes, Ranjit's father, Maha Singh, returned to his home from a trip one day to find his mother—Ranjit's grandmother—carousing with a group of men friends. Incensed by this ribald tableau, the outraged sardar later entered his mother's quarters and shot her dead, then lopped off one of her hands with his sword as a further gesture of his disgust.

Ranjit's father drank himself to death, some said out of remorse for having killed his mother. Others blamed his melancholia on his wife, whom he had always suspected of infidelity. He sometimes complained to friends that he doubted if Ranjit was, in fact, his son.

Hearing stories of his mother's adultery, Ranjit crept into her bedroom one morning only to find his worst suspicions confirmed. His mother's lover made his hurried getaway but left behind bits of clothing as telltale evidence of his act. Ranjit raged at his mother as she tried to protest her innocence. After a few days during which his anger mounted, Ranjit again entered his mother's apartment and, as she sat disheveled and half naked on her bed begging for mercy, slew her with his sword. He then tracked down his dead mother's lover and killed him as well. Ranjit is supposed to have commented that his act was just punishment for the crime and that "it was better that she should have died early than live a long life of guilt and shame."[3]

As was the custom, Ranjit Singh had been betrothed at the tender age of five. His bride-to-be was the daughter of a prominent and wealthy chieftain who had been killed by Ranjit Singh's father in battle. But the alliance, arranged by his mother with the girl's mother, Sada Kaur, was intended to bring two clans together for reasons of political power, and little thought was given to the wishes and emotions of either of the betrothed. In fact, the marriage, which took place when Ranjit reached his fifteenth year, was never a happy one.

The relationship between Ranjit Singh and his mother-in-law was turbulent. Sada Kaur was obsessed with power and wealth, and in young Ranjit she saw someone whom she believed could be a good medium through which to achieve her ambitions. He represented the power of a prominent Sikh clan, and her daughter's male heirs would, therefore, be beneficiaries of the combined strength of both clans. Sada Kaur thought that Ranjit Singh, seemingly an irresponsible boy interested only in hunting, would be malleable and accommodate himself to her well-arranged plans. To encourage his inattention to serious family matters, she arranged that from his earliest puberty he be kept well supplied with seductresses. She also encouraged his drinking, a vice he readily took to. But Ranjit Singh could not be so easily distracted. He quickly matured and exhibited a will of his own, even if he had acquired a taste for debauchery. But Ranjit Singh was shrewd enough to recognize his mother-in-law's talent for politics and saw the advantage of joining forces with her rather than opposing her.

While Ranjit Singh had gained Lahore, many of the Sikhs in the countryside, always individualists, did not give up their feudal autonomy easily. He was skilled at playing the game of Sikh politics, however, and his will prevailed. On April 12, 1801, Hindu New Year's Day, Ranjit made a fateful decision: he had himself proclaimed Maharajah of the Punjab. His forehead daubed with saffron, he rode regally through Lahore on the back of an elephant as his subjects showered him with gold and silver coins. A new nation was born, one that would fundamentally alter the balance of power in India's northwest.

The maharajah had taken the measure of the British and concluded that they would make better friends than enemies. In 1804, when he found himself wedged uncomfortably between a British force under General

Lake and and a Hindu Maratha army chased by Lake out of Delhi and into the Punjab, Ranjit Singh resorted to a daring strategem to assess the strength of this new trespasser on Punjab soil. He disguised himself as a simple Sikh soldier and personally reconnoitered the British lines. General Lake's officers spotted Ranjit by his one eye as the maharajah prowled about, and brought him before their commander. There is no record of what transpired between the two men, but they apparently got on famously, and it is believed that at this meeting the seeds of British-Sikh friendship were planted and a policy was born that would insist on alliance with the Sikhs. Once, while looking at a map of the subcontinent showing British territory colored red, Ranjit Singh commented realistically: "Soon it will *all* be red." There would be further tests of will and power, but the Sikh leader knew he had met his match in the Company raj. He vowed, however, to build an army equal to that of the British, particularly to acquire an artillery capability second to none, and to use European officers to help him in the process. If he had to share the Punjab with the British, he would share it as an equal. This, then, was the determined Sikh leader whom young Alexander Burnes was about to meet.

———— •-•-• ————

AS BURNES DREW NEARER TO LAHORE, AN EMISSARY SENT BY RANJIT SINGH graciously greeted him in the tributary state of Bahawalpur on the Sutlej River. Proceeding upstream, Burnes was greeted at Multan by an eleven-gun salute and, according to Sikh protocol, presented with a bag of gold coins. With a military escort provided by Ranjit Singh, the young envoy and his companions entered Lahore in grand style on June 18, 1831.

The next day Burnes and his colleagues, joined by Captain Claude Wade, political agent for the Punjab who had traveled overland from his residency in Ludhiana, and a platoon of Company soldiers as escort proceeded to the maharajah's palace for the ceremonial first visit to Ranjit Singh. The crowds were out in force to watch the procession led by the carriage brought by Burnes for Ranjit Singh—somewhat the worse for wear because of the long journey—drawn by the five giant dray horses. Burnes and his party, seated regally on elephant back, followed behind. As Burnes dismounted and stopped to remove his shoes at the threshold as custom demanded, he found himself suddenly in the "tight embrace of a diminutive and old-looking man—the great Maharajah Runjit Singh."

In behalf of the governor general, Burnes delivered a letter from the king of England. Touched by this honor, Ranjit interrupted the ceremony to order sixty cannons to commence firing an ear-shattering twenty-one-gun salute to His Majesty. The maharajah enthusiastically accepted the five dray horses, bigger than any horses he had ever seen. He called them "little elephants," and exclaimed that having seen their large shoes, the new moon just "turned pale with envy."

The preliminaries concluded, the occasion called for a party. True to form, Ranjit Singh treated his visitors to one of his famous orgies. As the Englishmen tried to restrain themselves despite a fiery brew laced with crushed pearls forced upon them, the royal bodyguard known as "the Amazons" lasciviously cavorted about, flourishing little bows and arrows— Sikh cupids shooting their shafts of love. A tipsy Ranjit Singh described his Amazons as the one regiment of his army that he could not discipline, nor did he want to. As the French traveler Victor Jacquemont had earlier described them: "They were a long way the prettiest girls I had seen in India, their lips were bright red from chewing betel and the rims of their eyelids were darkened with antimony."4 Burnes, no less entranced, marveled at the dancing girls "on whom grace and beauty had not been sparingly bestowed," and whose eyes, "finished specimens in gems, were black and bright."5

The nautch dancers of the Punjab and other parts of north India took pride in their art. While obviously calculated to arouse passion in the men who watched them, their performances had grace and required talent as well as long training. They were heavily made up and readily recognizable as professional dancers, but were not indecorously costumed—at least by today's standards of comparable performers. Their singing and rhythmic twirling, accompanied by musicians playing sitars and tablas, small hand drums, in a monotonous drone, had a certain hypnotic quality.

The nautch dancers were available for more private pleasures by favored guests and courtiers, but they were not considered prostitutes. In Ranjit Singh's court their graceful dancing often degenerated into less artful prancing about as the evening wore on as a result of being plied with brandy by the jaded maharajah. Ranjit Singh particularly delighted in provoking them to scratch and maul each other in unseemly brawls.

Ranjit Singh was a man curious about everything. He usually bombarded his guests with wide-ranging questions in an almost compulsive desire to inform himself about the world. But from Burnes he was particularly anxious to discover what British intentions were toward Sind, an area that he himself coveted. He had been pleased with his Company relationship since the treaty of friendship had been concluded, but apprehension now revealed itself as they discussed the strategic lands of Sind. Ranjit Singh was also concerned by his neighbor to the north, Afghanistan, a great trial to the Sikhs for centuries.

Ranjit Singh was an enthusiastic host and kept his visitors continually entertained and entranced. A feature event was the viewing of the great Koh-i-noor diamond, Mountain of Light, which flashed like fire and ice embedded in a large emerald arm bracelet worn by Ranjit Singh. Ranjit Singh was proud of his prize, the largest diamond then ever to have been found, whose previous owners included the great rulers of India, Persia and Afghanistan. Burnes gazed in awe at the Koh-i-noor, whose turbulent past was a story of invasion, bloody dynastic upheavals, greed and torture.

————— • - • —————

WITNESS TO THE TUMULTUOUS HISTORY OF THE INDIAN, PERSIAN AND AFghan ruling dynasties, and bellwether of power as conquerers seized it as a spoil of war, the famous gem has its own place in history as the supreme trophy for victors and is worth a digression. The source of the Koh-i-noor was probably a mine in the southern part of India at Kollur (in the modern Indian state of Andhra Pradesh). Called "the Great Moghul" when it reached the Moghul court, the diamond had been presented to Indian Emperor Akbar the Great in 1655 by a self-made ruler of Golconda in central India named Mir Jumla to gain royal favor. Emperor Shah Jehan later had an Italian court jeweler named Hortensio Borgio recut the priceless diamond to bring out its luster. Unfortunately, Borgio botched the job and in trying to repair its mangled facets reduced it from 787½ carats to 280 carats.

The Great Moghul was lost forever to the Moghuls when the Persian conquerer Nadir Shah seized it along with the famous Peacock Throne when he sacked Delhi in 1739. It was Nadir Shah who renamed the gem the Koh-i-noor and flaunted it as a prize of victory after he returned to Persia. In Nadir Shah's declining years he degenerated into madness, wreaking vengeance on peoples he conquered by erecting pyramids built from their severed skulls. His cruelties became so intolerable that he was killed in a palace coup, leaving Persia in chaos as claimants to the throne scrambled for power. Nadir Shah's grandson, the boy Shahrokh Mirza, held the throne only briefly before being blinded by rivals, but came into possession of the Koh-i-noor, whose brilliance he could no longer appreciate.

While Persia was wracked by dynastic struggles, an Afghan named Ahmad Shah Abdali, one of Nadir Shah's most loyal generals and leader of the great conquerer's Afghan levies, had found it necessary to flee back to his homeland. In a bid for power in Afghanistan, he soon conquered the important town of Herat and the province of Khorasan. Ahmad Shah made Khorasan a tributary princely state, wedged between Persia and Afghanistan, and entrusted it to the blind Shahrokh to rule as his vassal.

According to one story, Shahrokh gave the Koh-i-noor to Ahmad Shah in gratitude. Other stories variously have it that Ahmad Shah simply stole the Koh-i-noor, rationalizing that a blind man can get no pleasure from a beautiful gem that he is unable to see. Whatever the case, the famous diamond was now Ahmad Shah's and its new home Afghanistan.*

Ahmad Shah's political fortunes rose as he clawed his way to power amid the feudal chaos of Afghanistan. After several hard campaigns against rivals, Ahmad Shah emerged supreme, giving himself the title Dur-i-Durran, "Pearl of Pearls." In 1747 he joined the tribes in federation to found a true Afghan nation for the first time and establish for his Abdali clan a dynasty henceforth called Durrani. Ever after he has been known as Ahmad Shah Durrani and considered "father of his country." When he died of cancer, which had grotesquely disfigured him by eating away at his nose, he left his kingdom and the Koh-i-noor to his son, Timur.

After an unsteady twenty-year rule Timur died, and his son, Prince Zaman, emerged as the leading contender for power from among his twenty-two quarreling brothers. As Zaman Shah he inherited not only the throne of Kabul but the Koh-i-noor as well. Afghanistan was hardly a nation, however, with its principal cities—Herat in the west, Kandahar in the south and Peshawar in the east—only tenuously linked to the kingdom.

Zaman's reign came to an abrupt end when his half-brother Mahmud blinded him and seized the throne. The deposed Zaman was thrown into a dungeon, but he managed to scratch a hole in his cell wall with his dagger and hide the precious Koh-i-noor rather than give it to his successor. Zaman Shah had become but another in the succession of rulers whose possession of the fabulous diamond seemed to bring bad luck. When Zaman Shah's full brother Shah Shuja wrested power from Mahmud in 1803 and freed Zaman from prison, the grateful man presented him with the Koh-i-noor. Perhaps Zaman felt that by relinquishing the gem he could restore good fortune to his now-wretched life.

Zaman Shah's fortunes thereafter were never good, nor were his brother Shah Shuja's, having in his turn been overthrown and driven from Afghan-

*A pathetic footnote on the fate of Shahrokh Mirza reveals how Nadir's grandson by giving up the Koh-i-noor still could not rid himself of the curse believed to be on all who once possessed it. The avaricious Persian eunuch king Agha Mohammed, who had emerged as victor in the struggle for the Peacock Throne and was crowned in 1796 as the first shah of the Qajar dynasty, could not believe that Shahrokh no longer had the Koh-i-noor. When Agha Mohammed conquered Khorasan he had the unfortunate Shahrokh's head shaved so that he could pour molten lead into a circular dam shaped out of thick paste on his scalp in an effort to make him tell where the gem was hidden. However agonizing the torture, Shahrokh was, of course, unable to produce the Koh-i-noor, which by that time was in Ahmad Shah's hands.

istan. Alexander Burnes would soon hear the story at first hand from the exiled Shah Shuja, the next chapter in the saga of the Koh-i-noor and how it came to be Ranjit Singh's prized possession. On his way to report to the governor general, who was summering in the nearby Himalayan hill station of Simla, Burnes visited the deposed monarch in Ludhiana, where he and his blind brother, Zaman Shah, had lived for two decades under the protection of the British. Burnes had no more than protocol reasons for paying a call on them. He was simply passing through Ludhiana, then headquarters and seat of rule in the British part of the Punjab, and was interested in meeting this longtime Afghan ward of the Company.

———— •·•• ————

WHILE TRAVELING FROM LAHORE TO LUDHIANA, BURNES COULD REFLECT ON his two-month sojourn in Lahore. He had formed a high opinion of Ranjit Singh for all the maharajah's jaded life-style. Although an autocrat, Ranjit Singh was essentially humane; Burnes noted that he had never been known to punish a criminal with death. His style of governing was a combination of "cunning and conciliation." But from Shah Shuja he would hear less flattering views of Ranjit Singh; the Afghan exile had experienced too much of the Sikh leader's cunning and too little conciliation.

Chapter 3

SHAH SHUJA,
RESTLESS EXILE

WHEN ALEXANDER BURNES CALLED ON SHAH SHUJA, RESTLESS PEN-sioner of the British in Ludhiana, he found the former ruler of the Afghans with "dignity and prepossessing demeanour as when king,"[1] but he had run to fat and seemed melancholy. He had much to be melancholy about; since being forced from his throne in 1809 by his half-brother Mahmud Shah, his life had been an odyssey of futility as he dreamed of regaining power in Afghanistan.

Dressed in a tunic of pink gauze and wearing a green velvet cap studded with emeralds, Shah Shuja spoke to Burnes of his eagerness to return to his homeland. Despite the passing of more than a score of years, his lust for power had not diminished. He seemed interested that Burnes had visited Sind, an area for all intents and purposes independent but nominally still a vassal of the Afghans. He regretted that even though the emirs of Sind professed strong friendship and allegiance, they had done nothing to help him nor did they pay him his tribute due. Both Shah Shuja and his usurper, Mahmud Shah, were legitimately descended from the royal dynasty established by their illustrious grandfather, Ahmad Shah Durrani, and belonged to the same ruling clan of the Saddozai. There was little sense of cohesion within the clan and no nonviolent way to determine succession. Succession did not automatically pass to the eldest son but, theoretically at least, was determined by a ruler before his death or by consensus among his survivers. The problem was that Timur's twenty-three sons had split into factions at sword's points with each other. Making matters even more confusing, the vizier—or prime minister—Fateh Khan, was from the rival Barakzai clan and wielded more power in Afghanistan than the feckless Mahmud Shah himself. Shah Shuja could claim that he had been the legitimate ruler of Afghanistan and had been wrongfully overthrown, but *legitimacy* was a word with little meaning in the crazy-quilt tribal culture of Afghanistan.

In 1809 the Company's first envoy to Afghanistan, the astute Mountstuart Elphinstone, had found the young Shah Shuja a pleasing person with the "manners of a gentleman and possessing of great dignity," but his hold on the country had been so fragile that he never controlled more than a third of the nation ruled by his grandfather and was deposed before Elphinstone, with a now-worthless treaty in hand, had cleared the borders of the kingdom.

Shah Shuja's reign from 1803 to 1809, when he was forced into exile, had never been solidly based. He had unwisely abandoned his grandfather's strategy of enlisting tribal support within a framework of a federation permitting considerable local autonomy, and instead had tried to create a central, absolute monarchy like that of Persia. The result was feudal chaos among the tribes and clans, whose loyalty to the crown was never more than nominal and was the product of subsidies paid to them by the monarch rather than any sense of national consciousness. Afghan tribes neither understood nor accepted rule from Kabul. They would not tolerate interference with a way of life and local autonomy enjoyed for generations. To the warlike tribesmen, any central government was by definition the enemy. While tribes joined in common cause from time to time, usually when faced with a foreign enemy, their tranquillity and a semblance of loyalty to the crown normally had to be bought or maintained by sustained force.

For two years following his fall from power, Shah Shuja led the precarious life of a guerrilla marauder, trying to raise tribal levies and enlist Afghan chieftains to restore him to power. But the fickle tribesmen, susceptible to bribes and blandishments from his enemies, soon forsook him. Shah Shuja's trove of priceless gems, which he had taken from the

Kabul treasury when he fled the country, had provided the means to finance his filibustering—but it had also made him a tempting target for capture and robbery. Indeed, in 1812 he suffered the humiliation and agonies of being seized by the rajah of Kashmir, ruler of the beautiful mountain principality north of the Punjab claimed as vassal by both the Afghans and the Sikhs. Any hope he may have had of regaining his throne evaporated when the rajah threw him into prison. Seemingly another victim of the Koh-i-noor's curse, Shah Shuja languished while the rajah demanded the great diamond as price for his release. Shah Shuja had cunningly hidden the great jewel, however, and preferred to endure his wretched confinement rather than buy freedom with his most prized possession.

Ranjit Singh learned that the Afghan vizier, Fateh Khan, intended to march on Kashmir and seize both Shah Shuja and the Koh-i-noor. Having his own designs on Kashmir and having been promised the Koh-i-noor by Shah Shuja's wife if he rescued her husband, Ranjit Singh sent an expeditionary force to Kashmir. His Punjabi troops did, in fact, reach the imprisoned Shah Shuja first and brought him—and his fabulous diamond—back to Lahore. But the campaign had been costly to Ranjit Singh; his rivals, the Afghans, now held Kashmir.

Much pomp and ceremony had been lavished on welcoming the exiled Afghan leader to Lahore as Ranjit savored the thought of relieving his "guest" of the Koh-i-noor. On June 1, 1813, Ranjit collected his prize as the two men solemnly exchanged turbans signifying friendship in an atmosphere that was anything but friendly. They had stared sullenly at each other for an hour before the exasperated maharajah bluntly made his demand and Shah Shuja reluctantly produced the Koh-i-noor from the folds of his gown, wrapped in a well-worn cloth. Once again the coveted gem had changed hands, signaling a shift of fortunes[2]; it had found a new master to blind with its brilliance.

In Lahore Shah Shuja became the uneasy guest of the Sikhs as Ranjit Singh extorted other jewels from him and, more ominously, kept a tight surveillance over him. The maharajah, however, had good reason to watch his guest. His spies told him that Shah Shuja was now intriguing with the Afghans, secretly urging his old nemesis, the vizier, to send an army to capture Lahore. Shah Shuja denied these accusations, but in later correspondence with the British he admitted plotting against his host. With the ever-changing winds of political fortune, Ranjit Singh saw Shah Shuja as an Afghan intriguer in his midst rather than an ally, while Shah Shuja saw Ranjit Singh as a dangerous antagonist with designs on his native land. In a revealing letter to the British in Delhi, Shah Shuja wrote: "As we worship the same God, it is our duty to extirpate the tribe of infidels [Sikhs] who are so many in the garden of Runjeet." With little comprehension of British policy he added: "As soon as the flame of war shall have been lit and troops under Vizir Fateh Khan put in motion against that quarter, God willing, we shall soon . . . divide the Punjab between us."[3]

The British had no intention of turning against their Sikh ally, but were at least willing to play host to Shah Shuja's enormous zenana of some six hundred women when they suddenly appeared in Ludhiana. By bribing his guards Shah Shuja had managed to have his womenfolk smuggled out of Lahore in disguise and transported by bullock cart to the British Punjab outpost; now he devised an elaborate escape plan for himself.

Disguised as beggars, the shah and his two sons disappeared into the night on April 13, 1815, while a trusted servant dressed in the royal gowns impersonated him in bed to deceive the guards long enough for him to make good his escape. The fugitive Shah Shuja and his sons crawled through Lahore's sewers to emerge safely beyond the city wall. With a few followers who joined him, Shah Shuja struck out for the safety of the highlands to the north, where he found refuge with the rajah of Kistawar.

The royal fugitive spent some nine months with his protector concocting impractical plots to attack Kashmir until he finally concluded that such adventures were futile and he would be better off under British protection. In September 1816 he rejoined his wives and women in Ludhiana to enjoy a period of relative tranquillity as Company pensioner before plunging again into plots to regain his kingdom. Like his lost Koh-i-noor, Shah Shuja had found a new patron, but Burnes, after visiting him, concluded that the British had not gained much of an asset in their boarder.

"From what I learn," Burnes reported, "I do not believe the Shah possesses sufficient energy to seat himself on the throne of Cabool, and that if he did, he has not the tact to discharge the duties of so difficult a situation."[4] Burnes's opinion of Shah Shuja made on this occasion would prove important in his later conviction that the British should not try to put him back on the Kabul throne. He realized that the shah had never been very popular in Afghanistan and now had few tribal allegiances on which he could rely. Shah Shuja, he thought, was simply a frustrated expatriate dreaming of making a comeback. Nonetheless, the former king of Afghanistan had not been idle. Neither Burnes nor any other English official in Ludhiana, including political officer Claude Wade, was aware that he had secretly taken steps to regain his throne as early as 1827.

The British were often generous to ousted leaders of one kind or another, providing them with asylum in the event that they might have some future usefulness. In the case of Shah Shuja, Wade, at least, believed it was important that he be kept in reserve for the day Dost Mohammed fell from power in that perpetually unstable atmosphere of Kabul. But for the moment, official Company policy did not favor any adventures in Afghanistan that would alarm their new ally, Ranjit Singh.

Political maneuvering behind the Company's back was difficult, and the British agent in the Punjab, Claude Wade—Shah Shuja's host and keeper—could not permit any intrigues that he might propose. For this reason Shah Shuja, unbeknown to Wade, had in 1827 turned to an American freebooter, Josiah Harlan, who had suddenly appeared in Ludhiana. Harlan had been loitering about in Ludhiana at loose ends, having just been released from the Company army following the First Burma War, in which he served as assistant surgeon, when Shah Shuja first met and became impressed with him. Soon the two of them concocted an ambitious scheme to overthrow the Barakzai clan leader, Dost Mohammed, by then Kabul's ruler.

Wade was unaware of Shah Shuja's plotting with Harlan, but so was Shah Shuja unaware of Harlan's simultaneous efforts to sell his services to Wade as a Company spy. The British political agent instinctively distrusted Harlan and kept him at arm's length. The details of Shah Shuja's plot have been lost in the mist of history; all that is really known came from Harlan himself and is probably self-serving at the expense of accuracy. In an interview he gave to the *United States Gazette* in 1842, after he had left India,[5] he told how he had tried unsuccessfully to raise the tribes on the fringes of Baluchistan and seize a fort on an island in the Indus River from which to launch an invasion of Afghanistan. This mad scheme died aborning when Ranjit Singh's soldiers interfered and spoiled the would-be kingmaker's plan.

Shah Shuja did not give up easily, however, and in 1828 sent Harlan off again (or so Harlan later claimed), this time to foment an insurrection against Dost Mohammed in Kabul itself! The American was no more successful than he had been before, although for nearly a year he lived as a guest of Dost Mohammed's half-brother Nawab Jubbar Khan, with whom he actively intrigued.

Nothing came of Harlan's efforts to overthrow Dost Mohammed; Kabul's ruler proved too firmly entrenched in power. But unknown to Shah Shuja, the American soldier of fortune had at the same time secretly represented Ranjit Singh's interests at court. What Ranjit Singh did not know was that Harlan, behind his back, had secretly made a deal with Dost Mohammed to spy for him against the Sikh court in Lahore when he returned. Not content with this hopelessly tangled web of intrigue, Harlan misrepresented himself to Dost Mohammed as a British agent, which probably accounts for Dost's interest in having a relationship with him. In fact, the American bombarded Wade in Ludhiana with unsolicited intelligence on events in Kabul.

Oblivious to Harlan's multifaceted deception, Shah Shuja seemed pleased with the American's efforts on his behalf, even though unsuccessful, and when Harlan returned from Kabul, he rewarded him with the titles "King's Best Friend" and "Companion of the Imperial Stirrup." Ranjit Singh, no less satisfied with Harlan's performance as his secret envoy to Dost Mohammed, made him a proposition for employment as one of his provincial governors. "If you behave well, I will increase your salary," he promised, "if not I'll cut off your nose!"[6] Harlan accepted this challenging offer and in December 1829 became governor of the small remote frontier provinces of Nurpur and Jesota. This, however, would not be the last of Harlan's involvement in Afghan matters. He would soon play a curious role in the Sikh seizure of Peshawar from Dost Mohammed, an event that would profoundly jar frontier politics and seriously aggravate the British dilemma implicit in trying to keep Ranjit Singh's friendship without alienating Dost Mohammed. For the moment, however, only Wade saw through the American mountebank. He advised Calcutta not to have any further communication with Harlan, who was "endeavouring to impose himself on the Afghans as a British agent."[7]

Shah Shuja may have been fooled by Harlan, but by now he realized that adventurous mercenaries with dubious levies, hastily recruited, were not the answer to gratifying his ambition to regain power in Afghanistan. He would need British support and financial help to succeed. He had tried to ingratiate himself with Burnes during their meeting. "Had I but my kingdom, how glad should I be to see an Englishman at Cabool,"[8] he said. But Claude Wade, as political agent resident in Ludhiana, held the key to British policy for the frontier and, thanks in great part to his reporting, the British were, in fact, beginning to recognize that Shah Shuja might prove useful as an alternative if Dost Mohammed proved intractable or decided to throw in his lot with the Russians.

Wade was an able officer who knew his territory well. He had established a good relationship with Ranjit Singh and, as host to Shah Shuja in Ludhiana, had become progressively close to the Afghan exile. The answer to the Afghan problem, in his opinion, was to encourage divisiveness within the kingdom. Shah Shuja, "his man," could become a key player in such a scenario by stirring up opposition to Dost Mohammed. Alexander Burnes disagreed with this philosophy and would ultimately clash with Wade on the issue, but for the moment his talks with Shah Shuja had left him with an even stronger desire to visit Kabul and see the situation for himself.

Chapter 4

────────── ·•◦•· ──────────

MOHAN LAL,
LOYAL COMPANY
SERVANT

W HILE SHAH SHUJA CONSOLED HIMSELF WITH DREAMS OF GLORY, THE tempo of events was accelerating along the border. Soon after Burnes's visit to the governor general in the early autumn of 1831, Lord Bentinck in Simla received a goodwill delegation from Ranjit Singh, sent in reciprocation for Burnes's mission to Lahore and intended to reinforce the alliance between the British and the Sikhs. More specifically, the maharajah wanted to make sure that British objectives beyond the Indus would not be achieved at his expense.

Bentinck listened patiently to flowery salutations from Ranjit Singh, such as: "The nightingales of esteem warble in the meadows of attachment . . . rivers of devotion rush into oceans of affection." But the river of concern to Bentinck was the Indus, particularly where it rushed into the Arabian Sea, and based on Burnes's report, this was why the attitude of the Sind emirs, whose lands lay astride the Indus Delta, was important.

Then Bentinck had his own meeting with Ranjit Singh. His object was

While Shah Shuja, as ward of the British in Ludhiana, consoled hims
with dreams of glory and schemes of action, and his blind brother Zama
once long ago feared by the British, nursed old memories, the pace
Company diplomacy along the northwest frontier was quickening. Burn
gave his report to Bentinck at the Himalayan hill station of Simla som
one hundred miles beyond Ludhiana, where the governor general wa
staying to avoid the heat of Calcutta. Burnes had much to tell and his view:
greatly influenced Bentinck.

This was a golden opportunity for Burnes, an occasion to meet directly
with the governor general and impress him with the skill with which he
had handled the emirs of Sind and the maharajah of the Punjab. But of
more interest to Burnes was the opportunity to convince Bentinck of the
need for more intelligence on Afghanistan and unknown Bokhara beyond
the Hindu Kush, where reports had it that Russian agents were becoming
active. If successful, this journey would make Burnes's career, and he put
himself forward as the best person to conduct such long-range reconnaissance.

In fact, Bentinck did not have to be convinced; he was already under
pressure from London to acquire more information on Kabul and the
Central Asian khanates. Burnes wrote his sister on September 31, 1831:
"The Home Government have got frightened at the designs of Russia and
desired that some intelligence officer should be sent to acquire information
in the countries bordering the Oxus [River] and the Caspian; and I,
knowing nothing of all this, came forward and volunteered precisely for
what they want. Lord Bentinck jumps at it."9

to convince the maharajah that the Sikhs should abandon their designs on Sind and welcome British commercial shipping on the Punjab rivers. The meeting between the governor general and the maharajah took place on October 26, 1831, in the British Punjab town of Rupar on the banks of the Sutlej River just north of Ludhiana. Masters of pomp, the British staged the meeting with consummate skill; parodying the famous meeting between King Henry VIII of England and Francis I of France before the castle of Guines, France, in 1520, it has been described as taking place on "a field of the cloth of gold." Tents of red with curtains of yellow satin, hastily planted shrubs trimmed to look like small elephants and gaily caparisoned horses were but a few of the embellishments calculated to add a touch of grandeur to the occasion and create an aura of festivity. Ranjit Singh lent his own elegance to the event when he arrived at the head of sixteen thousand cavalry, including his personal guard of horsemen dressed in coats of mail.

For entertainment there were the usual Kashmiri nautch dancers provided by Ranjit Singh, and to his delight the English ladies of the governor general's party entertained him with more decorous English folk dances. Ranjit Singh threw a party climaxed by his Amazons throwing gold dust over the guests. But for all the ceremony and revelry, Ranjit Singh left the field of the cloth of gold with the realization that the British meant to control Sind and Indus navigation, in return for which he received only British assurances of perpetual friendship. Yet, on reflection, the maharajah could congratulate himself that, in fact, he had secured from the British something far more valuable: promises of noninterference with what he might do on the west side of the Sutlej River. This, in effect, was license to take Peshawar from the Afghans, an event soon to occur with far-reaching implications.

On December 23, 1831, Burnes, who had been waiting impatiently in Delhi, received his orders to travel the route he had so hopefully suggested to Bentinck. With one of his colleagues, Dr. James Gerard, assistant surgeon general from Calcutta, he would visit Dost Mohammed in Kabul, one of the most important trading entrepôts in Central Asia, then proceed onward through the Hindu Kush Mountains to the Afghan town of Kulum, from where he would take a diversionary trip without Gerard to the nominally tributary Afghan province of Kunduz. This journey would be undertaken in disguise to avoid detection by the inately hostile and rapacious ruler of Kunduz, who delighted in kidnapping infidels. After backtracking to the main route, he and Gerard would go on to Balkh and then to mythic Bokhara.

After Bokhara, Burnes and Gerard intended to travel some 150 miles eastward, more than a week's journey, to nearby Samarkand, the four-teenth-century capital of Tamerlane's empire and now vassal of the emir of Bokhara—if indeed this should prove possible. The plan called for them to return again to Bokhara and make their way through the Turkestan desert to Meshed; then from there Burnes would travel to the Caspian Sea coast before crossing the Alborz range southward to Tehran, where he would pay his respects to the shah and consult with the British legation before taking ship for India from the Persian Gulf. From Meshed Dr. Gerard would instead return to India overland by way of Herat, Kandahar and Kabul.

Burnes's mission was described as being essentially commercial—the opening up of the Indus River to British trade—although no one really believed that he could avoid political complications. Bentinck was eager for Burnes to meet Dost Mohammed in Kabul and assess him and the state of affairs in his turbulent capital. In addition to being considered one of the most important trading centers in Central Asia, its strategic value as a potential buffer between British and Russian spheres of interest was becoming increasingly apparent. Beyond Kabul, particularly in Bokhara, Bentinck wanted intelligence on an area virtually unknown to the British where Russian influence was beginning to be felt.

The Company was convinced that the Russians were on the verge of invading Khiva, north of Bokhara, then ultimately Bokhara itself, which would bring the czar's legions to the borders of Afghanistan. This meant that Kabul would become the fulcrum of British-Russian rivalry.

The province of Khorasan in eastern Persia, with its capital of Meshed graced by one of Shia-Islam's most holy shrines, was also important as the traditional Persian invasion route to Afghanistan via Herat. The Turkestan desert, stretching inland from the Caspian Sea to Bokhara, was a strong-hold of Turkoman and Uzbek slave dealers whose depredations provided a ready-made justification for Russian aggression to rescue its own nation-als held in bondage. This was a heavy intelligence burden for a twenty-six-year-old subaltern, but Burnes plunged into the venture with enthusiasm. Much of his success would depend on the services of his secretary and interpreter, a remarkable young man from Kashmir named Mohan Lal, who was fated to play a dangerous and critical role throughout the tumultu-ous period of British involvement in Afghanistan.

In 1808 Mohan Lal's father, a high-caste Kashmiri Brahman, ably served Mountstuart Elphinstone on his pioneering mission to Shah Shuja in Peshawar in a capacity similar to his son's role with Burnes. Through this connection, young Mohan Lal had come to the attention of Charles Trevelyan, an influential Company officer and zealous believer in English as the language of teaching, who sponsored him as one of the first half-dozen Indians privileged to be given an English-language education in Delhi as an experiment in bringing along natives who showed promise. Trevelyan later described Mohan Lal's career expansively as symbolic of the beginning of "one of the greatest moral changes that has ever taken place on the face of the globe." Among the first fruits of Trevelyan's pilot effort to breed an elite corps of Indian administrators fluent in English at the Delhi English College founded in 1828, Mohan Lal set a very good example; he was graduated first in his class and immediately taken into Company service.

Bentinck's administration was devoted to internal reform; the governor general wanted India to be governed for the benefit of the Indians, and foremost in his mind was education.* He believed in nationwide education in which instruction for the masses would be conducted in the vernacular tongues, but an elite would be taught English and English values. This "filtration theory" meant that higher education given the upper classes would trickle down to the rest of the population. Bentinck believed that English should also be a means for qualifying Indians for responsible jobs in government, a first step along the road to eventual self-government.

It is unfortunate that the role of Mohan Lal in the drama of the Great Game has received little attention in the various histories of this period. Imperial Britain was more interested in its own paladins and was rarely moved to put on pedestals the natives who helped them, but in the cooler light of retrospection Indian contributions should be recognized. As loyal assistant—perhaps alter ego—to Burnes for most of the famous explorer's career, Mohan Lal deserves to share the honors of exploration with him. Mohan Lal was usually right in his own judgments. He risked his life, however, for policies and actions of which he disapproved, and remained faithful to the Company despite its persistent folly. Unlike many others at the time, he never succumbed to the temptation to join the chorus of criticism after catastrophe struck. For all his service, he received little reward or recognition from Company officials in India who were all too willing to forget him once his usefulness was not required any longer. He was, in other words, the perfect Company servant—talented, loyal and long-suffering.

Fluent in Persian, Hindustani and English, Mohan Lal was admirably

*Bentinck's accomplishments also included the suppression of various Hindu practices that the British found abhorrent, such as *sati*, or widow burning, or, in some locales, infanticide. It was during his administration that the Thugs, or Tuggies—widespread gangs of religious zealots who preyed on travelers, strangling them with knotted handkerchiefs in the name of the Hindu goddess Kali—were suppressed.

suited to be Burnes's *munshi,* or secretary, and conduct correspondence with the native leaders they would meet. He knew the style, the ornate flourishes of language that had to be used to flatter potentates. Mohan Lal was first introduced to Burnes in Delhi in December 1831 and joined him and Dr. Gerard in Ludhiana soon afterward. In his best-selling memoir of the trip, Burnes introduced Mohan Lal simply as "a Hindu lad . . . who would assist me in my Persian correspondence." The "Hindu lad" would prove to be much more.

On the way to Kabul Burnes and his companions had to transit the Punjab and were welcomed in Lahore by Ranjit Singh. The maharajah was understandably curious about the purpose of this second trip of Burnes so soon after the first. Rather than excite his suspicions, Burnes told Ranjit Singh that he was simply returning to England on leave and wished to satisfy his own curiosity about the lands to the north; it was purely an "unofficial" journey. But Ranjit Singh, not so naïve as to believe Burnes, observed slyly that the knowledge gained would be useful to the British government as well as providing it with "other advantages which might derive from such a journey." And surely Ranjit Singh must have been apprehensive about agreements Burnes might conclude with his traditional enemies, the Afghans.

Mohan Lal described with awe Ranjit Singh's opulent court. The tent in which the maharajah received Burnes's party "was as if it had been the tent of an angel and not a man!" While Burnes and Gerard were seated regally on golden chairs, Mohan Lal took a more inconspicuous place at the durbar. Nonetheless, Ranjit Singh noticed him, even "confering on him favors and money."[1] Mohan Lal described Ranjit Singh as a "thin man" with only one eye "ever inflamed either by the use of opium or wine," but he kept beautiful dancing girls always with him to gratify this eye. "His long beard, which reaches his navel," was silvered by age.

Ranjit Singh again played the perfect host, insisting that his guests join in holiday festivities. There was a busy schedule of activities that gave the maharajah many opportunities to regale Burnes and his companions with fascinating tales of his exploits and adventures. But politics intruded and he dropped a cautionary comment to the effect that he would not like to see British vessels monopolizing the Indus and its tributaries. While any official significance to Burnes's trip had been downplayed, Ranjit Singh was under no illusion that the British were intent on opening up the Indus to commerce, and this worried him.

Burnes's stay was capped with the inevitable party. Captain Claude Wade, omnipresent political agent from Ludhiana, was in Lahore on other business but joined Burnes for the gala. The celebration took place in the grand and ornate palace, illuminated for the occasion with a myriad of candles flickering through glass bottles filled with colored water. Burnes told of the rich food and strong drink, details "easier to describe than the scene in which they took place."[2] The scene, in fact, was one of unbridled debauchery. As Ranjit Singh drank his exotic brandy and showered his Amazons with gold and silver, their dancing exhibitions degenerated into a free-for-all as the drunken, half-clad girls "tore and fought with each other."[3]

Mohan Lal was more frank than Burnes in describing Ranjit Singh's excesses. He later wrote of the "beautiful and delicate thirteen-year old boy, Heera Singh," always by Ranjit Singh's side, who had enormous power at court because of his favored position. The maharajah enjoyed the Amazons as a feast for his eyes, but at this stage of his satiated life only Hera Singh was allowed in his bedroom. Yet, despite Ranjit Singh's jaded indulgences, Burnes was again left with a high regard for him. "Without education and without a guide," Burnes wrote, "he conducts all the affairs of his kingdom with surpassing energy and vigour and yet he wields power with a moderation quite unprecedented in an Eastern prince."[4] Maintaining the charade that his journey was a private one, Burnes as a tactical device left to Wade, as official representative of the governor general, the task of getting Ranjit Singh's signature on a commercial treaty with the British, effectively denying him any claim to Sind.

Burnes's party began their journey to Kabul despite warnings by Ranjit Singh's mercenary generals, Claude Auguste Court and Jean François Allard. The way was filled with dangers for the unwary traveler. Court went so far as to write up a long list of instructions, what must be done and not be done, based on his own experience in the area. Above all, he warned them to conform to the manners and mores of the people. None of the dire warnings dismayed Mohan Lal; Burnes admired the "buoyancy of spirit and interest in the undertaking" he exhibited.

Mohan Lal's spirit was less buoyant when it came to suffering privations. "We never changed our clothes until they disappeared under filth and vermin," he complained. This was all part of the blending-in process Burnes insisted on. The slightest signs of affluence invited brigandage; only by appearing poor could one hope to avoid being robbed. Mohan Lal's privileged education had taught him the ways of an English gentleman; this was no way for a gentleman to travel. Betraying his disapproval, he reported: "Captain Burnes and Mr. Gerard used their fingers instead of knives and forks, and their hands for spoons, our towels were the sleeves of our shirts. We combed our hair with a piece of wood."[5]

There had been no official British mission to Afghanistan since Mountstuart Elphinstone's visit to Shah Shuja nearly a quarter of a century before, and this mission had taken the Company envoy only as far as Peshawar, the winter capital. Much had happened since then. Power had ebbed and flowed, depending on tribal allegiances treacherously bought and sold. But the upheaval that had brought the powerful Barakzai vizier, Fateh Khan, to a grisly end in 1818 and set in motion a civil war from which his much younger brother, Dost Mohammed Khan, emerged as strong man of Afghanistan in 1826, was of more than usual importance. Burnes, Gerard and Mohan Lal were to take the measure of this young warrior and determine what his rule might mean to British interests.

Chapter 5

DOST MOHAMMED,
EMIR OF
AFGHANISTAN

ALEXANDER BURNES AND HIS PARTY LEFT LAHORE FOR KABUL AND THE court of Dost Mohammed Khan on February 11, 1832. They paused in Peshawar for a month, as guests of Dost Mohammed's rival half-brother, Sultan Mohammed Khan. Sultan Mohammed resisted Kabul's rule, paying tribute instead to Ranjit Singh, who also claimed suzerainty over Peshawar. Peshawar, in fact, had become a serious point of contention between Dost Mohammed and Ranjit Singh. Since Burnes's objective was to make friends with Dost Mohammed, it was not politic for him to have stayed so long in Peshawar, but Sultan Mohammed, smothering him with hospitality, insisted.

Burnes found Sultan Mohammed to be an educated, well-bred gentleman whose open and affable manner made a lasting impression on him, although he was "more remarkable for his urbanity than his wisdom."[1] His reputed bravery was exeeded only by his prolificity. He had thirty wives and concubines and some sixty children—he could not remember exactly how many.

Two of Sultan Mohammed's sons gave Burnes a capsulized preview of Kabul: the city had a salubrious climate, handsome people and a fine bazaar. But it was expensive, they warned, the streets were often clogged with snow or flooded by an overflowing river, and there was an overabundance of immoral women. The boys giggled over an old Afghan saying: "The flour of Peshawar is not without the mixture of barley, and the women of Cabul are not without friends."

In Afghanistan adultery was a dangerous transgression, however—not a joking matter—as Burnes would witness in Peshawar. While making a tour of the town he came upon a gruesome sight: the mangled bodies of a man and a woman—the former in the process of dying—just thrown on a dunghill. From the angry crowd a man stepped forward, still holding a bloody sword and admitting to having killed the couple. He had been the woman's husband and had murderously assaulted her and her lover on discovering their tryst. The cuckolded husband explained to the assembled people that he had had no choice but to slay both his wife and her lover according to the code of the Afghans.[2]

As Burnes and his companions prepared to leave Peshawar on April 19, Sultan Mohammed attached one of his soldiers to the party for protection and provided them with six blank sheets of paper bearing his seal so that they could fill them out on the trip as needed. Burnes liked Sultan Mohammed; "nothing could surpass the kindness of this nobleman." The shrewd Mohan Lal, however, was less impressed, describing the governor as "notorious for his lewdness and always surrounded by females, both married and unmarried."

Burnes's party again dressed simply for the road in keeping with their efforts to appear inconspicuous. Burnes assumed the name Sikunder, the local rendering of Alexander, and hoped to pass himself off as an Armenian from India. Mohan Lal called himself Hasan Jan, a Moslem name to replace his obviously Hindu name.

Burnes wrote his mother from Peshawar: "Never was there a more humble being seen. I have no tent, no chair or table, no bed and my clothes altogether amount to the value of one pound sterling."[3] He was rapidly becoming an Afghan and learning Afghan ways. He had shaved his head and grown a beard; even his own mother, he felt, "would disown him" if she saw him. "I gird my loins and tie on my sword on all occasions," he wrote, "though I freely admit I would make more use of silver and gold than of cold steel." When entering the humble huts of the Afghans he would put his hand on his heart and utter with humility, "Peace be unto thee," according to Afghan custom. He found the Afghans "kind-hearted and hospitable" with no prejudices against Christians or Englishmen—a conclusion he would later discover was not altogether valid. He spoke their language flawlessly, observed their customs, denied he ever ate pork and abstained from spirits. Above all, he was solicitous of their religion. In short, he was the quintessential agent to work among the Moslems of Central Asia. Yet one day he would bring down on his head the wrath of the Afghans for flouting customs he knew so well.

Kabul fascinated Burnes. Soon after his arrival he toured the city soaking up its ambiance. An avid student of the history of this part of the world, he quickly sought out the tomb of Emperor Babur, who died in 1530 after establishing the Moghul dynasty of India. Preferring to be interred in Kabul, the city of his youth, rather than in Delhi, the city of conquest, he was buried beneath two slabs of marble on a hill a mile from the city. In 1640 a white marble mosque was built on the site with a clear stream running through it to commemorate the great leader, a descendant of Tamerlane. In his memoir Babur expressed his fondness for Kabul. With the soul of a poet he swore there was no place like it in the known world, and with the thirst of an imbiber he urged his readers to "send round the cup without stopping" while feasting their eyes on it. Notwithstanding Babur's rhapsodizing, an old Afghan saying states: "When the Devil was cast out of Heaven, he fell in Kabul." But Devil or no, Burnes, like Babur (whose Kabul was not so different than Burnes's), was attracted by the city and called it "paradise."

Burnes and Mohan Lal (poor Gerard was immediately confined to his bed by dysentery) were enchanted by the great bazaar—better than anything they had seen in India. At night the lamps hung in front of each shop shone brightly, illuminating the town. Mohan Lal thought the covered bazaar exceeded anything the imagination could conjure up: "The shops rise over each other in steps glittering in tinsel splendor till from the effect of elevation the whole fades into a confused and twinkling mass, like stars shining through the clouds."[4]

Kabul, a city of some sixty to eighty thousand souls, was a hodgepodge of two-story adobe houses, sprawled within a circumference of some three miles. Crooked streets meandered about the city in apparent disorder, creating a maze through which the Afghans went about their business. Kabul had been an important crossroads of commerce for centuries, and in the Char Chouk Bazaar along Kabul's main street, people of a dozen varieties noisily jostled each other as they bought or sold goods from all over. Every trade had its own section of the bazaar. There were the fruit bazaar, the leather bazaar, the booksellers, shoemakers, ironmongers and carpenters. Crowding the bakeries were Kabul housewives waiting for fresh, still-warm unleavened flaps of bread while criers ran through the streets shouting *"shahbash rhuwash"* ("glory to rhubarb"). Storytellers entertained the idlers, and mendicants intoned the glories of the Prophet.

Burnes commented on the fact that there were no wheeled carriages in Kabul. He was most struck by the robust people he saw who "sauntered about, dressed in sheep-skin cloaks [*pushtins*]." The children's "chubby red cheeks" glowed with good health while elderly people, worn by their hard lives, were bent and wrinkled. The city was densely built and had "no pretenses to elegance." Only a few houses owned by noblemen were graced with large walled gardens shaded by fruit trees and cooled by fountains. Bisecting the city was the normally tranquil Kabul River, which could, however, become savage in spate, as could the people who drew water from it.

The surrounding barren hills, sloping upward toward the snow-peaked mountains beyond, framed the city. The great Bala Hissar, citadel of countless rulers, was—and still is—poised 150 feet above the southeastern edge of the city. At its base was a vast enclosure whose walls and moats had fallen into disrepair by the time Burnes saw them. But higher on the conical mountain was the upper citadel, whose mighty walls circling its quarter-mile girth still stood staunchly on guard. Within this inner citadel was a smaller palace called the Kulah-i-ferangi, or European's Hat, because of its top-hat appearance as seen from the town below.

Sidling up to the Bala Hissar, as though seeking royal protection from the predominantly Moslem population, was the Armenian quarter, by then a small fraction of its once-considerable size and affluence. The Armenians had come with the Persian emperor Nadir Shah and had remained as traders and wine merchants when the great conqueror departed in 1738. But when Dost Mohammed banned drinking, he forced many of the Armenians out of work and obliged them to move elsewhere. The leader of the Armenian colony, one Simon Mugurditch, known by the Moslems as Suleiman, pleaded with Burnes to intervene with Dost Mohammed to legalize wine and spirits so that the remnant of the once-prosperous community could survive.

In the southwestern part of the city was the important Kizzilbash quarter, housing descendants of Nadir Shah's royal guard, whose origins can be traced to the Turkic-Tartar hordes that swept into Persia during an earlier time. Nadir Shah had left some of his Kizzilbash legions in Kabul to garrison the city after he left. The Kizzilbash, not part of the traditional Afghan clan structure, were a disruptive influence—sort of a wild card in the city's politics that was looked down upon by most Afghans but never ignored.

While not yet firmly enough in power to crown himself formally emir, or king, of Afghanistan, Dost Mohammed had emerged preeminent among the contenders for the Afghan throne and ruled most of the country with a strong hand. Burnes was curious about the man who would likely prove important to British strategy. Nawab Jubbar Khan escorted Burnes and Mohan Lal to the first royal audience—Dr. Gerard was still immobilized by dysentery and had to miss the occasion. Flanked by three of his sons and a covey of courtiers, Dost Mohammed received Burnes graciously. He asked him a wide range of questions: How many kings were there in Europe? How did they get on with each other? Was England's wealth solely a result of its India trade? The Afghan ruler was interested to know about China, whose western edge touched the eastern tongue of Afghanistan, known as the Wakkan Corridor; were the Chinese a warlike people, and why did they look so different? He wanted to know if European countries raised their armies by conscription, as he heard the Russians did.

While Burnes in the euphoria of his adventure took an immediate liking to Dost Mohammed, Mohan Lal saw in Kabul's ruler lingering traces of an earlier, darker side. Mohan Lal had praise for Dost Mohammed's astuteness, but intuitively he felt that the man was "not a character in whom one could place the confidence either of permanent friendship or political allegiance."[5] Someone who had killed many people, confiscated property and, despite oaths on the "holy soul of Mohammed," referred to the Koran as simply "leaves of a common book," was not good, although Mohan Lal conceded that such acts could have been the result of the "necessity of the times."[6] The necessities of the times were indeed demanding, as a glimpse of his early life reveals.

Dost Mohammed was not only the youngest of his fathers's twenty-one sons, but his mother, from the Persian Kizzilbash community, was looked down upon by the other ladies of the zenana. Generally ignored by his many half-brothers, Dost Mohammed in his youth had attached himself to his powerful and much older brother, Fateh Khan, the Barakzai vizier who served—or rather manipulated—Shah Mahmud. Young Dost Mohammed was content to serve Fateh Khan's household as a virtual slave, fetching the great man's water pipe and doing other such menial errands. But he made good use of this experience, gaining by his propinquity with the vizier a valuable education in guile and tribal politics.

Dost Mohammed's rise within the Barakzai clan despite his relatively humble beginnings could be attributed to more than simply basking in the vizier's favor. He was an exceptional young man whose qualities of leadership and bravery showed themselves early in life. There was, however, a darker side to his character.

Early in his service with Fateh Khan, Dost Mohammed was used to discipline enemies of the regime. To prove his zeal, on one occasion, when he was no more than fourteen years old, he killed a man in cold blood on mere suspicion. Dost Mohammed was also prone to drunkenness. It was not uncommon for him to while away his spare time in drinking orgies with other debauched cavaliers. The American mercenary Josiah Harlan, who came to know Dost Mohammed well, described the Afghan leader's pro-fligate youth in florid prose: "Surrounded by a crowd of drunken revellers maddened by the maniac draught of the frantic bowl, friend and colleague, master, man and slave, all indiscriminate and promiscuous actors in the wild, voluptuous, licentious scene of shameless bacchanals, they caroused and drank with prostitutes and singers and fiddlers, day and night, in one long interminable cycle."[7] This Hogarth-like scene, Afghan-style, does not seem to square with the Dost Mohammed whom Burnes met, nor was it characteristic of the ruler's more mature years, but his youthful excesses once rocked the kingdom.

It happened when Fateh Khan entrusted young Dost Mohammed with a devious mission to seize Herat. On the pretense of reinforcing the town that in 1817 had been threatened by a Persian invasion, Dost Mohammed and his army seized the city to bring it under Fateh Khan's control. Dost Mohammed captured the unsuspecting governor, a member of the rival Saddozai clan, and ordered the palace guard slaughtered. Then, going beyond the bounds of accepted rapaciousness, Dost Mohammed commit-ted the unpardonable sin of violating the zenana. He ripped the robes from one of the Saddozai noblewoman and seized her jeweled girdle. And, it was reported, "he treated her rudely in other ways."[8] Such provocation was the stuff of blood feuds in Afghanistan; the deeply offended, hysterical lady sent her defiled clothing to Kabul and demanded vengeance against the Barakzai clan.

Having inflamed the anger of the shah, Dost Mohammed found it prudent to flee to Kashmir while most of his many Barakzai brothers similarly sought safe haven from Saddozai wrath. But the vizier, taken unawares by Dost Mohammed's rash action in the Herat zenana, was seized by Shah Mahmud with encouragement from the Persians and held accountable for the young man's crimes as well as his own perfidy in ordering the overthrow of Saddozai rule in Herat.

Afghan vengeance was an awesome thing. The consequences of betrayal were worse than quick death. Crown Prince Kamran, Saddozai judge and high executioner in this case, personally stabbed Fateh Khan's eyes with the point of his dagger and had him scalped as a preliminary ritual of revenge. More than retribution was sought; the Barakzais had to pay the penalty for their disloyalty. Kamran and his father, Shah Mahmud, demanded that the dreadfully suffering Fateh Khan command his brothers, particularly Dost Mohammed, as perpetrator of the Herat atrocity, to give themselves up. This the vizier refused to do. He was loyal to his clan and courageous beyond belief.

An eyewitness to the torture inflicted on the vizier told a grisly tale to a British officer who recorded it: "Fateh Khan was brought into a tent in which sat a circle of his mortal foes." Each had a personal score to settle with the doomed vizier that lent terrible ferocity to their punishment. "They commenced by each in turn accusing him of injuries received at his hands, and heaping upon him the most approbrious epithets." Then khan after khan, each in his turn, stepped up to the bound prisoner, sword in hand. The first cut off one of his ears, the second sliced off the remaining ear. The third cut off his nose. And then his hands were amputated, "the blood gushing copiously from each new wound."9

Up to this point Fateh Khan had exhibited astonishing bravery and stoicism. But when they began to cut off his beard, the supreme symbol of manhood and dignity among Afghans, the vizier "burst into a passion of tears." He then had to endure his feet being chopped off, one by one, before he was put out of his misery by a knife to his throat.

Dost Mohammed felt obliged to avenge his older brother's terrible death and began his own march to power. For the next eight years civil war raged in Afghanistan, until in 1826 Dost Mohammed outwitted and outgunned his rival brothers to gain control of Kabul.

For all his youthful excesses, Dost Mohammed had the will to reform himself upon gaining power. Impressed with the challenges and responsibilities facing him, he performed the *Tuba,* a Moslem ritual of reformation, and insisted that his followers do the same. He foreswore drinking and outlawed spirits, assumed humble costume and in an abrupt change from his cavalier personality became courteous and kind. He made himself accessible to the common man and made a point of addressing their complaints. Dost Mohammed dramatically confessed his earlier sins and promised to lead a life of morality and austerity. Perhaps even more remarkable, he educated himself and mastered the teachings of the Koran.

Dost Mohammed was an impressive-looking man; Mohan Lal commented on his "tall stature and haughty countenance with his proud tone of speech." But he noted, "He trusts no one but himself, and is surrounded by numerous enemies, both of his own family and court." This latter, of course could be said of any Afghan ruler. Josiah Harlan's description of Dost Mohammed was more unflattering than Mohan Lal's. In the American's view, Dost Mohammed was a "monster of rapacity," whose eyes "had a feline glare when he looked full in the face of anyone." Harlan also accused him of vanity and of being susceptible to empty flattery. Despite Dost's reputation as a warrior, Harlan thought him essentially a timid soul, prone to crumble under pressure. Perhaps this was the consequence of sobering maturity. Harlan put it colorfully: "In youth he was bold from necessity, but probably the experience of years and the voluptuous excesses of luxurious leisure, in taking off the wiry edge from the sword of his ambition, dulled the instrument and deprived its temper."[10] Yet, wrote Harlan in his memoir, these very traits plus his understanding of the Afghan people and his "unprincipled readiness at despotic sway" made him "well adapted to govern the worse-than-savage tribes he had to command."

In his mid-forties, Dost Mohammed was tall, even by Afghan standards, and had a bowed look typical of his family. As described by Harlan, he had a Roman, aquiline nose, "finished with beautiful delicacy." He eyes were hazel-gray, his mouth "large and vulgar and full of bad teeth,"[11] and he had a rich black beard, dyed every Thursday in preparation for the Moslem sabbath.

This, then, was the man with whom Burnes would try to establish a relationship in the interest of buffering India from the Russians.

In Kabul Burnes and his companions were lodged in the house of Nawab Jubbar Khan, vizier and half-brother of Dost Mohammed—the same person with whom Harlan had earlier intrigued against Dost Mohammed in behalf of Shah Shuja. The Nawab would feature prominently in British-Afghan relations, and until disillusioned by British policy toward his country would be the Company's staunchest friend in court.

In a subsequent meeting, Dost Mohammed came to grips with politics. This time Burnes was accompanied by Dr. Gerard, who had recovered, and Mohan Lal. They all talked until well past midnight, Dost Mohammed describing frankly his domestic problems: the internecine conflicts that plagued Afghanistan and prevented him from restoring an uncontested monarchy. He expressed himself freely about his antagonistic neighbor, Ranjit Singh. Did the British have designs on Afghanistan, or would they join with the Afghans to eliminate the Sikh menace? The latter was the key question, one that would finally drive a wedge between Dost Mohammed and the British, but for the moment the talks were cordial, each man making an effort to be accommodating.

Burnes denied that the British had any hostile intentions toward Afghanistan; to the contrary, he said, they wanted a close relationship with the Afghans and help from them in dampening Russian ambitions south and east of the Caspian Sea. Burnes explained that Ranjit Singh was a friend with whom India had a treaty relationship that must be honored. But the subject of Ranjit Singh and his Punjab kingdom, which obsessed Dost Mohammed, impressed on Burnes the difficulty the British would have in trying to maintain friendly terms with these two neighboring rulers so hostile to each other. Both were important to the British in view of the Russian threat, but they were irreconcilable.

Burnes and Dost Mohammed got on well. The Afghan leader, in fact, invited Burnes to leave Company service and accept command of his army. This was surely a maneuver to bind the British close to him at the expense of Ranjit Singh. "Twelve thousand horse and twenty guns shall be at your disposal,"[12] Dost promised. Burnes, of course, refused.

Dost Mohammed made a deep impression on Burnes during the latter's three-week stay in Kabul. Now that a comparison was possible, the British envoy concluded that Dost Mohammed was a giant compared to the exiled Saddozai king, Shah Shuja. Burnes concluded prophetically that the dynasty of the Saddozai was finished unless it could "be propped up by foreign aid." The British must look for another family to rule Afghanistan, "and this, in all probability, will be the Barakzai, the clan of Dost Mohammed,"[13] he believed. The canny Mohan Lal, however, continued to be more measured in his view of Dost Mohammed. "I dare say he will side with that power which appears strongest in the field,"[14] Mohan Lal concluded realistically.

While Burnes was in Kabul a curious event occurred: news of an Englishman in distress in the mountains north of Kabul drifted in. The man turned out to be an eccentric, peripatetic missionary named Joseph Wolff, who had been enslaved by Afghan tribes after visiting Bokhara. But what had he been doing in Bokhara and how had he met with misadventure? With Nawab Jubbar Khan's intercession, Burnes managed to have Wolff rescued. When the poor missionary arrived in Kabul, it was even more apparent that he had been badly mistreated during his captivity. All his clothes had been taken from him and his horse was lost in a snowstorm, forcing him to walk to Kabul virtually naked. But none of this seemed to have dampened his missionary zeal when he arrived.

Wolff's story emerged. The son of a German Jewish rabbi, he had become British and adopted the Roman Catholic faith. Wolff had traveled widely in Asia preaching the Gospel of his adopted religion. On this particularly foolhardy journey to Bokhara and Kabul his objective had been to find the ten lost tribes of Israel, which, he was convinced, were somewhere in that part of the world. Burnes was bemused by the eccentric Wolff who had beaten him to Bokhara, but he enjoyed his company and learned much about the route his party was about to take. Mohan Lal, who complained that Wolff had tried to convert him to Christianity, was put off by his claim to have talked with Jesus Christ in Bokhara and Christ's prediction that the Vale of Kashmir would become the new Jerusalem.

Despite his claim to be in search of the ten lost tribes, Wolff curiously made little effort to look into the Afghan legend of the Ben-i-Israel, or Children of Israel, as many northern Afghans refer to themselves. The theory that the Afghans are descended from Jews who migrated or were transplanted eastward in an early diaspora centuries ago has never been proved, but the tradition still survives in Afghanistan and some Afghan customs do seem to bear a resemblance to those of the Jews.*

Wolff was really more interested in Christian sermonizing than in finding lost tribes of Israel, and Burnes cringed as he listened to the disputatious missionary debate a group of the city's leading Muslim clerics brought together by Dost Mohammed to argue the merits of Islam versus Christianity.

In the course of his stay Burnes established a good relationship with Dost Mohammed and learned much about his situation. Dost Mohammed learned just as much about Burnes, and could draw certain conclusions about British intentions. Just as the Russians from Orenburg, their farthest outpost on the edge of Central Asia, looked covetously southward to Khiva and Bokhara, and from their vantage point in Persia looked eastward to Afghanistan, the British looked northwestward from India to the lands drained by the Indus River and to Afghanistan. Dost Mohammed could uneasily conclude that his kingdom was becoming the fulcrum of imperial competition and that he could be caught in the middle. As Burnes headed toward Bokhara, the Russians could conclude that the British had ambitions in Central Asia and that his mission was a challenge they could not ignore.

---

*As Burnes heard the story, Nebuchadnezzar, after the overthrow of the Temple of Jerusalem, moved some of the Jews to the town of Ghor, northwest of Kabul. They later became known as Afghans because their leader, son of the uncle of King Soleiman's vizier, Azov, was named Afghana. But the community retained their Jewish faith until converted to Islam sometime during the first century of Islam.

Chapter 6

BOKHARA

THE PRINCIPAL ROUTE FROM KABUL TO BOKHARA WAS A RUGGED ONE, requiring the traveler to cross the mountainous Hindu Kush spine of Afghanistan. Caravans crawled westward from Kabul to Bamiyan through the rugged lands of the Hazara, a tribal remnant of thirteenth-century Mongols who scratched out a meager living as herdsmen and farmers. Then the way turned northward to Balkh of antiquity—"the mother of cities"—before crossing the Oxus and running northwestward through the Turkestan desert to Bokhara. This was a route that had attracted British interest since it might one day be used by Imperial Russian troops invading Afghanistan.

Not unlike another well-known nineteenth-century traveler, Sir Richard Burton, Burnes was in his element observing newly discovered peoples and their customs. Strategic and political intelligence was a game Burnes thoroughly enjoyed, particularly when he could immerse himself in the ways of the natives. Also like Burton, he reveled in the sexual side of life among the natives. The Hazaras, then more inclined to be libertine than most Afghan societies, seemed to hold particular fascination for Burnes. One sect of the Hazaras professed to be dedicated to purifying Islam, but, it was said, they spent much of their time after dark in bacchanalian sex orgies. Burnes had also heard that in some Hazara villages it was the custom for a husband to share his wives with guests. To his evident disappointment, this turned out to be untrue, although the womenfolk, unfettered by having to wear the burkha or veil, flaunted their considerable beauty and generally seemed "not to be very chaste." Mohan Lal was also swept away by the ladies' charms, admitting that he himself had "exerted his curiosity as far as decency permitted, but did not quite succeed."[1]

On reading Burnes's account of the Hazaras, with its suggestion of prurient interest, one is tempted to conclude that he wrote with the authority of personal experience. Had the trusting Hazaras not mistaken him and his companions for Persians of the Shia sect of Islam—a result of their light disguises—and realized instead that their visitors were foreign infidels, any sexual indiscretions on his part would probably have been severely dealt with. While amorous dalliance must have had its place with virile soldiers of the Company, Afghanistan, a land of Moslem zealotry, was not a place in which to experiment. Certainly Burnes's preoccupation with the women of Afghanistan would lead him into a perilous pastime.

On reaching Bamiyan, Burnes gazed at the ruins and relics of another age, two awesome colossi carved out of a rock escarpment, one 120 feet high, the other 70 feet high. Dating from the third or early fourth century A.D., the giant statues were centerpieces for other statuary from the Buddhist period. Surrounding the colossi were caves hewn out of the rock to accommodate Buddhist monks of the period. Buddhism had long since disappeared from Afghanistan, but it was nonetheless curious that the local inhabitants seemed uninterested in the evidence of an ancient culture all about them and quite unaware of its Buddhist origin.

After being warned in Kabul, Burnes had not wanted to risk a visit to Kunduz, infamous for the cruel caprices of its ruler, who had grown rich by slaving. But the mir had received word that there was a party of travelers from Afghanistan heading for Bokhara and insisted that they pay their respects to him in Kunduz. Fearing the worst, Burnes left his companions and all their baggage in the relative safety of a town some seventy miles from Kunduz and ventured forth on his risky detour with only the merchant, Nazir, who was now sorry that he had attached himself to their party in Kabul. Burnes pretended to be Nazir's servant, an Indian Armenian calling himself Sikunder Alaverdi—much to the distress of the frightened merchant, who was terrified at the thought of covering a dis-guised Englishman at the court of the mir.

Despite rumors that had already begun to spread in Kunduz, particularly in the Indian community, that Nazir's so-called Indian servant was, in fact, a European, Burnes's disguise held up. But had Murad Beg discovered that there was an English infidel in his midst trying to hide his identity, Burnes's days would have been numbered and unpleasantly spent: the mir's favorite way of disposing of prisoners was to put them in a pit filled with deadly poisonous creatures—scorpions and snakes—to die a slow and hideous death.

Mir Murad Beg was a villainous-looking Uzbek with harsh Mongol features and a perpetually brooding expression. That was all Burnes wanted to know about him at this point. Having survived his visit to Kunduz and his audience with the mir as an attendant of Nazir, Burnes was glad to leave the town as soon as he could and return to his companions waiting apprehensively for him so that they could resume their journey to Balkh and Bokhara. A local proverb expressed the sentiments of most travelers as well as those of Burnes: "If you wish to die, go to Kunduz." With great relief, on June 8 the reunited party reached Balkh, a satrapy of Bokhara but for the moment beyond the reach of the evil mir. This was the Bactria of antiquity, although now the place, victim of rapacious conquerers through the ages, bore little evidence of its ancient glory.

Near Balkh Burnes visited the melancholy grave of William Moorcroft, veterinary surgeon of the East India Company, who had died seven years earlier under somewhat mysterious circumstances.[2] In 1819 Moorcroft, accompanied by a geologist named George Trebeck and a Eurasian physi-cian named Guthrie, had set out on a pioneering journey of exploration to Kunduz and Bokhara from which they never returned. Except for an English trader named Anthony Jenkinson, famous for his early activities in Russia, who had visited Bokhara in 1558, and a Company official named George Forster, who had passed through these areas on his way to Russia in 1783, no Englishman had before been to Bokhara. It was not uncom-mon for Company officers to volunteer for such hazardous missions. The intelligence they gathered was valuable, but the Company reserved the right to disavow official sponsorship of such missions if they provoked political complications.[3] Certainly Moorcroft, Trebeck and Guthrie were generally assumed to have been British agents by the natives they met north of the Khyber Pass. Like Kim's horse-dealing friend, Mahbub Ali— alias C-25, secret agent of the India Survey Department in Kipling's classic story of the Great Game—Moorcroft should have expected that he would be under suspicion, particularly in view of the rash actions he took. He infuriated the governor general in Calcutta, for example, when en route he took it upon himself to encourage the chief minister of Ladakh and the khans of Peshawar to become vassals of the British—unauthorized actions certain to alarm the British ally, Ranjit Singh, who claimed suzerainty over both neighboring territories.[4]

Just how the three men had died was not clear, although they probably succumbed to disease. Most of Moorcroft's letters and journals had found their way back to Calcutta and were probably of benefit to Burnes as background before he set out for Bokhara. Moorcroft's reports had, in fact, made a considerable impact in London, where the British government took seriously—perhaps too seriously—his alarmist conclusions about the activities of Russian agents in Turkestan.

On June 26, six months after starting out on his epic journey to Central Asia, Burnes and his companions reached the fabled city of Bokhara, once graced by Tamerlane himself. The emir, Nasrullah Bahadur Khan, at first denied them even entrance to the city, but relented after Burnes sent him an artfully written appeal drafted by Mohan Lal. Bokhara was not the "paradise of the world," as the ancients described it, but after the searing desert he had crossed, Burnes thought it delightful.

The staunchly Islamic city of some 150,000 people was impressive. Two miles from the principal city gate and in the shadow of the emir's palace was the great bazaar of Bokhara, the Registan. Flanking the Registan on two sides were massive buildings, colleges for the learned, while on another side was "a fountain, filled with water and shaded by lofty trees where idlers and newsmongers assembled round the wares of Asia and Europe. . . ." Rising in the background was the city's most impressive building, the great mosque of Bokhara, whose minaret towered two hundred feet above the ground.

Burnes spent many of his evenings in the Registan. "A stranger has only to seat himself on a bench of the Registan to know the Uzbeks and the people of Bokhara," he wrote. As a major crossroads in Central Asia, one could see people of many races. Among others there were Persians, Turks, Russians, Mongols, Chinese, Indians and Afghans. Once could also meet Turkomans, Calmucks and Cossacks, who had come to town from the surrounding desert.

Bokhara was famous for its fruit. "One wonders at the never-ending employment of the fruiterers in dealing out their grapes, melons, apricots, apples, peaches, pears and plums," Burnes wrote. He gloried in the "moving mass of human beings." The crooked lanes of the city were crowded; only with difficulty can one move through them and "only at the risk of being run over by someone on a horse or donkey." When not jamming the streets, everyone seemed to be drinking tea in the shops.

In one section of town one could find bookstalls "where the learned, or would-be so, pore over tattered pages." Bokhara was a city of scholars, boasting scores of schools and colleges, the most famous of which was the College of King Abdullah. Students, many of whom were "old men with more hypocrisy, but by no means less vice, than the youths in other quarters of the world" lounged in front of their schools. As night fell, the "King's drum" beat, to be echoed by lesser drums throughout the city warning that no one was permitted to venture in the streets without lanterns, could be heard.

On a grimmer note, Bokhara had a slave bazaar in which Persians and people of other nationalities captured by Turkoman raiders were offered for sale every Saturday. The buyers had to satisfy themselves that the slaves were infidels, i.e., Shia-sect Moslems not from the Sunni sect, which dominated Bokhara, and were free of leprosy—almost as great a stigma as being a Persian Shia. Also for sale from time to time were Russians, mostly sailors captured in the Caspian Sea, whose hard-working nature made them highly prized.[5]

Burnes tried the public baths, picturesque places housed in vaulted chambers lit by domed skylights of colored glass, where one was "rubbed with a hair brush, scrubbed, buffeted and kicked," but withal refreshed by the experience. The baths were good places to pick up local gossip and generally get a feel for the city. Mohan Lal, no less inquisitive, visited the Jewish quarter, where some three thousand Jews lived. He was impressed by the beauty of the Jewish women, in his opinion the only attractive ladies in Bokhara. Burnes's tastes favored the Uzbek women, whom he found alluring. "The ladies of Bokhara stain their teeth quite black," he wrote, but underneath their veils were "many a lovely countenance, born to blush unseen." Again we see an Alexander Burnes who seems to know what he is talking about when discussing women. Shrouds covering the women protected them from being lusted after by men other than their husbands—or so their husbands thought. In fact, adultery was not uncommon despite the ultimate penalty of death if caught.

Burnes and his companions lived in very small and cramped quarters during their month-long stay in Bokhara. But as an ever-alert connoisseur of female beauty, Burnes saw at least one advantage: "it presented an opportunity of seeing a Turkee beauty, a handsome young lady, who promenaded on one of the surrounding balconies. . . ." To Burnes's delight, "Curiosity prompted her to steal a glance at the Ferangis," but she was too distant to indulge "in the sweet music of speech."[6] Considering the fact that only the head mullah of the city was permitted to mount the high minaret of the great mosque because of the vantage point these perches presented to seeing the ladies of Bokhara sunning themselves on their rooftops, Burnes's ogling was not without danger.

Punishments for a variety of crimes were severe in Bokhara. One could be executed for cursing one's mother, or be whipped unmercifully for not saying one's prayers. Smoking and drinking spirits were punished by various forms of public humiliation. Thieves and adulterers were thrown to their deaths from the minaret of the great mosque, while other transgressors of Moslem law could be condemned to the infamous vermin-infested pits to die a slightly more gradual death.

Burnes was never received by Emir Nasrullah despite efforts to obtain an audience, but he caught a glimpse of him one day leaving the mosque. The emir was unprepossessing, a gaunt and pale young man of about thirty years. Wolff had described him as a person of "deplorable morals," a sadistic homosexual who delighted in devising new forms of torture, and Burnes had heard nothing to change this description.

Burnes and his companions had been circumspect in their actions while in Bokhara, lest they provoke the capricious emir to clap them in prison. They had been clearly under suspicion from the outset: the vizier had summoned them for stern questioning. Burnes's story that he was a Company officer simply traveling home to England by way of Central Asia and Russia with no ulterior political motives had not been very convincing, although the vizier defended them after Burnes bought his support with a gift of a good English compass.

Burnes regretted that it was unsafe for him to journey on to nearby Samarkand. While thus far unmolested, Burnes did not feel it would be prudent to press his luck. The emir was quite capable of harming or even killing the members of the party on a whim or on the basis of some new suspicion. It was time to leave.

While Burnes had done little of a concrete nature to further British interests—there had been no basis on which to establish a commercial or political relationship—he had at least spent a useful month there, absorbing knowledge of the kingdom and its people, and getting some feel for the extent of Russian influence in that part of Central Asia. Considering Wolff's recent experience, Burnes had been lucky to emerge from Bokhara unscathed. The vizier, at least, had been cordial, and as they were leaving obligingly furnished them with a royal *firman,* ensuring safe conduct from the kingdom.

Burnes and his companions left the city in late July 1832, his reconnaissance objectives more or less achieved. For this feat Alexander Burnes would earn the sobriquet "Bokhara Burnes," by which an admiring British public would thereafter know him. However, the Russian reaction to his mission was anything but admiring. Unconvinced by the pretext that he had just dropped by Bokhara on his way home—particularly since he did not return by way of Russia—St. Petersburg considered it provocation, a trespassing in an area not yet in its grasp but within its sphere of influence.

Chapter 7

FATH ALI SHAH, PERSIA'S KING OF KINGS

Burnes's return route from Bokhara by way of Persia took him and his party through the bleak, waterless Turkestan desert east of the Caspian Sea. They had heard that the khan of Khiva, ruler of the steppes bordering the Aral Sea to the north, was campaigning in the area, plundering caravans and seizing travelers for slaves as his forces ominously moved southward toward the Persian border. Burnes and his companions, who found themselves in the path of the invading Khivans, had to wait a month before receiving assurances from the khan that they would not be molested and could proceed safely.

It was a depressing land through which they passed. A north wind continually whipped the desert. What few signs of life they encountered were slave depots where Persian slaves huddled in misery awaiting their fate. Whatever assurances Burnes had received from the khan of Khiva did not keep his party from being robbed by the local Turkoman tribesmen, nor did it spare him other misadventures, which included encounters with a camel gone mad and poisonous spiders with stingers as large as a scorpion's.

The forlorn group finally crossed safely into Persia and reached Meshed, principal city of Khorasan Province in the northeast part of the country. Meshed was the site of the venerated ninth-century Islamic shrine where the crypt of the Imam Reza, fifth in descent from the Prophet Mohammed's son-in-law, Ali, was—and still is—interred. As a holy city, Meshed was a place of religious fervor where devout, ecstatic pilgrims converged from all over. It would normally not have been a congenial place for a party of infidels. On this occasion, however, Burnes was greeted hospitably by the acting governor, son of Persian Crown Prince Abbas Mirza, encamped nearby with his expeditionary army in a village called Quchan as he prepared to met the Afghan Army of Herat in battle.

Burnes and his companions went on to Quchan to pay their respects to the crown prince himself and join him and his senior officers for breakfast. It was a diverse group that dined with Abbas Mirza: besides Burnes, Gerard and Mohan Lal, there was British Captain Shee of the Company's Madras Army, whom it seems had been lent to the Persians, and Polish mercenary officers Borowski and Beek, who were in the hire of the Persians.

The crown prince urged Burnes to plead his cause with the British government; his problem, put simply, was that he was without funds to pay and equip his army properly. He ingenuously claimed that he had taken the field to suppress the slave traffic carried on by the Turkoman tribes across the border. With tortuous reasoning he argued: "I am entitled, therefore, to the assistance of Britain, for if you expend annually thousands of pounds in suppressing the slave trade in Africa, I deserve your aid in this quarter where the same motives exist for the exercise of your philanthropy."[1] The crown prince, faced with the forces of Herat and possibly Khivan marauders as well, was presenting his own inept and faltering campaign against Herat as a philanthropic crusade against slavery deserving of British assistance for humanitarian reasons. Burnes was polite but not impressed with his argument.

On September 29, 1832, Burnes left his companions of the road, Gerard and Mohan Lal, to make their way back to India by way of Herat, Kandahar and Kabul, while he, according to plan, set out for Persia's Caspian Sea coast, an area that had eluded British reconnaissance yet was strategically important in view of Russia's domination of the Caspian.

From the Caspian coast Burnes traveled southward across the Alborz range to Tehran. This would be his first occasion to describe in person his epic journey to British officialdom. In Tehran, British minister Sir John

Campbell was fascinated by Burnes's firsthand account of Bokhara and the details of Crown Prince Abbas Mirza's problems in Khorasan.

Campbell had arranged an interview for Burnes with Persia's monarch, Fath Ali Shah, who was understandably eager to get news from the Khorasan front. Campbell and Burnes saw their interview as a protocol duty, but it did provide an occasion to impress the shah with the dangers to Persia of a Russian-dominated Central Asia.

BURNES WAS, OF COURSE, WELL VERSED IN RECENT PERSIAN HISTORY AND the trials of Fath Ali Shah during three frustrating decades devoted to parrying Russian threats and thrusts against his empire. It had been frustrating for the British to be unable to prevent the czar from establishing a dominant position in Persia and all that meant for the security of India. Russia had annexed Georgia, a vassal of the shah, in 1801, then by a crushing military defeat in 1812 had imposed on Persia the Treaty of Gulistan a year later, in which the Persians gave up much of their remaining claim to the Caucasus. In 1817 the Russians had pressed for even more concessions from Persia and the czar had sent to Tehran an awesome envoy, General Alexis Yermolov, to make his demands. Yermolov, "the Muscovy Devil," as the Persians called him, was no ordinary envoy—no ordinary man for that matter.[2] As commander in chief of all southern Russian armies and governor of the Caucasus, his giant physique and thunderous voice was backed by the authority of Russian military power. He was a mammoth man—allegedly descended from Genghis Khan,[3] mighty conquerer of Asia. The general's courage was legendary in the Russian Imperial Army. As chief of staff of the Imperial 2nd Army, he had distinguished himself in battle against Napoleon's legions. His awestruck troops swore that the enemy's bullets could not pierce him, and some said that his force of will was so powerful that he could stop his own heart from beating! Yermolov was proud to admit: "I relied on my wild beast's muzzle, my gigantic and terrifying figure and limitless voice; they [the Persians] were convinced that anyone who could shout so vociferously had good reasons to be obeyed."

What Yermolov had not been able to do by his bullying diplomacy, the Russian Army did by brute force. The Russians in 1827 defeated the Persians in battle and occupied Tabriz, the important capital of Persia's Azerbaijan province south of the Caucasus. The Treaty of Turkmanchai, signed the following year, ended all Persian claims to the Caucasus and marked the loss of its status as a fully sovereign nation. Turkmanchai changed the situation for the British as well. With peace on Russian terms, the British could no longer exploit Persian-Russian hostility to win over the shah to their side. Moreover, the Persians were resentful of the British for not having protected them from Russian aggression.

When the Duke of Wellington became prime minister of England and named Lord Ellenborough as president of the Board of Control overseeing Indian policy in September 1828, the Persian problem was reexamined both in London and in Calcutta. Russia was now in an enviable position. In Governor General Bentinck's opinion, Persia was not only in no position to impede Russia should the czar "take it into its head to invade India," but would probably help Russia as an ally.

As president of the India Board, Ellenborough was less apprehensive about any immediate Russian military threat, but saw the game as one of commercial rivalry. While he accepted the possibility of an eventual Russian advance to Kabul—either across Persia by way of Herat or via Khiva and Turkestan and down through the passes of the Hindu Kush—he did not think it would happen in the near term. More likely there would first be Russian commercial expansion into India's northwestern borderlands, and by watching this the czar's ultimate intentions could be foreseen.

Adding to British concerns was a Russian defeat of a Turkish army in the Caucasus that resulted in the Treaty of Adrianople, with Turkey giving the Russians possession of several ports along the Caucasus coast of the Black Sea. Coming in the wake of the Treaty of Turkmanchai humbling Persia, the Treaty of Adrianople humbling Turkey added to Britain's alarm and dramatized their seeming inability to contain Russian aggression.

To see to the enforcement of the Treaty of Turkmanchai, the czar in the autumn of 1828 sent a special envoy, Alexander Griboyedov, to Tehran.* Quite unexpectedly, this would lead to one of those explosive human dramas that the mullahs of the devout Shia sect of Islam in Persia are so apt to provoke by their zealousness. As Griboyedov and his entourage arrived at Tehran's gates, they encountered a turbulent mob observing the traditional rituals of the holy day Moharram in memory of a revered martyr. The crowd hypnotically chanted a traditional refrain and lacerated themselves with chains and whips. As the blood flowed from their self-

*A decade before these events, Alexander Griboyedov had been diplomatic secretary to General Yermolov. Griboyedov was quite a different kind of person than the hard-charging general. He was a sensitive, talented man who wrote plays, one of which had been a controversial, satirical comedy with the intriguing title *Woe Through Wit*, or *The Misfortunes of Being Clever*. Such liberal criticism of life in Russia under the czar was resented by the imperial court, and for a while this studious civil servant was under suspicion of having sympathy with the Decembrist conspirators of 1825 who plotted to overthrow Czar Nicholas.

inflicted wounds, their religious emotions mounted to a frenzy. Some who had reached a numbing state of masochistic ecstasy slashed themselves with swords and knives as they ritually re-created the martyr's death at the hands of an assassin. Suddenly Griboyedov's horse pulled up lame and the envoy had to mount another, a jet-black stallion. To the aroused crowd this was an evil omen; the Shia martyr had been murdered by a man on just such a black horse! With difficulty Griboyedov reached the Russian legation compound as the inflamed crowd swirled about him.

Cries of "holy war" erupted throughout the city as the pent-up frustration at Russian domination was vented in this strange incident. The crowds gathered outside the Russian legation seized on another "outrage"; they demanded that the minister relinquish two Armenian women who, claiming Russian nationality, had escaped from the harem of the shah's son-in-law and sought sanctuary until they could be repatriated to Armenia. When an Armenian eunuch from the shah's seraglio joined them seeking refuge in the legation, the fury of the mullahs became uncontrollable. Rumored to have been encouraged by British agents, the mullahs incited a street mob to storm the Russian compound. The eunuch was seized and torn to bits while Griboyedov with his Cossack guard tried futilely to defend the premises. Finally, the mob overpowered the legation. The hapless envoy and all but one of his staff were murdered. Their corpses were dragged triumphantly through the streets. This incident faded as the Russians accepted Persian official apologies. Being engaged in fighting the Turks at the time, the Russians had not wanted to complicate their situation by arousing further Persian animosity. But such episodes worried the British, who did not want to see the Persians provoke the Russians to tighten their grip on the country.

AGAINST THIS BACKDROP, BURNES PREPARED TO MEET WITH FATH ALI SHAH. One of the most vivid descriptions of Fath Ali Shah in royal regalia was provided by an English traveler who visited the Persian monarch in 1820. The King of Kings, he wrote, "was one blaze of jewels, which literally dazzled the sight on first looking at him." His crown was a three-tiered tiara "of thickly-set diamonds, pearls, rubies and emeralds, so exquisitely disposed as to form a mixture of the most beautiful colours in the brilliant light reflected from its surface." Spraying forth from the crown were black heron feathers "whose bending points were finished with pear-formed pearls of an immense size." Even larger—perhaps the largest in the world—were the pearls comprising two strings crossing the shah's shoulders. "But for splendour, nothing could exceed the broad bracelet round his arms and the belt which encircled his waist that blazed like fire when the rays of the sun met them."[4]

The shah's luxuriant black beard hid an autocratic and sybaritic soul, but perhaps he was no worse than most Oriental despots of his day. As Sir John Malcolm summed up the Persian royal attitude based on impressions gained during his two missions to Tehran: "Instructed to believe themselves born to rule, they conceived that they have only to enjoy the power which they inherit." In the rondo of power, kings "listen to the flatterers by whom they are surrounded till, enervated and subdued by a life of indolence and vice, they fall before a popular native chief or foreign invader."[5]

In those wonderful early Qajar Dynasty portraits of Fath Ali Shah's day, life-size in refreshing contrast to the miniatures that dominate Persian art, dancing women of the harem are often portrayed standing on their heads as though doing jolly cartwheels. Beyond range of the artists' canvases were even jollier scenes; Fath Ali Shah, it was said, happily whiled away the hours as, one by one, naked harem beauties swooped down a slide, especially made for the sport, into the arms of their lord and master before being playfully dunked in a pool.

Fath Ali Shah's regime was perhaps domestically more tranquil than most before him, but transgressors were severely and sometimes innovatively dealt with. The shah would have the teeth of a political dissident pulled out, then hammered into his head. When particularly angry he would don his scarlet "robes of wrath" as he meted out grisly punishment to the accused who stood quaking before him. It was not uncommon for fifty or more condemned men to be made to bow before him as executioners in a macabre choreographed scene lopped off their heads in perfect unison. Foreign envoys were sometimes "privileged" to see prisoners blown from cannons, although the diplomatic corps protested this kind of spectacle after one minister suffered a direct hit from a bloody chunk of flesh.

The shah was more than casually interested in Turkestan and Bokhara, where Burnes had just visited. The Turkoman tribesmen were forever harassing Persian caravans and taking slaves in the border area, but more seriously, the emir of Bokhara and the khan of Khiva had been on the verge of joining with Shah Kamran in defense of Herat and mounting a counter-campaign against the Persians in Khorasan. The Khivan army had, in fact, advanced as far as Merv, just north of Herat, before prudence—or fear of Russian retaliation against him—caused the khan to halt his forces.

Fath Ali Shah placed Burnes and Minister Campbell some forty feet from him in the audience chamber known as the Hall of Mirrors. The

"Attraction of the World," one of many honorifics used to flatter the shah, was dressed in black, against which the striking effect of his magnificent black-dyed beard was somewhat muted. The meeting began as the shah shouted a standard greeting: "Are your brains clear?" Not knowing quite how to answer, Burnes saluted smartly.

Fath Ali Shah was impressed that Burnes had visited so many places. "No Persian could endure the dangers and fatigues of such a journey," he exclaimed. He was interested in the affairs of Kabul, its ruler, Dost Mohammed, and his obstreperous brothers. He recognized the strategic importance of the Turkestan desert, the Hindu Kush mountains and the Oxus River as natural hurdles for any invasion of Afghanistan from the north.

The shah inquired closely as to how his son, Crown Prince Abbas Mirza, was faring in Khorasan. "Can the Persians hold back the Khivans and Turkomans?" he asked. Burnes gave the answer the shah wanted to hear: the Khivans and their Turkoman vassals "would be forced to fall at the Crown Prince's feet." But "What is your opinion of my son's army?" persisted the shah. "Is it efficient?" Burnes again avoided giving him the truth: "No Asiatic power could resist such armament."[6]

When Fath Ali Shah inquired of Burnes as to what he considered the most memorable experience during the journey, the diplomatic Scot replied extravagantly: "O Center of the Universe, what sight could have equalled that which I now behold, the light of your Majesty's countenance." Nothing much had been gained by the shah from his audience except an increased realization that the British and Russians were stalking each other and one day could collide.

After taking ship to Bombay from the Persian Gulf and traveling on to Calcutta, Burnes reported to Governor General Bentinck. This was an important meeting; on it hung policy decisions—and Burnes's career.

Bentinck listened carefully as Burnes gave an account of his journey and offered his views as to how each country visited during his odyssey should be handled. The governor general had not been among those who looked on the Russians with undue alarm; he had believed that the threat from the direction of Bokhara was at best "a very distant speculation."[7] But after hearing Burnes's somewhat overdrawn account of Russian activities in Central Asia, Bentinck joined the chorus of alarm that was already loud in London. He even became convinced that Calcutta was crawling with Russian spies. It now seemed more urgent to make secure Company relationships with both Sind and the Punjab. So important were Burnes's observations that Bentinck hurried him off to England so that he could report directly to the Board of Control at India House and to the British government.

In the meantime, Mohan Lal and Gerard were still in eastern Persia, where they found themselves in the midst of a tense situation as the Persian Army, led by Crown Prince Abbas Mirza and Herat's forces under the Saddozai ruler, Shah Kamran, squared off against each other. The Khivans were holding back, but a clash between the Herat Afghans and the Persians seemed imminent. However, neither side felt confident of victory, so Mohan Lal, as an agent of the British, was prevailed upon by the Persians to act as mediator. He met with Shah Kamran in Herat and extracted from him terms acceptable to the Persians. When he returned to the Persian headquarters from his successful mission to Herat he expected Abbas Mirza to hang on his every word in his eagerness to hear the results, but instead the crown prince asked him to describe in some detail the Battle of Waterloo. This apparent non sequitur was explained when the prince likened Wellington's victory at Waterloo to his own recent victories over marauding Turkomans. While a Persian Army band played martial music in the background, the vainglorious prince bragged of his recent campaign: "the road where 4,000 armed men dared not march, has been now made so safe that a woman may travel by herself without any danger, whatever."

In contrast with Burnes's flattering account of the Persian expeditionary force when he talked with the shah in Tehran, Mohan Lal deflated the crown prince with a blunt, honest assessment of the army's weaknesses: The Turkomans, he said flatly, could never be permanently subdued by the Persians without European help. "His royal Highness with elevated brows gazed at me," remembered Mohan Lal. Such a frank expression of opinion was not usual when talking to Persian royalty and the courtiers in attendance were transfixed. Abbas Mirza finally broke the spell of silence that had descended on his audience and exclaimed, "Wonderful, wonderful!" After a thoughtful pause he said, "How inscrutable are the decrees of Providence which has conferred so much power on an infidel!"

Mohan Lal had indeed handled himself well, revealing an exceptional talent for statecraft. The differences between his style and Burnes's was apparent. While Burnes had flattered the shah in Tehran by telling him that his Persian Army was well able to cope with Turkoman problem, Mohan Lal had spoken his mind boldly and frankly.[8]

Crown Prince Abbas Mirza showed his appreciation for Mohan Lal's services and his blunt assessment by bestowing on him the Persian Order of the Lion and Sun. He would soon be rewarded by his own government upon his return to India by being attached to Claude Wade's mission in the Punjab. But as the English public prepared to receive Burnes in London as the hero of untamed Central Asia, it was quite oblivious to Mohan Lal, who was still working his way toward Kabul on his way home. The talented Indian had shared Burnes's dangers as well as his triumphs, and had by himself performed the valuable task of achieving peace along the disputed Persian-Afghan border—albeit only temporarily. But native Company servants were not yet admitted to the British pantheon of imperial heroes. Public adoration would be reserved for Bokhara Burnes.

Chapter 8

A HERO
AND A FUGITIVE:
A STUDY
IN CONTRAST

THERE HAS ALWAYS BEEN AN AURA OF EXCITEMENT SURROUNDING EX-plorers who reach difficult goals. Burnes's mission had the added fascination of high politics; he had made a score against the Russians in the Great Game. His homecoming in November 1833 was a national event and he quickly became the lion of the London season. This intrepid young man from India had braved mountains, deserts, brigands and slavers to meet with exotic potentates and curry their favor in behalf of the empire. He had reached fabled Bokhara, whose very name conjured up time-worn fantasies of Mongol hordes and caravans lumbering across Asia bringing silk from Cathay.

Hostesses vied for the company of this most eligible bachelor in London. Burnes wrote his mother an effervescent letter in the midst of it all: "I have been inundated by visits from authors, publishers, societies and what not." The prestigious Royal Geographic Society admitted him to membership and celebrated his achievements. "I am a perfect wild beast," he wrote.

"People who pass say 'There's Mr. Burnes; there's the Indus Burnes.' " In another letter he wrote, "I am killed with honors and kindness, and it is a more painful death than starvation among the Uzbeks." But, of course, it was not really painful at all; Burnes loved every minute of it. What young officer would not enjoy basking in the spotlight of fame as he was lionized by the greats? Moreover, he could expect all this to be good for his career.

Burnes was feted by the East India Company Court of Directors at a banquet held in his honor at the London Tavern, and Charles Grant, president of the Board of Control for India, arranged a conference for Burnes with Prime Minister Lord Grey. The highlight of Burnes's stay in England was his audience with King William IV at the Brighton Pavilion, where His Majesty was in residence at the moment. Burnes captured the thrill of it in his diary. "From Castle Square I was taken to Lord Frederic Fitzclarence who led me to the Chinese hall," he wrote. "Mr. Burnes," cried a page as he announced him. "I passed through two rooms; a large hall was thrown open and I stood, hat in hand, in the presence of King William." The king greeted the young lieutenant effusively: "There was no bending of knees, no kissing of hand, no ceremony."[1]

Burnes produced a map of his journey. "I told him of the difficulties in Sindh, the reception by Runjeet, etc., but His Majesty was most interested in politics. I talked of the designs of Russia, her treaties, intrigues, agencies, ambassadors, commerce, the obstacles regarding the advance of armies," Burnes wrote in his diary. They talked of Lahore, Kabul, Bokhara, the Caspian, then the king led him to a larger map and made him go over it all again.

William IV flattered Burnes with personal questions as well: "Where were you educated? What is your age? What rank do you hold?" When he learned Burnes's age, he exclaimed, "Only twenty-eight, only a lieutenant; really sir you are a wonderful man!" William's words—"You have done more for me in this hour than anyone has ever been able to do"— were ringing in Burnes's ears as he left the audience. The king had also asked him to relate their conversation to Lord William Bentinck upon returning to India. "Lord Grey thinks as I do that you have come home on a mission of primary importance," and, he added, the prime minister "tells me that you have convinced him that our position in Russia is hopeless!"

If London had turned out for Burnes with banners flying, the reception in his hometown of Montrose in Scotland was even warmer. He was wined and dined by the town notables. His proud father shared in the festivities marked by endless toasts.

While in Montrose Burnes presented the academy that he had attended as a youth with £100, to be spent on prizes for deserving students. One letter of appreciation moved Burnes to reply in a self-revealing way: "That demon, ambition, I fear makes us climb the high hill as my great relative [Robert Burns] said 'not for the laudable anxiety of viewing an extended landscape, but rather for the pride of looking down on our fellows' . . . yet I feel I am working for my country's good."

His last dangling line suggests a transparent rationalization, but Burnes was an ambitious man. The mischievous genie of ambition would on more than one occasion cloud his better judgment. Yet ambition was the very quality that the East India Company sought in its officers. Robert Clive had won Bengal, Warren Hastings tamed south India, and Thomas Stamford Raffles founded modern Singapore with a drive fueled by ambition. The Company as seen by the directors in London may have been dedicated to turning a profit, but most of the officers in the field had visions of empire. How could they be expected to focus on the pitfalls of territorial expansion, how could they pause to consider the dangers of venturing beyond the Indus, when there was more glory to be had in "forward thrusting" than in minding the store? And the lionization of Burnes in England was proof enough to convince Burnes himself and others in the service, who watched his reception by an adoring public and admiring king, that there was more reward in derring-do than in quiet prudence.

To satisfy a popular demand for details of his great adventure, Burnes published an expurgated account of his journey to Bokhara while in England. A people already convinced that Russia was a menace to empire that must be contained eagerly read *Travels into Bokhara and a Voyage on the Indus,* making it an instantaneous best-seller. Bokhara Burnes's reputation was made.

Even the Athenaeum Club, "the Blue Riband of Literature," voted him to membership. And the grand old man of Afghan scholarship, Mountstuart Elphinstone, said: "I never read anything with more interest and pleasure." France too paid homage to the English hero when the French Geographical Society awarded Burnes its silver medal. It was said that King Louis Philippe had wanted to give him the Legion of Honor, but had not acted before Burnes returned to India.

A single sour note was sounded as Burnes's glorious homecoming drew to a close: Lord Ellenborough, the government's minister for Indian affairs, offered him for his next assignment a second secretaryship in Tehran. This was no promotion, nor did it otherwise appeal to Burnes, who wanted to return to Indian service. Burnes rejected the uninspiring assignment. When he was given as an alternative his old post in Kutch, still as number two in that barren, inclement outpost, he knew the bubble of herodom had burst. Ellenborough quickly lost interest in Burnes, laconically writing the newly appointed governor general, Lord Auckland: "What use should be made of [Burnes's] services in India entirely depends on you."

Ellenborough sensed in Burnes overweening ambition, something of a strutting peacock, and later recalled: "He [Burnes] was intensely vain and self-sufficient and he did that which he ought not to have done: acting as he was for a government to which I was opposed in Parliament, he wrote to me from Cabool upon the affairs of Afghanistan."[2]

WHILE BURNES HAD ENJOYED HIS HOUR OF TRIUMPH IN ENGLAND AND STILL hoped for better things despite Ellenborough's lack of interest in him, another intrepid traveler, calling himself Charles Masson, was pressed into duty by Claude Wade as agent in Kabul—a hybrid between resident and spy that carried the opprobrium of being a British representative without providing the protection of the Crown. Unlike Burnes, Masson for his own reasons sought anonymity, not acclaim.

Charles Masson was one of the more enigmatic figures in the Great Game. A self-taught archeologist and numismatist with an insatiable urge to explore, he spent years walking the length and breadth of Afghanistan.[3] He first came to the attention of British officialdom in the early summer of 1830, when he unexpectedly appeared at the British residence in the Persian Gulf port of Bushire. There he explained to the resident, Major David Wilson, that he had spent ten years traveling in the East, and had finally reached India from Europe by way of the Caucasus, Persia and Afghanistan before backtracking to Bushire. He also professed to be a citizen of the United States of America, originally from Kentucky. Masson's information, particularly his detailed description of Herat, excited interest on the part of the British resident, well aware of his country's steadily growing apprehension about western Afghanistan and Russian machinations in Persia since the Treaty of Turkmanchai.

Unknown to Wilson, the man claiming to be Charles Masson was not Charles Masson at all. He was not an American from Kentucky, nor had he reached Afghanistan by way of Tiflis in the Caucasus and Persia. He was James Lewis, an Englishman born on February 16, 1800, in Aldermanbury, London. His father had been an oil seller and his mother a member of a respected family of farmers and brewers named Hopcraft from Croughton. Beyond this, nothing has ever been discovered about James Lewis's first twenty-one years.

Lewis, or Masson as he will be called, had enlisted in the Indian Army in England and sailed for Bengal aboard the troopship *Duchess of Athol* on January 17, 1882. Upon arriving in Calcutta in July he was assigned to the Bengal European Artillery. He deserted from the ranks, however, and that was why he had assumed an alias and pretended to be an American whenever he had to explain himself to Englishmen. Desertion was a serious crime that would have brought severe punishment had he been caught and convicted by a court-martial.

Why an obviously well-educated man of good breeding had enlisted to become a ranker in the Indian Army in the first place has forever remained a mystery. As memorialized in Kipling's famous lines "Gentlemen rankers out on a spree/ Damned from here to eternity,"[4] it was not uncommon for men of good families in England to join the Indian Army to find anonymity or refuge below their station in the ranks. The "legion of the lost ones" and "cohorts of the damned," as Kipling called them, were usually fleeing from the law or some terrible scandal—or perhaps unrequited love. But if any of these reasons accounted for Masson's actions, there has never been a shred of evidence to substantiate it. He kept his secret well. Nor has it been discovered why Masson deserted in 1827 after taking part in the hard-fought British siege of Bharatpur. One can only speculate that the brutalized life in the ranks had proved unendurable to this man of considerable culture and education. Certainly, in light of the risks he subsequently took in Afghanistan, cowardice could not logically have been the cause of his desertion.

Masson's commanding officer, Major General Hardwick, remembered him as a diligent enlisted man whom he sometimes used to catalog zoological specimens incidentally collected in the field.[5] This was further evidence of Masson's intellectual bent. Whatever the case, Masson committed the crime of desertion and felt compelled to flee beyond the company's reach and live a new identity.

Masson's own account of his travels* before reaching Bushire and meeting Wilson, only much later revealed in his memoir, actually began in the autumn of 1827 when, after crossing the Great Indian Desert of Rajasthan, southwest of Delhi and Agra, he entered the tributary state of Bahawalpur, although in his memoir Masson put the date as 1826, a year earlier, apparently on purpose to help cover his tracks after deserting.

Masson did not reveal to Wilson or even later in his memoir that he had traveled with another deserter named Richard Potter, alias John Brown.[6] The two men had split up, however, after spending Christmas together near the Indus trade center of Dera Ghazi Khan. Potter headed for Lahore, where he planned to join the swelling ranks of European

Narrative of Various Journeys in Baluchistan, Afghanistan and the Panjab, first published in 1842.

soldiers of fortune hired by Ranjit Singh to bring his army up to continental standards, while Masson set out for Kabul by way of Peshawar, intent on distancing himself from the Company's dominions and exploring archeological sites, which fascinated him.

It took courage to travel through the robber-infested Khyber Pass. Whenever he could, he attached himself to a caravan for greater protection, but this did not guarantee immunity from attack by the untamable Afridi tribesmen whose hill villages overlooked the long pass. He helped his fellow travelers any way he could, usually by trying to alleviate their aches and pains with simple nostrums he carried or, at least, by his sympathy. In this way he repaid the food shared with him. On one occasion he was robbed by ungrateful Afridis whom he was trying to help. They took his cloak, his only protection against the sometimes harsh climate, and, even worse, stole his precious record book in which he kept notes of his journey and archeological observations.

By the time Masson reached Kabul he was in rags. The city he found was in the grip of a raging epidemic of cholera, so he stayed but a few days before going on to Ghazni, southwest of Kabul. It was here that Masson first met the Afghan leader, Dost Mohammed Khan—long before Alexander Burnes did. Ghazni was at the time threatened by the Kandahar chiefs, who had not yet accepted Dost Mohammed's rule, so he had gone there to take personal charge of the town.

Masson was much impressed with what he had heard about Kabul's ruler and wrote: "Dost Mohammed has distinguished himself by acts of personal intrepidity, and has proved himself an able commander, yet he is equally well-skilled in strategem and polity, and only employs the sword when other means fail." While flattering, this was an underestimation of Dost Mohammed's achievement in emerging supreme from the morass of Afghan tribal and fraternal infighting. During Masson's meeting with Dost Mohammed, the Afghan leader's looks did not readily suggest his true genius. Masson commented on his simple attire, in contrast with some of the costumes worn by courtiers who strutted about him, and admitted that he would not have imagined him "a man of ability, either from his conversation or his appearance."

Accompanied by a Pathan traveling companion, useful for his native language and knowledge of the land, Masson continued on to Kandahar. It was a disagreeable journey; Masson and his Pathan companion were viciously attacked by tribesmen along the route and barely managed to escape with their lives. Their assailants, suspecting Masson of being a foreigner and an infidel, screamed epithets as they circled around with cudgels and rocks. One tribesman struck Masson with a club and the others would have closed in for the kill had not friendly villagers rescued them. He now traveled alone, since his Pathan friend, considering the route too dangerous, abandoned him. The Pathan's instincts had been sound, as Masson discovered only twelve miles down the road when he was set upon and robbed. He wisely abandoned his intention to travel to Herat, instead turning southward toward the Bolan Pass through which he planned to return to the Punjab.

Unfortunately, this itinerary proved no safer than the road to Herat. A band of thieves mercilessly beat him and stripped him of all his clothes. Trying to survive the cold night by huddling naked over a small fire he had made from twigs, he repeatedly scorched himself. By morning his muscles, cramped from crouching close to the fire all night, were barely usable. He almost died of exposure and could not have made it through another night had it not been for a sympathetic soldier passing by who gave him a *pushtin,* or heavy sheepskin coat, for warmth. For the rest of his journey, Masson not only suffered the agony of stiff limbs but was also in pain caused by blistered feet worn raw by the rocky trail.

Once again he was attacked by robbers, who wanted to steal a battered pair of shoes which he had finally managed to beg. Only when he caught up with a caravan did he feel secure from the predators of the road, but his aching joints and sore feet prevented him from keeping up with the others and again he had to struggle on alone, begging food in the villages along the way.

As Masson had long since discovered, travel in Afghanistan could be risky. There were the marauders who infested the roads and would not hesitate to kill for a few coins or old clothes, but there were also the Good Samaritans, kindly fellow travelers who gave help when needed. And there were the villagers, willing to share their provisions even though they may not have had enough for themselves. Despite the unpleasant incidents that befell Masson during his years of wandering, he managed to survive. His obvious poverty was probably his best protection. Certain tribes noted for their rapaciousness had to be avoided or their lands traversed in the safety of large armed caravans, but in much of the country a lone traveler, even a foreigner, could travel freely.

In early 1829 Masson reached Lahore. He was now at risk. In Lahore Ranjit Singh's cadre of mercenary officers, mostly French veterans of the Napoleonic wars, were watched—and sometimes used—by British political agent Claude Wade. Keeping close track through his network of Company newswriters, or spies, in Lahore, Wade could easily spot any new European. Masson knew his presence would not bear scrutiny, but he took a chance on escaping notice.

The rainy season made the roads hopelessly soggy, so Masson accepted the hospitality of General Jean François Allard, French commander of Ranjit Singh's cavalry. A much-decorated officer in Napoleon's army, Allard had by this time been with Ranjit Singh nearly eight years. He had traveled to the Punjab from Persia after Waterloo, having been unsuccessful in finding service with the shah. It was rumored that Russian Minister Mazarwich in Tehran had urged the French officer to seek service with the Sikhs so that he could spy on them for the czar. But there was no evidence that Allard remained in contact with the Russians or played their game; certainly Ranjit Singh trusted him.

Masson passed himself off as a Frenchman with Allard, albeit one of Italian origin to account for any telltale trace of accent. (His fluency in French suggested that he must have spent considerable time in France during the mysterious missing years of his life's record.) During the several weeks Masson remained as Allard's guest, the two men became good friends. Somehow Masson evaded the scrutiny of Wade's spies even though he mixed with several of Ranjit Singh's mercenaries in the course of his stay in Lahore.

Among those whom Masson met were two other veterans of Napoleon's army: the Italian Jean Baptiste Ventura, and the Frenchman Claude Auguste Court. Ventura, who had come to the Punjab with Allard from Persia, was charged with command of the Sikh infantry, while Court, originally an artilleryman, rose to become Ranjit Singh's most senior foreign officer. Ventura and Court had taken a keen interest in archeology, so Masson had a common interest with them.

Masson spent the winter of 1829–30 in Sind, but, ever the wanderer, he left Karachi by ship for Muscat. From Muscat he sailed to Bushire, and it was soon afterward that he met Major Wilson. Having been careful to avoid Englishmen since his desertion, it seems curious that he would have run the risk of calling upon the Company representative. Time had passed, however, and perhaps he felt more confident, or perhaps he realized that to be evasive would only arouse suspicion. In fact, his appearance in Bushire would ultimately lead to his unmasking, but for the present Wilson accepted his fabricated story.

Wilson was fascinated by the enigmatic vagabond and his travels. Information about western Afghanistan was a rare commodity for the British, and Wilson urged Masson to record his experiences for the benefit of the Company. Masson knew he was taking a risk by doing so, but he could not easily refuse. His report was duly forwarded to Bombay with a copy to Colonel Henry Pottinger, resident in Kutch, who was Alexander Burnes's superior officer at the time and had been the first Englishman to explore Baluchistan and the Persian-Afghan borderlands in 1810. Masson's report, sent under cover of Wilson's dispatch of September 11, 1830, discussed Herat, Ranjit Singh, navigation on the Indus and the plight of the poverty-stricken Sind, all matters of timely importance that attracted considerable Company attention in Calcutta.

The more Wilson thought about Masson, the more he was curious about him. The "American" was clearly an educated man with a well-developed interest in archeology. But how did an American reach this part of the world on his own? He had no apparent means of support, nor was there any apparent motive beyond an innate love of exploration. But whoever this fascinating man was, Wilson saw his potential usefulness and convinced him that he should look up the British minister to Persia, Sir John Macdonald, then at the shah's court in Tabriz and responsible for reporting on western Afghanistan as well as Persia.

By the time Masson reached Tabriz, the minister had died in the terrible plague sweeping the Persian province of Azerbaijan. Major John Campbell, chargé d'affaires, was impressed with Masson, however, and advanced him official money so that he could continue his archeological research in Afghanistan—and also report on politically important developments.

Masson was grateful for the Company stipend; he could now travel with some dignity rather than as a mendicant. But travel still was not easy. Intending to reach Kabul by way of Sind, then northward through the Bolan Pass to Kandahar, he fell behind schedule when the ship on which he was traveling was not allowed to land in Karachi. The emirs of Sind, he learned, were suspicious of all British ships, believing that the large cargo crates they carried hid soldiers poised to invade their country. By landing at the less conspicuous port of Sonmiani, not far west of Karachi, Masson was finally able to go ashore and join a caravan bound for Kabul.

Masson arrived in Kabul on June 9, 1832, only a few days after Burnes, Mohan Lal and Gerard had left there on their epic trip to Bokhara. He found lodging with the leader of the Armenian community, Simon Mugurditch, who told him about Burnes's mission and the coincidental arrival of Joseph Wolff. People were still talking about the eccentric missionary's audacious religious debates with the mullahs and, more dramatically, how he predicted an earthquake that actually occurred, to establish him as a seer with supernatural powers.

Masson was not sorry to have missed Burnes's party. While lucky so far, encounters with fellow countrymen always increased the risk of his betraying himself. In fact, Company eyes were already secretly scrutinizing him. Claude Wade in Ludhiana had sent word to a Kabul agent, one Seyyid

Keramat Ali,[7] to report on Masson and his activities. The agent's first report told of a European whom he had seen in the bazaar on Christmas Day, walking barefoot and carrying a beggar's bowl. The man could have passed for a native fakir had it not been for his gray eyes and red hair— perhaps he was a Russian. Then Keramat Ali reported a curious story about the same man: dressed as a dervish, the stranger attempted to heal an Afghan boy suffering from palsy. As the boy's father watched, the "dervish" scribbled something on a piece of paper and threw it into a fire, announcing confidently, "Your son will recover."[8] Whatever and whoever the stranger was, Keramat Ali considered him suspicious. He was "shabbily dressed, without horse, mule or servant to carry his baggage as he traveled about the outskirts of Kabul looking at old ruins."

Masson kept himself busy with his archeological and numismatic exploration, digging in various sites outside Kabul, where he found rich lodes of artifacts. He soon attracted the attention of one of Dost Mohammed's sons, Akbar Khan, who took an interest in his country's antiquities. Thanks to the prince's friendship, Masson was able to gain access to areas otherwise denied him. Masson's discoveries also came to British attention. Henry Pottinger in Kutch was particularly interested, and provided him with official funds to finance his activities providing he would turn over all artifacts he found to the Company.

Martin Honigberger, a Transylvanian physician in Ranjit Singh's employ who was also an archeological enthusiast, visited Kabul in early 1833 to join Masson in a dig. Impressed with his new friend, Honigberger wrote Wade about Masson. Then Dr. Gerard, who had accompanied Burnes to Bokhara, revisited Kabul in March 1833 on his way back to India with Mohan Lal and met Masson. He too wrote Wade, praising Masson and commenting on his unique access to Afghan society. Wade's dossier on Masson was growing, but it was the American Josiah Harlan who caused his unmasking. As Masson had feared, Harlan, whom he had encountered in the Punjab in 1827, saw through his claim to be an American, and in early 1834 confided his suspicions to Dr. Gerard, who, in turn, passed them on to Wade. The British resident then checked Indian Army records and conclusively identified Masson as Lewis the deserter.

Wade's interest in Masson was not simply to apprehend a deserter; he saw him as the ideal candidate to replace Keramat Ali in Afghanistan. Keramat Ali was by this time not only thoroughly identified by the Afghans as a British agent in Kabul but, having involved himself in Afghan politics, he had become more a liability than an asset. Wade wrote the governor general on April 9, 1834: "Desertion is a crime . . . that scarcely ever admits of pardon, but if the severity of our laws is such as to preclude the extension of his Lordship's clemency to him, I still hope that I shall be excused for the correspondence I have opened with Mr. Masson and that, averting to his acknowledged talent and ability and light which his interesting researches are likely to throw on the present state of Afghanistan, I may be indemnified by government for any small sums of money which I may hereafter supply Mr. Masson."[9]

Wade received permission to press Masson to serve in May 1834 and in due course a king's pardon was granted him. The pardon was reward for accepting the dangerous role as British agent, but had he refused, he would have been court-martialed and doubtlessly sentenced to a long term in prison. Masson had mixed emotions; he was relieved to know that he was no longer a fugitive, but his role as agent, not entirely concealed, would detract from the trust his Afghan friends, including Dost Mohammed, had lodged in him. In his memoir he vented his feelings about being forced into service: "I might have supposed it would have been only fair and courteous to have consulted my wishes and views before conferring an appointment which compromised me with the equivocal politics of the country and threw a suspicion over my proceedings which did not before attach to them."

With little choice in the matter Masson was plunged into the thick of events in Afghanistan; archeology and numismatics would have to be put on a back burner while he assumed his role as a player of the Game.

Chapter 9

CONTEST FOR

PESHAWAR

WHILE ALEXANDER BURNES IN ENGLAND WAS REAPING THE REWARDS of fame, Dost Mohammed in Afghanistan faced two important challenges to his power. One was an effort by Shah Shuja to reclaim his Kabul throne by first seizing Kandahar, after which he hoped to march on the capital; the other was a bid by Ranjit Singh in 1834 to annex the important border city of Peshawar, in which the Sikh maharajah since 1819 had dominant influence but not sovereign control. Both issues would prove important in the Afghan course of events and be critical in determining British frontier policy.

In addition to keeping the tribes friendly—usually through some form of subsidy or internal political maneuvering—a firm grip on central power required any Afghan ruler in Kabul to exercise control over the other three important cities of Afghanistan: Kandahar in the south, Peshawar in the east and Herat in the west. Dost Mohammed's hold on Kandahar was tenuous; the ruling khans essentially ran their own affairs. Peshawar had eluded Kabul's control because its princely ruler, Sultan Mohammed

Khan, was at odds with Dost Mohammed—his half-brother—and enjoyed autonomy by maintaining a precarious balance between pressures on him from Dost Mohammed and Ranjit Singh. Peshawar, a town inhabited mainly by Pathan tribesmen, had traditionally been part of Afghanistan. Because of its strategic position as gateway to the Khyber Pass and its location near the Attock River, a tributary of the Indus, it was historically considered more important than Kabul and once was used as the country's winter capital. Dost Mohammed understandably wanted to include Peshawar in the Afghan realm, and this desire, amounting to obsession, dominated much of his career. At the same time Ranjit Singh saw Peshawar as key to the security of his Punjab kingdom.

Herat, far to the west, was at this time beyond Dost Mohammed's reach, since its rulers, the aging Shah Kamran and his devious vizier, Yar Mohammed, belonged to the hostile Saddozai clan. They ruled their virtually independent domain with a firm hand without reference to either their exiled Saddozai clan leader, Shah Shuja, or their Barakzai rival in Kabul, Dost Mohammed. But Herat was continually threatened by the shah of Persia, who claimed Herat as Persian territory. Herat also had special significance for the Russians as it could be used to flank Khiva and Bokhara, on which the czar had imperial designs. Kandahar too was of interest to the Persians and Russians, which gave the khans of that city leverage in playing them against Dost Mohammed to maintain their own power in the area.

This oversimplification of the hopeless maze of Afghan politics characterized the unsteady realm of Dost Mohammed in 1833, when Shah Shuja tried once more to regain power.

From his place of exile in Ludhiana, Shah Shuja had become restless as the years slipped by. He was well treated by the British, who provided him with an allowance large enough to support his substantial zenana. But the small Sikh town dominated by the British and under the close scrutiny of its eagle-eyed political officer, Claude Wade, was confining for the former Afghan monarch.

There was little to recommend Ludhiana to anyone. Located just east of Lahore on the banks of the Sutlej River, it had become an important garrison town, an advance concentration of British forces defending the Cis-Sutlej, i.e., the British-controlled Punjab south of the Sutlej River. If it had a reputation for anything, it was not as the site of asylum for the claimant to the Afghan throne, but as a hub for Wade's political and intelligence activities in the Punjab—and Afghanistan. It also had the dubious distinction of being a veritable bazaar devoted to providing women for British soldiers stationed there. Of the town's twenty thousand inhabitants, at least three thousand—half of the female population—were prostitutes. Some of the hill tribes were engaged in buying or stealing very young girls, who were then sold to the madams of Ludhiana who taught them the trade.

Since the British were not yet ready to assist actively Shah Shuja's efforts to return to Afghanistan, the Saddozai leader turned to Ranjit Singh for help. Despite their earlier falling out, the two men now saw advantage in working with each other: Ranjit Singh wanted Peshawar and Shah Shuja wanted his Kabul throne. Thus, on March 12, 1833,* the two leaders concluded a treaty in which Peshawar was ceded to the Sikhs—if the Sikhs could gain possession of it. In return for this Ranjit Singh promised to support Shah Shuja's effort to unseat Dost Mohammed in Kabul. But, being a ward of the British, Shah Shuja had to consider British wishes as well in going about his plans.

When Shah Shuja had appealed to the British in 1832 for help in restoring him to the Afghan throne, Governor General Bentinck archly replied that the British government "abstains from intermeddling with the affairs of its neighbors . . ." While Shah Shuja recognized the hypocrisy of this pious assertion, he could at least be grateful that the British had not forbidden him from taking action against Dost Mohammed on his own or with Sikh assistance. Official positions were one thing, official actions in practice were another; Shah Shuja knew that political agent Wade, his guardian and friend, favored the plan. It was, in fact, Wade who had put the idea in his head in the first place. And when, on Wade's advice, Governor General Bentinck approved Shah Shuja's request for a large advance on his pension to finance the venture, the Afghan exile could logically infer that he had tacit, if not formal or official, British encouragement to proceed. The Company had modified its policy of strict neutrality essentially because of Wade's energetic lobbying with Calcutta in behalf of Shah Shuja. While not ready to play a more dynamic and more obvious role in Afghan politics, the Company had been convinced by Wade that Shah Shuja would make a good replacement for Dost Mohammed, and thus it was willing to look on benignly while Wade did what he could to help by intriguing behind the scenes.

Dost Mohammed was not deluded. He could logically draw the conclusion that the British had at least acquiesced in his rival's undertaking when Shah Shuja left Ludhiana in 1833 at the head of a newly recruited army to invade Afghanistan. This was disturbingly inconsistent with the protestations of friendship just given Dost Mohammed by Alexander Burnes during the latter's recent visit. Kabul's ruler could wonder even more about where he stood with the British when Governor General Bentinck rejected

*In 1831 Shah Shuja had asked Ranjit Singh to help him regain his throne, but then the Sikh leader had demanded unacceptable terms.

his overture for an alliance of friendship. If the British sought good relations with Dost Mohammed, the professed purpose of Burnes's mission to Kabul, they were going about it in a very strange way.

Shah Shuja's route of advance in early 1834 skirted Ranjit Singh's Punjab and crossed the Indus River at a trading town in Sind called Shikarpur. Then, after marching through northern Sind (technically still a vassal of the Afghans to which Shah Shuja as claimant to the throne could claim tribute payments) and Baluchistan, the invading army crossed the Bolan Pass en route to Kandahar. The route through the Bolan Pass was taken for two reasons: as difficult as it was to cross the arid deserts of Sind and the mountains of Baluchistan, it was easier than the shorter Khyber Pass route defended by fierce Afghan tribesmen; second, Ranjit Singh did not want a foreign expeditionary force passing through his kingdom, even if it was that of an ally.

By early summer Shah Shuja's army, led by an Anglo-Indian mercenary named William Campbell, had reached Kandahar and driven its garrison from the city. Dost Mohammed rushed to the rescue of the Kandahar force from Kabul to meet Shah Shuja in battle. At dawn on the day of the clash between the two armies, Campbell skillfully maneuvered his infantry and drove Dost Mohammed's forces from the field. When the battle was rejoined the next day, Shah Shuja inexplicably fled the field on his elephant just as his general, Campbell, had gained the upper hand in the fighting. Seeing their leader in flight, the invading army disintegrated. It was a rout; Dost Mohammed's army plundered Shah Shuja's baggage train and fell upon his retreating forces, exacting a terrible toll of life as they fled southward. Campbell and many of Shah Shuja's other officers were wounded in battle and captured by Dost Mohammed. Shah Shuja's ambitious bid for the Afghan throne thus ended ignobly. When Dost Mohammed found among the battlefield debris incriminating evidence of Wade's intrigues in behalf of Shah Shuja—revealing letters inciting the tribes to rise in his defense—he could have had no doubt that the British had deceived him.

Dost Mohammed had won at Kandahar but paid a high price for his victory. While he had been preoccupied with Shah Shuja's advance on Kandahar, Ranjit Singh seized the opportunity to move against Peshawar. But, if the battle for Kandahar was decided by hard fighting, Peshawar's fate would be determined by intrigue and double-dealing. Peshawar's ambiguous status as an Afghan-populated autonomous principality, theoretically subject to Kabul but resisting Dost Mohammed's rule to pay deference and tribute to Ranjit Singh instead, made for a highly unstable situation.

Sultan Mohammed Khan, Afghan ruler of Peshawar, with the connivance of some of his brothers, had not only resisted Dost Mohammed's efforts to integrate Peshawar into the Afghan kingdom, but was plotting to remove Dost Mohammed from power in Kabul. To this end he had carried on secret negotiations with Ranjit Singh. Taking advantage of Sultan Mohammed's overtures, Ranjit Singh had his own plan: he sent his ablest commander, Hari Singh, with nine thousand Sikh soldiers on a "friendly" mission to Peshawar in May 1834. But instead of entering the town as friend and ally, the Sikh commander seized the town in a hostile act, forcing a surprised Sultan Mohammed to flee for his life. To his dismay, Sultan Mohammed found that he had been tricked by his "friend," Ranjit Singh, into capitulating without a struggle to a much smaller Sikh force.

The capture of Peshawar by the Sikhs was a terrible blow to the Afghans; one that Dost Mohammed could never get over. The loss of this town was not only a grievous assault on his pride; it also put the Afghans at a strategic disadvantage vis-à-vis the Sikhs. Dost Mohammed would not rest until he had regained Peshawar; he resolved to raise all the Afghan tribes to retake the city. In an effort to garner maximum tribal strength, Dost Mohammed crowned himself emir, or king, a title he had heretofore not claimed even though, in fact, he ruled most of the Afghans. He also declared himself "Commander of the Faithful," providing religious authority as well. Wrapped in these dignities, he launched an all-out holy war against the infidel Sikhs. By whipping up religious frenzy and judiciously distributing subsidies, he was able to amass a huge force of tribal levies who he hoped would make up in fervor what they lacked in discipline.

The ubiquitous Josiah Harlan, then Ranjit Singh's governor of the nearby Sikh province of Gujerat, suddenly appeared in Peshawar as the confrontation between Sikhs and Afghans approached a climax. His description of Dost Mohammed's holy crusaders hovering nearby in the Khyber Pass was graphic, if melodramatic: "Savages from the remotest recesses of the mountainous districts, many of them giants, promiscuously armed with sword and shield, bows and arrows, matchlocks, rifles, spears and blunderbusses, concentrated themselves around the standard of religion, and were prepared to slay, plunder and destroy for the sake of God and the Prophet, the unenlightened infidels [Sikhs]."[1]

To finance the campaign, Dost Mohammed had dunned the Hindus in his realm, particularly the moneylenders and bankers. Seizing on an obscure passage in the scriptures, he justified this extortion on the grounds that it is right to take the wealth of infidels so long as it is used to resist attacks by infidels.

Ranjit Singh rushed his full army to Peshawar to meet Dost Mohammed's host of tribal warriors. The Sikh force was formidable: there was Ranjit Singh's crack brigade, the Francese Corps, consisting of twenty thousand men under the command of the French Army veterans, Allard, Ventura and Court; augmented by twenty-four cannons commanded by an American mercenary, Alexander Gardner (whom we shall again encounter); and the rest of the Sikh army, sixty thousand strong, under Ranjit Singh's direct command.[2]

Charles Masson, as British agent in Afghanistan, witnessed events from the vantage point of Dost Mohammed's camp at the mouth of the Khyber Pass. According to Masson, Dost Mohammed was far from confident of winning a battle against the well-disciplined and well-trained Sikhs. While his force was large and for the moment exuberant at the prospect of fighting for a holy cause, Dost knew that the motley levies would disappear into the hills at the first sign of adversity.

The Afghan leader had hoped to induce the British to mediate the dispute over Peshawar. He had written both Wade in Ludhiana and the governor general himself on this subject, but not until the Afghan Army reached Jalalabad in early March 1835 as it prepared to attack the Sikhs at Peshawar was a reply received from the governor general. The reply was more than disappointing; it was infuriating. The British were clearly not willing to alienate their Sikh allies on the issue of Peshawar. But another factor in the British decision was uncertainty as to Dost Mohammed's flirtation with the Russians. Intelligence had been received that Dost Mohammed, in the miasma of Afghan politics, had solicited Russian help against both the Sikhs and their allies, the British, whose commercial penetration of Afghanistan he feared. He had even appealed to the Persians, his traditional enemies, for their support in his fight against the Sikhs for Peshawar.

Governor General Bentinck's letter to Dost addressed itself blandly to commercial relations with Kabul, but refused to entertain any thought of political agreement with the Afghans or help to them in taking back Peshawar. One of Dost Mohammed's trusted advisers erupted in anger when he read the governor general's letter, loudly accusing the British of even being pleased that the Afghans might be exterminated in battle. A witness to the scene, Charles Masson confessed that while the Afghan leaders were in this temper, "he was glad to retreat out of range."

Dost Mohammed moved slowly as he led his army toward Peshawar, hoping to receive overtures from the Sikhs to negotiate. Worried by the massed Sikh army, he compared himself to a "fly facing an elephant," and in public prayer asked God to grant him victory. Hazara tribal shamans, traditionally the Afghan magic makers, harking back to the custom of their

Mongol ancestors, brought out the burned shoulder blades of sacrificial sheep carcasses, arranging them in such a way as to assure success in battle.

Ranjit Singh was no more confident. He was awed by the size and fervor of his adversary, particularly since his allies, the British, were remaining on the sidelines with no intention of helping him. Rather than risk combat, the Lion of the Punjab played the fox instead and resorted to guile. He chose the American, Josiah Harlan, as his instrument in a trick to take Peshawar. The plan was for Harlan to meet with Dost Mohammed in the Afghan leader's campaign camp in the Khyber Pass in behalf of Ranjit Singh and pretend to enter into negotiations over Peshawar. But he was actually to set in motion a plot calculated to split Afghan leadership and, while pretending to negotiate in good faith, bribe the Afghan tribal host to desert.

Harlan met with Dost Mohammed in an atmosphere of distrust and suspicion. Increasing the tension of the negotiating session was the presence of Sultan Mohammed Khan, who, having been tricked by Ranjit Singh, had been forced to flee with his ten thousand troops to Dost Mohammed's camp. Dost Mohammed, however, distrusted his half-brother and suspected that Harlan would try to sow dissension between them. Even though Harlan swore on a Koran that this was not so, Dost shrewdly did not believe him. "Despite sweet words and promises, Harlan, like all *ferangis*, could be compared to a tree full of leaves which bore no fruit."[3]

Josiah Harlan was an adventurer whose whole career had been self-serving. But the American must, at least, be credited with having been able to compete with the Afghans on their own ground in their own game of labyrinthine scheming—often too complicated to comprehend. What followed, the defeat of Dost Mohammed in the Khyber Pass and the Afghans' irretrievable loss of Peshawar to the Sikhs, was the result of skulduggery worthy of the most devious Oriental intriguer.

As he met with Dost Mohammed, Harlan studied the Afghan leader's face carefully, searching in vain for any reaction suggesting that he knew what was afoot. The emir's delicately arched eyebrows framed hazel-gray eyes fixed only on Harlan in a feline stare.

As Harlan's charade of negotiating got under way, the emir was the first to broach the matter at hand: Peshawar. Whatever his private doubts, Dost Mohammed boasted that his Afghan force of 100,000 men was more than a match for the Sikhs. Harlan responded sternly: "If the Prince of the Punjab chose to assemble the militia of his dominions, he could bring ten times that number into the field." But, Harlan added, "he had chosen diplomacy, instead, to settle the differences between us."[4] Peshawar, he lied, was negotiable.

This enraged Dost Mohammed. Wagging his head, as he often did when angry, he threatened Harlan. But the American knew that the Sikhs held the high cards; Ranjit Singh had already induced Sultan Mohammed to defect and return to his side. Harlan also knew that Sultan Mohammed's considerable force, according to plan, would desert and steal away from Dost Mohammed's camp that very night under cover of darkness. Moreover, he knew that Dost Mohammed's Afghan levies, heavily bribed with gold by the Sikhs, were already beginning to drift back into the mountains, as Sikh troops stealthily moved in closer. When the massive desertions were discovered in the morning, the Afghan camp was thrown into confusion. "Without beat of drum or sound of bugle, or the trumpet's blast," Dost's forces had disappeared in "the quiet stillness of midnight," recalled Harlan, who was obviously pleased with his handiwork.

By daybreak the camp was virtually empty. A hundred thousand warriors whose frenzied cries only the day before had disturbed the silent Khyber defiles, were nowhere to be seen. Dost Mohammed's only course left was to retreat as rapidly as possible. According to Harlan, the emir was so flustered that he mounted his horse with the wrong foot and ended up sitting backward on the beast. It was said that as he fled from his camp, Dost Mohammed cast one last look in the direction of Peshawar and in his anger uttered a vile oath. A gloating Harlan boasted: "Machiavelli would have applauded."

In his fury that Ranjit Singh had outwitted him, Dost Mohammed seized Harlan, hoping to hold him for a large ransom—perhaps even for the return of Peshawar. He had second thoughts, however, fearing that this breach of the Afghan code of hospitality might disgrace him, and contrived to place the blame for the kidnapping of Ranjit Singh's envoys on Sultan Mohammed instead by turning the prisoner over to him. But the duplicitous governor of Peshawar, now having sensibly made his peace with Ranjit Singh, winner of the round, arranged to have Harlan returned safely to Lahore.

Mohan Lal, who had reached Kabul on his way back to India after his journey to Bokhara with Burnes and subsequent long journey homeward by way of Herat and Kandahar, was coincidentally on hand to watch Dost Mohammed return from his abortive Khyber campaign. He reported that the emir was in deep depression over his defeat and the loss of Peshawar: "There were no bounds to the sweat of shame and folly which flowed over his face, and there was no limit to the laughter of the people at his being deceived and ridiculed—he hung his head with great remorse and shame."[5]

The conclusion of this episode pleased Wade, who had been kept abreast of events by Masson's messengers. Having developed a close relationship and sympathy with Shah Shuja, political officer Wade had become progressively convinced that his ward was the man to sit on Kabul's throne. Shah Shuja's defeat at Kandahar had been disappointing, but at least Dost Mohammed had suffered a serious defeat in Peshawar. He believed that a unified country under Dost Mohammed would play into the hands of "British rivals [read, Russians] and deprive [the British] of the powerful means which have to be in reserve for controlling the present rulers of Afghanistan." The political agent explained to the governor general: "Our policy ought not to be to destroy, but to preserve and strengthen the different governments of Afghanistan [the feudal princes in Kandahar and Herat] as they stand." In short, divide and rule.

Harlan received no kudos from the British for his part in keeping Peshawar out of Afghan hands, however much Wade may have liked the results. While treachery was endemic in the area, and in this instance useful to British policy aims, Harlan as a free-lance intriguer was viewed by the British with distaste. It was one thing to play the Game for God and country; it was another to work for the highest bidder and change sides at will. Among the British, Harlan would suffer the stigma attached to most mercenaries and renegades in India, although this did not keep them from using him as it suited their purposes.

Harlan at this time was administering the Sikh province of Gujerat, nestled in the mountains north of Lahore—a step up in importance from his former charges, Nurpur and Jesotra. But suddenly, in October 1836, after seven years of working for Ranjit Singh, Harlan once again changed his allegiance; he defected to Dost Mohammed. Harlan gave a fatuous and unconvincing excuse for his abrupt departure from Ranjit Singh: "Monarch as he was, absolute and luxurious, and voluptuous in the possession of treasured wealth and military power, I resolved to avenge myself and cause him to tremble in the midst of his magnificence."[6] The truth was different. Harlan had fallen into Ranjit Singh's bad graces for perpetrating two outrageous scams: making counterfeit coins and pretending to convert common metal into gold.[7] But there was more to it than that. Ranjit Singh, stricken with paralysis of the tongue as the result of a small stroke, appealed to "Doctor" Harlan for help. The American infuriated Ranjit Singh by demanding an extortionist's fee before he would produce a "magic" nostrum he claimed to have, so the maharajah had him thrown out of his kingdom.

Arriving in Ludhiana, Harlan reported to the British political office, with which he had long corresponded secretly in his self-appointed role as British spy. He told the political assistant, Major Macgregor, of his ambitious plans. He explained that he was about to join Dost Mohammed in

Kabul to organize a new army to retake Peshawar from the Sikhs. Macgregor dismissed Harlan as an eccentric though enterprising man, whose plan to convince Dost Mohammed to launch a new war against the Sikhs was preposterous.[8]

Harlan's plan was not as wild as Macgregor imagined and was, in fact, welcomed by Dost Mohammed, who forgave him and called him "brother." He gave him command of his regular troops with the title General in Chief, and together they planed a new *jihad,* or holy war, against Ranjit Singh.

Harlan, who trained the new Afghan force, claimed to have taught Dost's son, Akbar Khan, the arts of warfare so that he could lead the campaign. In fact, Akbar Khan was no stranger to tribal warfare, as the British would later discover to their dismay. The Afghan force under Akbar Khan swept down upon the Sikhs at the town of Jamrud in the Khyber Pass in April 1837. The carnage on both sides of the battle was terrible. Masson reported that there had been a great slaughter of Afghans—some eleven thousand, including Dost Mohammed's oldest son, Mohammed Afzal. But the Sikhs lost half of their forces, some six thousand men, and Ranjit Singh's favorite general, Hari Singh, was killed in action. On hearing the news, the maharajah was said to have beat his chest in anguish and wept copiously.

The Afghans claimed victory at Jamrud, though the Sikhs did not admit defeat. Whatever the verdict, the Afghans had not succeeded in recovering Peshawar. After the battle, Harlan crowed: "The proud King of Lahore quailed upon his threatened throne as he exclaimed with terror and approaching despair: 'Harlan has avenged himself—this is all his work.' "[9]

Ranjit Singh was not quailing, nor did he probably waste much time in heaping vituperation on Harlan. But in the battle's results he saw good reason to draw even closer to the British; he needed their protection against further adventures by Dost Mohammed and the Afghans. Dost Mohammed, for his part, determined that he would give his friendship to whichever *ferangi,* British or Russian, was willing to help him regain Peshawar from the Sikhs. Shah Shuja could conclude from what had happened in Kandahar that he had little hope of regaining his throne unless the British were willing to assist him openly and dynamically—Sikh allies and British encouragement behind the scenes were not enough. The Great Game was assuming a new dimension for the British, one destined to engulf them in a political morass from which they could not extract themselves.

Chapter 10

POLITICIANS AND

BUREAUCRATS

WHEN IN MARCH 1835 THE TORY PRIME MINISTER, SIR ROBERT PEEL, fell from power and Lord Melbourne was named to head a new Whig government, the aggressive, adventurous Lord Palmerston became foreign minister to the anguish of the opposition. One prominent Tory was supposed to have blurted out: "I hope Palmerston can be made Archbishop of Canterbury, or anything that would keep him out of the foreign office." The new government appointed Sir John Hobhouse to be president of the Board of Control overseeing Indian policy, while Lord Heytesbury, recently appointed governor general of India by Melbourne's predecessor, Lord Peel, found himself removed from the job before he even had time to pack for the trip. In his place the Whigs named George Eden, Lord Auckland, as governor general. This would prove a fateful assignment, one that would one day be regretted.

This, then, was the political team that now faced the Russian problem in the East. The Whigs had canceled Heytesbury's assignment on the grounds that his recent service as British envoy to St. Petersburg had made him too soft on Russia. In fact, this was an unfair charge, but Lord Auckland, who had been First Lord of the Admiralty, was considered a "safe" man who would concern himself with India's internal affairs— meaning he would turn a profit for the Company rather than exhaust the treasury on frontier adventures. How disastrously inaccurate this estimate would prove!

Before turning over his Board of Control portfolio to Hobhouse, Ellen-borough had formulated his views on India policy, views based in great part on Alexander Burnes's report on Indus navigation, Afghanistan and Bok-hara—however much he disliked the precocious Company officer person-ally. In a secret dispatch to Calcutta, Ellenborough echoed Burnes's high regard for Dost Mohammed, and, again taking his cue from Burnes, wrote that he saw grave consequences if Ranjit Singh should, by humbling the Afghans, become too formidable. The Sikhs, he believed, could become a threat to India's northwest and require increased military expenditures "ruinous to our embarrassed finances." Ellenborough concluded: "It is our political interest that the Indus and its tributary streams should not belong to one state. The division of power on the Indus between the Scindians, the Afghans and the Sikhs is probably the arrangement most calculated to secure us against hostile use of that river. . . ."[1] And, like Burnes, he saw Afghanistan best playing the role as third leg of the three-legged stool under the stewardship of Dost Mohammed, providing the strongest possi-ble barrier to aggression from the west, i.e., Persia and Russia.

This was a policy at odds with the views of Claude Wade, political agent for the Punjab and the frontier, who favored a weak, divisive Afghanistan under "reliable friend, Shah Shuja," flanked by a strong Ranjit Singh, in whose enduring friendship with the British—and presumably his immor-tality as well—he had complete confidence. Wade had, in fact, grown partial to his two clients and had been infected with a bad case of parochi-alism.

Burnes's instincts about Dost Mohammed were better than Wade's. The Afghan ruler may have sent feelers to the Persians and Russians in his desperation to save Peshawar from the Sikhs, but he was quite aware that both countries were together scheming to take Herat. His position was difficult: on one side was the British colossus and its ally, the Sikhs; on the other was the Russian colossus and its ally, the Persians. Afghanistan was precariously sandwiched between the two. It was difficult enough for Dost Mohammed to control the Afghan tribes and clans, not to mention his own ambitious brothers, but to keep two great European powers at bay was asking a great deal. Burnes realized that if the hand of friendship could be extended to Dost Mohammed by the British, the Afghan leader would take the British side and resist Persian-Russian advances. Burnes had reached this conclusion, however, before Ranjit Singh's seizure of Peshawar; the loss of this important border town by the Afghans now loomed as a major obstacle to British-Afghan friendship.

The other fly in the Afghan ointment was Persia, which with Russian prodding seemed intent on taking Herat. To Governor General Bentinck, preparing to leave his post in May 1835, Persia had to be closely watched. In his valedictory dispatch to London from Calcutta, Governor General Bentinck wrote: "The advance of the combined [Persian, Russian] force would give them possession of Herat, the key to Cabul." If Herat were to fall, "The Afghan confederacy, even if cordially united, would have no means to resist the power of Russia and Persia."[2] This would presage defeat of the Sikh kingdom and all that could mean to the defense of India.

The departing governor general also warned of Russia's plans for Turkestan and Bokhara: "From the days of Peter the Great to the present time, the views of Russia have been turned to obtaining possession of that part of Central Asia which is watered by the Oxus and joins the eastern shore of the Caspian."[3] And after that the next Russian step would inevitably be toward Afghanistan. Seen through Russian eyes, the British initiative in sending Alexander Burnes to reconnoiter the Indus and scout out Kabul and Bokhara had been provocative. The Russians considered it a harbinger of British commercial aggression in Central Asia, an area that the czar felt was within his legitimate sphere of influence and part of Russia's imperial destiny. But in the British perspective, Russia had trespassed on its sphere of influence when it spilled out of the Caucasus and assumed a preeminent role in Persia.

The death of Fath Ali Shah in November 1834 introduced a new complication, however, one affecting the British and Russians alike; so for all their rivalry, the two countries could at least agree upon one thing: the successor to the shah.

The Persian crown prince, Abbas Mirza, had expired the year before during the autumn of 1833, leaving his son, Mohammed Mirza, as the logical heir apparent to the Peacock Throne. When he heard of his father's death, Mohammed Mirza had, in fact, halted his attack on Herat. His presence in Tehran was necessary to defend his birthright.

British Foreign Secretary Palmerston and the Russian ambassador, Prince Lieven,* in London quietly agreed that it would suit neither of their

*Palmerston, referred to by the London *Times* on occasion as "Lord Cupid" because of his propensity for romancing, was well connected with the Lieven family since the Russian envoy's wife, Dorothy, had been very close to him.

country's interests for Persia to degenerate into anarchy as a result of squabbling between rival claimants to the throne. Russian Chancellor Count Nesselrode also agreed with Palmerston that Mohammed Mirza should inherit power upon Fath Ali Shah's death. But this junction of interests did not signal a general warming of Russian-British relations, as Palmerston made clear to J. D. Bligh, British ambassador in St. Petersburg, when he wrote him that nations that do not mean to be encroached upon by Russia must "keep vigilant watch and have their horses always saddled."

The question that now bothered Melbourne's critics was whether the new governor general, Lord Auckland, could ride this political bucking bronco, saddled or unsaddled. Auckland's succession to office in India had not met with enthusiasm outside Whig circles and was, in fact, a sad mistake as later events would show. He had considerable standing in the party, but his prominence was not matched by ability.

The India establishment in London had become ingrown: Foreign Secretary Palmerston was a good friend of Prime Minister Melbourne and would ultimately marry the prime minister's sister, Lady Cowper, whom he had long admired; Prime Minister Melbourne was close to Lord Auckland's sister, Emily, who had accompanied her brother to India and exerted more influence on Indian policy behind the scenes in Calcutta than was good for the country—or for Auckland's reputation. Then, to complicate this already-confusing network of relationships, Lord Hobhouse, now president of the Board of Control for India, was a good friend of Lord Byron, who was carrying on with Lord Melbourne's wife. This all added up to a congenial-enough clique influencing Indian affairs, but not one with a grasp of the real situation in Central Asia. The man-on-the-spot, the governor general, inevitably had to call the shots, but Auckland, susceptible to influence from his Whig friends at home and disposed to accept advice from a coterie of advisers in Calcutta whom he imported as part of his entourage, was not the man for the job at this critical time.

Lord Auckland had prospered politically because of his steadfast support of the Whig party. He was hard-working and loyal; that was about as much as one could say for him. He looked forward to India as a place where he could quietly improve the Company's ward. As he said good-bye in London he "looked with exultation" on the new prospects opening out before him, providing him with the opportunity to "improve the lot of his fellow creatures by promoting education, improving justice, and bringing happiness to the millions in India."[4] These were fine words and Auckland meant them, but he had neither the energy nor the vision to carry out his programs, much less meet the terrible challenge that was about to face him on the northwest frontier.

Yet, for all his shortcomings, Auckland could perhaps have done a reasonable job had he not become a prisoner of his drawing-room confidants: political secretary William Hay Macnaghten; Macnaghten's assistant, Henry Torens; his private secretary, John Colvin; and these gentlemen's ally in court, Emily Eden, who delighted in whispering misguided advice in her brother's ear.

As Lord Auckland, accompanied by his maiden sisters, Emily and Fanny, sailed for India in September 1835, Henry Ellis was proceeding to Persia as special envoy to pay his country's respects to the new shah, Mohammed Mirza. Ellis took an apocalyptic view of things and his reporting soon rang alarm bells to add to the growing fear of Russia in England. According to Ellis, the shah was plotting new action to take Herat and Kandahar. Ellis had reason to believe that Shah Mohammed Mirza's ambitions even included the formidable citadel of Ghazni, within striking distance of Kabul. This, of course, sounded most sinister to the British.

Ellis kept up a drumbeat of warnings, and by January 1836 he reported that the Russian minister, Count Ivan Simonich, was blatantly lobbying at the Persian court in Tehran for a new campaign against Herat involving General Borowski, the Russian-controlled Polish mercenary who had figured so prominently in previous Persian operations in Khorasan aimed at Herat. With masterful understatement, Ellis concluded that Russian-influenced Persia could no longer be considered "an outwork for the defence of India," and in fact would more likely be the launching platform from which an attack on India would ultimately be made. By the terms of its own 1814 treaty with Persia, there was little Britain could legally do to intervene and prevent Russian-directed attacks on Afghanistan. Ellis, therefore, warned that his government might have to "submit to the approach of Russian influence through the instrumentality of Persian conquest to the very frontier of [the] Indian empire"[5] unless extraordinary measures were taken.

Lord Auckland was not convinced by Ellis's sometimes gloomy, sometimes alarming dispatches. The governor general saw expanded British commerce, not military confrontation, as the best means to penetrate Central Asia and counteract Russian influence there. But a shrill monograph entitled *Progress in the East,* written by Ellis's secretary, John M'Neill, galvanized London official opinion in favor of Ellis's pessimistic appraisal. M'Neill's paper may have been most significant for establishing a doctrinal justification for intervention: "The right of interference in the affairs of independent states is founded in this simple principle, that as self-preservation is the first duty, so it supersedes all other obligations."

More explicitly, he declared that the independence of Persia "is necessary to the security of India and Europe."[6]

Auckland began to be concerned when he heard from Ellis that an Afghan envoy in Tehran had tried to promote an alliance between the two countries, calling for Dost Mohammed to help Persia take Herat, ruled by his enemy the Saddozai clansman Shah Kamran, if Persia would assist Afghanistan against the Sikhs. The forfeiture of his claim on Herat, regrettable as it may have seemed to Dost Mohammed, was worth the gain of Peshawar. No alliance was in fact concluded, but the very idea of a Persian-Afghan agreement aimed at Ranjit Singh was disturbing to the Company. But, for all his concern, Auckland was not prepared to follow Ellis's suggestion that he defuse the situation by preemptively entering into an alliance with Dost Mohammed. The governor general felt that not only was Afghanistan still a weak confederation at best, a country on which one could not rely, but there were solemn agreements with Ranjit Singh that had to be honored.

Lord Auckland's reluctance to accept Ellis's dire predictions, much less his advice to reach out to Dost Mohammed, reflected Charles Metcalfe's influence, although Auckland did not like Ellis personally and this may also have been a factor in molding the governor general's attitude. Auckland, therefore, was relieved to learn that Ellis, whose mission had been only a temporary one to honor the deceased Fath Ali Shah and greet the new shah, was about to be replaced. But the new British envoy was none other than M'Neill, so Auckland could expect little change from Ellis's hard line. At least M'Neill, while basically a Crown appointment, would under a new arrangement be jointly sponsored by the Government of India. London's exclusive control of Persian relations would now end and the Government of India would regain some voice in British policy in this area.

Foreign Secretary Palmerston needed little convincing to embrace Ellis's pessimistic analysis and his conclusion that the Russians were a threat that had to be dealt with dynamically. Had Melbourne not restrained him, the foreign secretary would probably have plunged ahead with a favorite scheme: to arouse the Circassian tribes of the Caucasus against their Russian masters. As it was, the foreign secretary had gone far enough to cause the Russians to complain. In 1836, a Russian gunboat had intercepted the British ship *Vixen* in the Black Sea and found a cargo of arms destined for the guerrilla forces of Shamyl, Imam of Daghestan and leader of the Circassian anti-Russian movement.[7] Despite British official denials, this had caused a diplomatic incident that annoyed Melbourne, reminding him that his foreign secretary was quite capable of such adventures.

London was nonetheless now committed to a hard line. The Secret Committee of the India Office in June 1836 asked Auckland if it was not time "to interfere decidedly in the affairs of Afghanistan" and "raise a timely barrier against the impending encroachment of Russian influence?"[8] While phrased as a question, this was in fact an instruction, one destined to have far-reaching and unfortunate consequences.

Auckland, however, was a cautious man and still favored opening the Indus to navigation and trade as the best approach to the Russian problem, rather than run the risks implicit in intervening forcefully in Afghanistan. Metcalfe, about to leave India, was bombarding him with advice to avoid adventures beyond the Indus, and this made an impression on the governor general not easily counteracted by the Company directors or even Palmerston.

Burnes's reconnaissance had seemed to confirm the feasibility of riverine commerce—although there were those who argued to the contrary. But if the Indus was a centerpiece of Auckland's policy, he could not afford to sit by as the Sikhs cast covetous glances toward Sind. The governor general felt obliged to warn Ranjit Singh against making any move to annex Sind, so crucial to Indus River access. But in return for denying Sind to Ranjit Singh in an effort to keep a regional balance of power, Auckland felt he at least owed the Sikh leader support in defending Peshawar from the Afghans, and here is where the governor general's troubles began. It was this reasoning that made him unresponsive to a letter from Dost Mohammed requesting British help. The Afghan ruler—who, in fact, had written at the suggestion of British agent Charles Masson in Kabul—expressed the hope that Auckland, as new broom in Calcutta, would be more friendly to him than Bentinck had been when he allowed Shah Shuja to invade Afghanistan and attack Kandahar. Dost Mohammed phrased it nicely: "The field of my hopes, which had before been chilled by the cold blast of the times, has, by the happy tidings of your Lordship's arrival, become the envy of the garden of Paradise."[9] Auckland became less the envy of paradise, however, when he replied chillingly—and hypercritically—"It is not the practice of the British Government to interfere with the affairs of other independent states."[10] Considering that the British were interfering in Sikh affairs to prevent Ranjit Singh from moving against Sind, Auckland's letter was unconvincing. His reply was meant to be friendly, but, in fact, it could not have been more discouraging to Dost Mohammed.

Auckland did promise to send an envoy to the Kabul court for talks concerning commercial cooperation. This gesture, however well-meaning, disappointed the Afghan leader, who anyway was not enthusiastic about the prospect of British trade with his realm. He needed an ally against the Russian-Persian threat and wanted Peshawar, not trade, but saw in the governor general's offer an opportunity, at least, to plead his case in person with a British representative.

In early September 1836, Auckland plucked Burnes from his temporary oblivion in Kutch and ordered him to prepare for another mission up the Indus to Kabul in the hope that he could bring Dost Mohammed into the British trading orbit—euphemism for "sphere of influence"—or at least prevent undue Russian influence.

Events were now weaning Auckland away from Metcalfe's admonition against becoming involved beyond the Indus. Metcalfe's conviction that Ranjit Singh's Punjab sufficed as a northwestern buffer state and his belief that Sind, a weak collection of tribes and petty emirs, served no useful purpose and might better be absorbed by the stronger Sikh state, was neither convincing to Auckland nor the British government in London. Auckland now recognized that Afghanistan was the key.

Burnes, accompanied by Lieutenant Robert Leech of the Bombay Engineers and Lieutenant John Wood of the Indian Navy, sailed from Bombay on November 26, 1836. Soon the party would be joined by Dr. Percival Lord and Burnes's former companion of the road, Mohan Lal. Burnes's specific instructions were to open the Indus River to commerce and "establish in the countries beyond it such relations as should contribute to the desired end."[11]

Auckland had to resolve the dilemma for British policy implicit in Sikh-Afghan enmity, and Burnes, having done well on his previous journey to Kabul, seemed just the man to convince Dost Mohammed that he should content himself with British friendship since neither Persian-Russian adventures in Herat and Kandahar nor his efforts to retake Peshawar from the Sikhs could be tolerated by the Company. This was a tall order. Burnes's mission could hardly succeed.

Chapter 11

ALEXANDER BURNES,
HUMBLE PETITIONER

AS HE MADE HIS WAY UP THE INDUS RIVER, FIRST LEG OF HIS JOURNEY to Kabul, Alexander Burnes learned of startling new developments in which Dost Mohammed at Jamrud had tried once again but failed to wrest Peshawar from the Sikhs. In a letter to the governor general, a frustrated Dost Mohammed once more expressed his wish for British friendship and asked their help in recovering Peshawar. For the moment, this had only stimulated Auckland's influential secretary, Macnaghten, to warn Burnes against encouraging any political propositions along these lines when he met with Dost. The furthest Burnes could go would be to urge the Afghan leader to reach a reconciliation with Ranjit Singh. Charles Masson, as British agent watching developments in Kabul, later summed it up: Such guidelines were tantamount to "no instructions at all!" But Burnes was too exhilarated by his mission to be pessimistic. Nor did he yet realize how rigid Macnaghten could be in policy matters and how little the secretary would value his advice.

Macnaghten was the epitome of a good Company bureaucrat. While he had entered the service in 1809 as a cavalry cadet, he transferred to the Bengal Civil Service only five years later and attended the Company college at Fort William. He was a good student, excelling at languages, and soon revealed an exceptional aptitude for staff work. He spent eight years in the Office of Register of the High Court, quite at home with the voluminous paperwork the job entailed. Governor General Bentinck had taken him with him as a staff officer during a tour of the western provinces in 1830, during which he had his first taste of the frontier.

In 1833, during the preceding administration of Charles Metcalfe, Macnaghten had been put in charge of the Secret and Political Department of the secretariat—the name for the Company's foreign affairs section—where he gained a reputation as an ardent Russophobe. He remained in this position during the first year of Lord Auckland's regime before being named Chief Secretary of Government.

It was in Auckland's service that Macnaghten rose to power. His dispatching of Burnes to Kabul in the governor general's behalf, the moving of a pawn on the imperial chessboard, was the beginning of a drama that would plunge him into an Afghan nightmare from which he would not emerge alive.

The new British envoy in Tehran, Sir John M'Neill, dismayed by the prospects of a Persian-Russian grab for the important city of Herat, had hoped that Burnes's mission would bolster the confidence of Dost Mohammed in Kabul and encourage him to defend Herat against the invaders. It was not that M'Neill had any particular preference for Dost Mohammed as ruler of Afghanistan; like Ellis before him, he simply believed that a united Afghanistan was the best defense against Persian-Russian ambitions in that country, and Dost was the most likely leader to unify the Afghans. Auckland stuck to his conviction that there was advantage to a divided, weak Afghanistan and argued against M'Neill: "It cannot be in our policy to have the Sikh power on our frontier crushed by a strong Mohammedan union [in Afghanistan]."[1]

When Burnes reached Peshawar he was taken in hand by one of Ranjit Singh's foreign mercenaries, Paolo de Bartolomeo Avitabile, who as governor was charged with keeping order in that newly won frontier province.[2] At some point the Italian had become a secret British agent reporting to Captain Wade in Ludhiana, and certainly he was friendly and attentive to all Englishmen who came his way.

The Italian officer's techniques in subduing the Pathans of Peshawar were effective, if not pretty. He proudly showed Burnes the gibbets from which dangled the bodies of dissidents he had hanged to set an example.

Avitabile was a charming host, however, and with the help of eight cooks set a grand table for his guests. To Burnes he showed off his proudest possession, a sword that had once belonged to Akbar the Great, emperor of India. A tall man with a sensual face, the Italian lived well; erotic bedroom decorations portraying Indian dancing girls illustrated his leisure time.

Avitabile drove Burnes's party in his own carriages as far as Jamrud, on the border with Afghanistan, where they were met by an escort sent by Dost Mohammed to take them on to Kabul. At a rendezvous near Kabul, Burnes met for the first time the British agent Masson, who briefed him on what to expect at Dost Mohammed's court. Their talk left Masson despairing of Burnes's attitude, which he felt did not augur well for the success of the mission. It seemed clear that political matters, not commercial ones, were foremost in Burnes's mind despite the political restrictions placed on Burnes by Macnaghten—a hopeless situation in Masson's opinion. Masson had to alert Burnes to the fact that Dost Mohammed had been suspicious of his long stay in Peshawar on his way to Kabul; Dost seemed aware that the British were more intent on placating the Sikhs than on making friendly overtures toward him. But what discouraged Masson the most was the envoy's condescending attitude about Afghans. They "were to be treated as children," he said. Masson could only warn him that if that were the case, "he must not expect them to behave as men."[3] It also depressed Masson that political agent Wade in Ludhiana had undercut the mission. Wade was jealous and had by innuendo, at least, let it be known to Dost Mohammed that Burnes was not the right man for the job implying that he, Wade, could do better.

Entering Kabul on September 20, 1837, Burnes and his companions were warmly welcomed and treated with great pomp. The emir's son, Akbar Khan, greeted them with a finely turned out troop of cavalry, and escorted them on elephant back to their lavish quarters near the palace. But a ritual show of hospitality did not truly reflect Dost Mohammed's reservations about Burnes's mission.

At this, Burnes's initial meeting with Dost Mohammed—one of formal greeting, not substance—relations on the surface appeared to be cordial. Burnes considered his reception a gracious one and had the impression that Dost Mohammed appreciated the presents, "rarities of Europe," that he had brought. Actually, the Afghans, who still remembered the extravagant and exciting gifts brought by Elphinstone nearly two decades earlier, were not impressed. Burnes's trinkets were, in fact, paltry by any standard. Josiah Harlan, busy around Dost Mohammed's court, was aghast. For the emir's zenana there were pins, needles, scissors, penknives, silk handkerchiefs, toys, watches and musical snuff boxes "fit only to the frivolous tastes of savages or the wretched fancies of rude Afghans." Harlan recalled that Dost Mohammed, after the ceremony was over, shouted, "Pish!" as he threw the items on the floor in disgust. Harlan quoted the emir as saying angrily: "Behold! I have feasted and honoured this *ferangi* to the extent of 6,000 rupees and have now a lot of pins and needles and sundry pretty toys to show for my folly!"[4] Nor did Burnes's gifts to the emir himself, a brace of pistols and a spyglass, seem quite appropriate.

Masson was no more admiring of Burnes's performance. The envoy, in his opinion, was obsequious, prefacing his every remark with humbly folded hands and murmurings of supplication. Burnes quickly earned the public sobriquet of "Your Humble Petitioner" for his frequent repetition of this phrase in talking with Dost Mohammed. Nawab Jubbar Khan, the Company's friend in court, was distressed enough to advise Burnes tactfully against using so submissive a tone. As an Orientalist trying to act more native than the natives, Burnes was probably using the wrong psychology and had perhaps done so before as well.

At their first substantive talk Dost spoke bitterly of how Ranjit Singh had taken Peshawar from him while he was busy defending Kandahar from Shah Shuja's assaults. Burnes could only reply with banalities to the effect that Afghanistan and the Punjab "should live in peace." Certainly he could not promise that the British would unconditionally restore Peshawar to him.

Peshawar was, nonetheless, the principal point of discussion and contention. Dost Mohammed went as far as he could: he agreed to make peace with Ranjit Singh, even permit Peshawar to pay symbolic tribute to Lahore, provided that the strategic Pathan town be returned to him. Burnes's suggestion that Peshawar be made an autonomous principality had been firmly rejected; Dost Mohammed neither liked nor trusted his half-brother, Sultan Mohammed Khan, who ruled the city as Ranjit Singh's governor, but more important to him was the principle that Peshawar was rightly part of Afghanistan and should be unequivocally subject to the rule of Kabul.

Burnes soon received new instructions from Lord Auckland that, in effect, made agreement impossible. The most Dost Mohammed could hope for was British restraint of Ranjit Singh, but, as a condition of this, the emir would have to give up any idea of an alliance with Mohammed Shah of Persia—in short, he must ally himself with the British and forswear any efforts to play the Persians and Russians against them.

Burnes had sympathy for Dost Mohammed; the emir's bargaining was tough and he seemed to be auctioning his friendship to the highest bidder, but he was no more cynical than were the British. If the British were constrained by their Punjab Sikh relationship, Dost Mohammed was no less constrained by consideration for his Persian-Russian neighbors. Burnes sent off a dispatch to Lord Auckland by way of Wade in Ludhiana recommending that the British back Dost Mohammed as the only leader, however rigid in his demands, who was capable of reaching some kind of acceptable formula for settling the Afghan dispute with the Sikhs over Peshawar.

What Burnes specifically had in mind was a deal in which Peshawar would be returned to the Afghans *after* Ranjit Singh's death. The decrepit Sikh leader was in very bad health, on the verge of death, and the chances of his empire staying together after his death were dismal. This should have been obvious to all who had pinned frontier security to the Company's alliance with the ailing Ranjit Singh. Burnes was right: the power equation would inevitably be changed radically by the Sikh maharajah's death. Either chaos would reign indefinitely in the Punjab as it broke up in confusion or, more likely, the British would take over the Punjab and Sind along with it (which, in fact, happened). In either case, a friendly Afghanistan under a strong leader would be important to India's security.

On October 31, Burnes sent Macnaghten a message reporting on "very gratifying" meetings with Dost Mohammed. The emir, he wrote, had expressed his extreme distress with the Kandahar khans' flirtation with the Persians, and offered to take any steps necessary to stop it, including doing battle if need be. And Dost reiterated his eagerness to be friendly with the British. But Burnes's reporting did not make a dent in the Company's mind-set.

As intermediary for Burnes's reporting, Wade had the opportunity to annotate his dispatches from Kabul before they reached Macnaghten and Auckland. This Wade did to the detriment of Burnes's case for Dost Mohammed. And Wade's bias in favor of Ranjit Singh and Shah Shuja colored his own reporting to Calcutta, in which he missed no opportunity to downplay Burnes's opinions. If Wade prejudiced Burnes's position by his heavy overlay of opposing views, Macnaghten in Calcutta was guilty of even more egregious assaults on objectivity. As Company policy hardened against Dost Mohammed, he actually struck from the record Burnes's arguments in favor of the Afghan leader!

Burnes became more involved with the Kandahar problem than Calcutta liked. Encouraged by Dost's attitude and some indications of flexibility on the part of the Kandahar chiefs, Burnes went beyond his authority to send Lieutenant Leech to Kandahar with offers of British protection from Persian attack—even money—if they would abandon their intrigues with the Persians and Russians. When Macnaghten heard of Burnes's initiative, he had his assistant, Colvin, severely rebuke him: "His Lordship [Auckland] is compelled to disapprove, and in the future conform punctually on all points to the orders issued for your guidance."[5] Auckland would later see the logic of Burnes's strategy and admit that his envoy had been right, but at the moment he believed that Burnes had become too involved and had moved too far out in front of Calcutta's official policy.

But Burnes's problems were just beginning; on December 19, a Russian agent, Ivan Victorovich Vitkevich, suddenly arrived in Kabul.

Chapter 12

IMPERIAL JOUSTING

IN KABUL

I F THE BRITISH WERE CONCERNED ABOUT RUSSIAN DESIGNS ON TURKESTAN and Afghanistan, the Russians were no less concerned about British objectives in the same areas, whether commercial, strategic or both. And since the British had again sent Burnes to Kabul, the Russians felt they had to match this move. Their knight would be an intrepid Lithuanian named Ivan Victorovich Vitkevich, whose grasp of Central Asian politics was as good as Burnes's and his bargaining position better. But just who was Vitkevich and from where did he come? Only a little more is known about him today than when, phantomlike, he suddenly came to British notice in 1837.

As an eighteen-year-old youth of the Vilna nobility, Vitkevich began his career in Orenburg, Russia's frontier garrison at the southern limits of the Ural Mountains, north of the Caspian Sea. He was a convicted criminal, sentenced to this remote gateway to Central Asia for having been a member of a secret organization called the Black Brothers, dedicated to freeing Lithuania and Poland from the czar's rule. Found guilty of writing revolutionary letters to his teachers and scribbling seditious graffiti on the walls and buildings of Krazhiai, where he attended school, Vitkevich had been sentenced to death. But Grand Duke Tzarevich Konstanin Pavlovich, regent of Poland, showed mercy on him because of his youth and commuted the sentence to military duty in the Orenburg Independent Corps.

Arriving in Orenburg in April 1824, Vitkevich endured six years of hard service as a simple soldier, but during this period, as time permitted, he studied the customs of Central Asia and mastered Persian, court language of Bokhara, and the Kirghiz language of the steppes. In this way he attracted the favorable attention of his superiors, who needed linguists in conducting relations with the obstreperous independent tribes of Transcaspian Central Asia.

Having proven good at negotiations with the Kazakh chieftains near Orenburg, Vitkevich was promoted to noncommissioned officer in 1830 and assigned to the Orenburg Boundary Commission. He became a valuable addition to the commission and was recommended for promotion to officer in 1831. With the cloud of a rebellious past still hanging over him and because of brief suspicion that he might have been involved in an insurrectionary plot in Orenburg, his promotion was not approved until 1834, when he was transferred to the Orenburg Cossack Regiment. Here he was in his element as his commanding officer, Count Vasili Alekseevich Perovski, urgently required intelligence on Turkestan for a planned Russian military campaign against Khiva.

The vast Kirghiz-Kazakh steppes, which cradle the Aral Sea, more than one hundred feet higher than the Caspian, occupy the Transcaspian region from the Ural Mountains in the north to Khiva and Turkestan in the south. The Kirghiz-Kazakh tribes, or hordes, as they were known, thrived on brigandage and slaving much to the exasperation of their nominal Russian masters, and kept the Orenburg garrison busy dispatching small punitive campaigns that did nothing to solve the problem.

It was a harsh land that made service there onerous. The summers were scorching and the winters bitter cold. Tamerlane's hordes had perished there by the thousands. Though a short autumn was depressingly rainy, the area was generally cursed with unremitting dryness, and what little groundwater existed was salty. The soil, a mixture of clay and sand, was uncongenial to livestock, forcing the tribes to keep constantly on the move to find forage for their cattle. This was the country across which the Russians would have to march before reaching Khiva.

As Burnes had seen in Bokhara during the midsummer of 1832, slaving and brigandage were growing problems for the Russians. Tribal slave raiders enjoyed a brisk business raiding Persian caravans venturing northward, but Russian subjects—mostly Caspian Sea sailors—brought premium prices in the slave markets of Bokhara and Khiva because of their reputation for diligence and survivability. The British feared that on the pretext of suppressing slave trading, the Russians would extend their influence in a region disturbingly close to India.

An 1834 Russian mission to Bokhara undertaken by a Baron Demaisons had determined that the emir of Bokhara would remain neutral in the event of a conflict between Khiva and Russia, but there was still much to be learned before sending a Russian army into the hostile and desolate steppes that lay beyond Orenburg. Vitkevich was just the man to collect the required intelligence on this area he knew so well.

Vitkevich set out for Bokhara in November 1835. One account of his trip had him arriving in Bokhara by mistake after losing his direction in a snowstorm, but this unlikely story may only have been a cover excuse invented to lessen the emir's suspicions of Russian intentions toward his kingdom. Whatever the case, Vitkevich arrived in Bokhara in January 1836.

What Vitkevich accomplished in Bokhara cannot be seen clearly through the mist of history, but his mission must have been considered a success, for on his return he was promoted, and in 1837 he was made adjutant to Count Perovski, by then governor general of Orenburg. This was the prelude to Vitkevich being given the most important assignment of his career—and sadly his last: a mission to Dost Mohammed's court in Kabul to meet the challenge posed by Burnes. It was time for jousting at close quarters.

———— •·•• ————

VITKEVICH HAD FIRST BEEN SPOTTED, QUITE COINCIDENTALLY, BY BRITISH Major Henry Rawlinson when the latter was traveling across eastern Persia in early November to deliver an official message to the Persian Army, then poised to march on Herat. Rawlinson and his small party had lost their way in the low mountains of Khorasan when they came upon another party of horsemen. They were in Cossack uniforms, obviously Russian. When they stopped for breakfast, Rawlinson approached the officer-in-charge, "a young man of very fair complexion with bright eyes and a look of great animation."[1] A language barrier feigned by the Russian officer interfered with conversation, but Rawlinson was made to understand that their destination too was Mohammed Shah's expeditionary army headquarters near Meshed. When the two men later met more formally at the shah's camp, the Russian, speaking flawless French and Persian, was introduced as Captain Vitkevich from Orenburg. Rawlinson learned that Vitkevich was, in fact, on a mission to Kabul, and was just passing through the Persian camp. On hearing this, the Englishman returned posthaste to Tehran to give the startling news to M'Neill.

The British learned that Vitkevich had reached Tehran in September 1837, where he received his final instructions from the Russian minister, Count Simonich. After his brief stop at Mohammed Shah's camp in Khorasan, he made his way to Kandahar to intrigue with the chiefs. From there he proceeded to Kabul, pretending as Burnes had that his mission was purely a commercial one. Dost Mohammed still cherished hopes that he could reach an acceptable agreement with the British, so he kept Vitkevich at arm's length.

In his eagerness not to compromise his conversations with the British envoy, Dost Mohammed went so far as to ask Burnes whether or not he should receive the Russian agent at all. Knowing that this was meant as a gesture, Burnes magnanimously advised the emir that he should at least be hospitable, but in his mind he knew that Vitkevich was a complicating factor and a very unwelcome visitor.

Burnes invited Vitkevich to Christmas dinner—the least show of civility one Christian could make to another in an alien land at Christmastime. The two rivals got on well; Vitkevich "was a gentleman and an agreeable man of about 30 who spoke French, Turkish and Persian fluently," recalled Burnes. Both having been to Bokhara, they had that to talk about even though they avoided discussing their respective missions to Kabul. The two men never met face-to-face again. Burnes regretted this but knew it was "impossible to follow the dictates of my personal feeling of friendship toward him . . . lest the relative positions of our nations should be misunderstood."[2]

Vitkevich bore a letter to Dost Mohammed, liberally sprinkled with gold leaf, purportedly from the czar himself, as well as one from Count Simonich in Tehran. The czar's letter acknowledged Dost Mohammed's earlier message to him and rather noncommittally promised that Afghan traders would always be welcome in Russia. Masson, who managed to steal a copy, suspected the letter was a forgery since it lacked the czar's signature, but Mohan Lal was convinced that it was genuine. Whether or not the czar actually wrote the letter was unimportant; it clearly came from top levels of the Russian government and vouched for Vitkevich as an agent with authority to make promises to the Afghans—very generous ones.

BURNES WAS NOT AS FORTUNATE IN THE BACKING HE RECEIVED FROM HIS government. By the end of January 1838 he had Auckland's response to Dost Mohammed's plea to the British, and conveyed to the Afghan leader an unwelcome position with which he profoundly disagreed. Calcutta had rejected every formula suggested by Burnes; Auckland's cheerless words extinguished all hope for Dost Mohammed: "In regard to Peshawar, truth compels me to urge strongly on you to relinquish the idea of obtaining the government of that territory." Adding insult and implied threat to disappointment, Auckland continued: "Ranjit Singh has acceeded to my wish for the cessation of strife and the promotion of tranquility, if you should behave in a less mistaken manner toward him."[3]

Josiah Harlan claimed to have been present at court when Dost Mohammed described the terms of Lord Auckland's "didactic and imperative ultimatum" to his ministers. The emir, who had genuinely wanted an accord with the British, was mortified. The letter was passed around to all present, including Harlan, and "an embarrassing silence ensued." The leader of a pro-Persian faction at court proclaimed that the governor general's ultimatum left no alternative but to eject Burnes from Kabul. Another faction, more kindly disposed toward the British, took issue with this, its spokesman calling for renewed negotiation. Never hesitant to attach more importance to himself than was warranted, Harlan claimed that the emir's council had unanimously agreed that *he* should assume the burden of negotiating with his fellow *ferangi*, Burnes. But the British envoy rejected Harlan's overtures, perhaps not taking the American mercenary seriously and considering that it would be humiliating to deal with the Afghans through a dubious American freebooter.[4]

Charles Masson had been critical of Burnes from the beginning. The envoy's philandering particularly bothered Masson, especially after Dost Mohammed's counsellor, Mirza Sami Khan, smirkingly offered to fill his house with "black-eyed damsels" in emulation of Burnes's ménage. Close to the people because of his long residence in Kabul, Masson knew the effect that Burnes's activity was having. Dost appeared to ignore the whole thing, not wishing to upset his negotiations with Burnes, and perhaps feeling that the envoy's liaisons, often with high-born ladies, could even be used to influence the British position. Harlan, at least, was convinced that Dost Mohammed used "every subterfuge that duplicity could suggest . . . to work upon the English agent."[5]

Burnes himself admitted his fascination with Afghan women: "Their ghost-like figures" with their shrouding garments made him melancholy, but he knew that their talents behind closed doors "amply amend for all such somber exhibitions in public."[6]

Even making allowances for life on the frontier, which forced him to spend months on end away from appropriate female companionship, he took risks he should not have taken under the circumstances. Protection of womanhood from the illicit lusts of men is a tenet of Islam. The veil was encouraged by Mohammed himself for this reason and nowhere was the veil more shrouding than among the Afghans. Burnes knew all this well; he was the expert on Central Asia, and he had seen at firsthand the fatal punishment for adultery in Bokhara and Afghanistan. Yet he would allow sexual temptation to prejudice his missions and ultimately lead him to an untimely death.

If Burnes's personal life was reprehensible, his professional performance was not much better in Masson's opinion. Burnes, he thought, had over-reacted to Vitkevich's arrival, and was completely taken in by lies and exaggerations concerning the Russian's mission purposely leaked to him by the emir's court "to rouse his mind." According to Masson, Burnes was so depressed by Vitkevich's presence that "he bound his head with wet towels and took to the smelling bottle." It was "humiliating to witness such an exhibition and the ridicule to which it gave rise."[7]

Wet towels and smelling bottles may not have been a very useful way to cope with the Russian threat, but Masson minimized the significance of Vitkevich's mission. The very presence of this Russian agent was convincing evidence that the Russians had no intention of letting the British get the upper hand in Kabul. Even in London, well removed from the jousting field of Kabul and presumably capable of cooler judgments, the British government felt it necessary to protest Vitkevich's mission through its ambassador in St. Petersburg. Masson also disapproved of Leech's mission to Kandahar, and Lord and Wood's mission north of the Hindu Kush to Kunduz, knowing that this kind of reconnaissance would be viewed with suspicion by Dost Mohammed. Masson's valedictory summation of the mission as it was coming to its ill-fated end was highly critical and exaggerated in its condemnation of Burnes: "Thus closed a mission, one of the most extraordinary ever sent forth by a government, whether as to the singular manner in which it was conducted, or as to its results." As a parting shot at Burnes, he wrote: "The government had furnished no instructions, apparently confiding in the discretion of a man who had none."

Harlan, in his postmortem of events, was even more unkind in his assessment of Burnes's performance: "The utter and deplorable incapacity of the English agent originated a line of bewildering policy, commenced in the feebleness of a narrow mind and finished with a deluge of misery and blood."[8]

In fairness to Burnes, Masson's and Harlan's criticisms were aired in memoirs long after the events they criticized, and in both cases were probably influenced by grudges against the Company. Moreover, as the British searched for reasons to explain the failure of their Afghan policy, there was a general atmosphere of recrimination.

Burnes's mission should be judged in light of the fact that it was preordained to be futile by the Company's mind-set. Burnes was convinced that Dost Mohammed genuinely considered his interests to be bound up with the British; he had rebuffed "alluring promises" from the Persians and had held off Vitkevich until he despaired of British reasonableness. Considering this, Burnes found a solution: delay decision on the all-important issue of Peshawar until the rapidly ailing Ranjit Singh died and his kingdom, sure to disintegrate, ceased to be an ally that needed appeasing. Calcutta would not listen, which exasperated Burnes. In fact, Burnes had much to blame the government for.

The sin of bad judgment is as dangerous as it is reprehensible in statecraft, but purposeful distortion of the record is perhaps worse, and it was this that angered Burnes. Put bluntly, the record of Burnes's mission was altered in Calcutta to fit Company policy preconceptions. The envoy's conviction that an understanding with Dost Mohammed was possible despite British obligations to the Sikhs was systematically expunged from the record (and did not appear in the blue books that later officially chronicled the events leading up to the Anglo-Afghan War). Burnes wrote eloquently, albeit privately, about official digging of "the grave of truth." "The character of Dost Mohammed has been lied away; the character of Burnes has been lied away—both by the mutilation of the correspondence of the latter,"[9] he wrote in evident anger. Burnes accused Calcutta officialdom of doctoring the Company record, "the sheet anchors of historians, to misrepresent the conduct of Dost Mohammed and so justify their after conduct toward him."[10]

Mohan Lal had a lower opinion of Dost Mohammed than did Burnes. Dost, in Lal's opinion, was treacherous. Mohan Lal's negative views of the Afghan leader were used out of context to counteract Burnes's opinions and support similar views held by Wade and Macnaghten. But Mohan Lal was loyal to Burnes; unlike Masson and Harlan, he blamed the failure of the mission on Russian intrigues and Dost Mohammed's double-dealing rather than on Burnes's performance. As one of the first Indians to be entrusted to a responsible diplomatic and intelligence role, Mohan Lal was scarcely in a position to question his "betters' " actions and judgments, certainly not those of his friend Burnes. And Mohan Lal's use of the word *double-dealing* was an unduly pejorative way of saying that Dost Mohammed, like most Eastern rulers faced with Western threats to their kingdom, in self-defense had but one real weapon: play imperial predators against each other. This time-honored tactic preserved for both Persia and Afghanistan some semblance of independence through the years.

Mohan Lal, busy gathering intelligence on the Russian mission in Kabul, could not help but be dismayed by what he found. This, perhaps, made it more difficult for him to assess the longer-range significance of events as they unfolded before him. But things undeniably did look black for the British as Dost Mohammed began his calculated lionization of Vitkevich and conspicuously sped Burnes on his way. His last words to Burnes conveyed his hatred for Ranjit Singh, whose befriending by the British so upset him: "I can't do that brute any real harm, but I will torment him a good deal before I have done with him."[11]

Burnes departed on April 26, 1838—even before Lord and Wood returned from their survey trip to Kunduz in the north. The dejected envoy believed that his personal relationship with Dost Mohammed had, at least, survived the breakdown of negotiations, but Harlan remembered otherwise. The American claimed that in his presence Dost Mohammed expressed himself in strong words after Burnes's departure: "The greatest error of my life lay in this, that I allowed the English deceiver to escape with his head!"[12]

What lay behind Dost Mohammed's strong sentiments was more than hyperbole or momentary anger. Masson revealed that the last days of Burnes's mission were marked by incidents of hostility; Masson's house was assaulted and tradesmen refused to deal with Burnes. More seriously, the powerful Ghilzye chieftains, who held sway east and south of Kabul, had become aroused by the prospects of growing British presence and influence in Afghanistan. Afghans have never welcomed foreign infidels, so upon hearing of British overtures, the tribesmen became alarmed that the British posed a threat to their religion and way of life. The Ghilzyes, as it was learned later, had exerted strong pressure on Dost Mohammed to execute Burnes—their way of meeting the problem. When Dost Mohammed said to Harlan at the time, "Fool that I was, I have ruined my affairs by making myself pivot of foreign diplomacy,"[13] he meant just this. Burnes had then had a closer brush with death than he realized.

At the end, Dost Mohammed turned a cold shoulder toward the mission and, according to Masson, there were "some indelicate exposures" on the part of certain of Burnes's colleagues that made an undignified, hasty departure advisable. Masson was referring to philandering by members of the mission, including Burnes, which had contributed to the Ghilzyes' attitude toward the infidel "Kaffirs," as they referred to the British.

As Burnes left town, taking Masson with him since in this atmosphere the British agent's usefulness in Kabul seemed to be over, Vitkevich stepped into the limelight to reap the rewards of British failure.

VITKEVICH'S INSTRUCTIONS WERE TO CONVINCE BOTH THE KHANS OF KANDA-har and Dost Mohammed in Kabul that their protection from foreign enemies and their internal security depended on reaching a treaty with the Russians. Only Russia could restrain the Persians, now besieging Herat, from seizing Kandahar and ultimately Kabul. Since Persian temerity was a product of Russian encouragement, this was circular reasoning at best, and a threat at worst. Like his rival, Burnes, Vitkevich had an intelligence mission as well. He was to assess British influence in Afghanistan and the feasibility of British commercial navigation on the Indus. The Russians were also interested in tribal and regional antagonisms such as those between Kabul, Herat and Kandahar. The mission's objectives were to have been secret, known only to a few top Russian officials, and Vitkevich had had to travel to Kabul under the assumed name of Ibrahim Bey in the disguise of a Khivan merchant to mask his movements until he arrived in Afghanistan.[14]

Vitkevich's offer had had little appeal to Dost Mohammed so long as the Afghan ruler had hope of British help in regaining Peshawar from the Sikhs, particularly since the price of Russian friendship could mean the loss of Herat. But with Auckland's rejection of his overtures, Dost Mohammed became more interested in the Russian offer, particularly after Vitkevich promised support in seizing Peshawar.

Mohan Lal's intelligence efforts in Kabul had been effective even if Burnes's negotiations had not. By bribing Vitkevich's messengers he was able to intercept most of the Russian's dispatches, including a long and particularly comprehensive message to Simonich in Tehran. The message revealed that Dost Mohammed was clearly trying to play the British against the Russians, telling Vitkevich that a Russian accord was impossible because of British offers to force the Sikhs to give up Peshawar and British promises to help him prevent Herat from falling into Persian hands. Vitkevich was not taken in by Dost Mohammed's wiles, however, and soon learned of Lord Auckland's negative reply to Dost Mohammed in February rejecting all that Burnes had negotiated with the Afghan leader. The Russian agent accurately attributed Auckland's refusal to pressure Ranjit Singh on the question of Peshawar to the Persian siege of Herat, now in full swing.

Significantly, Vitkevich in his intelligence appraisal of Afghanistan saw with more clarity than did the British the problems that would be encountered by India if it sought to invade that country, difficulties of rugged terrain and warlike people. But, he assured Simonich, the "English have appreciated the full importance of this country in a political point of view, and have spared neither trouble nor expense to gain a footing in Afghanistan."[15] The Russian agent pointed out that since 1832 there had been an established English agent (Masson) in Kabul, but that he had left with Burnes, perhaps indicating the extent to which Burnes's mission had irretrievably lost the game to the Russians in Kabul.

Masson, not privy to all of Mohan Lal's intelligence, refused to believe that Vitkevich had letters to Ranjit Singh as well and intended to penetrate the British sphere of influence to beard the Lion of the Punjab in Lahore. Masson also believed that some of the more alarming reports about the Russians were forgeries—false information intended to impress the Afghans and demoralize the British. In Masson's opinion, Burnes had been duped despite abundant warnings. "On fifty occasions I had to protest against the delusive intelligence he forwarded without explanations,"[16] Masson recalled. Loosing one of his more venomous shafts at Burnes, Masson wrote that based on "some of these very items of intelligence, which the most arrant blockhead in Kabul would have rejected as fallacious, and which no one, I venture to say, would have dared to make to me, a Government of India and a British ministry [in London] justify the monstrous policy they followed." Masson persisted in believing that Vitkevich's mission was simply an intelligence one, intended only to discover what Burnes was doing in Kabul; "that he achieved more was owing to the folly of Burnes, himself."[17]

With historical hindsight, the British were overreacting to Russian moves in Afghanistan and did not give due credence to the fact that Russia had just as much right to cry "Provocation" as did the British. Russian actions were thus defensive, or at least reactive, but they were no less troubling. Burnes may have overestimated the threat represented by Vitkevich's mission, but Masson, because of his antagonism toward Burnes, underestimated it and weakened his case by heaping vituperation on his antagonist.

Vitkevich had arranged with Dost Mohammed a treaty promising that the Russians would guarantee the return of Herat to the Barakzai rulers of Kandahar as soon as it was wrenched by the Persians from the Saddozai regime of Shah Kamran and his powerful vizier, Yar Mohammed—an ingenious but not convincing justification for the Persian attack on Herat. Then, on his way back to Russia by way of Persia, Vitkevich obtained adherence to the treaty by the chiefs of Kandahar, on whom he lavished money and made extravagant promises with regard to Herat. Of course, this was a discouraging development from the British point of view, but even Dost Mohammed began to realize that there were pitfalls to joining the Russian camp, and soon he would also realize what British alienation would mean to him.

When Vitkevich arrived in St. Petersburg toward the end of April, the British heard that Nesselrode praised him and recommended him for promotion. Vitkevich had, in fact, outscored Burnes in Kabul and deserved Russian acclaim. The Russian chancellor was supposed to have taken steps to award him a monetary prize and, best of all, restore his status as a nobleman. If true, he had traveled far from his days as a student revolutionary banished to remote Central Asia.

But was this a true account of Vitkevich's reception? Within a week of his return to St. Petersburg and on the very day he was to be received by the czar himself, Vitkevich committed suicide by blowing out his brains in a hotel room. He left no note to explain his motives. Making matters worse, he destroyed all the valuable notes he had taken on his journey before committing the fatal act. According to one account, Vitkevich killed his Kazakh servant, who was with him in the room, before taking his own life. There seemed to be no good explanation for this strange human drama.

John Kaye, exhaustive chronicler of Afghan events, wrote that Nesselrode was concerned by strong British protests and by the European political implications of Vitkevich's mission, so repudiated the agent and refused to see him.[18] Nesselrode disingenuously claimed he "knew of no Captain Vitkevich, except an adventurer of that name, who, it was reported, had been lately engaged in some unorthodox intrigues in Caubul and Caundihar," a patently unconvincing denial. Fearing the fate of being sacrificed for the greater needs of country, Vitkevich was plunged into deep and fatal despair, according to Kaye.[19] Later investigations, based on evidence given by the director of the Asiatic Department of the Russian Ministry of Foreign Affairs, revealed a much different account of Vitkevich's death. The director, whose testimony could of course have been fabricated, wrote Vitkevich's friend and superior officer General Perovski in Orenburg, claiming that the unfortunate agent had revealed suicidal tendencies while passing through Persia and had told the Russian traveler Prince Saltikov that he would eventually shoot himself—an odd thing to say in view of his successful mission.

On the eve of his death, Vitkevich seemed in good spirits and left instructions with the hotel desk to call him early in the morning.[20] A contemporary Russian writer named Pol'ferov, who had a flair for the dramatic, wrote that just before his death Vitkevich had been visited by a certain Tyszkiewicz, a Polish underground partisan whom he had known from his revolutionary student days. Tyszkiewicz, according to this account, berated Vitkevich for being a spy and a traitor to Polish nationalism, serving the hated Russian czar and abandoning the struggle to free the "dear motherland from slavery."[21] This set Vitkevich to brooding, and later that night in a fit of remorse he burned all his information and shot himself.

Pol'ferov did not say how he had come to know this. The mystery surrounding Vitkevich's death was no closer to a convincing explanation. Nesselrode, faced with a complaint from Palmerston, found it expedient to deny official sanction of Vitkevich's actions in Afghanistan. Could the czar's government have had him murdered, then announced it was suicide to avoid any chance of Vitkevich revealing the truth? That he had left no suicide note and his servant, witness to what occurred, was also found dead with him, not to mention the curious fact that all his notes were burned, perhaps suggest an execution by the government. Certainly George Buist, editor of the *Bombay Times,* who wrote a detailed history of the British campaign in Afghanistan, suspected officially directed murder.[22] But then, in the murky recesses of nineteenth-century politics and espionage, many mysteries have defied explanation by historians—usually because the governments involved wanted it that way. To call Vitkevich a martyr would probably be overdoing it, but he was nonetheless among those who, one way or another, forfeit their lives in the Game.

Vitkevich had worked in the service of Russia not for patriotic reasons and not for glory but because he had had no choice but to make the best of a harsh exile—although he doubtless felt professional pride in his achievements. Burnes, to the contrary, loved his calling as a "political," and was certainly moved by patriotic motives. But, having tasted glory after his Bokhara trip, he had also dreamed of new victories ahead to nourish his ambition and vanity. This mission, however, had been a frustrating one. For Burnes, this was more than a policy failure; it was a blow to his career. This time he could not return a hero. A fellow officer, Eldred Pottinger, instead emerged as the imperial champion of the day.

Chapter 13

ELDRED POTTINGER,
HERO OF HERAT

A T ABOUT THE SAME TIME THAT ALEXANDER BURNES ARRIVED IN KABUL on his ill-starred mission, the Persian Army, led by Mohammed Shah himself, was approaching Herat, some five hundred miles to the west as the hawk flies. Herat was strategically important as the western gateway to Afghanistan and therefore India beyond. Located in the northwestern corner of Afghanistan, near the neighboring Persian city of Meshed to the west and the Turkestan desert to the north, it was part of a region straddling Iran and Afghanistan known as Khorasan and seemed always in contention between the two countries. With its crumbling citadel rising from the town, Herat commanded the strategic tri-junction of Afghanistan, Persia and Turkestan, and for this reason attracted the Russians and British alike. It seemed particularly important to the British now that it was once again a target for Persian attack. Earlier predictions in Calcutta that Russia would exploit its preeminence in Persia and use that country as a cat's paw to seize Afghanistan seemed to be coming true.

The Persians, augmented by a curious battalion recruited from among "Russian deserters" in Persia and commanded by Russian "military advisers," were intent on capturing the autonomous province of Herat from its Afghan ruler of the Saddozai clan, Shah Kamran. Next on the Persian agenda for conquest was Kandahar to the southeast—then perhaps even Ghazni northeast of Kandahar, key to Kabul itself. Shah Mohammed's plan, inspired by the Russian envoy in Tehran, Count Ivan Simonich, envisioned reducing Dost Mohammed to vassalage, in return for which the Persian monarch would help him recapture Peshawar from the Sikhs. For now, however, Shah Mohammed contented himself with trying to bring about the downfall of Shah Kamran and the capitulation of Herat.

Throughout most of 1836 Shah Kamran had been campaigning with little success against Turkoman tribes and, more recently, had been engaged in an inconclusive attack against a fortress in a remote corner of southeastern Persia—to the annoyance of the Persian shah whose territory was being violated. When Shah Kamran heard of the Persian advance on Herat, he rushed back to defend his city.

Watching the Herat army as it returned to its garrison to bolster the town's defenses against the impending Persian attack was a man sometimes calling himself a horse trader from Kutch, sometimes claiming to be a seyyid, or Moslem holy man. He was neither. He was, in fact, a British artillery lieutenant seconded to the political service named Eldred Pottinger. Unlike Burnes, Pottinger had attended the Company school for military cadets at Addiscombe in England, a converted country estate near Croydon. The "gentlemen cadets" at Addiscombe, all between the ages of fourteen and sixteen, were a high-spirited lot whose revels were the bane of the town. Young Pottinger was no exception and regularly drew extra drill for minor breaches of discipline. Caught in a more serious prank that involved a window-shattering explosion on the parade ground, Eldred was very nearly expelled from the academy. He managed to survive, however, and graduate with his class. Almost immediately, he sailed for India to join the Bombay Artillery and launch himself into what would be a tumultuous career.

Like Burnes and many other young officers who grew bored with cantonment life without combat, Pottinger applied to the political service while serving with the Kutch Irregular Horse. Kutch, because of its ambiguous status on the Arabian Sea near the Sind border, was an interesting place in which to serve. It was, of course, Alexander Burnes's post as well, although in 1836, when Pottinger joined the mission, Burnes was about to leave on his mission to Kabul. The resident heading the Kutch mission was Henry Pottinger, Eldred's uncle, who had many years before made a name for himself by his explorations in Baluchistan and western Afghanistan.

Henry Pottinger was receiving alarming reports of Persian intentions toward Herat, so when his nephew, Eldred, volunteered to conduct reconnaissance in the endangered province, he readily gave him his permission. There was a pressing need for better intelligence on this likely flash point in the uneasy relations between the Persians and the Afghans, with all this could mean to British-Russian rivalries in the area, and it required the eyes and ears of an Englishman, not simply some native informer of unknown loyalty.

Herat was a dirty, unprepossessing town of some thirty thousand dispirited people, which, with its surrounding countryside, constituted Shah Kamran's autonomous realm. The aging Saddozai prince was the last of his clan to rule an Afghan principality and keep alive the rivalry with the Barakzais, who had gained ascendancy in Afghanistan under Dost Mohammed.

Characteristic of East Indian Company frontier officers, Eldred Pottinger had a lust for exploration and saw the Afghan passes beyond the Indus and the lesser-known regions of western Afghanistan as exciting challenges. But, typically, the Company disavowed Pottinger's journey; it must appear to be his own personal excursion. If he found himself in trouble or created an incident, it must not be blamed on the Company. Just as St. Petersburg publicly denied that Vitkevich's mission to Kabul had been anything more than a commercial one—the same euphemism used by the British to explain Burnes's mission to Kabul—and claimed that he had exceeded his instructions by negotiating political agreements, the British would steadfastly protest that it had nothing to do with Pottinger's fortuitous presence in Herat as the Persians prepared to lay siege to the town. Such pretenses did not fool anyone but were, nonetheless, rules of the Game.

As Pottinger watched the returning Afghan troops enter Herat's gates, first the aging and infirm Shah Kamran carried on a litter, then his well-mounted cavalry, followed by a more motley infantry, he saw Yar Mohammed, Shah Kamran's vizier and the real power in Herat. This was the man with whom Pottinger must contend. In his younger years Shah Kamran had given himself over to a life of debauchery. He had considered the women of the town his for the taking, and had employed roving bands of brigands to plunder Herat households of their treasures to satisfy his greed. But as he grew old, he had been obliged to delegate rule to Yar Mohammed, his vizier. Yar Mohammed, however, was no more estimable than Shah Kamran. To quote the historian Kaye: "If there was a worse man in Central Asia, I have not yet heard his name."

Eldred Pottinger now considered his own situation. To attempt to sustain his disguise as a native of Kutch would be difficult, and dangerous if he were found out. On his way to Herat from Kabul he had had a close call when a Hazara chief became suspicious of him. (British disguises rarely fooled the Afghans for long; they were useful to avoid being conspicuous while traveling, but not to sustain a false identity.) Before that Dost Mohammed himself was perturbed to hear that an English officer in disguise had hurriedly passed through Kabul bound for the Herat stronghold of his Saddozai enemy, Shah Kamran—particularly at the very moment that Burnes was lingering unaccountably in Peshawar, the other Afghan town that had so maddeningly eluded his grip. Masson in Kabul, who had not been forewarned that Pottinger would be passing through, was forced to do much explaining to convince Dost that he, Pottinger and Burnes were not conniving in some dark plot against him.

Yet, for Pottinger to present himself to Shah Kamran and Yar Mohammed as a British officer at this particular time would surely have political implications in Tehran. Pottinger, nonetheless, elected to announce his presence frankly. Yar Mohammed, who instantly realized the value of having a British officer in Herat implying British support at this critical time, welcomed Pottinger—so heartily that the English officer was not allowed to leave! Pottinger wrote Burnes, who by this time had arrived in Kabul on his ill-fated mission, informing him about the predicament.

Throughout early November 1837 Yar Mohammed feverishly prepared for the Persian onslaught. Grain was collected and stored within the town in anticipation of a siege before the countryside was put to the torch to prevent its use as a source of food by the attackers. Pottinger pitched in to improve the town's defenses: the citadel walls, which had fallen into disrepair, and the moats encircling the town.

On November 23, the Persian siege began. The advance guard of ten thousand men, the first of three divisions, brought into position an impressive artillery park, including a giant sixty-eight-pounder. That behemoth, however, soon exploded from its own might, and the Persian bombardiers, despite their Russian mentors, proved anyway to be bad marksmen. Persian mortars, appropriately enough using marble chipped from tombstones as shot, were more effective. Cavalry from both sides sallied forth from time to time but accomplished little for the effort.

Afghan patrols flushing unsuspecting Persian pickets brought back the severed heads of their victims as grisly battle trophies. Pottinger, of course, thought this barbaric. War in Central Asia was often undisciplined slaughter and an excuse for gratuitous cruelty. Pottinger remembered with revulsion that on the day after Christmas Shah Kamran had sent off all Persian prisoners to Turkoman slavers, while Mohammed Shah retaliated by having his Afghan captives ripped open and forced to bury their heads in their own entrails before dying of shock or suffocation. The Persians could probably have taken Herat easily had their attacks been concentrated and sustained rather than sporadic. As Pottinger commented: "I could not understand what kept the Persians back. They had an open breach and no obstacle which would have checked British troops for a moment."[1]

Pottinger, who was everywhere at once, propping up defenses, advising on tactics and exhorting the soldiery to greater effort, also involved himself in trying to negotiate a peace. Shah Kamran accepted his offer to serve as an intermediary with the Persians, but the old man's state of health had not permitted him to do more than sputter incoherent ravings when he tried to give him instructions. Kamran's message for the Persians, as best Pottinger could understand it, was ominous from a British point of view: "raise the siege, retire and give me the troops and guns I want; and I will give you, on my success, Herat." In effect, Herat's ruler wanted to convey to the Persians the suggestion that they ally themselves with him against the Barakzai rule of Dost Mohammed. For all his senility, Shah Kamran shrewdly reasoned that Herat was a reasonable price to pay for the greater Afghan throne.

Pottinger also received instructions from Yar Mohammed and his ministers as they received him while soaking themselves in the *hammam,* or communal bath. What the vizier had to say was not much clearer than the befogged bathhouse where they talked. Hedging his bets, Yar Mohammed urged Pottinger to assure the Persians of his "affection." Like Shah Kamran, he believed that the threat from Persia and the Russians was, after all, no worse to contemplate than the threat posed by Dost Mohammed and the Barakzai clique in Kabul. Pottinger could find little to rejoice about from a British perspective; the Herat rulers seemed more interested in making a deal with the Persians against Dost Mohammed than in negotiating a peace.

On reaching the Persian lines, Russian General Samson, commanding the Persian siege, received Pottinger hospitably, although he was under no illusion about British intentions to spoil his game. It was ironic that an English officer and a Russian officer sipped tea together while their respective clients were locked in war. The Game did not prevent its players from acting in a civilized way toward each other despite their nations' rivalry.

Pottinger sought out his fellow countryman Colonel Charles Stoddart, whom he knew had been sent to Mohammed Shah's camp by British Minister M'Neill in Tehran as liaison officer with instructions to dissuade the Persians from their course of action—and to keep an eye on the Russians who were behind it. Stoddart was as delighted as he was totally surprised to discover that Pottinger was the peace emissary sent by Shah Kamran to the Persian camp. Pottinger, no less pleased, recorded in his journal: "No one who has not experienced it can understand the pleasure which countrymen enjoy when they thus meet—particularly when of the same profession and pursuing the same object."[2]

The two Englishmen's meeting with the Persian shah was most unsatisfactory. Working himself into a frenzy of vehemence, Mohammed Shah made it clear that he would settle for nothing less than total surrender; negotiations were over before they began. When Pottinger returned to report the Persians' rigid position to Shah Kamran, the sick and crotchety old ruler erupted in "a gasconading speech" of abuse. Obviously, no progress toward peace had been made.

Mohammed Shah's vizier approved a new initiative suggested by the Russian commander, Samson: if Herat would contribute troops to the Persian Army, Mohammed Shah would not interfere with Shah Kamran and Yar Mohammed's administration of the province. Mohammed Shah would thus become a benign suzerain of Herat to the benefit of both. The real objective, explained the Persian emissary, was to have both sides united under "the Defender of the Faith" to conquer India and Turkestan. While, in fact, the Afghans recoiled at the thought of a Persian garrison in Herat, any possibility that there could be an alliance between the Russian-dominated Persians and Herat filled the British with alarm.

Enter Sir John M'Neill, British minister to the Persian court, as would-be peacemaker. With his deputy, Major D'Arcy Todd, and a baggage train of six hundred camels he arrived in the Persian camp from Tehran to reason with Mohammed Shah. The minister brought a letter of greeting from Queen Victoria, who had just mounted the British throne upon the death of King William IV. Although Mohammed Shah was not pleased with British intervention, he agreed to another round of mediation in Herat to be conducted with the Afghans by Todd.

In fact, M'Neill himself soon visited the city as well to talk at length with Pottinger and Yar Mohammed. The spectacle of three English officers, M'Neill, Todd and Pottinger, conducting shuttle diplomacy between the two warring camps was upsetting to the Russians and brought the czar's minister, Count Simonich, rushing from Tehran to Mohammed Shah's camp to protect their interests. The Russians now played their hand, distributing liberal bribes to keep the Persians from listening to British peace efforts. As a result, the siege of Herat was intensified and Persian-Russian intrigues in Kandahar were renewed.

With Simonich at the Persian shah's campaign headquarters near Herat, M'Neill's status rapidly deteriorated. The British envoy was harassed and humiliated by the Persians at every turn. And by late May 1838, Herat's morale had been dangerously eroded by the prospect of Persian victory. The assembled Afghan chiefs in Herat were so discouraged that they considered offering themselves as vassals to the Persians rather than resist what they now considered inevitable defeat.

For all he had done to help the people of Herat defend their city, Pottinger's finest hour was now. Despite his own feelings of despair, he exhorted the vizier to have faith that the British would somehow prevent the Persians from taking Herat. Despite an appalling deterioration of conditions in the city—food shortages, plummeting morale and general disillusionment—Pottinger kept the town's defense alive and prevented the disheartened Yar Mohammed from throwing himself into Russian arms.

M'Neill's position in Mohammed Shah's court had by now become intolerable. On June 7, the British broke relations with the Persians and M'Neill left the shah's camp, intending to exit Persia by way of the Turkish border. From Meshed, M'Neill sent Todd ahead with an urgent dispatch for Palmerston, acquainting the British foreign secretary with what he considered the mortal threat facing India should Herat fall to the Persians. "If we do not seize the present opportunity to check the advance of Persia and to close the door against her on the side of Afghanistan, we must prepare at no distant time to encounter both Persia and Russia in that country," he warned. Making matters worse, Count Simonich had announced Russia's intention to attack Khiva and Bokhara.

M'Neill painted an alarming picture. If Russia gets a "military footing in Khiva before we shall have rescued and secured Herat," he wrote, "we must retire on the line of the Indus, and send out ten or fifteen thousand more European troops to India."[3] M'Neill now called upon Lieutenant Colonel Stoddart to lead a mission to Nasrullah, emir of Bokhara, in response to growing British apprehension that Russia planned to invade Khiva. Since slavery provided a convenient pretext for the czar to push his frontier southward from Orenburg into the Transcaspian steppes, Stoddart's orders were to convince the emir that he should release Russian slaves so as to deprive the Russians of an excuse to invade his lands. Stoddart was empowered to promise the emir that he could rely on the British to come to his rescue if attacked by a foreign power, i.e., Russia, and assure him that British activity in Afghanistan was not a threat to him.

Stoddart arrived in Bokhara on December 17, 1838. He was a brave soldier but a poor diplomat, and ran roughshod over the sensibilities of the emir. At best, the cruel and perverted Nasrullah was difficult to deal with, as Moorcroft and Burnes had earlier discovered, but Stoddart's brusque refusal to show deference fatally soured his reception at court.

Stoddart ineptly maneuvered himself into the bad graces of the new vizier as well and was seized and thrown into a dungeon, forced to endure near starvation and noxious vermin for two months until he agreed to embrace Islam. But his ordeal was not over. His precarious position, now more hostage than envoy, would cause the British to focus even more intently on that inhospitable land beyond the Hindu Kush and Russian intentions toward it.

Meanwhile, M'Neill before he left made Pottinger official British representative in Herat. With M'Neill's mission at an end, someone with official status had to cope with the still-ongoing war between Persia and Herat, thus Pottinger, "private" explorer and self-appointed helpmeet to Herat, suddenly metamorphosed into British resident.

A week after M'Neill's departure on June 14, the Persians, with Russian prodding, began a furious new offensive. Three times the Persians breached the town walls only to be thrown back. The prospects of survival seemed bleak in Herat, while in Calcutta and London the thought of losing another round with the Russians was alarming. Pottinger was a one-man band, propping up Yar Mohammed's resolve and marshaling Herat's defenders to resist the worst attack yet on their ramparts. The Afghans were despondent; when the Persians launched what was intended to be their definitive assault on June 24, there was little spirit left with which to meet it. The fate of Herat was teetering on the brink of disaster.

Once again Pottinger thrust himself into the fray. The key to the defense lay in Yar Mohammed, but the vizier seemed to have given up. Only with Pottinger's spirited prodding did he rouse himself from despair and rally his forces to the town's defense. At one point, Pottinger had to haul Yar Mohammed by the scruff of his neck back to the field of battle. Then, with Pottinger's oaths ringing in his ears, the vizier suddenly seemed possessed of new spirit. He literally ran up and down the line beating his troops with a cudgel, forcing them to attack as he loudly pleaded with Allah to help. In a final upwelling of zeal, the Afghan defenders repelled the Persians, inflicting on them heavy casualties and forcing them to flee. Their commander, Borowski, was killed in action and Samson, who led the batallion of Russian deserters, was wounded. The tide was turning in favor of the British.

Suddenly a new development gave the British a distinct edge over the Russians in Herat. Governor General Auckland, it seemed, had ordered the Bombay government to send a modest force into the Persian Gulf as a precaution in the event that M'Neill's efforts to negotiate a peace failed. However tardy Auckland's actions had been, the naval ships *Semiramis* and *Hugh Lindsay,* carrying a battalion of Royal Marines and units of the 15th, 23rd and 24th Regiments, sailed into the port at Kharack Island just off the Persian mainland near Bushire in the nick of time. Although the British gesture was a small and essentially defensive one, it had a strong impact on the Persians. By the time news of the British action reached Mohammed Shah, the Persians perceived it as a major expedition launched against them.

Under instructions, M'Neill, who had not gotten far in his withdrawal from the country, ordered Stoddart to deliver a British ultimatum to the shah: further advance against Herat or elsewhere into Afghanistan would be considered an act of hostility against England, and if the siege was not lifted, Persia would be held accountable. When the shah asked, "If I don't leave Herat there will be war, is that not it?" Stoddart replied, "It *is* war!"

The British also complained to Russian Count Nesselrode in St. Petersburg of Simonich's action in having exhorted Mohammed Shah to attack Herat, and of Vitkevich's prodding of Dost Mohammed in Kabul to take Peshawar, as well as his intrigues with the Kandahar chiefs calculated to win them over to the Persian side. Nesselrode, as seen, disowned Vitkevich; as for Simonich, the Russian chancellor explained unconvincingly that on his own initiative the Russian envoy had simply tried to help a state friendly to Russia—certainly his actions had not been approved by St. Petersburg.

Suddenly, from the Herat citadel, the town defenders could see the Persians folding their tents and retiring their artillery. Yar Mohammed, on the verge of surrendering, took heart, now realizing that Herat had survived. While the Persian shah's decision to lift the siege of Herat could mainly be attributed to British military and diplomatic pressure, the town had Eldred Pottinger to thank for having kept the resistance alive and Yar Mohammed from capitulating. Pottinger's achievement at Herat contrasted starkly with Burnes's lack of success in Kabul, yet Burnes had gained a knighthood while Pottinger was given a much more modest Order of the Bath.

Russian efforts in prodding the Persians to attack Herat had been in vain, but still ominous in British eyes was the Russian intention to invade Khiva and Bokhara, which would push their zone of control closer to the borders of northern Afghanistan. Even more pressing was the problem of Afghanistan.

PART II

All the Queen's Horses and All the Queen's Men

Chapter 14

TO WAR

IN MAY 1838 GOVERNOR GENERAL AUCKLAND MADE A FATEFUL DECISION to remove Dost Mohammed from power by force and replace him with Shah Shuja. The immediate reason had been the Persian siege of Herat, a dramatic demonstration that the shah, with encouragement and assistance from the Russians, had designs on Afghanistan. The Persian King of Kings himself was in the field leading an army against Herat; his commander was a Russian officer and the Russian minister to Persia was in busy attendance at the Persian campaign headquarters. Before British gunboats landed in the Persian Gulf to change the power equation and intimidate the shah into abandoning his campaign, the British might well have assumed that Herat was doomed; after that Kandahar, whose khans were already intriguing with both the Persians and the Russians, would fall, and perhaps Ghazni as well. Then Kabul itself would be at Persia's mercy. That, at least, was what the shah was boasting—and behind the shah, accounting for his brazen confidence, was the czar of Russia. The shah's ultimate strategy was to leave Dost Mohammed no choice but to join him, more as vassal than as ally, in taking Peshawar.

Of course, there was an underlying Russophobia that had permeated official thinking in both Calcutta and London and provided distorted lenses through which the Herat crisis was seen. The Russians had moved inexorably through the Caucasus since the century began and now enjoyed a strong position in Persia. And recently the British had learned that the czar planned a Transcaspian military campaign southward from Orenburg, Russia's advance garrison at the edge of Central Asia, to conquer the khanate of Khiva and perhaps Bokhara as well, pushing Russian influence southward from the Aral Sea toward Afghanistan.

There were other causes for concern having nothing directly to do with Persia and Russia but infecting official thinking with a virus of apprehension. Burma and Nepal, within the Company's sphere of influence, were being troublesome. Even more worrisome was India itself, where the Company was aware that the rise of Dost Mohammed revived hopes among Indian Moslems that a Moslem savior from Afghanistan might sweep across the Punjab and rescue them from the infidel British raj. The vast Hindu majority, by contrast, feared such a possibility. Whatever their differences and however fanciful their reasoning, an inchoate conviction was taking hold in both communities that the British raj was coming to an end. From the Company's point of view, it would not do to lose face by reverses in Afghanistan. All of this was only part of a larger body of native dissatisfaction that manifested itself in many ways, particularly in the powerful medium of unfathomable rumor—and would erupt disastrously in the Great Indian Rebellion of 1857. But at the moment Calcutta's concern for the internal tranquillity of the subcontinent was at least one factor contributing to the decision to take Draconian measures in Afghanistan.

The attitudes and prejudices of Auckland and his close advisers must also be blamed for the specific course of action adopted by the Company. Beginning with the premise that Sikh friendship must be maintained at all cost, Auckland saw himself faced with three alternatives. The first was to confine the government to defensive measures needed to protect the Indus Valley and leave Afghanistan to its fate. This, Auckland feared, would give the Russians and Persians a free hand to "intrigue on our frontiers." Second, the British could support Dost Mohammed, but this would alienate Ranjit Singh. The third option, the one he chose, was to encourage and help Ranjit Singh invade Afghanistan and restore Shah Shuja to the throne. It would become evident that Auckland's decision was more the product of his chief secretary William Macnaghten's thinking than his own. The removal of the Afghan monarch was hardly an appropriate response to a Persian attack on Herat, an autonomous principality acknowledging no allegiance to Kabul and headed by a superannuated prince of the rival Saddozai clan. Moreover, as the British magazine *Spectator* pointed out, Shah Kamran, the ruler of Herat, had, in fact, provoked the Persians by invading their province of Seistan south of Herat and carrying off twelve thousand of its inhabitants and selling them as slaves. But the decision to replace Dost Mohammed with Shah Shuja, whose ability to sustain himself in power without British troops was doubtful, was the most glaring mistake of all. Dost Mohammed's demand for Peshawar, stolen from him by Ranjit Singh, and his flirtation with the Russians after Auckland rejected his friendly overtures may have been annoying to the British, but they did not constitute provocation enough to justify what the British now planned to do in Afghanistan.

Burnes had been dismayed to learn of the proposed expedition to Afghanistan when he reached the hill station, Simla, on his way back from Kabul. The decision had been made without waiting for him to report in person and contrary to his advice by dispatch. In fact, Macnaghten's aides intercepted him before he reported to Governor General Auckland in Simla and "prayed him to say nothing to unsettle his Lordship; that they had all the trouble in the world to get him into the business, and that even now he would be glad of any pretext to retire from it."[1]

Burnes was not able to convince Macnaghten of his views, and without his agreement he had no hope of changing Auckland's opinions. In a letter to Macnaghten, Burnes had reiterated his old argument, asserting: "It should be our object to make Cabool in itself as strong as we can make it, and not weaken it by divided power."[2] A strong Dost Mohammed, Burnes still argued, could keep the country together and resist Russian or Persian encroachment, but a country split into feudal principalities and tribes would invite Russian intrigue aimed at picking them off piecemeal with no great difficulty.

Burnes's views were rejected by Macnaghten and the others of the "drawing room cabinet" surrounding the governor general. However illogical, Auckland's decision became the order of the day, and Macnaghten was on his way to Lahore by the end of May 1838 to enlist Ranjit Singh's collaboration in this bold plan of action. As chief architect of the policy, Macnaghten forged ahead, convinced he was right, even though the cautious Auckland was beginning to be haunted by nagging doubts.

Burnes, with Mohan Lal in attendance, was ordered to join Macnaghten for the talks with Ranjit Singh. Auckland had been annoyed with Burnes for his outspoken criticism of him, but the governor general realized that the young envoy, who had "done his best with zeal and ability" in Kabul and had a good grasp of the problems, would be valuable to Macnaghten.

Auckland, as usual, felt strongly about the need to obtain Ranjit Singh's full cooperation rather than risk doing something that could upset relations with the Punjab, India's first line of defense. Would Ranjit Singh look with equanimity at the British leapfrogging over him to establish a position in Afghanistan? Auckland ruffled Macnaghten's ego when he sent him a note of warning admonishing him to be careful. The governor general needn't have worried, however; the now sick and aging Sikh maharajah, "teetering on the brink of the grave," responded positively, particularly welcoming Macnaghten's proposal that the British formally affiliate themselves with his four-year-old alliance with Shah Shuja against Dost Mohammed. "This would be adding sugar to milk," said Ranjit, who shrewdly saw advantage in such an arrangement.

Macnaghten offered Ranjit Singh two alternative courses of action: restore Shah Shuja by a Sikh Army without British help, or act together with the British. Macnaghten made it clear that Auckland preferred that the Sikhs act independently, but the maharajah predictably elected the second alternative to keep the British fully involved. The envoy sketched out a plan of invasion in which a Sikh Army would force the Khyber Pass while Shah Shuja would lead his forces, raised with British help, through the Bolan Pass by way of Kandahar—the long way around. But it soon became evident that Ranjit Singh had little faith in the success of such a campaign without the main burden of combat being borne by the British. Moreover, he could see clearly that it made no sense to put his army at risk in a venture that could easily fail. In the end, the Sikh leader would for the most part back out of his military participation in the proposed invasion, and spare his Khalsa warriors the terrors of a major attack through the Khyber with its fierce Afghan defenders.

As usual, Ranjit Singh put on a good show for his visitors. Captain W. G. Osborne, military secretary to Lord Auckland, offered the liveliest account of the festivities.[3] Ranjit Singh's army, twelve thousand infantry and two thousand cavalry, was a source of pride to him and he showed it off in one grand review. He admitted that not all was perfect in his force; some regiments had been disbanded because of mutinous acts. One of the problems was the irregular payment of wages; even the European mercenary officers were kept in arrears of their pay so that they would not desert. Another problem was corrosive intrigue as Ranjit Singh seemed to be nearing the end of his life. On parade, however, the infantry, under the command of the Italian General Ventura, turned out smartly. Dressed in white with black crossbelts and red or yellow turbans, the soldiers were a colorful sight as their straight line stretched nearly two miles into the horizon.

The Sikh artillery was also impressive. Having watched how decisive British cannons were in battle, Ranjit Singh was determined to have an artillery second to none. The battery of fifty-three horse-drawn nine-pounders made from brass in Ranjit Singh's own foundry was trained and led by the American Alexander Gardner. Osborne judged the Sikh artillery to be the most powerful part of the Sikh Army and inevitably it gave a good account of itself. In an exhibition of marksmanship the gunners regularly shredded the target curtains at more than two hundred yards. "If only Dost Mohammed could see this," boasted Ranjit Singh as he put on the exhibition for his visitors.

It was in the midst of Macnaghten's mission, on June 14, that news arrived from Persia that British minister M'Neill had broken relations with Persia and departed the shah's camp near Herat. Wildly exaggerated reports had also reached the Sikhs, telling of a Russian Army marching to the assistance of the Persians besieging Herat. Ranjit Singh bombarded Macnaghten with questions about this development: Can the English beat the Russians? How many troops could the Russians put across the Indus River? What would the British do if the Russians tried to invade India?

Ranjit Singh lightheartedly belittled the Russian threat. "It would be great fun" to take on the Russians, he said, particularly if there was plunder to be had. But the maharajah's true concern about developments in Herat was more seriously reflected in his decision to join with the British and Shah Shuja in a revised treaty calling for the removal of Dost Mohammed. The new trilateral pact negotiated by Macnaghten specified that Shah Shuja would give up Afghan claims to all territory currently held by Ranjit Singh—Peshawar and Kashmir being the most important provinces in question. He would also relinquish the Afghan claim of suzerainty over the emirs of Sind. While Ranjit Singh and Shah Shuja would be addressed as equals, the latter would yearly send symbolic tribute to Lahore in the form of prize horses and an assortment of delectable fruit. Shah Shuja agreed not to enter into negotiations with any foreign state without the consent of the British and Sikh governments, nor would he disturb the Persian frontier. He would be content to leave Herat a Saddozai preserve titularly under the aging Shah Kamran, although, in fact, ruled by his vizier, Yar Mohammed. The three parties agreed that the enemies of one would be the enemies of each.

On his way back, Macnaghten stopped off in Ludhiana to obtain Shah Shuja's agreement to the arrangements made with Ranjit Singh. The prospect of regaining power obviously excited the old man; at last the

British were willing to help him gratify his long-held ambition. After a little pro forma grumbling over details, Shah Shuja affixed his seal to the new treaty.

Auckland had sent Macnaghten to Lahore on his own authority. London had been less than helpful in sending him guidance, reticent to take an initiative in this unpredictable situation, but in a message on August 2, both the Foreign Office and the Board of Control for India approved after the fact all that Auckland had done. Replying to M'Neill's counter-recommendation that the British instead invade Persia from the Gulf and march on Tehran, Palmerston disagreed. He was in favor of the "great operation" planned against Afghanistan. Ranjit Singh's forces would "drive the Persians out of Afghanistan and reorganize that country under one chief." Afghanistan, he was convinced, would make a better buffer than Persia. "We should have the same kind of geographical pull upon such a state that Russia has upon Persia,"[4] he explained. The score would be evened with Russia. If the British invaded Persia it would only provoke the shah to turn even closer to the czar and it could lead to British-Russian conflict in which the Russians, with their shorter supply lines, could very well win.

Initially, it had not been anticipated that British Indian Army forces would be used in the invasion of Afghanistan; Ranjit Singh's forces supplemented by levies raised by Shah Shuja with British financing would suffice. But as the summer of 1838 wore on, it became apparent that Indian Army forces were needed if the venture were to succeed. Commander in Chief Sir Henry Fane had grave qualms about invading Afghanistan and argued against it, but if his views were to be ignored and this risky operation undertaken anyway, it should at least be done properly, and this meant that the Indian Army would have to bear the brunt of the action. At this point it was hoped that Sikh Khalsa forces could simultaneously invade in force through the Khyber. Because of Ranjit Singh's sensitivity about Company forces crossing his territory (he feared an adverse reaction from the Khalsa), the Bengal Army and Shah Shuja's levies, marching from the Punjab to Sind on the first leg of its march, would have to swing far south, bypassing the maharajah's domain to cross the Indus near Shikarpur. At the same time elements of the Bombay Army would arrive in the Sind seaport of Karachi by sea and march northward to join them at Shikarpur before proceeding onward. This meant trespassing on Sind and Baluchi territory before crossing the difficult Bolan Pass to reach Kandahar in Afghanistan. While this much longer route was arduous, it had two advantages: it would avoid the Khyber Pass, infamous for its wild, indomitable defenders, and it would provide an opportunity to cow the troublesome

Sindis, who might otherwise be a threat to Indus River navigation and the southern supply line to Afghanistan. As Burnes put it: "The Scinde orange is to be squeezed."[5]

Auckland announced his intentions toward Afghanistan in a declaration on October 1, 1838, referred to as the Simla Manifesto. This landmark announcement came as a shock to the British public, causing dismay and raising a storm of protest from the press. On a matter as important as war it was strange that the Whig government in England did not exercise a more energetic direction of policy rather than allow Calcutta to blunder on, particularly since there was no clear consensus of public opinion in England on this issue.

Auckland's declaration was an unconvincing rationale for his Afghan policy—a potpourri of distortions and dubious reasoning. It blamed Dost Mohammed for having made an "unprovoked" attack on Ranjit Singh, but made no mention of the fact that the Sikh maharajah had earlier seized Peshawar from him. It found fault with Dost Mohammed's desire to retake Peshawar as an "unreasonable pretension." The Persian siege of Herat, which by the time the manifesto was issued was within days of being lifted, was already flagging. For diplomatic reasons, mention of Russia was studiously avoided even though fear of that country's Central Asian ambitions was underlying the proposed action. Auckland feebly reasoned that Mohammed Shah's attack on Herat provided justification for the British to attack Afghanistan. Twisting logic further, the incredible document asserted that the integrity of Herat "should be respected"[6]— somehow it was wrong for Persia to seek to gratify its irredentist claims at Afghan expense, but it was not wrong for the British to encourage fragmentation of Afghanistan.

Auckland had been reluctant to take the big step of invading Afghanistan, but, according to Masson, was talked into the fateful decision by "certain females, aides-de-camp and secretaries." This referred to the governor general's strong-willed sisters, Emily and Fanny Eden; William Macnaghten, the drafter of the Simla Manifesto; and his acolytes, Henry Torens and John Colvin. But however influential this group may have been, it was Auckland's decision and its success or failure would in the first instance be his responsibility.

By September 9, when the Persians finally abandoned their siege of Herat and the crisis had passed, it would seem to have been a time to reconsider the invasion of Afghanistan since the original casus belli had disappeared. Burnes still argued that Dost Mohammed would abandon his flirtation with the Russians and Persians if the British could find some formula for Peshawar acceptable to him, and that he would make an infinitely more capable ally than Shah Shuja. The Secret Committee of the East India Company's Court of Directors on October 24 did in fact give Auckland authorization to make one more cautious overture to Dost Mohammed.

Auckland, however, chose not to make a final effort and issued another announcement declaring his intention to proceed with his plans despite the lifting of the Herat siege by the Persians. He was by this time committed to the policy of invasion and had British cabinet approval. At his summer retreat in the Simla hills he was under the exclusive influence of his trio of closest advisers, all strong advocates of the plan. Such proponents of the forward policy argued that while Herat had been saved from Persian clutches by British pressure on the shah, the problem of a Russian-dominated Persia still existed; only by controlling Afghanistan could the Russian menace be contained. Moreover, the Persians still held a few minor forts within Afghan-claimed territory, and Russian agents continued to intrigue with the khans of Kandahar and would probably do the same at Dost Mohammed's court in Kabul. "Russian agents are notoriously active in Afghanistan,"[7] Auckland wrote the governor of Madras, explaining his actions.

Much of the press in England howled its protests while several old India hands bitterly complained about Auckland's decision. The governor general's predecessor, Lord Bentinck, thought it was "an act of folly"; the Marquis Wellesley called the "wild expedition" an "act of infatuation"; and the venerated Duke of Wellington considered the decision a prelude to "a perennial march into the country."[8] Metcalfe, always conservative when it came to adventures beyond the Indus, feared that an expedition to Kabul would "bring Russians down on ourselves." But old Mountstuart Elphinstone, who in 1809 had led the first British mission to the Afghan leader, Shah Shuja, just before the latter lost his throne, predicted more accurately his fate if restored to power: "If you send 27,000 men up the Bolan Pass to Candahar (as we hear is intended) and can feed them, I have no doubt you will take Candahar and Caubul; but for maintaining him in a poor, strong and remote country among a turbulent people like the Afghans, I own it seems to me to be hopeless."[9]

Auckland had committed four unpardonable mistakes that were to cost the British dearly. He had been obdurate in dealing with Dost Mohammed, who genuinely wanted some kind of accommodation with the British; instead Auckland had based British policy on the ailing Sikh leader, Ranjit Singh, whose alliance with the British—even his kingdom itself—could obviously not long survive his imminent death; he had overestimated Shah Shuja's capacity to control the Afghans; and he had overridden his commander in chief's advice not to commit British troops to invading Afghanistan. It was no less tragic that Palmerston and the Whig government did not see the fallacy of Auckland's decision and step in to prevent it.

Undeniably, the Russians had encouraged the Persian attack on Herat and, despite protestations to the contrary, Vitkevich had been a Russian agent bent on manipulating Dost Mohammed and the khans of Kalat. But from a Russian point of view, it was the British who were the initial aggressors: Pottinger had interfered at Herat and a squadron of British warships had landed on Persian territory in the Gulf, while Burnes, fresh from his provocative adventure in Bokhara, had tried to convince Dost Mohammed to ally himself with the British against the Russians and had sent Leech to Kandahar to bring the chiefs there into camp as well. Considering all this, it was unconvincing for the British to complain of "intolerable provocation."

Despite his opposition, Burnes now reconciled himself to going along with the governor general's policy—in fact, he seemed to leap eagerly on the bandwagon. It is the fate of public servants almost everywhere to implement policies with which they may not agree. If this were not so, a civil service would quickly degenerate into an undisciplined shambles. But could Burnes have done more than he did to prevent the disastrous course set by Auckland and Macnaghten? Did he betray his convictions in the interest of career?

On September 10, 1838, Burnes wrote a revealing letter from Simla, where he was consulting with the governor general. Having "implored the government" to accept his recommendations without success, he claimed to have been faced with Auckland's insistence that he recommend an alternative position. He replied equivocably to the governor general: "Self-defense is the first law of nature. If you cannot bring round Dost Mohammed, whom you have infamously used, you must set up Shah Shuja as a puppet and establish a supremacy in Afghanistan, or you will lose India."[10]

As for the Persians' retreat from Herat, which removed the principal justification for Auckland's decision to invade Afghanistan, Burnes in a letter to Hobhouse in December dutifully rationalized that the Persian withdrawal did not remove the danger to Herat. Russian Captain Vitkevich had lavishly bribed the Kandahar chiefs, he reminded Hobhouse, and encouraged them to join with the Persians. Burnes argued that the Persians and Russians would still prevail in western Afghanistan if the British did not act quickly. In sum, Burnes justified his new line on what he considered to be pragmatic reasoning: Since London and Calcutta refused to do it his way, they must at least do it their way rather than do nothing at all.

Personal motivations were, in fact, important in Burnes's actions: If Auckland and Macnaghten were determined to launch an invasion of Afghanistan, he did not want to be left out of the show. To have continued as a critic and naysayer would have blighted his promising career and relegated him to obscurity. Having just received a double promotion to lieutenant colonel and been honored by a knighthood, Burnes hoped to be made principal political officer for the expedition. Having reversed field, he now spoke optimistically, almost recklessly, about Shah Shuja's chances for success: "The British Government have only to send him to Peshawar with an [British] agent, and two of his own regiments as an honorary escort and an avowal to the Afghans that we have taken up his cause, to ensure his being fixed forever on the throne."[11] The ambitious Burnes could now imagine himself by Shah Shuja's side, almost single-handedly taking over and ruling the kingdom. This would be another opportunity to gain glory.

Burnes's hope of becoming the chief political officer was soon dashed. Macnaghten was given that plum and gazetted with the pretentious title "Envoy and Minister on the part of the Government of India at the Court of Shah Shuja-ul-Mulk."* Angered and disappointed, Burnes threatened to resign from the service and go home to England because he felt slighted, but he had not been willing to resign over a nobler matter of policy and principle. This fact casts a long shadow over any pretense that duty and loyalty to service had made him fall in with Auckland's mistaken policy. On calmer reflection, Burnes consoled himself with the thought that his "friend," Dost Mohammed, was fortunately to be "ousted by another hand" than his, and succumbed to Auckland's blandishment that he remain. Subordinate to Macnaghten, Burnes would serve as "Envoy to the Chief of Kalat or other states." In practice this meant that Burnes would pave the way for the invading British Army, enlisting the cooperation of the Sind emirs and Baluchi khans, through whose territories the army must march, particularly the influential khan of Kalat, whose cooperation would be critical as the army approached the dangerous Bolan Pass.

*A correspondent of a London newspaper had an explanation as to why Lord Auckland, against his better judgment, had agreed to the plan to invade Afghanistan. Knowing that Macnaghten would want the post of political envoy accompanying the expedition, the "real rulers of India," Auckland's sisters, Emily and Fanny, who found Macnaghten socially tiresome, wished his place to be taken by Torens, whose fashionable wife was their close friend, thus convinced Auckland to proceed with the invasion. (George Buist, *Outline of the Operation of the British Troops in Scinde and Afghanistan*, Bombay: Bombay Times 1853, p. 71.) While this explanation is most unlikely, these kinds of stories were typical of the frivolous high society in Calcutta that clustered about the governor general.

Burnes hoped that he would replace Macnaghten soon after they reached Kabul on the assumption that the latter would be returning to India. In the meantime, he was swept along on the wave of exhilaration felt by the expeditionary force, grandly dubbed "the Army of the Indus," as it prepared for the first foreign campaign waged by Indian Army troops since the Burma War a dozen years before. It would also be the first war of empire since the young Queen Victoria mounted the throne.

To Alexander Burnes, the thrill of the hunt made up for his basic disagreement with its rationale: his anticipation of new laurels was stronger than his concern for the consequences. This, in fact, was the watershed of Burnes's career. Vainglory and death lay ahead.

Chapter 15

MARCH TO KABUL

T HE FIRST DECADE OF THE NINETEENTH CENTURY WAS A GOLDEN AGE
of exploration and distant reconnaissance for the Company; fearless young
officers blazed new trails into the unknown and pitted their wits against
native potentates from another time and culture. John Malcolm's early
mission to Persia, Charles Metcalfe's mission to Ranjit Singh binding the
Punjab to the Company by treaty, and Mountstuart Elphinstone's probe
into Afghanistan, among other signal achievements, had been historic
milestones in the progress of empire and had bred a generation of giants
destined to govern India. This was a time when Russia inexorably pushed
southward through the Caucasus toward Persia, and the British reacted
with alarm: India seemed to be in jeopardy. That Russia gained preeminence in Persia, humbling the shah under the terms of the Treaty of
Turkmanchai in 1828, bore testimony to an inescapable law of geopolitics:
military power close at hand is more persuasive than diplomatic finesse.
This, however, did not detract from the personal valor and skill of these
early Company pioneers.

Alexander Burnes, his Indian aide, Mohan Lal, Eldred Pottinger, Charles Masson, Charles Stoddart, Arthur Conolly and others who braved Central Asia in the third decade of the century served in the tradition of their illustrious predecessors two decades before. Imperial Russia had also fielded brave agents in this epoch, such as Vitkevich, to probe the steppes and mountains of Central Asia beyond the immediate reach of the czar's armies. So long as the outriders of empire on both sides operated behind a curtain of diplomatic propriety, or even resorted to more Machiavellian wiles, neither the British nor the Russians were committed, and if either overstepped the bounds, the matter could be resolved in London or St. Petersburg; Central Asia was a playing field, but it was essentially a European contest. What then occurred, however, introduced a more dangerous dimension to the Game: the British resorted to naked force and invaded Afghanistan. This stretched the rules of the Game as well as good judgment and incurred enormous penalties for the transgression.

Enter now the warriors, unleashed to impose the Company's will, to succeed where intrepid political agents had failed. Inept leadership carrying out misbegotten policy in the fourth decade would doom the enterprise, but first there would be days of glory and false hope as the warriors gallantly dashed onto the field with banners flying.

At a time when marching off to war was a festive occasion, an opportunity for an expeditionary army to flaunt its plumage, ninety-five hundred men of the Bengal Army strutted gloriously on the parade ground of Ferozepore. This was the Company's forward-most garrison in the Punjab, ninety miles west of Ludhiana on the Sutlej River, bordering Ranjit Singh's realm. Much like a peacock inviting attention to himself, this was the Company's way of announcing its imminent invasion of Afghanistan. (Appropriately enough, in India the peacock is regarded as the steed of Kumara, Hindu god of war.) On this memorable twenty-eighth day of November 1838, throngs of spectators could thrill to the parading redcoats marching up and down again. Gracing the occasion was the host, Ranjit Singh, escorted by his Sikh cavalry charging and wheeling for the benefit of his honored guest, Lord Auckland. With them in spirit were fifty-six hundred men of the Bombay Army, who would sail from Bombay to the mouth of the Indus and march northward to link up with the Bengal Army at Shikarpur, the ancient caravan crossroads of northern Sind, before striking out together for Afghanistan by way of the Bolan Pass in Baluchistan.

The British governor general was first greeted by the maharajah's foreign minister, who favored him with such florid phrases as "The luster of one sun [Ranjit Singh] has long shone with splendor over our horizon; but when two suns come together, the refulgence will be overpowering." A lesser sun shone more dimly in nearby Ludhiana, the British edge of the Punjab where Shah Shuja waited restlessly for his call to glory, a summons to lead his levies to Kabul. Uninvited to the celebration, he could console himself that soon he would be the centerpiece of the invasion. To give the would-be king at least a semblance of autonomy and to pander to his pride, the British had recruited and trained an army of some six thousand men, which he could call his own even though it was encadred by officers seconded from the British Indian Army. Shah Shuja and his force were to accompany the Bengal Army in the van, to give the illusion that he was the central character in this drama, regally reclaiming his rightful throne.

Ranjit Singh's elaborate durbar, or royal audience, at Ferozepore, welcoming the British expeditionary force, was a ceremonial symbol of British-Sikh solidarity in Afghan matters.[1] But the wily maharajah, contrary to earlier hopes, was content to let the British do all the fighting. He had reneged on the agreement that a Sikh force would participate in the expedition. Moreover, he would not allow the British to cross his territory to take the short route to Kabul through the Khyber Pass; instead they must take the long way around by way of Kandahar and the mighty Afghan fortress at Ghazni before reaching Kabul.

The climax of the festivities at Ferozepore occurred on November 29, when the two leaders, Ranjit Singh and Lord Auckland, exchanged formal visits. Units of the Bengal Army were lined up to form an avenue of honor leading to Lord Auckland's tent. The Bengal infantrymen were wearing their heavy red tunics with white crossbelts and colorful shakoes while the horse artillery troopers were resplendent in brass dragoon helmets and white buckskin breeches stuffed into high jackboots. The Sikh chiefs, dressed in gold embroidery that flashed blindingly in the sun, pranced about on their chargers. Bands played uncertainly as the maharajah and his entourage mounted on elephants were met by Lord Auckland in his diplomatic uniform of somber navy blue. But suddenly confusion broke out as British and Sikh dignitaries in the festooned howdahs were jostled by skittish elephants excited by the noise and crowd. Ranjit Singh was rescued from the melee and hustled safely into the governor general's tent. But even there, officers eager to see the show crowded about until forcibly removed by two companies of British soldiers.

The maharajah graciously accepted the state gifts offered by Lord Auckland, seeming to appreciate most a portrait of Queen Victoria painted by the governor general's talented sister, Lady Emily Eden. In a spontaneous gesture honoring the British queen, Ranjit Singh ordered his artillery to fire a one-hundred-gun salute. Just as everything seemed to be going well, the feeble old ruler stumbled over a pile of shells and fell flat on his face

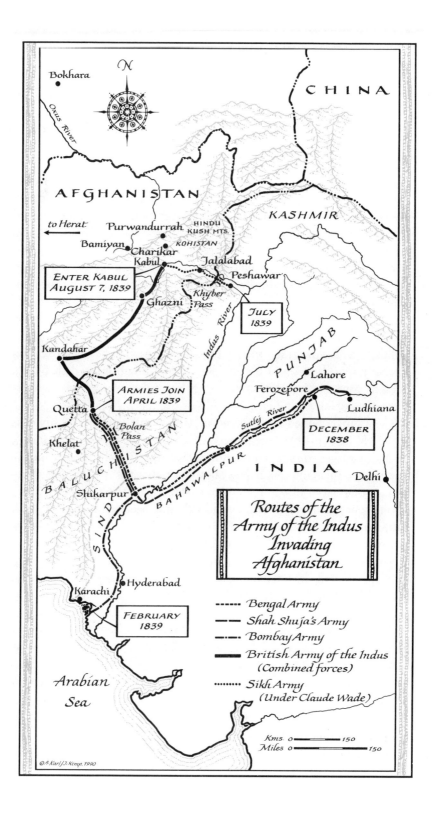

Bokhara

CHINA

N

Oxus River

AFGHANISTAN

KASHMIR

to Herat Purwandurrah HINDU KUSH MTS.
Bamiyan Charikar KOHISTAN
Kabul Jalalabad
  Peshawar
ENTER KABUL AUGUST 7, 1839
Ghazni Khyber Pass
JULY 1839

Indus River

Kandahar

PUNJAB

Lahore
Ferozepore
ARMIES JOIN APRIL 1839
Quetta *Sutlej River* Ludhiana
Khelat Bolan Pass **DECEMBER 1838**

BALUCHISTAN

Shikarpur BAHAWALPUR INDIA Delhi

SIND

Routes of the Army of the Indus Invading Afghanistan

Hyderabad
Karachi
FEBRUARY 1839

------- Bengal Army
— — Shah Shuja's Army
—·—· Bombay Army
━━━ British Army of the Indus (Combined forces)
·········· Sikh Army (Under Claude Wade)

Arabian Sea

© A. Karl / J. Kemp. 1990

Kms. 0 ——— 150
Miles 0 ——— 150

before the muzzles of the British guns. Auckland personally helped him up, but the incident was considered a bad omen by the Sikhs, and perhaps it was, since the decrepit Lion of the Punjab died not many months later.

On the second day of the ceremonies, Lord Auckland returned Ranjit Singh's visit. Lady Emily Eden recalled that the maharajah, looking "exactly like an old mouse with grey whiskers,"[2] sat curled up on his settee in a faded crimson gown, holding one foot in his hand so that his favorite courtier, the young Hera Singh, could fondle it. A Sikh band tried to play the British national anthem in honor of the occasion but somehow skipped every other note. Lady Eden thought the musical result, nonetheless, had its own charm.

The ceremony was enlivened by an unseemly exhibition of scantily clad dancing girls sprinkled with silver dust. That evening things became even more boisterous. Emily Eden and the other British ladies present were thoroughly shocked by the spectacle of wanton nautch dancing by a bevy of Sikh Amazons—Ranjit Singh's "bodyguard." "All the satraps in a row and these screaming girls," she wrote of the occasion in her memoir, "and the old tyrant drinking in the middle!" Ranjit Singh insisted that Lady Eden try some of his potent brew. "One drop," she complained, "actually burnt the outside of my lips. I could not possibly swallow it."[3]

Ranjit Singh gloried in the occasion. It was really *his* day. As frivolous as the old Lion may have appeared during the evening's entertainment, he had managed things more adroitly than the British. He had neatly maneuvered them into pulling his chestnuts out of the Afghan fire. Moreover, in the matter of pomp and circumstance, a specialty of the British, he outshone his ally. The British officers "came back rather discomfited," Lady Emily Eden noticed. Ranjit Singh had almost as many troops as the British and "they were quite as well disciplined—rather better dressed" as they carried out their intricate maneuvers. Writing frankly, Emily Eden recalled: "Nobody knows what to say about it, so they say nothing except that they are sure the Sikhs would run away in a real fight. It is a sad blow to our vanities."

Ailing and drunken profligate though he was, Lady Eden admired Ranjit Singh: "He has made himself a great king; he has conquered a great many powerful enemies; he is remarkably just in his government; he has disciplined a large army; he hardly ever takes a life . . . and he is excessively loved by his people."[4]

Lord Auckland and his party accompanied Ranjit Singh to Lahore, where more formalities and festivities took their toll on the ailing maharajah. He became quite ill on Christmas Eve, perhaps suffering a small stroke. Emily Eden thought he looked to be near death's edge. It was ironic that just as the British were about to invade Afghanistan, a dramatic affirmation of their having chosen Ranjit Singh over Dost Mohammed rather than trying to reconcile their differences, the old maharajah was on the verge of dying. But within a few days he rallied enough to distribute glittering farewell presents to his guests and send them all happily on their way. This exhibition of Eastern splendor concluded, it was time for the army to march.

The size of the expeditionary force was pared back when news arrived reporting Persia's abandonment of its attack on Herat. The threat from the west had evaporated. General Sir John Keane, commander in chief of the Bombay Army, rather than the higher ranking Sir Henry Fane, commander in chief of all Indian forces and second in rank only to the governor general in the Government of India, would assume overall command of all forces once the Bengal and Bombay armies joined up. Fane was not in the best of health and his term of duty in India was about to expire, so the reduction of the force's size gave him a welcome excuse to turn the baton over to Keane. It was planned that the Bombay contingent, 5,600 strong under Lieutenant General Sir John Keane, would disembark at the mouth of the Indus in Sind; the 9,500 men of the Bengal Army, led by Major General Sir Willoughby Cotton, would march down from Ferozepore; and Shah Shuja's 6,000 levies, under Major General Simpson from Ludhiana, would rendezvous on the Indus, crossing that great river near a fortified island called Bhakkar to reach Shikarpur. The entire force of some 21,000 fighting men was grandly dubbed the Army of the Indus.

As the Bengal Army, led by the Queen's 16th Lancers, resplendent in their light-blue tunics with silver buttons, set out from Ferozepore on its twelve-hundred-mile march to Kabul, it presented an astonishing spectacle, one reminiscent of the grand armies of emperors in the bygone days of Moghul glory. The column stretched thirty to forty miles as it made its way through the desert of the princely state of Bahawalpur en route to the Indus. Dramatically elongating the column was a veritable moving city of camp followers, perhaps more than forty thousand at the outset although it was difficult to keep track of their numbers.

As the term was then used in India, camp followers were the servants, artisans, shopkeepers and assorted menials of all kinds—not to mention their wives, children and indigent relatives—who were thought necessary to support an expeditionary force. They were, literally, the butcher, the baker and the candlestick maker. Bearers, cooks, sweepers, camel drivers, grooms, blacksmiths, tailors, milkmaids jostled one another as they went about their duties or plied their trades. Of course, there were also the fiddlers, nautch dancers and prostitutes to entertain the troops. It was a rule of thumb that the Bengal Army on the march was accompanied by five camp followers per soldier; the less pretentious Bombay Army averaged a more modest three per soldier.

The number of beasts of burden needed to carry supplies for the army and its horde of followers stretches imagination. The Army of the Indus started out with hundreds of bullocks to draw the supply carts, 8,000 horses and some 30,000 camels. The camels may have been ideal for the desert but were a catastrophe in the mountains where they could not keep their footing. It was estimated that before reaching Kabul some 5,000 of them had died. Countless others were stolen by Baluchi predators or wandered off in confusion. It would have been infinitely better to have used donkeys and mules.

While in the beginning the march was described as "halcyon" by one ecstatic chronicler, troubles soon arose. Desertions among the Bengal Army camp followers as they trudged through the Bahawalpur desert grew steadily more common as the poor wretches wracked by dysentery began to realize the ordeal ahead. Making matters worse, they often stole camels as they faded into the desert never to be seen again.

Indian sepoys also began to desert as the Bengal column approached the Indus River. The expedition may have struck Auckland as a "military promenade," as he once referred to it, but as seen from the lowly vantage point of the Indian sepoys it was an ill-omened campaign, not because it might prove difficult but because crossing the Indus River meant venturing beyond Hindustan, an act forbidden by their religion and one certain to cause them to lose caste. The Hindu troops were also uneasy because of wild rumors that they would soon meet in battle a vast Russian host, whose appearance on the Indian side of the Afghan passes would signal a general uprising of the hated Moslems throughout India and a revival of Moghul suppression of the Hindus.[5]

Accounts of imperial wars during the nineteenth century were for the most part written by and from the perspective of the officers. Rarely can we read of events from the point of view of long-suffering British rankers. Rarer still is it possible to see things through the eyes of a native soldier. But one of the most extraordinary memoirs describing military events in nineteenth-century India was written by Sita Ram Pande, a sepoy of the Bengal Native Infantry.[6] Having served in the campaign against the Gurkhas, the Hindu nationalist armies of the Marathas, the maurading Pindari tribesmen and the Sikhs, Sita Ram now found himself seconded to Shah Shuja's levies as a noncommissioned officer in the invasion of Afghanistan.

Sita Ram, a Brahmin, or highest-caste Indian, was a very religious man. His father, a farmer of Oudh province in north-central India (now called Uttar Pradesh), was a man of prominence in his village. Sita Ram received an early religious education from a village priest and was taught to read and write in Hindi. But it was his uncle, a jemadar (lieutenant) in the infantry of the Company Bahadur, as the Indians then referred to the East India Company Army, who influenced the young man and inspired him to follow a military career. His uncle had "such a splendid necklace of gold beads, and a curious bright red coat, covered with gold buttons." He would spin wonderful tales of military valor which, Sita Ram remembered, "inflamed his breast."

The Bengal Army at the time of the Afghan campaign was still an army of spit and polish, so to be made to serve in the hastily assembled and poorly trained levies of Shah Shuja was a letdown for Sita Ram, even though he was given a havildar's rank (sergeant) and drew premium pay.

Sita Ram's memories of the campaign are probably representative of the exaggerated impressions held by most Indian Army sepoys. "The Russians were said to have an army of hundreds of thousands and untold wealth," he recalled, and their soldiers were of enormous stature, as "brave as lions." The end of the Company's rule was predicted by the sepoys, for how could it withstand the Indians, much less the Russians, with only twelve or thirteen regiments of Europeans "in all of India"?[7]

Before encountering the trials of the Sind desert and the Baluchi highlands, the British officers, unlike the sepoys, considered the campaign a pleasant excursion. Glory was in the offing—they could hope. In the meantime they enjoyed all the amenities of home. There were damask table linens on which sterling silver flatware places were set. The officers enjoyed fine wines and Manila cigars (one regiment devoted two camels to carrying their supply of cigars). After a long day's march they dined by candlelight on imported jams, pickles, potted meats and freshly shot partridges served by bearers after refreshing themselves with a shower replete with Windsor soap and eau de cologne.

This all required transport. One brigade boasted no less than 60 camels devoted to carrying personal belongings and such niceties. It was said that General Keane and his staff needed 160 camels to carry supplies for their personal use. There were brass bands to entertain and native whores to ply their trade among grateful soldiers. The 16th Lancers even brought their best hounds so that they could fox hunt along the way. All soldiers knew they were perpetually stalked by disease or quicker death on the battlefield, but in the meantime life should be enjoyed as much as possible—at least by officers.

Alexander Burnes had been charged with arranging for the Indus crossing although he had not succeeded. It was, in fact, his assistant, Mohan Lal, who finally negotiated successfully with the Sind chieftain, Mir Rustam Khan, for the use of the fortified Bhakkar Island, key to safe passage across the wide-flowing river, and gained his cooperation in erecting a bridge of boats at a narrows called Rohri. Burnes had been delinquent in having the essential boat bridge prepared before the army arrived. Only through herculean efforts by the engineering corps was the cumbersome army able to avoid further delay in crossing the Indus. Sita Ram recalled with horror passing over the bridge to the "dreaded other bank of the Indus, trodden for the first time by the Hindustani sepoy." The Bengal Army safely crossed the Indus to Sind, where, as Sita Ram with his Hindu prejudice put it, "The people of the country were all Mohammedans . . . and everything belonging to them was unclean."[8]

One advantage to the route through Sind was that it provided the expeditionary force with an excuse to coerce the tribal chiefs of Sind, extorting from them tribute payments to Shah Shuja in contravention of a treaty earlier reached with them by the British. This British breach of trust was pointed out by Colonel Henry Pottinger, who had been the one to sign and seal the agreement in the first place and had the disagreeable task of explaining its "suspension" to the emirs. Governor General Auckland wrote callously: "The interests at stake are too great to admit of hesitation in our proceedings." Guns would be used if subvention could not subdue the Sind emirs; Britain's will would be done. Macnaghten righteously rationalized: "No civilized beings had ever been treated so badly as were the British by the princes of Sind." But, as John Kaye, chronicler of the invasion, parodied Macnaghten's remark to criticize British action: "no civilized beings had ever before committed themselves to acts of such gross provocation."[9] Hyderabad, principal city of Sind to the south, was a particularly tempting target for General Cotton; the booty to be stripped from the houses already had his troops' blood up in anticipation. Macnaghten, at least, had the good judgment to countermand Cotton's orders and prevent such a gratuitous outrage so that the Bengal Army could get back to the task at hand.

Burnes was still grumbling about government policy as the march to Afghanistan got under way, and this put him at odds with Macnaghten. Burnes declared to the envoy that he "could not proceed with the Army to Kabul to dethrone Dost Mohammed whom he considered a friend."[10] This was but an excuse; he simply did not want to travel with Macnaghten, who had taken the job he coveted and whom he anyway detested. For that matter, Macnaghten was no more eager to travel with Burnes. General Cotton, however, insisted that Burnes was essential to negotiating safe passage through Baluchistan and would not permit him to remain behind in Shikarpur.

General Cotton set out westward for the Bolan Pass without waiting for Keane and the Bombay Army, who were working their way up from the mouth of the Indus where they had landed. Macnaghten had insisted that Cotton ignore his instructions from Keane and move out immediately, arguing that intelligence had been received predicting a massing of the Baluchis to oppose them in the Bolan Pass if they delayed too long. This decision forced upon him deeply upset Cotton, but he was even more disturbed that Macnaghten had assumed supreme power, even in military matters. The bickering between Macnaghten and Cotton was symptomatic of a schism between the politicals and the military over the matter of control; the political officers had been given more authority than the generals liked. The politicals also came under fire for not locally requisitioning and stockpiling enough foodstuffs along the line of march. This had proved difficult in view of severe shortages among the tribes, who could barely feed themselves much less provision an army. Commander in Chief Sir Henry Fane, who had observed the trials of the Army of the Indus in Sind just before he left the column to embark for England, was nonetheless moved to write Auckland criticizing the appalling lack of logistical foresight. Keane blamed Burnes, specifically, for failing to set up adequate stores and tried in vain to delay the advance until the shortfall could be rectified.

Leaving the 2nd Brigade under Major General William Nott temporarily at Shikarpur to protect the rear, the Bengal Army began its difficult march to Dadur at the entrance to the Bolan Pass on February 23, 1839. The route ran through 140 miles of the salt-encrusted Sind desert, where water was scarce and grass for the livestock was virtually nonexistent. Nor could relief be expected at Dadur. There was a local saying: "Oh, Allah! Wherefore make hell when thou has made Dadur." The sixteen days to Dadur took a severe toll in camels. And if the cattle driven with the column to provide food did not die of heat or starvation, they were rustled by marauding Baluchis.

Sita Ram recalled that as the going became more difficult, the sepoy army was rife with talk of mutiny. "Our sufferings were frightful and the livers of all Hindustanis were turned to water."[11] Seen through the eyes of a native trooper, the oppressive heat "was worse than a tomb." Fear of the Baluchis kept desertions lower than otherwise would have been the case, but many nevertheless abandoned the march and straggled back to India. The British soldiers of the queen's units were long suffering, but no happier with their lot. They could not share the luxuries enjoyed by their officers. Their swallow-tailed uniforms of heavy red serge, buttoned up to the chin to hold their heads erect, were cruelly hot in the searing desert, and their heavy packs were a crushing burden.

If the march had been difficult, Dadur was a nightmare; the temperatures hovered around the 100-degree mark as Baluchi snipers picked off camp followers and careless sepoys. When a hospital wagon was brutally attacked, Cotton ignored Burnes's advice not to return fire (lest the natives become "hostile"!) and permitted his harassed troops to shoot any Baluchi who came near the train.

The food situation was the most worrisome. Instead of a ten-day supply awaiting the force at Dadur, enough to carry it through the Bolan Pass, the local tribesmen had produced but one day's supply. Part of the problem was Cotton's premature march from Shikarpur undertaken on Macnaghten's advice. And, understandably, the tribes were less than cooperative with an army that foraged on their already-barren lands. With only a few days' rest, Cotton's force pushed on in the hopes that the food situation would be better in Quetta at the other end of the pass.

On March 16 the weary column resumed its march, now climbing the tortuous sixty-mile stretch leading to the Baluchistan highlands, famous in frontier lore as the Bolan Pass. The advance column, made up of the Horse Artillery, the 2nd Cavalry and the 13th Light Infantry (Prince Albert's own), led the army through the savage gorges. The jagged rocks of the pass provided good cover for the Baluchi mountaineers trying to pick off stragglers. Ever present was another danger: a flash flood could, without warning, inundate the troops trapped in the narrow defiles with no way to escape. Jagged flintlike rocks made walking difficult and lamed the beasts of burden, so that much of the baggage had to be discarded.

It was a cruel march. Camels dropped from fatigue and lack of food; the rotting carcasses of dead camels littered the line of march. A depleted camel train meant that even less supplies could be carried.

On March 26, the half-starved and thirst-parched column finally reached Quetta, but with their food supplies nearly exhausted. The Army of the Indus, so grand on the parade ground of Ferozepore, so buoyant as it began its march, was now a wretched rabble of worn-out and dispirited men. John Kaye's chronicle of the march, with the benefit of contemporary testimony, caught the misery of the scene: "The sufferings of the present were aggravated by the future; and as men looked at the shrunken frames and sunkened cheeks of each other, and in their own feebleness and exhaustion felt what wrecks they had become, then hearts died within them at the thought that a day was coming when even the little that was doled out to them might be wholly denied."[12]

Baluchi Prince Mehrab, khan of Khelat and master of the Bolan Pass, only reluctantly agreed to cooperate with the British force. Burnes and Mohan Lal by bribery had extracted an agreement from him, but it had not been easy nor did it eliminate the problem of predatory tribes along the route of march. There had been much intrigue among the various undisciplined chiefs, who quarreled over their share of the bribes. And the burden on the fragile tribal economy presented by the huge invading army was understandably resented.

A Baluchi plot to murder Burnes, whom they blamed for the imposition, failed only because he unexpectedly departed from Khelat. Mohan Lal was left to play the main role in negotiating the treaty with the Baluchis. He had to bargain hard and talk tough, provoking the Baluchi leader to complain: "British have soldiers to frighten with their arms, and agents to cause alarm by their tongues."[13]

Mir Mehrab Khan not only resented the despoiling of his lands by the foraging British Army but disapproved of British efforts to seat Shah Shuja again on the throne of Kabul. While Mehrab Khan was less than helpful, perhaps even treacherous, he at least warned the British of their folly in trying to restore Shah Shuja to power. With considerable prescience he said: "You may keep him by main force for a time on the throne, but as soon as you leave the Kingdom, your Shah Shuja will be driven beyond its frontier."

In the meantime, Shah Shuja's army and the Bombay contingent, led by the expedition's commander in chief, Sir John Keane, were making their way through Sind and toward the Bolan Pass to join up with Cotton and his exhausted Bengal Army. General Keane was having the same difficulties experienced by Cotton as his food supplies dwindled to the danger point, but his troops struggled through the long pass, belatedly to join the Bengal contingent on April 4 near Quetta. As Keane took overall command of the combined force, he was dismayed by the situation in which the Army of the Indus found itself. Cotton's Bengal troops, he discovered, had nearly exhausted their supplies and his own Bombay units were not much better off. Making a bad situation worse was Cotton's leaden pessimism. A prophet of doom, he predicted that disaster would befall the army if it pushed on toward its goal.

Macnaghten was so annoyed at Cotton for his defeatist attitude that he dashed off an angry note to the governor general. "Sir W. [Willoughby] is a sad croaker," he complained. "Not content with telling me we must all inevitably be starved, he assures me that Shah Shuja is very unpopular in Afghanistan and that we shall be opposed at every step of our progress." But even Macnaghten, whose faith in Shah Shuja seemed boundless, was beginning to realize that Afghan support could be gained only by liberal distributions of bribes. Learning from Burnes's experience with the Baluchi khan of Khelat, he reported to Lord Auckland: "considerable sums must be expended . . . here we are at the mercy of the Baluchis." Yet, the fact remained that the Baluchis had refrained from seriously attacking the vulnerable column in the Bolan Pass. Had they done so, passage would have been impossible.

Keane had no choice but to push on to Kandahar, hoping the stores would hold out and they would not be met by serious resistance along the way. It was not a happy army that now moved forward. Keane, as a British Army officer only temporarily serving in India, was not popular with the officers of the Indian Army, who resented serving under the command of a "Queen's officer." General Nott of the Company army, angry to be left behind again to protect the rear, this time at Quetta, was particularly outspoken, claiming that Keane's appointment "has paralysed and nearly given a death blow to the enterprise." Keane's objectionable manners also grated on his subordinates. One officer, Major Henry Havelock, complained of the general's "open parade of private vices and affected coarseness of language," which he felt "were only a cloak for darker features of his character."

Sita Ram was appalled at the dissension he saw in the Army of the Indus. "The Bombay Commander in Chief [Keane] and the Bengal general [Cotton] quarrelled," he wrote, and "all the Bombay officers looked with contempt on the Bengal Army." As for Shah Shuja's levies, with which Sita Ram was serving, they were despised by all as "irregulars."[14] But despite its problems, the Army of the Indus under Keane now struggled forth uncertainly toward Kandahar, where the first real Afghan resistance was expected.

Between Quetta and Kandahar there was another cruel barrier, the Kojuk Pass, and rumors reached the column that the Afghan Kandahar chiefs were massing their forces there. But with the help of a large bribe arranged by Mohan Lal, one of the chieftains, Haji Khan Kakar, with his tribal following defected to the British. This so demoralized the other chiefs that they fled to Persia, causing Afghan resistance in Kandahar to collapse. But if the Afghans did not prove an obstacle, geography did. The field guns had to be dragged up and lowered down from the precipices by exhausted soldiers desperate with thirst. When small trickles of water were found, the streams were usually brackish and mud-clogged. The Bengal troops suffered the most; they were not used to this kind of climate and terrain. Sita Ram wrote of the jackals who "grew sleek and fat by their attendance" at death. But worse, "There was no wood with which to perform the funeral rites when a Hindu died, and he was far from holy Benares and the pure Ganges." Now Sita Ram understood why it was forbidden for Hindus to cross the Indus.

Crossing the Kojuk Pass was an achievement of endurance. In places the towering rocks nearly met overhead, plunging the trail into near darkness.

Had the Afghans chosen to attack here, it would have been a slaughter, but strangely they did not. The steep climb made it difficult to drag the nine-pounders forward, but inch by inch progress was made. Losses were severe, however; some three thousand more camels were lost, and untold ammunition had to be blown up or abandoned for lack of transport.

Luck and dogged determination had brought the army through. The campaign had not been well planned or well executed. Considering the terrain and sparseness of food and fodder along the route, it would have been a torturous march at best, but faulty logistics made matters worse. Burnes was blamed for not having negotiated better support from the Baluchis and for not providing better intelligence on the conditions to be encountered. On May 4 that ordeal was over and the Army of the Indus could gratefully pitch camp on the lush meadows outside Kandahar. The leader of the city's defenders, Kohun Dil Khan, and his brothers had fled to Persia rather than fight.

A longer than expected stay of two months in Kandahar, awaiting the harvest so that food stocks could be replenished, provided Shah Shuja with an opportunity to posture regally. Any homage paid him in Kandahar was more a product of gold liberally spread about by the British than of devotion. Shah Shuja had been permitted to lead the forces triumphantly through curious crowds into the city, but a grand ceremonial review of the troops by the would-be monarch proved a failure as only a hundred Afghans turned out to watch. Once again it became evident that success in this venture could be bought only at enormous expense. Sita Ram summed it up simply: "The truth began to dawn on us that despite all the assurances Shah Shuja had given us . . . that the Afghans were longing for his return, in reality they did not want him as their ruler."[15] The Afghans particularly resented his return as a ward of foreigners: "He had shown the English the way into their country . . . they would use it as they had done all Hindustan and introduce their detested rules and laws." Sita Ram had a better understanding of the situation than did Macnaghten.

The campaign thus far had been costly in terms of human life. While military casualties were few on the march from Ferozepore to Kandahar, thousands of camp followers, many ill suited for the march, had perished. More than seven hundred horses died, requiring a remounting of the Bengal Brigade in Kandahar, and most of the cattle and camels did not survive the march. Kandahar had proven a good respite, although the stay there was longer than expected and provided the Afghans with more time to organize their defenses. Nott was brought up from Quetta now to hold Kandahar, while on June 27 the Army of the Indus resumed its march— not yet knowing that on the same day Ranjit Singh died in Lahore, to mark the end of a valuable relationship with the Sikhs and a change in the power equation in the Punjab.

Still ahead, 230 miles away, was the town of Ghazni, with its massive fortress guarding the approach to Kabul. This would pose the greatest combat challenge yet for the expeditionary force. Reinforced by new Afghan troops commanded by Dost Mohammed's son, Hyder Ali Khan, the fort was considered impregnable. Despite this, Keane elected to leave his siege artillery, the eighteen-pounders and heavy howitzers, behind in Kandahar—just when he needed it the most. Bad intelligence belittling the strength of the Ghazni defenses may have been one reason for this strange decision; Burnes had even sent Keane word that the Afghans had abandoned the fort altogether.

On July 21, Keane, who had ridden ahead with his staff to reconnoiter Ghazni, gazed with dismay at the battlements perched upon an escarpment 280 feet above the surrounding plain. The town itself was encircled by two stone walls, 30 feet high, flanked by impressive towers. In the center rose the citadel, certainly not abandoned, which had to be breached if the Army of the Indus hoped to pass. Screen walls had been erected to protect the walled city's gates and a moat dug to give additional protection from attack. It was a disheartening sight and Keane might have realized his folly in leaving the heavy artillery behind. After laboriously dragging it over two passes, this was the one place where it would have been useful. Just as disturbing was the plight of his troops, already on half-rations, with provisions for only two more days. This meant that a prolonged siege was impossible. Keane could not bypass the fort, leaving the Afghans to harass the rear, nor could he retreat with only two days' rations. He had no choice; he must attack the bastion without benefit of siege artillery to breach the massive walls.

By this time Keane had had enough of the politicals, whom he blamed for his problems, and in exasperation turned the responsibility for supplies over to his military staff. Keane wrote Macnaghten a letter advising him that he was also forming his own intelligence service. "I have never seen the like in any army," he ranted as he accused the politicals of incompetence and of trying to succeed by negotiations when the sword was required.

British luck held in Ghazni. A nephew of Dost Mohammed, Abdul Rashid, crept secretly into Keane's lines to desert and provided valuable information on Ghazni's defenses. More than luck was involved, however. Notwithstanding Keane's criticism of intelligence gathered by the political officers, the defection of the traitorous nephew was the handiwork of Mohan Lal, who had recruited Abdul Rashid as a spy during his duty with

Burnes in Kabul. Abdul Rashid revealed the great fort's one weakness, the Kabul gate, which was lightly defended. Determined to take immediate advantage of his information, Keane quickly re-formed his army for a night attack on this vulnerable position.

Despite a spirited cavalry attack and heavy bombardment by Afghan artillery, Keane was ready to attack at dawn on July 22. A storming party under Brigadier Robert Sale, destined to play a pivotal role in future events, moved forward in the dark while the main column took their positions as skirmishers on the flanks. It was important to move rapidly if the essential advantage of surprise was to be achieved. This became particularly important when Keane learned that Macnaghten had already imparted the plan to Shah Shuja, whose venal courtiers surely included one or more spies reporting to the enemy. Moreover, Keane now knew that Afghan reinforcements sent by Dost Mohammed were within a day's march of Ghazni.

By just after midnight the attacking units were before the town gate to provide protective fire while a party of engineer volunteers crept forward to lay the charges. Fortunately the night was stormy and the movement of the men could not be heard above the wind and rain. Captain Peat, lieutenants Durand and Maclean, three sergeants and eighteen sappers lugged three hundred pounds of powder into position against the gate before retreating quickly as a seventy-foot fuse was fired. The gate blew open, lighting the night, and British troops rushed forward. But just as success was within grasp, Brigadier Sale ordered retreat to be sounded, fearing that the rubble of the collapsing gate had barred entrance to the fort.

Captain Dennie was the real hero of Ghazni. Despite the confusion created by Sale, Dennie's storming party, flailing away with their sabers and bayonets, slashed their way into the fort; and bugler Wilson, on his own initiative, blew the signal for attack, which propelled the rest of the force to follow.

Brigadier Sale* had gathered his wits about him and was in the forefront of the general attack when he was struck down by a saber cut in the face. He wrestled in the dirt with his assailant, slicing his hand on the Afghan's blade as he tried to deflect its thrusts. Major Kershaw, who saw his commander's predicament and rushed to his rescue, ran the Afghan through, but the hardy tribesman continued to fight until Sale finally killed him.

Later, events would contrive to make Bob Sale of the 13th Foot one of

---

*Sale was actually a colonel, but as commander of the 1st Brigade he assumed the position of brigadier. "Brigadier," in fact, was more a title than a rank and was given to any officer, regardless of his actual rank, if he commanded a brigade.

the few heroes of the Afghan War, and indeed he was a brave officer. He was not brilliant, however, and his performance at Ghazni typified his blundering. But his men loved him for his courage, which often bordered on foolhardiness. The sobriquet "Fighting Bob" was earned in the First Burma War in 1823 for always being at the head of his troops in battle, due to which he inevitably drew fire and was wounded.

Following Burma, Sale had assumed command of the 13th Light Foot, a British royal regiment that had become notorious for the depravity of its troops. Many of the draftees had been recently released from prison in England, which perhaps accounted for a rash of murders that took the lives of several unpopular noncommissioned officers. On more than one occasion Sale himself received anonymous death threats. He handled these situations by facing his troops on the parade ground, waving the threatening letter and ordering them to fire a volley of blanks—a perfect opportunity for the would-be assassin with real shot in his musket to gun him down. Following the volley, a very much alive Bob Sale would taunt for-whom-it-may-concern for not having had the courage to kill him.

Fighting Bob had been delighted that the 13th had been selected to join the Army of the Indus. No red-blooded officer wanted to miss this action, which promised glory, but Sale was particularly pleased to be in the van as commander of the 1st Brigade.

Some twelve hundred Afghans died in the defense of Ghazni before resistance ended. A few survivors escaped, but sixteen hundred were taken prisoner. The Afghans had nonetheless fought bravely. The governor of Ghazni, Hyder Ali, among the last to be captured, probably spoke for his people as well as himself when he told Keane: "Kill me if you like, but if you let me go, I shall ever be found as your enemy . . . and drive you all out of Kabul!"[16]

With one glaring exception, the Army of the Indus treated their captives with exemplary restraint. The exception occurred when Shah Shuja ordered fifty captives to be beheaded. A British officer chanced to come upon this scene of carnage and described it with horror to Macnaghten: "There were 40 or 50 men, young and old. Many were already dead, others at their last gasp, others with their hands tied behind them; some sitting, others standing awaiting their doom; and the King's executioners amusing themselves with hacking and maiming the poor wretches indiscriminately with their long swords and knives." This act of brutality did not augur well for wise stewardship of Afghanistan by Shah Shuja, nor would the Afghans forget it.

After the fall of Ghazni, the way to Kabul was open. The demoralized forces of Dost Mohammed were rent by desertion; any plans the emir had to defend Kabul at its gates had to be abandoned. Dost Mohammed sent to Ghazni Nawab Jubbar Khan, the Company's best friend in the Afghan court, to treat with the invaders. Burnes and Mohan Lal cordially received him, fondly exchanging reminiscences, but their peace negotiations did not go well.

The Nawab's proposition was that he should continue as vizier under Shah Shuja—this, he felt, was the least the British could do for their old ally. Moreover, his presence in the government would improve Shah Shuja's chances of acceptance on the part of certain Afghan factions. There was no flexibility in the British position, however; if Dost Mohammed gave himself up he could expect honorable asylum in India, and the same treatment would be given Nawab Jubbar Khan. If not, they both would be considered fugitives to be tracked down by the British.

Stung by his rejection by the British, whose cause he had so faithfully supported at court, Nawab Jubbar Khan angrily informed Burnes that he would remain with his brother, Dost Mohammed; they would rather "fling themselves on British bayonets" than accept the protection of the *ferangis* in exile. The vizier's last words to Burnes and Mohan Lal were: "You have brought him [Shah Shuja] by your money and arms into Afghanistan. Leave him now with us Afghans and let him rule us if he can."[17]

Tribal support for Dost Mohammed rapidly melted away, with many of his officers abandoning him to jump on Shah Shuja's bandwagon. The British could be grateful that Dost Mohammed had miscalculated. He had sent most of his army toward the Khyber Pass under the command of his ablest son, Akbar Khan,* believing the main British attack would come from that direction. With the defeat at Ghazni, where he discovered that the main British force was concentrated to march on Kabul, Dost hastily recalled Akbar Khan. But this permitted a smaller British-officered Afghan force—titularly under Shah Shuja's son, Prince Timur, for political effect but actually commanded by British political agent Claude Wade—to breach the Khyber without difficulty.

As Keane's army approached Kabul, the ubiquitous American, Josiah Harlan, once again emerged, this time claiming to be empowered by Dost Mohammed to meet with Macnaghten and Burnes to arrange some kind of peace. He also claimed to be commander in chief of Dost's Afghan army, and apparently the emir had, in fact, given him this eleventh-hour appointment as the Afghan forces were collapsing. Burnes ignored Harlan, suspecting quite accurately that the American, not unused to switching sides, was more interested in arranging a new position for himself in the court of his old friend and employer, Shah Shuja. Harlan was sent packing

*Dost Mohammed's son's full name was Mohammed Akbar Khan. The shortened version, Akbar Khan, is being used here since it was how the British referred to him most often at the time.

by the British, who paid his passage home to Philadelphia to make certain he would go.

The Company had little use for Harlan. He was a nuisance at best and a troublemaker at worst. Ranjit Singh had been responsible for attracting most of the foreign adventurers to the Punjab. They served him well, building a strong modern army. While the British may have been uneasy about this, Ranjit Singh was an ally unlikely to use his force against them. Moreover, the mercenaries for the most part were predictable in their actions as military officers; several of them were even helpful to the British, secretly providing the Company with intelligence on the Sikh court. But Harlan's duplicitous role made him unpredictable; he kept popping up when least welcome, playing roles at odds with Company interests.

Harlan was a turncoat and the British did not admire turncoats, who changed loyalties with few qualms of conscience and played their own little games in a discordant accompaniment to the Great Game. Yet the games of nations were no less duplicitous and very often more hypocritical. Harlan's motives, if not his actions, were at least straightforward: he wanted to survive and prosper. It was a wonder that Harlan did survive in the dangerous world beyond the fringe of empire.

Harlan and Burnes, perhaps typical of their respective types, had little in common except that both were ambitious and both were adventurous. Harlan had sworn no oath of fealty to any nation—except implicitly as needed for survival. This was not admirable in an age of patriotism, but it was at least honest. Burnes was loyal to his country and was an able servant of empire, but tugging at him was the genie of ambition, perhaps less devoted to cause than to glory.

On August 2, Dost Mohammed and Nawab Jubbar Khan fled to the north, pursued by a small British force under Captain James Outram. Thanks to treachery on the part of Outram's Afghan guide, the emir and Nawab Jubbar Khan made good their escape and disappeared into the Hindu Kush, ultimately to find uneasy refuge with the emir of Bokhara. However self-serving Harlan was during the collapse of Dost Mohammed's reign, he at least left a good account of the drama attending Dost Mohammed's flight as the British approached the capital. "A crowd of noisy, disorganized troops insolently pressed close to the royal pavilion," recalled the American. "A stranger handed the vessel for his Highness's ablution, and he mournfully performed for the last time within his tent the ceremonials of his religion. His prayers finished, he commenced putting on his turban, his horse ready at the door of his tent." Now in danger from his own guards, Dost Mohammed shouted: "Hold, will ye not give me time to tie my turban?" As the emir rode off to the north toward Bamiyan, "a dark scowl of desperation met his eye from those who were wont to fawn upon his kindness and flatter the once-potent chief."[18] Suddenly a magazine exploded, fired by Dost Mohammed's mutinous troops. According to Harlan, who could not resist romantic embellishment, "The Prince turned his horse toward that dense cloud, which seemed like a shadow enshrining his glory, and plunged into the screening veil that obscured his fallen fortunes and protected him from pursuit."[19]

Except for a small garrison of twelve hundred men left at Ghazni, Shah Shuja with his levies and the Bengal and Bombay divisions, nearly twenty thousand strong in all, entered Kabul with ostentatious pomp on August 7, 1839. The restored monarch, mounted on a white charger, dressed in his finest gown garnished with his best jewels, led the parade. Following close by were Macnaghten and Burnes in diplomatic uniform and Mohan Lal wearing a magnificent outsize turban for the occasion. Then came the senior military officers in their dress uniforms. But there was no enthusiasm from the street.

Major Henry Havelock wrote of the people's reaction to Shah Shuja: "An ocean of heads spread out in every direction, the expression of countenances indicated a ready acquiescence in the new state of things." But the British escort, an unwelcome infidel legion, suffered "a shower of maledictions." When Shah Shuja reached his palace in the Bala Hissar, he rushed up the main staircase to his apartments in childish delight; after thirty years in exile he was once again emir.

Shah Shuja's son, Prince Timur, and Claude Wade, leading a Khyber force made of nondescript and unreliable Sikh troops feeling rudderless since Ranjit Singh's death, and some Afghan levies picked up along the way after having been induced to rise in support of Shah Shuja (for opportunistic, if not true, partisan reasons), made it through the Khyber Pass by bribing the Afridi tribesmen. They reached Kabul soon after Keane's main force arrived.

The Army of the Indus had achieved its objective; Shah Shuja was back on his throne. Governor General Auckland was created an earl, Sir John Keane was made a peer—Lord Keane of Ghazni—Claude Wade was knighted and Macnaghten was made a baronet. From a military point of view, the Army of the Indus had acquitted itself well despite the logistical failures, the lack of harmony among the top officers and the twin nightmares of insufficient food and tribal harassment. Human casualties from the physical hardships had been distressingly high among the camp followers, but Afghan resistance had proved unexpectedly light. The real problems, however, lay ahead.

Chapter 16

STAFF AND DISTAFF

Garrisoning the army of the indus in kabul posed an immediate problem. As winter approached the troops could not be left with only the protection of their light campaign tents. The logical place for a military cantonment was the defensible citadel within the Bala Hissar, perched high above the city commanding its eastern approaches. Strongly recommended by the engineering officers—and most every other officer of the brigade for that matter—Macnaghten cast the only dissenting vote against garrisoning the troops in the Bala Hissar because the king had made it clear that he would need the space to accommodate his large zenana about to arrive from the Punjab. Unfortunately, Macnaghten had his way; Shah Shuja was not to be disturbed.

The word *harem* has too often been identified in romantic stereotypes as a fantasy of vaulted, ornate halls and marble baths squirming with voluptuous beauties in seductive attitudes meant to catch their master's eye. Shah Shuja's zenana, to use the Hindi word, was anything but this.

It was a working household, albeit a large one, of some three or four hundred women. Reflecting the ruder tribal society of the Afghans, it did not have the grandeur of the imperial Moghul court, or even the courts of lesser maharajas in India. In Kabul the royal ladies and their attendants went about the daily business of living without much pomp or pretense. There were the royal wives and children, countless concubines and their second-class children, handmaidens, menials and assorted servers such as artisans, musicians and Islamic teachers for the children. Standing guard over the king's womenfolk were the eunuch guards, wily masters of intrigue, whose access could be and often was used to personal advantage. If the zenana was not ornate, it was cumbersome and burdened Shah Shuja's palace administrators with a logistical problem of no small dimension.

Brigadier Sale and his engineering officer, Lieutenant Henry Durand, had already ordered reconstruction of the citadel, perched on the highest promontory within the Bala Hissar, to barrack the 13th Infantry when the king made his objections known to Macnaghten. Shah Shuja considered it an indignity to have foreign soldiers overlooking his zenana from their elevated vantage point in the citadel, even though they were there to protect him.

General Cotton, who had argued with Macnaghten over many issues during the course of the march, strangely did not strongly protest the political officer's decision to erect a cantonment on the exposed plain north of Kabul. Perhaps the general was less than resolute because he was about to return to India. Dissent would have done little good anyway since he did not have the authority to overrule the envoy; he had not inherited the same overall command authority that had been vested in General Keane before the commander in chief returned to India in November 1839.

Cotton's Northern Command included the important British garrisons at Ghazni and Jalalabad as well as Kabul itself, but Macnaghten had sole authority over Shah Shuja's troops, by then under the military command of British Brigadier Thomas Anquetil in Kabul. General Nott, as head of the Southern Command, had jurisdiction over Kandahar and the subsidiary garrisons at Quetta, Khelat, Dadur, Gundava and Ghiresk, vital to the protection of the important Bolan Pass supply route. The cumulative effect of this divided command was to subordinate military decisions to the political judgments of Macnaghten. This was not a happy situation from the military point of view. The politicals were troublesome enough as it was, but to have them given this kind of power was maddening. The command structure during the important first winter of occupation became all the more cumbersome when in October 1839 Macnaghten had

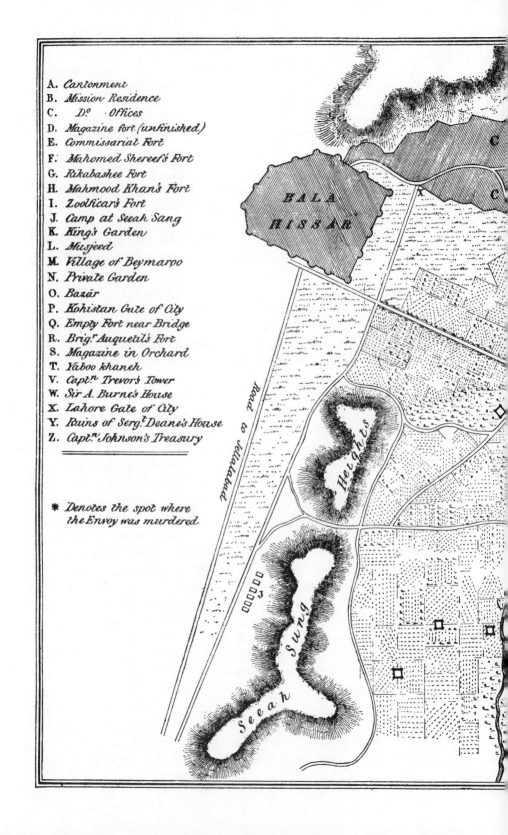

A. Cantonment
B. Mission Residence
C. Do. Offices
D. Magazine fort (unfinished)
E. Commissariat Fort
F. Mahomed Shereef's Fort
G. Rikabashee Fort
H. Mahmood Khan's Fort
I. Zoolficar's Fort
J. Camp at Seeah Sang
K. King's Garden
L. Musjeed
M. Village of Beymaroo
N. Private Garden
O. Bazār
P. Kohistan Gate of City
Q. Empty Fort near Bridge
R. Brigr. Auquetil's Fort
S. Magazine in Orchard
T. Yaboo khaneh
V. Captn. Trevor's Tower
W. Sir A. Burne's House
X. Lahore Gate of City
Y. Ruins of Sergt. Deane's House
Z. Captn. Johnson's Treasury

✱ Denotes the spot where
the Envoy was murdered

BALA HISSAR

Road to Jellalabad

Heights

Seeah Sung

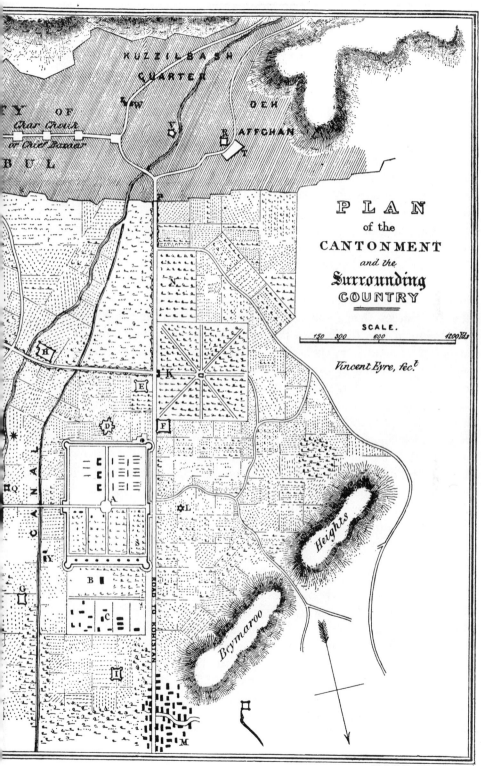

KUZZILBASH QUARTER

OF

CITY

...TY OF
Char Chouk
or Chief Bazaar

...BUL

New Deh
N
O

R AFFGHAN
T

PLAN
of the
CANTONMENT
and the
Surrounding
COUNTRY

SCALE.
150   300   600   1200 Yds

Vincent Eyre, fect

N

CANAL

H

E

K

D

F

A

Q

L

S

Y

B

Heights

G

C

Beymaroo

M

J. & C. Walker. Lith. 9. Castle St.

to accompany Shah Shuja to the more temperate climate of Jalalabad, leaving Burnes in Kabul as principal political officer.

The role of political officer had not been formalized until recently and was an outgrowth of northwest frontier campaigning, in which the difference between a political or diplomatic mission and a military mission was blurred. Usually operating far from a headquarters with which he was linked only tenuously by native message carriers, or *cossids,* the political was apt to wield more power than his military escort liked. In Macnaghten's case, his closeness to Governor General Auckland gave him more than usual authority, limited only when the howls of his commanders became so strident they could no longer be ignored. Macnaghten certainly never thought it necessary to consult Calcutta in the disagreement over where the cantonment would be located.

The cantonment, designed to accommodate about ten thousand troops, the force estimated as necessary to protect Shah Shuja, and, of course, the inevitable camp followers,* was hurriedly erected from the ground up on the flat plain less than a mile north of the city between the Kabul River and the main road to Kohistan Province. The rectangular cantonment, about twelve hundred by six hundred yards, surrounded by a low parapet and ditch that could be mounted by any Afghan "with the facility of a cat," as one officer muttered disparagingly, offered little or no protection. It was vulnerable to half a dozen small forts located nearby, which in the event of hostilities could be occupied by Afghans to bottle up the British force. A detachment, placed on the lee side of the Siah Sung Hills about a mile east of the cantonment, was intended as a screen against attacks launched from that direction, but the unattended Behmaru heights, much closer to the encampment and looming over it on its western flank, offered an inviting vantage point for Afghan attackers.

Only a few British officers lived in town rather than in the cantonment. Alexander Burnes maintained his political residency on the edge of the Kizzilbash quarter in the congested center of town. This brought him nearer to the Afghans; and for an officer in his position it was useful to be free of the confining atmosphere of the cantonment. Mohan Lal occupied a house only a few doors away, convenient for discreet meetings with his spies and informants. Across the lane from Burnes was a "tower," or small fortified building, in which Captain Johnson, Shah Shuja's paymaster, and a handful of armed guards kept the royal treasury. Such a vulnerable location rather than the better protected Bala Hissar was chosen

*The Army of the Indus when it set out from India consisted of approximately 21,000 fighting men and an estimated 38,000 camp followers, an appalling number of whom perished along the route to Kabul or deserted rather than face the perils of the march.

Imperial Outrider

East India Company political officer Alexander Burnes, popularly known in England as "Bokhara Burnes" for his exploratory mission into Central Asia, met a violent death in the streets of Kabul when tribal leaders vented their bitter opposition to British interference and took revenge against an "infidel" who had taken liberties with their women. He is portrayed here by fellow officer Lieutenant Vincent Eyre wearing native Bokharan costume.

Kings

Maharajah Ranjit Singh, hard-living, one-eyed "Lion of the Punjab," who welded the Sikhs together as a nation for the first and last time in the early nineteenth century. He was the antagonist of the Afghans from whom he took the strategic frontier city of Peshawar. He also took from the Afghan ruling dynasty the fabled Koh-i-noor, then the largest diamond in the world.

His dashing cavalrymen, shown below, led his troops into battle.

Emir Dost Mohammad, the leader of the Afghans who was deposed by the British in favor of Shah Shuja in 1839, returned to power after British forces in Kabul were annihilated during their ill-fated retreat in 1842.

Shah Suja, Afghan king, who was assassinated by enemies after his British protectors left Kabul.

Street scene, Kabul

Companymen

George Eden, Earl of Auckland, the governor general of India on whom blame for the British debacle in Afghanistan during 1841–42 has generally been placed. A victim of bad advice and his own bad judgment, Auckland left India in disgrace in 1842 to be replaced by Lord Ellenborough.

Sir William Hay Macnaghten, principal architect and ultimate victim of Auckland's disastrous policy toward Afghanistan. As East India Company envoy to Shah Shuja and political officer, Macnaghten's misjudgments continued to plague British fortunes in Kabul and led to his own murder.

Freebooters

General Josiah Harlan, American freebooter who frequently changed sides during the events leading to the First Afghan War, serving Sikhs and Afghans alike. As the British Army of the Indus trimphantly entered Kabul in 1839, Harlan was acting as head of Emir Dost Mohammad's crumbling army.

Alexander Gardner, Irish-American mercenary in a uniform of his own design, who commanded Maharajah Ranjit Singh's well-trained artillery in its battles with the Afghans. He also served as a British agent.

Agents

Scottish Academic Press Ltd./George Pottinger

Viktorovich Vitkevich, (*top left*), Russian agent at the court of Dost Mohammad, Emir of Afghanistan, in early 1838. He outscored his rival, Alexander Burnes, in Kabul but met a mysterious death in St. Petersburg either by suicide or murder.

At about the same time British major Eldred Pottinger (*top right*) became the "hero of Herat" by holding at bay a Russian-backed Persian Army besieging Herat in western Afghanistan.

Mohan Lal (*left*), intrepid Indian agent, helped Burnes fence politically with Vitkevich. He returned to Kabul with the Army of the Indus and remained there in 1842 to perform invaluable intelligence duties after the Kabul garrison left on its fatal evacuation.

Hero and Heroine

Brigadier Sir Robert "Fighting Bob" Sale, commander of the Jalalabad garrison in 1841–42, who staunchly resisted Afghan attacks. Fighting with General Pollock to rescue the British hostages still held near Kabul in 1843, Sale emerged as a hero of the disastrous Afghan affair. Among those he rescued was his wife, Lady Florentia Sale, who had endured harsh Afghan captivity to keep a remarkable diary chronicling the horrors of the First Afghan War. The sketch of Lady Sale was made by fellow hostage Lieutenant Vincent Eyre.

Gateway

The British Army of the Indus invading Afghanistan in 1839 enters the Bolan Pass on its way to Kandahar, Ghazni and the British goal, Kabul. Transit through these rugged gorges was made possible by a fragile agreement with Baluchi tribesmen who, however, all too often honored it in the breach.

Hostile Land

Rising in the background is the almost impregnable fortress and citadel of Ghazni reduced by the British Army of the Indus during its 1839 invasion of Afghanistan to clear the way to Kabul. In the foreground are two historic minarets.

Kabul from the heights of the Bala Hissar, or Citadel, of the city.

Generals

Major General William George Keith Elphinstone, old and ailing commander of the British army in Kabul at the time of the 1841 uprising and fatal 1842 retreat. His indecision contributed to the British debacle at the hands of the Afghans.

Brigadier John Shelton, choleric second-in-command of the British cantonment in Kabul at the time of the Kabul uprising, disgraced himself by poor leadership during the crisis in 1842.

Major General Sir William Nott, commander of the British garrison in Kandahar, who was able to resist repeated Afghan attacks and keep open the supply line through the Bolan Pass. He joined Pollock in Kabul as part of the army of retribution and burned the Kabul bazaar to teach the Afghans a lesson.

Surrender

Dost Mohammed, fugitive emir of Afghanistan, rides out of the mountains behind Kabul and unexpectedly surrenders to British political agent Sir William Hay Macnaghten in 1840, leaving leadership of Afghanistan's rebellious tribesmen to his son, Akbar Khan.

Murder

As he tries to escape, a frenzied Afghan mob murders Alexander Burnes in front of his house near the Kabul bazaar, sparking an uprising that would culminiate in the destruction of the British Army in Kabul.

Lieutenant Bird, trapped within a fort near Kabul held by hostile Afghans, survived by barricading a door until rescued, but was killed only fifteen miles from Jalalabad and safety during the army's disastrous retreat in 1842.

Predator and Prey

Akbar Kahn, Dost Mohammed's son, murdered Macnaughten, forcing the British to evacuate Kabul and run the fatal gauntlet of hostile tribes.

Afghan tribesmen, led by Akbar Khan, drag an artillery piece to the top of Behmaru Heights overlooking the vulnerable British cantonment on the flat plain outside Kabul. British efforts to capture this strategic position proved futile. Watercolor by J. A. Atkinson

Disaster

An Afghan horseman with saber
raised bears down on women and
children near Jagdalak during
the retreat of the British Army
from Kabul.

Afghan tribesmen with their long-barreled *jazails* outgunned the British and had the advantage of fighting from rocky promontories where English muskets could not reach them.

A few survivors of the 44th Foot who reached Gandamak took their last stand on the barren rocks before being massacred, as memorialized in W. A. Wollen's dramatic painting.

Last Survivor

"Remnant of an Army," Lady Butler's dramatic painting of Dr. Brydon's approach to the British fort at Jalalabad. Brydon was the last and only survivor of the retreating British Army in 1842 excepting those few taken captive or held hostage by the Afghans until rescued by a British army of retribution led by General Pollock.

because it was near Brigadier Anquetil's fort, headquarters detachment of Shah Shuja's army. Of course both Anquetil's headquarters and the treasury should have been located in the Bala Hissar, but Shah Shuja's aversion to troops cluttering up the palace premises made this impossible. Similarly, Shah Shuja had insisted that the grain stores for his army be removed from the Bala Hissar. Instead the stores were kept in a fortified compound on the edge of town under the command of Captain Colin Mackenzie and guarded by twenty sepoys, fifty sappers and ninety locally recruited cutthroats. Between Anquetils's fort and Burnes's house was another tower, manned by Captain Robert Trevor, commander of Shah Shuja's Life Guards, and a small guard force.

The Kabul cantonment soon became the scene of a flourishing recreational life. Cockfighting, wrestling, horse racing and other sports helped the officers while away their leisure time during garrison duty. Shah Shuja was cajoled into offering up one of his prize swords to be given the best rider in a gymkhana exhibition of horsemanship. The lucky officer to win was Major Daly of the 4th Light Dragoons. Friendly Afghans joined the British in steeplechase races and watched as baffled spectators while the British played cricket. There had been fox (jackal) hunting until the 16th Lancers and their "hounds" returned to India with General Keane. Even the fierce winter of 1839–40, which took its toll on the Indian sepoys unaccustomed to such cold, had its compensation as the British learned to ice-skate on the Kabul River. Captain George Atkinson, in that day famous for his lampoon of army cantonment life in words and pictures called *Curry & Rice,*[1] seemed to think that sports were at the core of cantonment life because they were extensions of English schoolboy—or even earlier—exposure to games. War was just a grander game for grownups to play. Gymkhanas and horse races were particularly popular and were imprinted on British children from earliest age when nannies put their little charges on rocking horses to keep them amused. This prepared them for cross-country hunting later in life. Atkinson's pack of hounds, typical of Indian cantonments everywhere, were probably much like those of the 16th Lancers: "a miscellaneous assortment of indescribables, rejoicing in unabbreviated ears and ambiguous genealogy."[2]

Another sport tolerated by the command was infinitely less harmless. Certain British officers soon discovered in Kabul the joys of Afghan women. Black burkhas, tentlike shrouds that covered the Afghan ladies from head to toe—even their eyes were hidden by latticework stitching—were meant to protect them from lustful male eyes. In practice they provided a foolproof disguise, permitting the women to slip into British officers' quarters for their assignations in perfect anonymity. British society in India was once characterized in the popular London magazine *Vanity Fair* as "Duty and Red Tape; Picnics and Adultery," but the British womanizing in Kabul would have political implications and prove more lethal than the fun-loving and doubtless frustrated British officers realized.

As seen by the native Indian sepoy, the situation was an open scandal. Sita Ram had his own simplistic explanation for the behavior of many Afghan women willing to risk the punishment of death for their adulterous behavior. They liked the British officers "because they were fair; they pride themselves in Kabul on being fair, and the whiter a woman's skin is, the more beautiful she is considered to be." Another theory was that Afghan grandees sent their wives to British officers as spies to discover British intentions, although there is little basis for this. Still another theory was that the Afghan ladies in many instances felt neglected by bisexual or homosexually inclined husbands in what was essentially a man's world. Reflecting a native Indian soldier's attitude, Sita Ram philosophized: "How true it is that women are the cause of all evil!" But, whatever accounted for the accommodating nature of many Afghan women, the wages of sin came high in Kabul and, as Sita Ram observed, "more than one officer was stabbed or fired at" by jealous husbands.[3]

Gossip that reached England had Alexander Burnes as one of the prime offenders. He had certainly attracted attention to his menage of dark-eyed damsels during his earlier mission to Kabul. Living in the center of the town amid its narrow, twisting alleys, Burnes's life-style divorced from the cantonment was as well suited to sexual assignations as it was to clandestine meetings with spies and informants. Mohan Lal, however, loyally denied such allegations against his friend and chief. In his memoir Mohan Lal claimed that Burnes and the other officers sharing his bachelor establishment—Burnes's newly arrived brother, Lieutenant Charles Burnes; his military secretary, Captain William Broadfoot; and, for a while, political officer Lieutenant Robert Leech—had no need to cuckold Afghan men to find their pleasure, since they had brought with them from India Kashmiri girls, thinly disguised as servants. But whether Burnes and his housemates maintained an imported zenana of Kashmiri women or loved off the land was a fine distinction for Afghans to make in the face of the rampant rumors implicating him.

Mohan Lal may have tried to spare Burnes's reputation by dampening exaggerated rumors about his personal life, but in describing the widespread misconduct of other British officers blamed on his leniency, Mohan Lal condemned his friend in an even more telling fashion: as political officer, Burnes had failed to correct a serious situation imperiling the entire cantonment. His handling of Afghan protests was insensitive and unfair;

he invariably took the side of his fellow officers and dismissed the complaints of Afghan chiefs who had been cuckolded by them. Burnes's excuse, "I am hardly to blame because I have no responsibility [i.e., authority]," was not convincing.

It may have been easy for British officers to rationalize their behavior in Kabul—and indeed they had been without women for a long time. But Burnes certainly knew Afghan mores and the dangers of adultery in that society. Moreover, he was aware that he, personally, was being blamed for the scandal by the Afghans.

Most dangerous of all, Burnes by his actions had made a blood enemy of one of Kabul's most influential chiefs, Abdullah Khan, head of the Achakzai clan. Abdullah already bore a grudge against Burnes for other reasons, but after Abdullah Khan's favorite concubine had been lured to the bed of an English officer and Burnes refused to do anything about it, the wrath of the Achakzai chief exploded; he declared a blood feud against Burnes, which demanded satisfaction by death. Other similar cases, including one involving Abdullah Khan's brother, whose fiancée had been stolen by an English officer, added to the smoldering anger of the Achakzais. Burnes now embodied all they hated about British rule; moreover, this was an issue around which chieftains of other clans could rally as well.

Afghan men did not take kindly to their womenfolk being tampered with by the "cursed Kaffirs," but they were upset in a different way by the sudden arrival of British wives. To the Afghan, this signified a British intention to settle down for a long time in their country. What had been billed as a temporary expedition to seat Shah Shuja safely on his throne now took on the trappings of a permanent occupation.

Toward the end of 1839 Macnaghten began the flow of British wives to Kabul when he had his wife escorted from Calcutta. Social life in the cantonment then took on even more luster. Band concerts, occasions for dressing up in the evening to promenade within the cantonment, and the inevitable amateur theatricals were now organized to help distract the officers from the grimmer side of duty. The prototype of the behind-stage prompter particularly fascinated George Atkinson in *Curry & Rice:* "Weep," shouts the prompter in an amateur theatrical to a young soldier whose lackluster female impersonation had infuriated him. "Confound it, can't you weep?"[4] roared the prompter again, this time so loud that the whole audience heard and burst into laughter at the best performance of the play.

As wives arrived, more servants from India came to swell the ranks of the already burdensome camp followers. Lady Macnaghten brought much of her Calcutta household so that as wife of the envoy she could properly hold court in her residency bungalow. She brought with her jewels and finery even though her audience of less than a score of fellow officers' wives was too small to make it really worthwhile.

Eldred Pottinger, as he was passing through Kabul en route to Kohistan in the north, where he had been posted as political officer, noticed that the exposed location of the Macnaghten house, adjoining but outside the cantonment perimeter, made the garrison vulnerable to attack. Later events would prove Pottinger's observation to be an accurate one, but for the moment the British seemed more intent on reproducing in miniature the kind of cantonment they had been used to in the peaceful garrison towns of India than on securing their position. There was some logic to the Company approach, even if it did not prove appropriate under these circumstances. Used to being surrounded by overwhelming native populations where it would have done little good to isolate themselves in fortified bastions, they relied on an aura of invincibility—in reality, bluff—to control their subjects. But the warlike Afghans were quite a different people and, as it would turn out, the British leaders in Kabul were indifferent bluffers.

Second in rank among the wives was Brigadier Sale's wife, Florentia, who arrived in early 1840 to join the colony of wives—several with children. She shared quarters assigned to them, "the best and most commodious" in the cantonment, with her twenty-year-old daughter Alexandrina, who was about to marry Lieutenant (Brevet Captain) John Sturt of the Royal Engineers. "Fighting Bob" Sale was at this time second in command of the Kabul force, but Lady Sale's elevated place in society was as much a product of her formidable personality as it was of her husband's rank. She was a remarkable woman.

Florentia Wynch, whose parents and grandparents had been Company civil servants, was born in Madras in 1787. She married Captain Sale, then of the 12th Foot, in 1808 to begin her active life as a soldier's wife. All began tranquilly enough away from India in Mauritius, England, and Ireland, but they returned to India in time for Bob Sale to fight in the First Burma War. Florentia remained in Calcutta with their five children (five others had died in infancy or childhood).

In 1826 the Sales had enjoyed cantonment life together in Agra. As wife of the commanding officer, Florentia had the advantage of status, but she emerged as a personage in her own right, referred to behind her back as "the grenadier in petticoats." Then came the Afghan invasion, which took Bob off again, but now Florentia was reunited with her husband in Kabul, if only briefly, and could try to create some semblance of a home for him on the bleak Afghan plateau. The Sales' forty servants, brought from India, made for a smooth-running household, and favorite pieces of furniture carried from India graced their quarters. Florentia's pride was her garden, where Bob could indulge himself in his favorite hobby, gardening.

While the British officers and their ladies re-created as best they could the kind of lively society they knew in Calcutta, a feeling of unease was beginning to creep in to nag at them. Lieutenant Sturt, in charge of the cantonment public works, brought home rumors heard from his laborers that rebellious tribes were stirring restlessly in the hinterland, and Burnes and Mohan Lal, with their network of provincial agents, were hearing no less disquieting reports revealing the true temper of the times.

Lady Sale, who had sharp eyes and acute ears, conscientiously kept a daily journal in which she recorded everything of consequence, and, being an army wife, she had a good grasp of military matters. She would only occasionally lapse into simple domestic affairs in recording her daily observations. She wrote of such things as quarrels over the rent charged them by brigade headquarters, and the usual gossip heard in any small town was occasionally grist for her mill. On several occasions she found time to rave about the fruits and vegetables in her garden. Never did she make any attempt to muffle her stinging criticism of the bumbling she saw about her.

The marriage of Lady Sale's daughter Alexandria to Lieutenant Sturt was a joyous event in due time to be blessed by news that a child was on the way. Life in the rude cantonment went on and several other children were raised and born in this most unsuitable nursery for British children. Sacred rather than profane love with Afghan women flourished in a few cases. Captain Robert Warburton, an officer of the Bengal Artillery, fell very much in love with a niece of their fugitive adversary, Dost Mohammed, and the two were joined in holy matrimony as Burnes and Macnaghten dutifully witnessed the sacrament. (Their first son became a distinguished Indian Army officer, best known for his service policing the ever-unruly Afghan tribes of the Khyber Pass from 1879 to 1898.)

The British were rapidly learning what it meant to be an alien invader of a Central Asian country far from their bases. Keane's campaign had been blessed with exceptional luck. Had the Bolan Pass been defended, or had there not been advance intelligence betraying the secrets of Ghazni's defense, or if Dost Mohammed had not diverted his main force to Kabul's approach from Peshawar and the Khyber, things could have gone very differently.

British luck seemed to hold during the initial phases of their occupation as well despite Shah Shuja's growing unpopularity and conspicuous misrule. Lulled into a false sense of well-being, the Company planned to withdraw from Kabul the entire Bombay Army contingent and a few units of the Bengal Brigade as well. With Kabul and Kandahar under British control and Dost Mohammed a fugitive in the Hindu Kush, it seemed safe to dissolve the large Army of the Indus and replace it with smaller garrison forces. While the Company had planned to leave no more than ten thousand men, a force considered adequate to preserve Shah Shuja's position in Kabul if not to police the remoter parts of the country, it soon became apparent that the king could not survive for long without British forces to maintain the garrisons in two other principal cities, Jalalabad and Kandahar, as well as in subsidiary outposts required to keep open the supply lines. One such was Quetta, south of Kandahar, required to protect the Bolan Pass; another was Ghazni, which had to be garrisoned to keep the route between Kandahar and Kabul open.

The Bombay Army division under General Wiltshire began its march home by way of the Bolan Pass on September 18, 1839. It had been ordered to take time to mount a punitive campaign en route against the Baluchis, whose chief, Mehrab Khan, was suspected of treachery. The Baluchis were not the only troublemakers; the Ghilzye tribes, despite a generous subsidy given them, were not reliable and could pose difficulties for elements of the Bengal Army retiring by way of Jalalabad and the Khyber Pass. There was, in fact, ferment spreading throughout the country.

But it was not only Afghanistan that worried the British; events to the north, reminders that it had been the specter of a Russian threat that had propelled the British into Afghanistan in the first place, were of growing concern as well. Less than three months after their triumphant entry into Kabul, the British received disturbing news that the Russians from Orenburg were advancing on Khiva, the strongest of the Transcaspian khanates!

Chapter 17

FRAYING AROUND
THE EDGES

I T WAS IN OCTOBER 1839 THAT ELDRED POTTINGER, STILL IN HERAT AS political agent, became the first to hear that a Russian Army was about to set out from the advance Russian garrison in Orenburg to attack Khiva. The British march to Kabul was to be matched by a Russian move against the chronically troublesome khan of Khiva, who preyed on Russian travelers and interfered with Russian trade ambitions in Central Asia. More important, this action was meant to serve notice on the British that Central Asia was a Russian sphere of influence. Auckland's Simla Manifesto, launching the British invasion of Afghanistan, had particularly caught the czar's attention with a phrase justifying the expedition as an effort "to give the name and just influence of the British Government its proper footing among the nations of Central Asia."[1]

The Russian blueprint for action south of the Aral Sea had been drawn up by a special commission appointed by Czar Nicholas I to study the problem. Its recommendations, submitted on March 24, 1839, called for an expedition against Khiva to be launched under cover of conducting a scientific study of the Aral Sea, but the timing of the operation would depend on how the British fared in Afghanistan. Assuming a successful expedition, a trustworthy Kazakh sultan would be installed in Khiva as ruler with the understanding that Russian slaves would be released and Russian trade favored.[2]

General Perovski, governor of Orenburg, issued a proclamation on November 26, 1839, as his army was about to depart, giving the reasons for the expedition. He did not hide behind any subterfuge of scientific inquiry, but forthrightly announced his intention to establish "the strong influence of Russia in the neighboring khanates "for reasons of trade" and above all "to prevent the influence of the East India Company, so dangerous to Russia, from taking root in Central Asia." And, if this was not clear enough, he added that Russia's purpose was to "redress the balance shaken by the British advance on Kabul." Perovski further announced that other Central Asian rulers had to be prevented from joining Khiva "by means of threats and promises of English agents."[3]

Russia asserted a claim to Khiva on the grounds that from the early eighteenth century it had been ruled by khans of the so-called "Little Horde" of the Khirghiz people, tributaries of Russia. Not until the beginning of the nineteenth century did "intruding" Uzbeks dominate Khiva. And, according to St. Petersburg, Russia's geographic proximity to Central Asia gave it a right to monopolize all trade there. Whatever the rationalizations were, at the heart of the matter was political and commercial rivalry between Great Britain and Imperial Russia.

Petrovski's expedition, 5,000 strong, marching through a pitiless land now covered with winter snow, could expect fierce resistance from 500,000 Khivan tribesmen and another 500,000 tributary nomads. It would probably have failed under the best of conditions, but no one anticipated that the winter of 1839 would be one of the worst on record, or foresaw that disease would decimate the ranks to stop the Russians in their tracks before they engaged the enemy. Even before reaching the Ust Urt plateau between the Aral and Caspian seas, the survivers were forced to turn back to Orenburg. This was a debacle of the first magnitude.

Not yet knowing of the Russian military catastrophe, the British in Kabul and Calcutta were alarmed. Macnaghten, overreacting, began talking about sending a British expeditionary force northward beyond the Hindu Kush, possibly all the way to Bokhara, "to meet a Russian attack on Afghanistan." Colonel Stoddart's mistreatment in Bokhara also preyed on his mind as reports filtered in that the capricious emir was cruelly playing with the British envoy, alternating feigned hospitality with gross abuse. Macnaghten did send a detachment as far as Bamiyan, north of Kabul, and dispatched an officer from Herat as envoy to deliver to the khan of Khiva an offer of an alliance.

Auckland, reacting more realistically, dampened Macnaghten's forward-thrusting instincts. The cautious governor general was aware that the Russians were for the moment getting on relatively well with the British in Europe. It was no time to provoke an incident. Still another reason for not entertaining thoughts of any new adventure was the likelihood that Russia would hesitate to stretch its supply lines to risk an invasion against Afghanistan. When news reached Calcutta that the Russian expedition, defeated by the elements, had collapsed, this reasoning was amply vindicated.

London, nonetheless, worried about Russian intentions in Central Asia. Palmerston, always suspicious of the Russians, urged Auckland to give serious thought to the possibility of Khiva succumbing to the czar's pressure to become a Russian dependency. "It seems pretty clear," Palmerston wrote, "sooner or later the cossack and the sepoy will meet in Central Asia,"[4] and fitting policy to prediction, he thought Herat should be made a British outpost and Shah Shuja's control extended beyond the Hindu Kush.

Alexander Burnes thought otherwise. In a revealing letter to a friend he confessed that he could quite understand why Russia would want to free enslaved Russian subjects in Khiva; moreover, he saw grave consequences if the British overcommitted themselves in Afghanistan. "The man who recommends the cantonment of a British or an Indian soldier west of the Indus is an enemy to his country,"[5] he wrote in an outpouring of frankness. But in a letter to another friend a month later, he gloomily recognized that because of the British occupation of Kabul things had probably progressed beyond the point of no return: "England and Russia will divide Asia between them, and the two empires will enlarge like the circles in the water till they are lost in nothing." Because the fugitive Dost Mohammed had been invited to stay in Bokhara by the emir "at the instigation of Russia," Burnes foresaw British occupation of Balkh on the northern edge of Afghanistan by the following May.

Macnaghten's sword-rattling was curbed by the military. The outspoken Nott thought the idea of marching to Bokhara completely mad; the army had no reserves closer than the British Punjab, and the Sikhs by now, following Ranjit Singh's death, were an unreliable ally. In a note to Burnes, Macnaghten groused: "We are supine, whilst our inactivity will probably be the cause of our ruin,"[6] and tried unsuccessfully to talk Burnes into what would have been a useless and dangerous mission to the Russian

Army as it marched toward Khiva. Anyway, the problem disappeared for the time being when Perovski met disaster and turned back. The Russian catastrophe was revealed to the public on March 13, 1840, and the British could breathe a little more easily.

Other problems beset the British in Kabul as news of Dost Mohammed drifted in. From being a guest of the emir of Bokhara, from whom he sought sanctuary, Dost Mohammed had become a virtual prisoner. But he had just escaped and was now inciting the northern tribes, particularly the Uzbeks, to rally to his standard. Just as worrisome, Yar Mohammed in Herat, with predictable ingratitude for British help in lifting the Persian siege, was now intriguing with the Persians in violation of treaty pledges. The devious vizier, who resented the presence of British agents in Herat and dreamed of advancing his own fortunes, secretly invited the Persians to join forces with him to throw the infidel British out of Afghanistan. Macnaghten argued for Draconian measures to keep the Persians from again attacking western Afghanistan, where their influence could menace Shah Shuja's rule and spoil the British position in the country. Auckland, however, vetoed Macnaghten's proposal to take Herat by force and get rid of Yar Mohammed. He instead sought to solve the problem with a carrot rather than a stick by increasing the subsidy being given the double-dealing Yar Mohammed.

The Baluchis were the next to raise the standard of revolt. The British having felt compelled to seize Khelat to chastise the Baluchi chief, Mir Mehrab Khan, and keep the Baluchis from harassing their supply line through the Bolan Pass, made matters worse by killing him in battle. Rather than chastising the Baluchis, Mir Mehrab's death made the tribe even more incorrigible, and the late mir's son, Nasser Khan, led an insurrection.

Charles Masson suddenly appeared in Khelat in April 1840 en route by caravan to Kabul. He was now his own man. "Pudding-headed political agents and arbitrary envoys and ministers" had so exasperated him after the collapse of Burnes's mission to Dost Mohammed that he quit British service and moved to Karachi in Sind. Soon, however, his attraction to Afghanistan and its archeological treasures waiting to be discovered beckoned him.

In Khelat Masson soon heard strange, almost unbelievable stories from the natives about the British political agent there, Lieutenant William Loveday. His "alleged enormities could not have been committed without knowledge of his superiors," wrote Masson to a friend, yet it was inconceivable that they would tolerate them.[7] It was said that Loveday had killed a tribal chieftain with no more justification than that the man had looked at him disrespectfully, and he regularly set his vicious dogs on innocent townfolk.

Masson remembered vividly his first visit to the obviously strange Loveday. The agent bade him sit on the floor while he occupied the only chair in the room. "After all," he said to Masson, "you are used to sitting on the ground." Masson was disgusted by Loveday's recitals of how he had blown rebellious tribesmen from cannons, while Loveday was offended by Masson's frankly expressed opinions on British mismanagement of Afghan affairs. Their meeting was a disaster and Masson vowed not to go near the objectionable man again.

It obviously riled Loveday that Masson avoided him and spent much of his time in Khelat collecting evidence to prove that the late Mir Mehrab Khan may not have been the blackguard the British had made him out to be. While it was true that the khan had been unable to control completely the marauding Baluchis who harassed the unwieldly Army of the Indus as it made its way through the Bolan Pass during the invasion, no serious attack had been launched by them as it might have. Some of the evidence of Mir Mehrab's alleged treachery, Masson thought, may have been forged by rivals to discredit him.

That the British made no effort to recognize their mistake and make amends for the death of Mir Mehrab Khan to his son, who had taken over leadership of the tribe, was in Masson's opinion attributable to the necessity "to preserve unsullied the reputation of Lord Auckland's clique and to conceal their incapacity."[8] Such views were too much for Loveday, who sent off a dispatch branding Masson a Russian spy.

When a vengeful band of some twelve hundred Baluchis attacked Khelat, Masson pitched in to help bolster the town's defenses while Loveday, immobilized by indecision, did nothing. As the siege grew worse, Masson urged Loveday to leave while he could. Despite abundant warnings that treachery was afoot in the town and that the people on whom he relied planned to betray him to the attacking Baluchis, Loveday chose to stay. Both Loveday and Masson, who had also remained behind rather than abandon his countryman, were betrayed and imprisoned in the "Chamber of Blood," locally infamous as the traditional place of executions.

As the Baluchi insurgents rampaged through the countryside they took Masson and Loveday with them in manacles and forced them to bear the taunts and jeers of the people. The two prisoners sent frantic messages by runners they bribed to Captain Bean, the British agent in Quetta, describing their predicament. Masson by chance discovered at this time that Loveday had earlier denounced him to Bean, who in turn reported to Macnaghten: "The mystery of Mr. Masson's appearance at Khelat at the period of the present outbreak, combined with his clandestine residence at that place, has given rise to suspicions in my mind."

Masson was released by the Baluchi insurgents to carry their demands to the British garrison in Quetta, while Loveday was kept as a hostage. But Masson's ordeal was not over. Captain Bean incarcerated him on orders from Macnaghten, who believed the malicious charges. The prisoner's appeal to the unsympathetic Macnaghten and the governor general's office was given little consideration.

In the meantime, Loveday's plight was daily growing worse at the hands of the Baluchis. Nasser Khan kept the British agent chained to a camel's pannier. The sun cooked his near-naked body, while his chains cut cruelly into his flesh with every lurch of the beast. When a British rescue force from Kandahar approached Khelat, the hapless Loveday was cut down by the tribesmen before they fled. His would-be rescuers found his head severed from his still-warm body. Loveday's intemperate behavior, in some ways comparable with Burnes's misconduct while at Dost Mohammed's court, had consequences far greater than he or his superiors ever seemed to realize. Having no other evidence on which to draw conclusions, Afghan tribesmen considered the actions of a lone British resident to embody the policies and actions of his nation.

Masson was finally cleared of the ridiculous charges against him and released in January 1841, but by this time his plan to proceed to Kabul was out of the question. Having looked on with dismay at the comportment of Burnes during his last mission to Dost Mohammed, and now Loveday's, Masson returned to England an angry man, more determined than ever to publish a memoir criticizing official policy and practices in Afghanistan.

A new threat to the British now loomed in the Punjab as it became obvious that succession to the late Ranjit Singh, who had died as the Army of the Indus crossed into Afghanistan, could not be easily resolved. The Punjab, until now a reasonably reliable and stable ally on India's northwest frontier, had lapsed into chaos. It was rapidly disintegrating as rival factions fought for power in bloody plots and counterplots. The British now missed the old Lion of the Punjab.

It was unfortunate that Auckland, on advice of Macnaghten and Wade, had relied so heavily on this all-too-mortal leader whose days had obviously been numbered even as they reached agreement with him on Afghanistan and whose lineal successor was a fool. As events in the Punjab unfolded, it became obvious that the great buffer would crumble unless the British stepped in and moved their own Indian border up to the Indus. As India's most revered emperor, Akbar the Great, once said, "The Indus is the moat of Agra." The Indus now seemed to be the moat of Calcutta, where the Government of India followed the chaotic events in the Punjab with dismay.

What emerged in the wake of the great Sikh's death was a dramatic validation of Burnes's original conclusions that an independent Punjab would not endure his death, hence the nettlesome issue of Peshawar need not have prejudiced negotiations with Dost Mohammed. With the Punjab in disarray, Auckland's strategy was going badly awry.

Chapter 18

TURMOIL
IN THE PUNJAB;
DANGER BEYOND THE
HINDU KUSH

O<small>N JUNE 27, 1839, AS THE BRITISH ARMY OF THE INDUS WAS STILL</small>
struggling toward Kabul, Ranjit Singh's corpse was placed on a sandlewood
funeral pyre designed like a ship with sails of silk and brocade. His principal
wife, three lesser wives and seven slave girls leaped into the fire with their
late master to perish according to the cruel ritual of sati. The ashes had
hardly cooled before a power struggle began among the several rivals for
the Punjab throne. The drama of succession was one of intrigue, murder
and mayhem, with plots as ornate as they were implausible—and confusing.[1]

This incredible story is a complicated one featuring a myriad of players,
a few with lead parts but most only spear carriers—in the literal sense of
the stage-jargon phrase. Basically, however, it was a three-cornered contest
between Ranjit Singh's Sikh heirs, by and large a feckless lot, the Sikh
Army, or Khalsa, and Gulab Singh, the Hindu Dogra rajah of the tributary

state of Jammu, who, with his brother Dhyan Singh, had long been influential at Ranjit Singh's court.*

On his deathbed Ranjit Singh named his only legitimate biological son, Kharak Singh, as his successor. Kharak Singh was a dolt and an opium addict, quite incapable of ruling the Sikhs—nor would he for very long. Before dying, Ranjit Singh had also insisted that Rajah Dhyan Singh be made prime minister. He and his brother Gulab, as leaders of the Dogras, had to be placated if the Punjab was to remain unified, but with Ranjit Singh gone, this created a Dogra power block rivaling the Sikhs.

Court intrigues became even more elaborate as plot and counterplot unfolded. Kharak Singh was deposed in a palace coup engineered by the Dogra leader, Dhyan Singh, and replaced on the throne by the maharajah's son, Nao Nihal Singh. Gradually poisoned by his enemies, Kharak Singh suffered a lingering and painful death. On November 5, 1840, the wretched man died, but his ruling son did not himself live out that day.

The fateful day had begun normally enough as Kharak Singh was placed on his funeral pyre and cremated with one of his wives and eleven slave girls. (Lord Auckland's sister, Emily, could not resist a catty comment when she heard the news in Calcutta: "I fancy Kharak's wives found him rather a bore, for only one of them thought it necessary to burn herself."[2]) But Nihal Singh, walking hand in hand with a friend, was felled by falling masonry when an archway under which they strolled suddenly collapsed. The friend was killed instantly by the stone, while the injured young maharajah was rushed into the palace by Dhyan Singh for first aid; he died almost immediately. But was it an accident? More probably, Dhyan Singh had seized this opportunity to have Nao Nihal Singh murdered while being attended for his injuries.[3] This seemed to be one more move in the Dogra's master plan for manipulating succession in order to achieve power himself.

During his very brief reign as maharajah, Nao Nihal Singh had not been helpful to the British. In collaboration with the Khalsa military brotherhood, he had managed to evade most of the terms of the Tripartite Treaty, which called for Sikh cooperation in the British occupation of Afghanistan. Not only had Sikh troops not been deployed in sufficient strength on the northwest frontier to protect the supply line to Kabul by way of the Khyber Pass, but they were providing haven for certain of the Afghan Ghilzye chieftains hostile to the British and Shah Shuja. The British had

*The Dogras, or Hill Rajputs as they are sometimes known, of the principalities of Jammu and Kashmir are probably the descendants of the Central Asian invaders of the Indian subcontinent in the second millennium B.C. While some Dogras were converted to Islam and some to Sikhism, most are Hindus. In this context they are any of the non-Sikh Dogras of Jammu.

also uncovered secret correspondence between the Sikh court and other tribal enemies in Afghanistan.

Macnaghten was frustrated by the Sikh problem. In his correspondence with Calcutta he railed at Sikh intransigence. "The plot is thickening," he complained in April, "and we shall find ourselves in a very awkward predicament unless we adopt measures for macadamizing [i.e., making more reliable] the road through the Punjaub."[4] Probably on the basis of intelligence provided the British by the American mercenary Alexander Gardner, who was close to the Dogra faction of the Lahore court, Macnaghten was convinced that the Dogra leaders were behind the increasing dissidence in Afghanistan.[5] When Sher Singh became maharajah after Nao Nihal Singh's death, Macnaghten recommended dissolving the Tripartite Treaty binding the Punjab to Shah Shuja and the British, since it had ceased to have any meaning.

It was becoming obvious that a British conflict with the Sikhs at some point was inevitable. In the meantime, the leaders of the Punjab, struggling for power, continued to war among themselves. It was a moot point whether Khalsa antagonism or general chaos was worse from the British point of view.

In the kaleidoscopic and violent turnover of Punjab leadership following Nao Nihal Singh's sudden death, the eldest of the surviving Sikh princes, Sher Singh, had but the flimsiest claim to the throne of Lahore since he was not a biological son of Ranjit Singh. Confusing the picture further, the loyalties of the Dogra kingmakers were ambiguous; the Dogra clan leader, Gulab Singh, backed Maharani Chand Kaur, mother of the now-dead Nao Nihal Singh. Yet Gulab's brother, the powerful Prime Minister Dhyan Singh, declared himself in favor of Sher Singh. While the maharani held possession of the royal palace in Lahore and the national treasury, including the famous Koh-i-noor, Sher Singh proclaimed himself maharajah and prepared to march on Lahore to take his prize. Gulab stayed with the maharani—and the treasures of the kingdom—while his brother, Dhyan, remained in the Dogra mountain stronghold at Jammu supporting Sher Singh's troop buildup in preparation for the contest.

In fact, however, the split in the allegiances of the two Dogra brothers was an illusion. This was but a tactical device to ensure that Dogra power survived no matter who won the struggle for succession. Dhyan Singh and Gulab Singh's long-range strategy was still to establish Dogra supremacy in the Punjab; by dividing the Sikhs they hoped to seize the reins of government themselves.

With Nao Nihal Singh's death the British saw all pretense of legitimacy evaporate. Lord Auckland, on Macnaghten's advice, declared the Tripartite Treaty with the Sikhs and Shah Shuja at an end. This was formal recognition of what had become painfully apparent: the kingdom of Lahore would henceforth be more a trial than a tribute to British power, and would certainly gravely prejudice the British position in Afghanistan.

Alexander Gardner, who had cast his lot with the maharani in Lahore, was given command of the 3,000-man garrison of mainly Dogra troops headed by Gulab Singh and entrusted with the defense of Lahore and the maharani. But despite the maharani's control of Lahore's massive citadel, the coming contest was weighted in favor of Sher Singh, who had raised an impressive army of 150,000 men.

Leading his army, Sher Singh advanced on Lahore at dawn on January 13, 1841. Gardner heard a tremendous roar issue forth from the Khalsa army as Sher Singh planted his standard on a hill outside the main city gate. The American remembered a deafening salute that lasted for more than an hour marking Sher Singh's self-enthronement and signifying obeisance by the commanding officers of the Sikh Army. Here unfolding were tableaux of medieval battle about to be joined.

The maharani cowered in her chambers, sick with terror, while Gardner prepared Lahore's flimsy defenses to meet the Khalsa horde poised to attack. As usual, treachery was the real enemy of the defenders: disloyal soldiers let Sher Singh's soldiers into the city gates, permitting them to mount their attack on the citadel itself at close range. Gardner described the predicament: "Destruction stared us in the face . . . two heavy siege trains of 40 guns each were laid against the fort, while 800 horse artillery pieces were drawn up on the broad road immediately in front of us."

Gardner was in despair; the situation seemed hopeless for the defenders of the fort. As he peeked through a chink in the Hazuri Bagh gate he saw the fort surrounded by a "sea of human heads." In nearer focus he saw fourteen guns placed within twenty yards and pointed straight at the gate: "I had not time to warn my artillerymen to clear out of the way when down came the gates over our party, torn to shreds by the simultaneous discharge of all fourteen guns." The grim picture was described in all its horror by the American: "Seventeen of my party were blown to pieces, parts of the bodies flying over me. When I had wiped the blood and brains from my face, I saw only one little trembling *khasi* [soldier]."

Whether it was the very hopelessness of the situation or the instinctive reaction of a professional soldier at bay, Gardner sprang into action. He hurriedly asked the surviving soldier for a portfire with which to fire the cannons. Gardner recalled: "The soldier just had time to give it to me and I had crept under my two guns when with a wild yell some 300 Akalis [Sikh zealots] swept up the Hazuri Bagh [gardens] and crowded into the gate." The Akalis "were packed as close as fish." Just as the crowd was rushing in, their swords high in the air, Gardner managed to fire his guns and literally blew the Akalis into the air. Gardner and three artillerymen, who were still alive, reloaded. "Our next discharge," the American remembered vividly, "swept away the hostile artillerymen who were still at the fourteen guns outside and who had remained paralyzed by the destruction of the Akalis."[6]

The shock of Gardner's carnage caused Sher Singh and his force to draw back. The Dogra defenders on the parapets "seemed that day not to miss" as they peppered the fleeing Sikhs. No less than 2,800 soldiers, 200 artillerymen and 180 horses lay dead on the field of battle.

But Sher Singh's fallback did not spare the defenders of the fort from a tremendous pounding by expert Sikh artillery as soon as it had regrouped. The walls of the fort and palace were being reduced to rubble; the defenders could not hold out long.

Dhyan Singh, the Dogra prime minister of the kingdom, who had been biding his time in the northern principality of Jammu while fighting raged in Lahore, suddenly appeared on the scene. With both sides having sustained heavy losses, he judged that this was the time to mediate a peace between the new maharajah, Sher Singh, and Maharani Chand Kaur, who had tried but could not expect to defend her throne against the usurper. Having remained loyal to Maharani Chand Kaur during the siege, Gulab Singh had earned the right to speak for her, while his brother Dhyan Singh, in fact his ally, pretended to be an impartial arbitrator. The two Dogra brothers thus carried out a clever charade of negotiating while they manipulated and controlled the settlement to their advantage.

The agreement specified that Chand Kaur, having assumed the role of ruling maharani upon her son Nao Nihal Singh's death, could remain as titular head of state—a ceremonial queen mother—but Sher Singh, the usurper, would reign as maharajah. The real power behind the scenes would be shared by the Dogra brothers on one side and the leadership of the Sikh Army on the other in an implicit but uneasy partnership.

The first order of business was to divide the treasury. During the fighting Ghulab Singh had shrewdly taken possession of the Koh-i-noor for "safekeeping" and now brought the famous jewel to the table to use as a bargaining chip with the new monarch, Sher Singh. Gardner, a witness, described Gulab's masterful negotiations: "He presented the Koh-i-noor to the reigning monarch, and took credit for saving the royal property."[7] But for his services Gulab insisted on being given a charter to an enormous tract of land. And, not satisfied with this, he walked off with the royal coffers as well—hardly an equitable division, but a commentary on the strength of the Dogra faction in the new scheme of things.

As the weeks went by Sher Singh proved to be no improvement on the earlier maharajahs who had established fleeting claims to power. He spent these critical early days of his reign in unbridled debauchery, while the victorious Sikh Khalsa got more and more out of hand. Nor could the foreign mercenary officers control the Sikh soldiers, who ran riot through the city, plundering and attacking those whom they considered enemies. Responsible officers who tried to interfere were shot on the spot.

The situation was rapidly deteriorating in Lahore, but Lord Auckland, probably wisely, was unwilling to do anything that might risk war with the Sikh Army. It was no time to become more involved in the Punjab morass with problems looming in Afghanistan.

Maharani Chand Kaur was so depressed by her loss of status and her lack of any real authority that she wrote the British secretly, inviting them to occupy the Punjab. She paid dearly for her treachery, however, when her slave girls dropped a great flagstone on her, killing her instantly as she was luxuriating in her bath. It seemed likely that Dhyan Singh had bribed the girls to carry out this dark deed in behalf of Maharajah Sher Singh. He then had the tongues of the slave girls cut out before they were executed, giving rise to rumors that he feared their testimony would implicate him in the murder plot. Certainly, Dhyan Singh was the one who stood to gain the most by Chand Kaur's death; by this act he was one step closer to achieving his goal of placing his son on the throne.

AS MUCH AS SIKH PROBLEMS ON HIS EASTERN FLANK TROUBLED MAC-naghten in Kabul, he felt even more threatened by events to the north. Campaigning in the Hindu Kush, Dost Mohammed posed a serious threat as he tried to foment rebellion against Shah Shuja, and the mad Nasrullah, emir of Bokhara, seemed no closer to releasing his British hostage, Colonel Charles Stoddart.

Alexander Burnes had written of Bokhara following his visit there in 1832: "I cannot concur with the Arabian geographers, who describe it as the paradise of the world." Nor could Stoddart as he languished there. One of those who worried most about Stoddart's fate was Captain Arthur Conolly, Macnaghten's cousin and a zealous Bengal cavalry officer whose obsession was Central Asia. It was Conolly who first referred to British-Russian rivalry in Central Asia as "the Great Game." Determined to visit Khiva and Bokhara to press the British empire's cause and to rescue Stoddart, he used his memorable phrase in a letter written during the summer of 1840: "We are on the eve of stirring times; but if we play the great game that is before us, the results will be incalculably beneficial to us and to the tribes whose destinies may change from turmoil, violence, ignorance and poverty to peace, enlightenment and varied happiness."[8] Stirring times indeed lay ahead, but they would hardly prove beneficial.

By this time Conolly was no stranger to exotic travel. In October 1829, after home leave in England, he had set out from Moscow, determined to return to his post in India by way of the Turkoman Desert—resolutely setting his face "toward Asia," as he put it. Unconvincingly disguised as an Indian merchant, the young romantic and his native traveling guide, Seyyid Keramat Ali, had finally made their way to Herat in 1830 after a frightening encounter with Turkoman slave-dealing bandits. From Herat Conolly traveled on to India through the Bolan Pass and presented to the then governor general, Lord Bentinck, a report describing how an overland invasion of India from Central Asia could be mounted by the Russians. But he was really more interested in some sort of grand antislavery crusade in Central Asia than in simply stopping a Russian advance. The slave trade, which had almost claimed him as a victim in Turkestan, incensed him, and with rare understanding among the British he saw "under what strong provocation Russia was labouring and how impossible it was, with any show of reason and justice, to deny her the right to push forward to the rescue of the enslaved people."9

Assigned to Cawnpore (Kanpur) in north central India, Conolly began a correspondence with Alexander Burnes, whose recent trip to Bokhara had excited him. If Conolly felt any jealousy because his owns travels had not earned him the same fame, he did not betray it. He was, at least, rewarded for his daring travels by being assigned to the Political Department, where his demonstrated talents could best be put to use.

Conolly's career was briefly interrupted when a tragedy of the heart struck. He wooed a high-born lady in India, daughter of a senior Government of India official, and in 1838 followed her home to England with every intention of wedding her. But, alas, something went wrong with the romance and their betrothal came to a sad, sudden end. Conolly tried to convince himself that "with God's comfort, he should not fail to find happiness in a single life."10 In practice that would mean pursuing his passion for Central Asia.

When the British were preparing to invade Afghanistan in 1839, Conolly set his sights a notch higher, urging Whitehall to send an envoy— namely himself—to Khiva, Bokhara and Kokand. There he would try to reach trade agreements, convince the rapacious natives to stop their slaving and spread the Gospel of Christ—an ambitious plan of action. Back in India by the end of 1839, Conolly next tried to convince Auckland that he should send him to the Central Asian khanates. But Afghanistan was by this time the government of India's focus, so in the spring of 1840 Conolly had to be satisfied with an assignment in Kabul, where the Hindu Kush still separated him from his goal. That Macnaghten was his cousin gave him hope, at least, that he could still talk the Company into sending him on to Khiva and Bokhara. "God," he was convinced, "seems now to be breaking up all the barriers of the long-closed East for the introduction of Christian knowledge and peace."[11]

If God was on Conolly's side, Alexander Burnes was not. He considered it folly to provoke Russia in Central Asia when it was by no means certain that Afghanistan itself could be controlled, or even the Punjab, closer to home. Burnes scoffed at Conolly's idea of "purifying Tartary." And if Russia were to be kept at bay, it should be done in the chanceries of London and St. Petersburg, not by trying to convince the "barbarous hordes" of Central Asia to give up slavery in the hope that it would eliminate the czar's need to intervene.

When intelligence of General Perovski's planned expedition to Khiva reached the British, Royal Artilleryman Captain James Abbot was dispatched to Khiva, arriving there in January 1840 in an effort to convince the khan of Khiva to release the Russian slaves, removing any pretext for the impending Russian invasion. The khan did, in fact, agree to release the Russians if Perovski's expedition were called off, but the situation was changed when the Russian expeditionary force foundered in the desert before reaching Khiva. Anyway, Abbot had been unable to reach the retreating Russians to transmit the khan's terms. This was just as well, since the British captain had exceeded his instructions by promising the khan a defensive treaty with Britain if he would resist Russian aggression. Poor Abbot was captured by Turkoman tribesmen and nearly killed before he could escape. His mission had been anything but a success.

Burnes was scathing in his assessment of Abbot's mission, describing it as "the most unhappy step taken during the campaign." Abbot's actions in Khiva, Burnes believed, placed the British "in a position far more equivocal than Russia had been placed in by Vitkevich being here [Kabul]." By now Burnes was convinced that the British had no business in Khiva and Bokhara.[12]

Lieutenant Richmond Shakespear was nonetheless sent to Khiva in June 1840 to set right Abbot's misrepresentation, which had infuriated the Russians, and to attempt to get the Russian slaves released. He accomplished single-handedly what General Perovski and his army had failed to do; he negotiated the release of some four hundred Russian prisoners and personally escorted them safely to Orenburg. As could have been foreseen, the Russians were anything but grateful for Shakespear's accomplishment; it was humiliating to have the British intervene in Russian affairs, even if it had been to Russia's benefit, and it was worrisome that their British rivals were in cordial contact with the khan of Khiva, particularly when viewed against the backdrop of the British presence in Afghanistan.

While all this was going on, Conolly fidgeted enviously in Kabul, trying to promote his own mission to Central Asia. But Burnes continued to oppose any such mission. He wrote sarcastically to a colleague, Dr. Lord, that his "flighty" friend would "regenerate Toorkistan, dismiss all the slaves, and look upon our advent as a design of Providence to spread Christianity . . . yes, with the wand of Prospero!!!"[13]

When startling news reached the British that under duress Stoddart had embraced Islam and been humiliated by a public circumcision ceremony, Conolly's religious sensibilities were deeply offended. No greater calamity could befall a British officer and fellow Christian soldier. Burnes, however, was still against any idea of a rescue mission and wrote that if Conolly went to Bokhara to seek Stoddart's release, he will simply "stand a fair chance of keeping Stoddart company."

In drinking a toast to the unfortunate Stoddart's health during a party at the officers' mess in Kabul one evening, Burnes sneered at the prospect of "our gallant and unfortunate countryman being released by *Baron Bokhara.*" This snide reference, delivered with emphasis as noted, was humiliating to Conolly, who wrote his friend Rawlinson: "How very much English gentlemen let themselves down by these vulgar outbreaks." But by August 1840, in another letter to Rawlinson, Conolly could rejoice: "Hip, hip Hurray! I do believe that I am going [to Bokhara] now!"[14]

Burnes may have been ungracious, but he was right. It was now evident that the British would have difficulty sustaining themselves in Kabul, much less being able to cross the Hindu Kush and the cruel deserts of Turkestan. Now Conolly wanted to rescue Stoddart single-handedly! It was all very frustrating for Burnes to realize that as Macnaghten's deputy, his opinions carried little weight. He could well wonder what good he was doing in Kabul.

Conolly was indeed ordered to Bokhara, with a mission to explain British policy in Afghanistan to the emir, express the British desire to establish closer relations with his country and press for the release of Stoddart. With premonitions of death, Conolly made one last gesture toward his unrequited love before leaving when he wrote Thomas Robertson, lieutenant governor of the Northwest Frontier Provinces, asking him to assure his ex-fiancée that if he met death in Tartary, it had not been courted "in consequence of his disappointed love for her." "Explain to her," he added, "the cause I go upon is one which every man must be proud and eager to peril his life for." Then, in a poignant farewell, he hoped she would find "the best gifts on earth [to] make her eternally happy in heaven where all separations and disquietudes will be healed."[15]

On his journey Conolly was accompanied by Shah Shuja's appointed envoy to Khiva, a "scrubby-looking, sallow little man with a scant beard

and a restless eye, which seems to indicate all the disposition of intrigue."
Also in the party was the Khivan ambassador to Kabul, returning home.
Escorted by a detachment under Brigadier Dennie being sent to reinforce
the garrison at Bamiyan, Conolly at last saw the Hindu Kush, an object
of his dreams. From Bamiyan Conolly and his party struck out northward
alone for Merv (Mary), entrepôt for slave trading, where he blanched at
sights in the slave market "enough to shame and sicken the coarsest heart."
There he heard bazaar talk that Shakespear's successful mission to obtain
the release of Russian slaves in Khiva was but a harbinger of a British
invasion of all Central Asia as "deliverers of all who are in bondage."

Conolly reached Khiva in early 1841, but the khan, exuberant over the
failure of the Russian invasion, was unwilling to forswear future slaving.
The next stop was Kokand, where a letter from Stoddart awaited him,
inviting him to Bokhara in behalf of the emir—and written on his orders.
Only after entering Bokhara on November 10, 1841, by which time it was
too late, did Conolly realize that "The Khan [emir of Bokhara] caused
Stoddart to invite me here" and "pent us both up here to pay him as a
kidnapper for our release or to die by slow rot."[16] The emir was convinced
that the two Englishmen were advance scouts preceeding a British invasion.

A Russian mission in Bokhara led by Colonel Butenef did what it could
for Stoddart and Conolly despite the rivalry between the two countries.
Faced with the perils of Bokhara, fellow Christian soldiers—albeit from
different sects—could find common cause whatever their official differences. While Stoddard still had some semblance of freedom, Butenef had
housed him in his mission for the added safety this provided, and had pled
his case for release.* Before Conolly arrived, Stoddart would even have
been allowed to leave Bokhara by way of Orenburg under Cossack protection, but he felt that to owe his release from town arrest to the Russians
would be dishonorable.

Without reliable communications with Kabul, Conolly and Stoddart
could not fully realize that their own fate in Bokhara hung on the fortunes
of the British in Afghanistan. As storm clouds gathered there, the emir
looked less kindly on his British "guests." It was becoming apparent to him
that Shah Shuja could not survive without British force to prop him up
and that the British position itself was becoming more precarious as tribal
hostility spread throughout Afghanistan.

*Russian Colonel Butenef had a high regard for Stoddart, whom he described as "a very
clever, well-educated and agreeable man."

Chapter 19

GATHERING CLOUDS

Alexander Burnes the exuberant young lion, fired with ambition by his triumphal visit to London, metamorphosed into Burnes the dispirited cynic in Kabul. The problem was inaction. As Macnaghten's understudy, he knew his lines but had no opportunity to act. He had been considered for a mission to Herat bearing guns and money to buy off the troublesome Saddozai leaders, but this did not appeal to him. Burnes preferred to wait for Macnaghten to return to India, which the envoy had announced he would do, so that he could take his place. Burnes had been promised the job, so he elected to wait out Macnaghten's departure even if it meant more time in limbo.

Time dragged on without Macnaghten leaving, however, and with every day that passed Burnes's discontent grew deeper. He had time to brood about his treatment. It upset him that the British advance to Kabul had earned honors for most everyone but himself. Burnes's craving for recognition was addictive. The fame gained from his epic journey to Bokhara had to be replenished. A life of idleness in Kabul, in which he found himself generally ignored, was starving his ego.

Burnes also had time to worry about an Afghan policy that he now realized was failing. He confided his state of mind on a variety of subjects in correspondence with his good friend Percival Lord, who was now stationed north of Kabul at Bamiyan, advance listening post both for Russian activities in Central Asia and for Dost Mohammed's filibustering in the Hindu Kush. Burnes was concerned by intelligence revealing continuing Russian designs on Khiva and Bokhara, but, as he wrote Lord in November 1839, the proper British response should be to strengthen their position in Afghanistan rather than take provocative steps north of the Oxus, as Macnaghten seemed intent on doing. "We had better look out, seeing the Dost is loose," he wrote. And Herat, he pointed out, was in a fragile position with Yar Mohammed Khan "being tampered with by the Russians."[1]

In December Burnes again unburdened himself in a letter to Lord. He blamed Macnaghten for the obvious fact that things were going wrong. Misjudgment ruled the cantonment, particularly as it pertained to Shah Shuja's prospects. "Sheets of foolscap are written in praise of the Shah's contingent [Shah Shuja's army]," he wrote Lord, and "as God is my judge, I tremble every time I hear of its being employed." Burnes added: "From all this I see that Shah Shuja never can be left without a British army, for his own contingent will never be fit for anything."[2]

By January 1840 Burnes's patience was wearing thin. "I have begun the year with a resolution of making no more suggestions, and of speaking only when spoken to," he wrote Lord. He now blamed Auckland for everything. "Lord Auckland took a step in sending an army into this country contrary to his own judgement and he cares not a sixpence what comes of the policy, so long as he gets out of it,"[3] Burnes complained. Despite Macnaghten's plea for more troops, Auckland replied unrealistically: "It is your duty to rid Afghanistan of troops and leave Shah Shuja to defend himself." Burnes criticized the governor general for trying to conciliate Yar Mohammed in Herat with larger bribes instead of disciplining him for his perfidy.[4]

In his despair, Burnes cynically advised his friend Lord to "be silent, pocket your pay, do nothing but what you are ordered, and you will give satisfaction. They will sacrifice you and me without caring a straw." Burnes accused Auckland of not wanting to hear the truth, so he wrote Lord that he would not be part of a "chiming-in" simply to support the official view. "I can go a good way," confessed Burnes, "but my conscience has not so much stretch as to approve of this dynasty—but mum—let that be between ourselves."[5]

Burnes's confidences were revealing of himself as much as of his views. He was now willing to complain in private but not officially speak his conscience. To do so would be futile, he rationalized, but unmentioned was his fear that as a dissenter he might jeopardize his chances of replacing Macnaghten to become himself all-powerful British proconsul. There could be no glory in naysaying. Better let things drift and fester until he could take the baton.

But would Burnes be chosen after all to replace Macnaghten? Burnes found the suspense maddening. He whiled away the time reading the *Annales* of Tacitus ("his lessons are of practical use"), Horace Walpole's *Letters* ("How inimitable") and *Sir Sidney Smith's Life* ("All great men have more or less charlatanerie"). Revealingly, he quoted Guizot's *Life of Washington* in a letter: "In men who are worthy of the destiny [to govern] all weariness, all sadness is weakness." He questioned his own qualifications: "Am I fit for supreme control? I sometimes think not, but I have never found myself fail in power when unshackled."[6]

For all his discouragement, Burnes's life was very civilized. In the mornings he and a dozen or so other officers who dropped by ate a "Scotch breakfast" of smoked fish, salmon grills, devils and jellies—all imported, of course. They would then chat over imported fine cigars. Burnes often entertained at dinner as well. "I can place before my friends my champagne, Madeira, sherry, port, claret, sauterne, not forgetting a glass of curaçao and maraschino," he bragged. And all the way from Aberdeen came hotchpotch and hermetically sealed salmon. Aside from its professional advantages, Burnes enjoyed living in the heart of town. For a man of his temperament cantonment life would have been stifling.

There was no lack of indications that tribal ferment was rising in the provinces of Afghanistan. Dost Mohammed, having escaped from the clutches of his host-turned-captor, Emir Nasrullah Bahadur of Bokhara, was free to gather around him a resistance force of about six thousand Uzbek tribesmen north of the Hindu Kush. By late August 1840 his tribal partisans had become strong enough to force a detachment of Shah Shuja's 4th Gurkhas to fall back from its vulnerable outpost at a place called Bajgah to the British-commanded garrison at Bamiyan. The Bajgah affair made Macnaghten anxious, but rather than take it as a sign of more profound trouble brewing, he blamed the officer in command of the Gurkhas for losing thirty to forty men in that "awkward business."

The next ominous development was the defection of a regiment of Shah Shuja's native infantry to Dost Mohammed, making it obvious to even the most optimistic British officer that without the continuing presence of British Indian Army units their puppet would be helpless. As Burnes had long believed, the shah's Afghan levies simply could not be trusted. Macnaghten in despair wrote Auckland: "We have just heard that the whole country between [Kabul] and the Oxus [River] is up in favour of Dost Mohammed." The Kohistan area, threatening the small British garrison at Bamiyan and too close for comfort to Kabul itself, was on the verge of revolt. Macnaghten predicted all too accurately: "our attention will probably be distracted by risings in different directions at the same time."[7] Because of the threat, Colonel Dennie was sent to reinforce the now-vulnerable garrison at Bamiyan, arriving there with a relief regiment on September 14. More serious, Kabul city itself would be in danger if Bamiyan fell; the capital then would surely rise against Shah Shuja and the British and be joined by the tribes to the north.

The causes of popular dissatisfaction should have been obvious to the British, but overconfidence blinded them to the seriousness of the problem, while maladministration inflamed the Afghans' natural hatred for infidel foreign rule. It was apparent to most Afghans that despite Shah Shuja's pretense of ruling, the British were in charge, and this rankled. Yet, in an effort to bolster Shah Shuja and present him as a sovereign ruler, the British permitted his administration to abuse his power and mismanage affairs rather than step in to correct the abuses and by so doing advertise their role as the real rulers.

Shah Shuja's vizier, Mullah Shakur, was an incompetent retainer who had come with him from Ludhiana exile; his memory was failing and his abilities, if they ever existed, had atrophied. The feckless old mullah permitted corrupt officials to fleece the merchants and overtax the farmers. And before Macnaghten finally insisted on his ouster, he mischievously spread the word that the British would not allow Shah Shuja to take the reins of power. His whispering campaign helped to discredit Shah Shuja, turn opinion against the British, whom he accused of suppressing the Moslem faith, and drive a wedge between the two. His inept policies also kept grain prices high, causing suffering as well as resentment among the people. Inflated wages were paid by the British for services to the cantonment, luring the farmers from their fields and thus creating further food shortages and higher prices.

Shah Shuja resented his puppet role. He had neither the respect of his people nor that of his British masters. For all the deference shown him by Macnaghten, few other British officials respected him and he knew it. The crusty General Nott was the worst offender in this regard; Macnaghten was particularly upset at his obvious contempt for the royal family. When Nott refused to call on Shah Shuja's son Prince Timur, governor of Kandahar, Macnaghten complained to Lord Auckland: "If such an outrage . . . is to be tolerated and justified, there must be an end to our efforts to make it be believed that Shah Soojah is the King of this country." Apparently unwilling to believe the excesses of Shah Shuja's court, the British envoy added petulantly: "I regret to say, there is a feeling too prevalent amongst the officers against his Majesty. . . . I hope that though they may not be compelled to treat the Royal Family with becoming respect, they will not be permitted to offer them a direct insult with impunity."[8]

Nott's dislike of Prince Timur was understandable. While the general tried to keep order around Kandahar, the corrupt prince fanned the fires of discontent by plundering his people. When Nott caught some of Timur's agents in the act of pillage, he had them flogged publicly—to the joy of the victims but to the outrage of Timur and his father, Shah Shuja.

Symptomatic of the unrest, the militant western Ghilzye tribesmen, living astride the route between Kandahar and Ghazni, erupted in revolt in the spring of 1840. Punitive detachments sent by General Nott succeeded in subduing them temporarily, but it had been a close call, with the fate of Kandahar itself hanging in the balance as ten thousand hostile tribesmen rallied nearby.

Then the Baluchis, intent on avenging the death of their late leader, Mir Mehrab Khan, attacked Quetta and harassed the British convoys, imperiling the southern supply route to India. A British column was ambushed by the Baluchis and wiped out. And in another incident a large supply convoy escorted by some five hundred infantry and two hundred Irregular Horse was decimated when Baluchi mountaineers showered large boulders upon them in a narrow pass.

Stripped of the Bombay Army units, some forty-five hundred men who had left in September 1839, the British garrison in Kabul was inadequate to contend with the rising tide of tribal unrest. It could do little to support the outlying posts now subject to tribal harassment in the north, although it had sent Colonel Dennie to reinforce Bamiyan in the nick of time. As the small garrison tensely awaited an attack by Dost Mohammed, news arrived on September 17 that advance units of his Uzbek cavalry were entering the valley only six miles away. The next day Dennie, at the head of four companies of Gurkhas, two Horse Artillery guns and four hundred Afghan Horse, sallied forth to meet this threat. What Dennie found facing him, however, was not simply a vanguard but Dost's entire army, six thousand strong and made up largely of fierce Uzbek tribesmen vastly outnumbering his own troops!

Dost Mohammed's Uzbek's retreated under Dennie's withering artillery fire and were relentlessly pursued by his cavalry. Dost Mohammed and his son Akbar Khan narrowly escaped by riding hard, but left behind a discouraging number of casualties. Dennie's victory was a tonic to the British in Kabul and a great relief to Macnaghten, whose burden of adversity was resting heavily on his shoulders. He wrote Major Rawlinson: "I can assure you I was beginning to be nervous, and I entertained great apprehensions that Afghanistan was about to be convulsed from one end to the other."9

Burnes's friend Dr. Percival Lord, as political officer at Bamiyan, rushed to take advantage of Dennie's victory by convincing the area's tribal leader, the wali of Kulum, to break with the tribal insurrection. This was a loss for Dost Mohammed but the Afghan leader was resilient; he bragged that he was "like a wooden spoon: you may throw me hither and thither, but I shall not be hurt." He moved his base to the Kohistan area near Kabul, by then in a state of insurrection against the Kabul government.

Brigadier Sale, accompanied by Alexander Burnes, launched a punitive campaign against the Kohistanis, hoping to catch Dost Mohammed in their snare. This was for Burnes a happy respite from inaction. The force handily captured a place called Tutumdrah on September 29, and routed the rebellious Kohistan chieftain, Ali Khan. The only British casualty was Sale's aide, Edward Conolly, who died of a bullet to his heart before he could know the fate of his brother Arthur in Bokhara. Sale, however, had only scattered his adversaries, who survived to fight another day. When the British pursued the Kohistanis, they simply melted away. Burnes was particularly disheartened by the inconclusive results of their campaign against these elusive rebels. With Dost Mohammed at large and the Kohistani tribal force intact, Bamiyan was no longer defensible and the British withdrew the garrison to Kabul, where preparations to resist a siege were stepped up.

Shah Shuja now felt insecure with Dost Mohammed marauding so near the capital. Macnaghten too became fretful. In a fit of petulance he criticized Burnes and Sale for "sitting down" before a fortified position only twenty miles from Kabul, "afraid to attack it" with their two-thousand-man column, and then allowing the enemy to escape. The envoy, at last beginning to awaken to the reality of Shah Shuja's rule, also railed at his performance and was heard to say: "Shah Shuja is an old woman, not fit to rule his people."

The worst blow fell on November 2 in the valley of Parwandara, just north of Kabul. Taking advantage of a poorly conceived British cavalry maneuver, Dost Mohammed rose in his stirrups and exhorted his followers in the name of God and the Prophet to drive the infidel British from the land of the faithful. As he shouted "Follow me or I am a lost man," his cavalry advanced at a gallop so resolutely that the British native troops broke and fled despite the best efforts of their officers to rally them. Dost Mohammed's thundering Uzbek and Kohistani horsemen seemed to have terrified them. Pursued by Dost's saber-wielding horsemen, the fleeing force was badly cut up as its soldiers fled toward the protection of their guns. Political officer Lord, felled by a rifle shot, was finished off by a dagger thrust to his heart. Other British officers, who also found themselves abandoned by their troops, bravely faced the enemy alone but were slain as they fought their overpowering assailants. Only two seriously wounded officers made their way back.

Appalled by what he saw, Burnes on November 3 sent off an urgent dispatch to Macnaghten in Kabul by native runner—one of the intrepid *cossids* used by the British to maintain communications—urging the envoy to recall the badly mangled force to Kabul, where it could at least help defend the capital from what he considered certain attack by Dost Mohammed. Burnes, who had never believed that the British could pacify Afghanistan "at the point of a bayonet," was now even more convinced of this and was finally moved to press his views on Macnaghten.

Macnaghten was taking his evening gallop near the cantonment when Burnes's alarmist message was delivered to him. But even as he contemplated the bad news of Dost Mohammed's victory, the melancholy envoy was astonished to see the emir himself, with only one attendant, suddenly emerge from the gathering dark and ride toward him. This was an eerie coincidence.

Dismounting from his horse, the deposed ruler handed his sword to the startled envoy and kissed his hand in a gesture of surrender. This sudden, unexpected stroke of good fortune just as he was pondering the consequences of Parwandara filled Macnaghten with chivalric impulses. He handed the emir's sword back to him and comforted him with promises of good treatment at the hands of the British. But Dost Mohammed's son, Akbar Khan, was still at large and, as events would soon reveal, the Afghan rebellion was just beginning.

What had caused Dost Mohammed to give himself up just as he won his proudest victory? Perhaps he felt that Parwandara would only provoke the British to redouble their efforts to capture him.* Dost Mohammed probably preferred surrender with honor at a pinnacle of success to an inevitable and humiliating defeat. And the fate of his womenfolk, by that time captured and sent off to the Punjab by the British as hostages, may have worried him. Had he been able to foresee that the British would not

---

*Burnes claimed that Dost Mohammed had given himself up because of a letter he had sent him promising good treatment in exile and a generous stipend.

prove invincible, and that his son, Akbar Khan, would at least for a while savor the fruits of victory, he might have bided his time.

A change in military leadership worsened the fortunes of the British in Afghanistan at this critical period. Sir Willoughby Cotton was in poor health and had to leave. Nott in Kandahar should logically have replaced him, but the undiplomatic, outspoken general was not on good terms with Macnaghten and was in Shah Shuja's bad graces. Instead, Auckland chose Major General William Elphinstone, an old and gout-ridden "Queen's officer" who had arrived in India two years previously and taken command of the Benares Division of the Bengal Army stationed in Meerut near Delhi. While having had no Indian battle experience, Elphie Bey—as Lord Auckland's sister, Emily, affectionately called this old friend of the family—was an amiable soul, liked by his troops. In the best of times he had not been a decisive leader, but now poor health plagued him. Certainly he was not of the caliber of his first cousin Mountstuart Elphinstone, whose distinguished career in India had been well launched by his pioneering mission to Shah Shuja's court in 1809.

When Auckland offered the Kabul post to William Elphinstone in November 1840, the old general had not been enthusiastic, but to the surprise of many he accepted—apparently out of a sense of duty. Auckland had written him: "I hope that you find the bracing hills of Cabul more congenial to your constitution than the hot plains of India"—as if this most savage land in the world was some kind of spa where ailing generals could take the waters.

John Colvin, Auckland's private secretary, cheerfully wrote Macnaghten that Elphinstone was "the best general we have to send you," even if he had seen no real Indian service. The general's passivity appealed to the cautious Auckland, who did not approve of aggressive campaigners in Afghanistan forever straining in their harnesses, itching to take on the tribes. He wanted a conciliatory officer of Elphinstone's quiet temperament. The calamitous selection of Elphinstone to command in Kabul must be blamed on the Horse Guards, Army Headquarters Command in London and arbiter of senior appointments, which was talked into it by Fitzroy Somerset, future Lord Raglan, best remembered for the "Charge of the Light Brigade" fiasco in the Crimean War. Auckland, however, has unfairly borne the blame in most accounts of these events.

The ailing general had good military instincts, but his inherent passivity, aggravated by his weakened constitution, did not permit him to argue strongly with Macnaghten, even on purely military matters.

The Horse Guards must also bear responsibility for sending Brigadier John Shelton to India, but it was Auckland who chose him for second-in-command in Kabul. Shelton, who had lost his right arm in the Peninsular Wars, was a thoroughly unpleasant man. Colvin forewarned Macnaghten that he was known to be something of a tyrant, and when the brigadier arrived in Afghanistan toward the end of 1840, his style did nothing to dispel that reputation. He showed his stripes while bringing up the 44th Queen's Regiment from India through the Khyber Pass, where he drove his men nearly to the breaking point. But Shelton did get results; by his efforts he subdued several hostile forts along the route of march, suffering only nine British casualties.

Any hope that two very different personalities might complement each other was dashed when Elphinstone arrived to take command in April 1841. Shelton took an immediate dislike to his new commander and was painfully obvious in showing his utter contempt for him. Understandably, Elphinstone did not trust such a man. So as 1841 got under way a command whose two most senior officers were barely on speaking terms was unpromising of success.

In the meantime, Auckland was having problems with London. Early in 1841, he received a rebuke from Sir John Hobhouse, chairman of the Court of Directors of the East India Company. Upset that the Bombay contingent had been withdrawn in September 1839, Hobhouse took the economy-minded Auckland to task for having reduced the British garrison too much before Shah Shuja's levies were prepared to shoulder the burden. "We pronounce our decided opinion," he wrote, "that for many years to come, the restored monarchy will have need of a British force, in order to maintain peace in its own territory and prevent aggression from without."[10] Hobhouse with good sense believed that it would be better to abandon Afghanistan altogether and make "a frank confession of complete failure" rather than try to stay on with an inadequate force, as Auckland seemed to favor.

Hobhouse was also distressed by the bad feeling between Macnaghten and Burnes, which revealed itself by their frequently conflicting views on policy. While the chairman tended to side with Macnaghten on most issues, he believed that Shah Shuja had not been controlled tightly enough and thought that more British intervention in the administration of the country was necessary. He wrote Macnaghten: "We do not see how it is possible so to choose the public functionaries and to make such arrangements in Afghanistan as shall conceal the fact that the British are masters of the country."[11]

HERAT WAS A TEST OF BRITISH RESOLVE IN EARLY 1841. THE BRITISH RESIdent there, now Major D'Arcy Todd, tried to bring Yar Mohammed to heel by demanding he cease his intrigues with the Persians and Russians. When Yar Mohammed refused to yield to discipline, even after his British subsidy was slashed, Todd on his own authority broke relations with him and precipitously closed his mission in February.

Todd had hoped that British troops would be dispatched from Kandahar to deal with the recalcitrant vizier of Herat. But this was not the course of action Auckland wanted to take. Todd was instead chastized in a stern note from the governor general, accusing him of taking actions "at variance with all the orders received by him" and "inconsistent with the most obvious dictates of sense and prudence."[12] Despite advice from his commander in chief, Sir Jasper Nicolls, who had replaced Keane in Calcutta, Auckland refused to commit British troops to Herat. The army at its presently reduced strength had all it could handle without adding Herat to its burden.

Despite all that was happening, Macnaghten remained optimistic; Dost Mohammed's surrender had been an intoxicating elixir. Perhaps he just wanted to keep up a good front so as not to spoil his chances of taking up the coveted post of governor of Bombay, which was recently promised him. Or perhaps he simply misjudged the situation. How could he write to London that the Khyberis, who terrorized all who tried to traverse the famous pass, had abandoned brigandage and were now settling down as peaceful merchants? It was not easy to agree with his judgment: "The whole country is as quiet as one of our Indian chiefships."[13] No less guilty of unjustified optimism was Foreign Secretary Palmerston. While campaigning in Tiverton during the general elections of July 1841, he took credit for the "success" of government policy toward Afghanistan, a country "so perfectly tranquilized and so entirely satisfied with our management that Englishmen might travel from one end of it to the other without fear of danger."[14]

General Nott in Kandahar, who now had to keep one eye on Herat in addition to watching his already troublesome command, grumbled ominously: "Unless several regiments be quickly sent, not a man will be left to note the fall of his comrades."[15] And from the farther perspective of London, the redoubtable old Duke of Wellington was convinced that the British position in Central Asia was "precarious and dangerous." But most prophetic of all was Colonel Dennie, now with the 13th Light Infantry in Jalalabad, who wrote with eerie prescience: "You will see: not a soul will reach here from Cabul except one man, who will come to tell us the rest are destroyed!"[16]

PART III

Disaster
and
Retribution

Chapter 20

UPRISING

THE SUMMER OF 1841 WAS FADING; INTIMATIONS OF THE COLD KABUL winter to come could be felt in the autumn air. It was not the weather, however, but the chilling effect of a hostile population that troubled the British. General Nott's punitive campaigns against the western Ghilzye tribes in May and August had been taxing, and Dost Mohammed's son, Akbar Khan, was still stirring up the tribes to the north against Shah Shuja and the British. British forces now found themselves in a policeman's role, contrary to what Auckland wanted. The prospects of Shah Shuja ever being able to control the country without British assistance were becoming dimmer despite Dost Mohammed's surrender. Shah Shuja's public image as a British puppet and his gross mismanagement had alienated the tribes. One must wonder, then, how Macnaghten could have blundered so badly as to cut tribal subsidies at just this time.

General Nott was having trouble enough keeping open the longer route to India by way of Kandahar; now Macnaghten had put at risk the only other supply line, the short route to Peshawar through the Khyber Pass, by depriving the eastern Ghilzye tribe of its agreed-upon allowance—the price of safe passage. Tribal subsidies had long been a way of life in Afghanistan, where central authority—on those rare occasions when there was any—was achieved by tribal federation stuck together with the glue of money. Every Afghan ruler had understood this, but Macnaghten, intimidated by the mounting cost of occupation and probably oversensitive to Auckland's obsession for economy, chose to ignore this time-proven precedent.

Macnaghten had never favored large subsidies to the tribes for another reason: they encouraged the tribes to consider themselves autonomous. He believed that central authority under the shah imposed by force was preferable to tribal federation. It would be more effective, he believed, for the shah to play one tribe against another, relying on their natural feuds and jealousies to keep them from finding common cause against the throne, than simply to buy their allegiances.

London was becoming seriously concerned by the cost of occupying Afghanistan: £1.25 million per year. Talk of total withdrawal from Afghanistan—acknowledging the failure of the enterprise—was being heard in London as early as the spring of 1841. Under such pressure Auckland called his Supreme Council into session in March to discuss the problem. Somehow, the Company's military representatives on the council, never enthusiastic about the Afghan venture, were not included in these deliberations, and Auckland, with his civilian advisers unfettered by military arguments, made the fatal decision to continue the occupation of Afghanistan.

This put Macnaghten in a difficult position. While he had been loud in his insistence that the abandonment of Kabul would be an "atrocity," the ability of the British to remain was diminishing as tribal dissidence grew. Yet Auckland continued to preach economy, which meant denying Macnaghten the wherewithal to survive. Whatever hopes Auckland had had that a bond issue floated in Calcutta would pay for the occupation were dashed when it failed to sell. Macnaghten too was at fault, however; while he had asked the governor general for five additional regiments, including two Queen's regiments, in August, he had allowed himself to be talked into canceling the request by Burnes shortly thereafter. The reason why is not clear.

The eastern Ghilzyes who commanded the rocky gorges between Kabul and Jalalabad on the route to Peshawar were the first to react to the reduction of subsidies. Macnaghten had summoned the chiefs in early October 1841 to break the news that their eighty-thousand-rupee subsidies would be halved. The Ghilzye response was simple and entirely predictable: they savaged the first supply caravan to come along—within ten miles of Kabul. The British found themselves suddenly isolated, their most vital link with India severed.

This was a particularly awkward moment for the Macnaghtens and Elphinstone to be marooned in Kabul. Along with Lady Sale and her daughter, Mrs. Sturt, they had planned to accompany a returning brigade scheduled to leave Kabul with the sick and wounded under Brigadier Sale's command at the end of October. Elphinstone had requested relief because his health could no longer withstand the rigors of Kabul. He suffered from gout, fever and rheumatism, and could scarcely mount his horse without help. He pathetically told one of his officers: "I am unfit for it, done up, body and mind."

If Elphinstone had reached the end of his long career, Macnaghten looked forward to the apogee of his. He was to receive the greatest prize awarded in the India service: the governorship of the Bombay Presidency. The Ghilzye uprising at just this time was an embarrassment since he had confidently predicted tranquillity. In a dispatch to Auckland he wrote: "We are in as prosperous a condition as could have been expected." This misanalysis was particularly galling since Burnes, slated to replace him as envoy, had officially disagreed with him in a definitive assessment written in August. Macnaghten was provoked to send Auckland the snide observation in his dispatch: "Sir Alexander, of course, wishes to prove the contrary, since by doing so, when he succeeds me his failures would thus find excuse and his successes additional credit."[1]

Macnaghten refused to see the symptoms of trouble right under his nose in Kabul. Dr. Metcalfe on one occasion had been forced to flee an Afghan assailant, and Captain Robert Waller narrowly escaped death at the hands of a would-be assassin. A trooper in the Horse Artillery was shot dead and an unwary infantryman had his throat cut in other grisly incidents that told the temper of the times.

A halfhearted attempt to negotiate with the Ghilzyes, not surprisingly, came to nothing since Macnaghten's peacemaker was secretly one of the ringleaders of the revolt. Still, Macnaghten remained optimistic. On October 8 he sent off a dispatch to Auckland assuring the governor general that the Ghilzyes could easily be suppressed and that he fully anticipated being in Bombay by mid-December. "The rascals," he promised, "will be well trounced for their pains."

The trouncer would be Brigadier "Fighting Bob" Sale, whose brigade was ordered to open the road to Jalalabad and Peshawar. The planned return of Sale's brigade to India under the new circumstances was another miscalculation. Macnaghten and Elphinstone were faced with a dilemma: the vital supply line to Peshawar had to be kept open, but Sale's brigade was now needed in Kabul. It is tempting to suspect that Macnaghten and Elphinstone for their own different reasons were so eager to return to India that they glossed over the seriousness of the situation facing Kabul so that Sale could proceed to tame the Ghilzyes and escort them home safely before winter closed the passes to them.

The 35th Native Infantry under Colonel Thomas Monteith, vanguard of Sale's brigade, would lead off to clear the Khoord Kabul Pass, less than ten miles east of Kabul. Accompanying the 35th would be a hundred sappers, crack troops led by a remarkable young officer, Captain George Broadfoot, whose men worshiped him despite—or because of—the iron discipline he enforced. His account of the confusion surrounding Monteith's departure not only betrayed the bankruptcy of Elphinstone's command but also illustrated the icy relationship that existed between the decrepit commander and Macnaghten. Trying to get coherent orders and some estimate of the conditions he could expect so that he could plan his ordnance requirements, Broadfoot found himself shuttling between the two men, each passing the buck to the other.

Poor old Elphinstone confessed that he had no knowledge of what Monteith's column could expect. Exhausted by only a brief conversation with Broadfoot, the general excused himself and sent him off to see Macnaghten. The envoy was equally unhelpful, protesting that he "was no prophet," and testily sent the captain back to Elphinstone. The general could only murmur sadly that he was being treated as a mere cipher. On still another visit to Macnaghten, the envoy snapped at Broadfoot that he need not go at all if he feared the Ghilzyes. Broadfoot was enraged by this slur on his courage and stomped back to Elphinstone, but the old man had by now retired to his sickbed. Bewailing the mistreatment he received from Macnaghten, the general's last pathetic words to a frustrated and disgusted Broadfoot were: "For God's sake clear the passes quickly, that I may get away. . . ." Sale was equally frustrated in trying to requisition new percussion muskets lying unused in the cantonment arsenal, so his troops had to be satisfied with old guns that were no match for the Afghan *jazails*.

George Broadfoot's concerns about the strength of the Ghilzyes was soon borne out. The vanguard 35th under Monteith, which departed Kabul on October 9 with eight hundred men, bumped into a hornet's nest at the Khoord Kabul Pass, suffering heavy casualties as the tribesmen perched high in the jagged defile unmercifully peppered them. To rescue Monteith's men, Sale on October 11, with Her Majesty's 13th Light Infantry regiment, moved up from Boothak at the mouth of the pass, where he had been waiting to be joined by the 37th Infantry. Sale finally forced the Khoord Kabul Pass, but it had been a costly affair. The force suffered sixty-seven casualties, including Sale himself, who took a ball in his left leg.

Sale's brigade had been weakened by the sudden defection of Shah Shuja's cavalry, the *hazir-bash*, or "ever-ready," which was seething with treachery and was anything but ready to fight for the British against their compatriots. When they were sent back to Kabul in disgrace, Lady Sale was moved to quote Sir Walter Scott: " 'At a word it may be understood / They are ready for evil, not good.' "[2] But the others, particularly the men of the 13th, had fought well, scaling the rocks to gain vantage points from which to return Ghilzye fire.

On October 22 the Ghilzyes fell back to a fort in Tezeen, just east of the town of Khoord Kabul, which anchored the pass at its southern terminus. Just as Sale was about to attack in Tezeen, an ideal place in which to corner them and break the back of the uprising, their crafty leader, Khoda Bakhsh, sued for peace. Sale's political officer, Captain George Macgregor, had Sale call off the 13th Regiment, resplendent in their red coats, just as they were ready to charge. The terms of the Ghilzye "surrender" as negotiated by Macgregor were very lenient under the circumstances. Khoda Bakhsh could keep his fort intact and, astonishingly, Macgregor took it upon himself to promise a restoration of their subsidies if the Ghilzyes would police the passes and keep them clear for the British. The fox was back in the chicken coop.

In fact, the Ghilzye surrender had been a trick to avoid Sale's attack at a moment when the tribe was vulnerable, and to give the rest of the Ghilzyes along the route to Jalalabad time to assemble and join the fray. Macnaghten was furious when he learned of Macgregor's trusting treaty, and, indeed, the folly of the political officer's act soon became apparent when Sale's column was viciously attacked on October 26 as it continued on toward Gandamak to clear the route.

Many were sacrificed in the running battle with the treacherous Ghilzyes. But the worst was yet to come. A political fuse cord had been lit by Macgregor's act of appeasement; his renewed promises of subsidies only convinced the Afghans that the British had made a craven purchase of protection rather than fight. It was interpreted as an admission of weakness. The explosion at the end of the cord was about to occur in Kabul.

On October 26, when Sale began his dangerous march to Gandamak, the 37th under Major Griffiths retraced its steps toward Kabul, where it intended to pick up Elphinstone, Macnaghten and his wife, Lady Sale and some invalided soldiers before rejoining Sale's brigade for its march to

Peshawar and on to India. Before Griffiths could reach Kabul, however, the regiment was set upon by the Ghilzyes in the Khoord Kabul Pass and barely made it though to Boothak, where it paused to regroup. The truce negotiated by Macgregor no more protected the 37th than it did the rest of Sale's brigade.

While Sale's force was facing grave problems along the route, cantonment life during the closing days of October 1841 was in turmoil because of preparations being made for the imminent change of command. Eager to take control of political matters, Burnes could hardly wait for Macnaghten to leave; it was still cheerfully assumed that Sale could take care of the troublesome Ghilzyes, so plans for the envoy's departure would not be affected. And on the military side, General Nott was finally going to take supreme command from the departing Elphinstone even if Shah Shuja did not like him. Most everyone in the cantonment looked forward to that change except, perhaps, Shelton, who had wanted the position himself.

Change of command also meant a reshuffling of senior housing assignments. This, of course, would cause a flurry of packing by those leaving, and a good deal of competition for the best houses by those staying. On the eve of her departure Lady Sale was preoccupied with the fate of her garden, so lovingly tended by her husband when he had not been out fighting unruly tribesmen. She prided herself on her sweet peas and geraniums, the envy of the cantonment. "If not cut off by frost," the sweet peas "will give a good crop next month,"[3] she wistfully noted in her diary. Now what would become of her vegetable garden, with its fine cauliflowers, artichokes and turnip radishes; and who would tend the fruit trees imported from Turkestan, which bore such delicious fruit—pears, peaches and Orléans blue plums, unequaled anywhere in the world?

<hr>

DURING THE EVENING OF NOVEMBER 1, ALEXANDER BURNES'S HOUSEHOLD in town was experiencing another kind of turmoil. Burnes had just returned from congratulating Macnaghten on his imminent departure and, with no little cynicism, the "profound tranquility" that the envoy insisted prevailed when Mohan Lal burst in on him with ominous intelligence. A few days earlier Mohan Lal had warned Burnes that a tribal confederacy had been formed and could erupt in violence any moment despite the Ghilzyes' promises of peace made so solemnly to Macgregor. Now Mohan Lal told of a conspiracy in Kabul, triggered only a few minutes earlier by a cabal of rebellious chiefs organized by the influential Achakzai clan chief, Abdullah Khan, who had vowed to kill Burnes for the latter's many outrages against him. Not only had Burnes taken no action to give the chief satisfaction for the humiliating circumstances surrounding the seduction of his favorite woman, but on one occasion Burnes had called him a dog and threatened to have his ears sliced off for suspected treachery—insults not easily forgiven by an Afghan.

Burnes found Mohan Lal's urgent warnings irritating and vowed not to let them spoil his euphoria that night as he relaxed with his military secretary, William Broadfoot, brother of George Broadfoot, who had gone off with Sale's brigade, and his own brother, Lieutenant (Doctor) Charles Burnes, recently arrived in Kabul. But Mohan Lal insisted that his information was firsthand; one of the conspirators, in reality one of Mohan Lal's agents, had rushed from the fateful meeting to warn him that Burnes would soon be consumed in "flames of fire." The vindictive Abdullah would have his revenge on his arch-nemesis, "Sikunder" Burnes—using the Afghan version of the name Alexander.

Close on Mohan Lal's heels, a friendly Afghan arrived to tell essentially the same story, predicting that Burnes would be dead before dawn if he did not seek shelter in the cantonment. A third person to warn Burnes that night was his good friend Naib Mohammed Sharif, who offered to send his son with a guard of a hundred reliable men to prevent the attack. Even Burnes's servant knew of the plot after being warned by an anonymous caller at three o'clock in the morning on November 2. The caller had said: "Inform your master immediately that there is tumult in the city and the merchants are removing their goods and valuables from the shops."[4] Just before dawn still another bearer of bad news, Shah Shuja's new vizier, Osman Khan, called on Burnes, begging him and his housemates to take refuge in the Bala Hissar.

Despite these forewarnings, Burnes stubbornly refused to leave his house. Confident that Afghans would not harm him—after all, he was a "friend of the Afghans"—and unwilling to exhibit fear or believe that the British forces at hand could not protect him, he resisted all entreaties to flee to the safety of the cantonment or the Bala Hissar.

Burnes's faith in the Afghans was unshakable. Only a week before he had written in his journal a defense of their behavior, likening them to unruly Scottish highlanders, tough but admirable in many ways. "I have often wondered at the hatred of the [British] officers toward the Afghans," he wrote. "They surpass their western neighbors, the supple, lying Persians; their northern ones, the enslaved Uzbeks; their eastern, the timid Indians; and their southern ones, the fierce, savage Beloochis."[5]

Burnes was convinced that "so long as there were 6,000 men within two miles of him," he could be rescued if worst came to worst—"neither the envoy nor the general would permit him to be sacrificed."[6] But he at least took the precaution of sending a message by runner to Macnaghten on the eve of his departure asking for help, and confiding to Mohan Lal that perhaps "the time has arrived that we must leave this country."[7]

Burnes also sent a last-minute message to the arch-villain of the drama, Abdullah Khan, promising to address his grievances if he would call off the gathering mob. Abdullah's response was decisive: he murdered the messenger on the spot!

Shortly after dawn broke, a small group screaming for blood gathered in front of Burnes's house. The beleaguered "Sikunder" appeared on his balcony overlooking the street, where angry men were rapidly gathering, and attempted to reason with them. He shouted that he would reward them handsomely if they would spare the lives of his friends. This offer, if heard at all above the din, had no effect since by now the mob had grown unruly and was breaking into paymaster Johnson's house next door to loot the treasury. Luckily, Johnson was not there, having spent the night at the cantonment.

Still hoping to calm the crowd, Burnes had ordered the small twenty-eight-man treasury guard detachment not to interfere in his defense, but when William Broadfoot was killed by a sniper, the soldiers began to fire in desperation. Nothing, however, could stop the surging mob that now set fire to the stables behind Burnes's house and forced its way into the garden.

An unknown Kashmiri who suddenly appeared implored Burnes and his brother to follow him, promising he would lead them to safety in the fort a quarter-mile away where Captain Trevor and a small detachment had barricaded themselves against their attackers in what had by now become a citywide uprising. With no alternative, Burnes accepted the word of his would-be rescuer, who had hurriedly sworn on his Koran that he was a friend. But no sooner had Burnes and his brother left the house through the back door, lightly disguised as Afghans, and slipped into the street, when their "benefactor" betrayed them to the mob, shouting: "This is Sikunder Burnes!"

According to Burnes's servant, a survivor of the household who claimed to have witnessed the ensuing slaughter, a mullah struck Alexander Burnes with his sword, then killed Charles Burnes before the howling mob hacked them both to pieces. The sepoys of the guard detachment were overwhelmed and also cut down before they could escape.

Mohan Lal, watching the mayhem from his nearby rooftop, avoided Barnes's fate by the thinnest margin. As the crowd began to descend on his house, he crawled through a hole in his garden wall to his neighbor's courtyard and from there fled into the street. He intended to seek help from the friendly chief of the Kizzilbash, Shirin Khan, but was recognized and intercepted by the mob as he ran through the narrow alleys. He would have been slain on the spot had not a friend, the Nawab Mohammed Zaman Khan, come along by sheer chance and rushed to his rescue. Mohan Lal literally hid under the balooning skirts of the Nawab and escaped with him to the sanctuary of his women's quarter.

In the meantime, the cantonment had become alert to the uprising. The usually imperturbable Lady Sale, packing her bags in her bungalow, had noted on the eve of the uprising a gang of Kohistani tribesmen rushing toward the city from the northeast. And on the morning of the fateful day her servant, having run from the city to escape the mobs, breathlessly reported that "all was in commotion in Cabul; the shops were plundered and the people were all fighting."[8] Indeed, flames could be seen rising from the city and shooting could be heard.

Lieutenant Sturt, Lady Sale's son-in-law, was sent off to notify Shah Shuja of the crisis. It had been difficult enough to reach the palace because of the throngs of demonstrators clogging the road, but as the captain leaped from his horse at the main gate, he was set upon by an Afghan who stabbed him three times in the face. Bleeding profusely, Sturt rushed into the court, sword in hand, to deliver his message before allowing himself to be helped back to the cantonment for medical attention.

Shah Shuja, who then seemed to be at a loss to understand why the British had not done something already, acted with dispatch, if not wisdom, by sending into the city a regiment of his Indian troops under command of the Anglo-Indian William Campbell. The soldiers tried to fight their way through the narrow, twisting alleys, but found themselves hopelessly engulfed in an angry sea of demonstrators and looters who surged through the streets while snipers shot at them from the rooftops. Casualties were heavy, some two hundred being killed. As Campbell's force tried to extricate themselves, they became separated from their cannons, which could not be dragged around the tight turns in the narrow streets and had to be abandoned. When the regiment finally broke out of the city and fell back to the Bala Hissar, it was spared further mauling only because Shelton had finally arrived with a detachment and could cover its retreat.

Elphinstone and Macnaghten had been in complete confusion ever since Burnes's hastily scrawled note was received. An indecisive Macnaghten asked his military secretary, Captain George Lawrence, what they should do. Without hesitation Lawrence urged that a British regiment be immediately dispatched to rescue Burnes and put down the uprising, but the envoy dismissed this proposal as "one of pure insanity and under the circumstances utterly unfeasible."

General Elphinstone's report of events that day made reference to a proposal that Brigadier Shelton, with two regiments and guns, proceed to the Bala Hissar and "operate as might seem expedient." The general, immobilized with indecision as usual, did not know what to do, so it had been Macnaghten who issued the order. But second thoughts, reflected in his negative reaction to Lawrence's suggestion, caused the envoy to countermand even this wishy-washy instruction almost immediately and send explicit word to Shelton that it had been "deemed impracticable to penetrate to Sir Alexander Burnes's residence." And, as seen, by the time Shelton reached the Bala Hissar, Shah Shuja's troops were in full retreat from the city after an abortive and costly effort to reach Burnes.

Lawrence in his memoir written years later[9] told a more complete story of Shelton's role in the crisis. Shelton was pointlessly lobbing shells into the city from the Bala Hissar when Lawrence found him. On his own initiative, the envoy's secretary urged Shelton to lead his troops into the city to restore order and, if it was not already too late, rescue Burnes—regardless of Macnaghten's wishes. After all, as political agent it was not Macnaghten's place to command the military in such an emergency. Lawrence's humor had not been improved by a close call; a sword-flourishing Afghan had attacked him as he approached the Bala Hissar. By good horsemanship and good luck Lawrence had dodged his assailant and made it to the Bala Hissar, but he was in no mood to suffer laggards gladly. When he arrived he could see that Shelton "with incapacity stamped on every feature of his face was almost beside himself." Shelton's excuse for inaction was that his force was inadequate. After an angry exchange, Lawrence could only conclude that Shelton was, in fact, "quite paralyzed and would not act," at least not without orders from Elphinstone, who was incapable of issuing them at this moment of crisis.

Indecision continued to wrack Elphinstone, so no British punitive force was sent into the city on that terrible day. The dithering old general could only write a note to Macnaghten (whose office was right next door), lamely excusing himself from taking action. "We must see what the morning brings," he scribbled. By evening the massacre of Burnes, his brother and Broadfoot was known to Elphinstone, but the news seemed to have done nothing to bolster his resolve.

Macnaghten was not pleased with his own performance that day. If he was guilty of misjudging the situation, at least he was honest enough with himself to admit it. In a letter never posted—and only much later found—the envoy confessed, "I may be considered culpable . . . for not having foreseen the coming storm." Macnaghten, however, could not resist placing part of the blame on Burnes and wrote: "I can only reply that others, who had much better opportunities of watching the feelings of the people, had no suspicion of what was coming."[10] In fact, Burnes, with the help of Mohan Lal's intelligence, was one of those who had sensed trouble, but ambition too often interfered with his judgment; self-confidence and his eagerness to replace Macnaghten caused him not to ring alarm bells that might make the envoy postpone his departure.

THE SEVERAL CAUSES OF THE KABUL UPRISING WOULD ONLY BECOME CLEAR in retrospect, although there were the wise ones who had predicted it. Wise only after the fact, Macnaghten attributed the immediate cause of the revolt to a seditious letter addressed by Abdullah Khan to several influential chiefs in Kabul accusing the British of designing to "seize and send them all to London." And at the fateful meeting of the chiefs on the eve of the uprising, a forged order from Shah Shuja had been produced calling for the death of all infidels. It was thus made out that even the British puppet had turned on his masters.

The fundamental cause of the tribal rebellions and the Kabul uprising was a deep-seated resentment of foreign infidel intrusion, but there were several contributing factors. Surely Macnaghten's policy of withholding tribal subsidies and his refusal to accept the need for federation, not strong central control, were critical mistakes in judgment. And trying to police a large and impossibly rugged country of tribal warriors contributed to public antagonism and unrest. Poor military leadership offered by Elphinstone and Shelton and, more specifically, an irresolute response to the attack on Burnes must be blamed for not nipping the revolt in the bud. Shah Shuja's maladministration also played a role in the upheaval that took place.

That Burnes was the first focus of the Kabul uprising, if not an underlying cause, can be attributed in part to the fact he had become a symbol of the invasion and in part to his own comportment. He had made an enemy of Abdullah Khan and other influential chiefs by his own philandering and by tolerating the libertine behavior of other officers in a society where such things were punishable by death. The Afghan chiefs considered themselves honor-bound to seek revenge.

This was a sorry requiem for a brave and talented player of the Game whose comrades made no effort to save him. Surely, his transgressions pale in significance when compared to the political and military blunders of others. But he was indicted and sentenced by the Afghans in their own way and paid the supreme penalty to a society that resented foreign interference in their private lives as much as in their tribal affairs.

Burnes's sin had also been his unfaithfulness to his own good judgment in forsaking political policy in deference to ambition. Could he have done more to save his country and countrymen from the tragedy about to engulf them in Afghanistan? His best and most honest answer to that question was perhaps contained in a letter he wrote toward the end of 1839 when he admitted that after having failed to convince his government of the importance of backing Dost Mohammed, he "did advocate the setting up of Shah Shuja." But he added, "When was this? When my advice had been rejected." Burnes admitted that at the outset he had "looked only to personal advantages," but now, "with an onerous load upon me, the holy and sacred interests of nations, I begin sometimes to tremble at the giddy eminence I have already attended." Perhaps he feared he would again trip over his shoelaces from running too hard as he did in his school days.

In another letter he questioned whether he had been right to avoid correspondence with his numerous influential friends in England, or "even with Lord Auckland." Had he lobbied for his views, he would perhaps have undercut Macnaghten, and for all his ambition, this deterred him. Yet his retreat into cynicism, biding his time until he assumed the envoy's mantle, was surely wrong. At least he did not live to witness the consequences of his inaction at a critical time.

Chapter 21

DESPERATION

SHORTLY BEFORE DAWN ON NOVEMBER 3, THE BRITISH CANTONMENT was roused by the call to arms. Scouts had just reported great swarms of tribal insurgents approaching Kabul from the direction of the Siah Sung Hills. As dawn broke, clouds of dust on the horizon seemed to herald their advance; battle posts were manned to defend the cantonment against an anticipated attack by the hostile host of Afghans. But as the force came into view, the men of the cantonment erupted in cheers; they had recognized the colors of their own 37th Regiment and heard the beat of their drums.

Major Griffiths, left by Sale to hold the entrance to the Khoord Kabul Pass with the 37th, had brought his men back in orderly fashion, baggage, wounded and all, while fending off a running attack by three thousand Ghilzyes intent on annihilating them. For this the major earned the respect of the cantonment that day; he had shown quality of leadership rare in Kabul command. Elphinstone had urgently ordered Griffith's return from Boothak, where the regiment was still recovering from its mauling in the pass, as soon as news of the Kabul uprising reached him. Every man available was needed to defend the cantonment.

As relieved as the British were to see the 37th rather than a horde of hostile Afghans, there had in fact been a massing of the tribes in the nearby hills. Among the chiefs was Nawab Jubbar Khan, once the best friend of the British in Kabul, but since Macnaghten rebuffed him near Ghazni as the Army of the Indus approached Kabul, he had been active in the ranks of the enemy. The British presence and the systematic alienation of the Afghans by Macnaghten's inept policies provided such chiefs with a common cause, which for the moment distracted them from their usual internecine squabbling.

The road between the cantonment and the city was already clogged with tribesmen flocking to the cause, or at least eager to share in the loot. In a show of force unconvincing for its inadequacy, Major Stephen Swayne and three companies marched out to regain control of Kabul before the insurgency, swollen by the influx from the hills, grew even larger. But well short of the Kabul Gate, the British column was driven back by angry mobs that overwhelmed them.

It had been folly to think that Swayne's meager detachment could deal with the mass of rebellious Afghans careening about the city. When a determined column of well-trained British troops could have saved the city at the insurrection's birth, Elphinstone had dithered. Now that the revolt had grown to awesome proportions, the general sent an inadequate force on a hopeless mission. Making matters worse, confused commands prevented Brigadier Shelton's detachment at the Bala Hissar from linking up with Swayne's force as planned. Under the circumstances, the three companies had been lucky to escape annihilation.

Not so fortunate were Lieutenant Richard Maule and his adjutant, Lieutenant Wheeler, commanding a regiment posted some twenty miles north of Kabul at a place called Dardurrah. Although warned of an attack by a vastly superior force of Kohistani tribesmen, the two men remained staunchly at their post. When the horde descended on them, the regiment fled, leaving Maule and Wheeler at the mercy of their assailants. Both were killed while defending themselves.

Adding to the gloom of that terrible day, intelligence filtered in from Kohistan that Major Pottinger, resident at Charekar, and his 4th Gurkha regimental escort were in serious danger. Several officers had already been killed in skirmishes with the hostile Kohistani tribesmen, and the small, beleaguered outpost was rapidly running out of water. Elphinstone's reaction to the news was typically unhelpful. "This is most distressing," he told

Macnaghten. "Can nothing be done by the promise of a large reward to any of the Kohistani chiefs?"

Such humiliating exhibitions of British impotence only encouraged the Afghans to greater militancy. While most of the chiefs had cowered in their houses on the day following the uprising, fearing retribution by an overwhelming British force, now they realized that the *ferangis* were on the defensive. The tribes had only to circle for the kill—then pounce.

At least the frightening events had cured Macnaghten of his excessive optimism. No longer Pollyanna, he realized that he was faced with a major insurrection with countrywide ramifications, not simply a spontaneous, isolated incident soon to die down. He moved himself and his wife into a tent on the cantonment from his adjacent bungalow for greater safety and to reduce the perimeter that would have to be defended against the rising hordes already pouring into the city. It was now obvious to the envoy that the revolt of the eastern Ghilzyes was linked to the Kabul uprising, as Mohan Lal had insisted all along.

A more coherent picture of what had happened in Kabul in the confusion of the fatal day of uprising began to come into focus. Burnes's house and Captain Johnson's treasury had not been the only quarters attacked by the mobs. Isolated outposts in the city had also borne the brunt of Kabul's eruption. Captain Colin Mackenzie on that fateful day of November 2 had been startled to see rush into his compound a naked man covered only with his own blood from saber and gunshot wounds. As officer in charge of Shah Shuja's supply depot, Mackenzie was housed with his stores in a fort on the northern edge of the city known as Qilai Nishan Khan. The shooting that morning had alerted him to trouble and caused him to call his guard force to arms. But this bleeding man before him, a victim of the street violence, was a courier who had risked his life bringing formal warning from Macnaghten.

Mackenzie had managed to barricade his fort only moments before it was attacked by a howling mob of Afghans. But by noon his troops were running dangerously low on ammunition, having had to repel several assaults by his besiegers. Although Mackenzie sent frantic messages by runners who managed to slip out of the fort unobserved, asking desperately for ammunition and reinforcements with which to defend his fort, Elphinstone rejected any thought of sending a relief column that might "expose his men to street firing."

By the second day, November 3, Mackenzie's chances of survival were slim. One wall of the fort could not be defended because of the hail of bullets from Afghan sharpshooters perched nearby. Tunneling Afghans, whose shovels could be heard beneath the walls, would break through any moment, and the besiegers were building a bonfire beside the gate to burn it down. It was not surprising that some twenty of Mackenzie's soldiers tried to sneak out the gate and take their chances in flight. But grabbing a double-barreled shotgun, Mackenzie challenged the mutineers before they could flee; cocking his gun ostentatiously, he threatened to shoot the first man to disobey. He later wrote of this harrowing experience: "They saw that I was determined, for I had made up my mind to die, and they obeyed."[1]

After two sleepless days and nights, the loyal leader of the guard, who was by then out of ammunition, wearily informed Mackenzie that he was willing to die if necessary, but advised that further resistance was useless. Mackenzie agreed, and by the grace of God and his own courage, he broke out and brought the group, including women and children belonging to the sepoy guards, safely to the cantonment after fighting most of the way.

At the same time, some five hundred yards east of Mackenzie in town, Captain Trevor, his wife and seven children were trapped in their fortified tower by the mobs. They held out for two days, thanks to help given them by the friendly Kizzilbash chief, Shirin Khan, but when their cries for help went unheeded by the British, the frightened family, with only a small sepoy escort, stole forth hoping to reach the cantonment safely by a circuitous back-alley route. A marauding Afghan rushed the group and slashed out at Mrs. Trevor with his saber. Only because a mounted trooper by her side shot forth his arm to deflect the blow was her life spared. By this act of gallantry the sepoy's hand was chopped off, but as badly wounded as he was, blood gushing from the stump, he did not abandon his charges until they reached the cantonment.

That Elphinstone at this stage of jeopardy did not muster his strength to move all the British and their supplies to the defensible Bala Hissar can be blamed in large part on Macnaghten's stubborn reluctance to inconvenience Shah Shuja. Soon the British would pay dearly for Macnaghten's misplaced concern for his client, but already it was painfully obvious that another early mistake, that of locating the commissariat beyond the perimeter of the cantonment, was rapidly becoming a catastrophe. Captain Skinner, chief commissariat officer, had warned the command about this error when the cantonment was first set up, but his protests had been brushed aside.[2] Now the British could think of nothing but their stores, tantalizingly just beyond their reach. The vital commissariat, housing a three-month supply of food and clothing, was guarded by a British junior officer, Lieutenant Warren, and eighty Indian sepoys. Not only was it unsafe to travel between the cantonment and the commissariat because of marauders, but because the road was commanded by the so-called

Mohammed Sharif Fort, newly occupied by the rebellious Afghans. Lady Sale, always uncompromising in her comments and shrewd judgments, noted in her journal at the time that they had only three days' provisions within the cantonment: "Should the Commissariat fort be captured, we shall not only lose all our provisions, but our communications with the city will be cut off."[3]

At the beginning of December, about a month after Burnes's murder, Lady Sale's quite accurate version of the terrible events reached the governor general's sister, Emily Eden, in Calcutta by private letter—almost as quickly as the official report did. Lady Sale, it seems, had sent the news to her worried husband on the march by secret courier and he had forwarded her letter to Emily Eden, who had passed it around Calcutta. Lady Sale's opinions also made depressing reading in Calcutta if we are to assume that she used language similar to the accounts recorded in her journal. On November 3, she recorded: "No military steps have been taken to suppress the insurrection nor even to protect our only means of subsistence [the commissariat fort] in the event of a siege. The King, Envoy and General appear paralysed by this sudden outbreak: the former is deserted by all his courtiers and by even his most confidential servants, except the Vizier, who is strongly suspected of having instigated the conspiracy; and suspicion attaches to his Majesty . . ."[4] Upon hearing such gloomy news from Lady Sale, Emily expressed herself as being alarmed about the fate of the British women in Kabul, now at the mercy of the Afghans—"such savage people."

Afghan insurgents swarmed into the Shah Bagh, or King's Garden, adjacent to the Mohammed Sharif Fort and directly across the road from the commissariat, making the quarter-mile distance to the commissariat even more difficult to navigate. This effectively isolated Warren, making his position untenable. On November 4, the alarmed lieutenant sent a note to Elphinstone warning that if he and his men were not reinforced very soon, he could not hold out. The Afghans were already assembling ladders for the escalade.

By evening Elphinstone finally stirred himself to send a small detachment, much too small in the opinion of his staff officers, who begged him to recall it before it was decimated by the withering fire coming from the Mohammed Sharif Fort and the Shah Bagh. As usual, Elphinstone had not understood and had underestimated the problem. He did recall the relief detachment, but not before it was badly mauled. After another detachment was sent out, this time a cavalry column, it was also forced to turn back with heavy casualties. Only now did it occur to Elphinstone that without first taking the Mohammed Sharif Fort, Warren and his men could not be reinforced nor the stores saved. Had he moved promptly before the fort was occupied by the Afghans, he could have prevented the tribes from massing in the Shah Bagh and retained control of the vital stretch of road linking the cantonment with its supplies. Now it would take a major operation to dislodge the Afghans from their new bastion. But unless this was done, the single gate to the commissariat would remain squarely in the rifle sights of a host of Afghans.

With mounting horror, the British staff realized that Elphinstone had, in fact, reconciled himself to giving up the commissariat. Incredibly, he did not seem to realize that this meant condemning the cantonment to starvation and depriving the growing number of wounded of medicine. By the time his officers convinced him of the absolute necessity of rescuing the supplies, it was too late. Warren had fled!

Lieutenant Warren had been able to hear the enemy mining the walls, and watched helplessly as many of his sepoys slid down the walls and deserted out of fear. None of his messages to the cantonment had been answered. He later claimed that he had never received the order calling upon him to stand fast and await the arrival of a new and larger relief column scheduled for the early hours of November 5. So in desperation he and other survivors had escaped from the fort by tunneling under the walls during the night of November 4 and dashing to the cantonment under cover of dark. Warren had abandoned his post and left the vital supplies to be plundered by the Afghans, a chargeable offense, but since a court-martial would only raise the issue of Elphinstone's negligence in handling the situation, no charges were brought against him. Through indecision and procrastination Elphinstone was at fault for losing British supplies; whatever lingering hope there may have been now seemed gone. From the cantonment the troops could see with despair throngs of Afghans rushing to the abandoned commissariat to loot its contents. Like jackals ripping the flesh from the carcass of its prey, the Afghans carted away sack upon sack of precious foodstuffs, the very sustenance of cantonment life. Although it was too late to save the provisions for the commissariat, the capture of the Mohammed Sharif Fort was still vital to the defense of the cantonment and plans were at last made to attack it.

Escape from the cantonment would now be costly. As Lieutenant Eyre noted starkly in his journal, they were "unable to move out a dozen paces from either gate without being exposed to the fire of some neighboring fort."[5]

The most charitable thing that could be said about Elphinstone's pathetic exhibition of incompetence was that he seemed too sick to think, much less function. Only the day before he had fallen from his horse from weakness. In his deteriorating physical and mental state, defeatism was now added to incompetence. Only three days after the outbreak Elphinstone was moved to send a note to Macnaghten saying: "It behooves us to look to the consequences of failure. . . . You should, therefore, consider what chance there is of making terms if we are driven to this extremity."[6]

Lieutenant Eyre, eyewitness to the Kabul tragedy as it unfolded, later assessed Elphinstone's role with more sorrow than anger. "It would be the height of injustice to a most amiable and gallant officer not to notice the long course of painful and wearing illness which had materially affected the nerves and probably even the intellect of General Elphinstone," he wrote in his journal. But Eyre did not answer the question as to why the ailing general did not recognize his state of health and turn command over to Shelton. Not until November 9 was Shelton summoned from the Bala Hissar to *share* command with Elphinstone, an arrangement that could never work under the best of conditions, and one that under these conditions would only contribute to disaster.

While defeatism and indecision wracked the cantonment, Mohan Lal wove his webs of political intrigues in town. No one knew more Afghan chiefs than did Mohan Lal, or understood Afghan politics better. He was now well positioned to serve Macnaghten in a very special way. Undoubtedly, the Indian agent could have escaped to the cantonment, but the envoy needed him there to carry out his secret political-action plans.

Mohan Lal's rescue from the mob by Nawab Mohammed Zaman Khan, who like a large mother hen hiding her chick beneath her feathers had hid him beneath his ample gown, was an act of courage, and to give him refuge in his zenana was even more dangerous. Mohan Lal, however, soon moved to the house of Shirin Khan, whose quarters were not only safer but would also provide him with the propinquity he needed to work on the Kizzilbash chief and convince him to remain loyal to the British. Continuing friendship with the Persian Kizzilbash community, or at least its benevolent neutrality, was now essential to the British. From Shirin Khan's house, Mohan Lal also secretly negotiated with certain Ghilzye chiefs with the object of sowing discord among them.

A message from Macnaghten to Mohan Lal on November 7 revealed the general thrust of the envoy's political strategy. Macnaghten enclosed two letters, one for Shirin Khan, the other for Mohammed Hamza, formerly Shah Shuja's governor of the Ghilzyes, now a leader of the rebellion. "You may assure them both," Macnaghten wrote to Mohan Lal, "if they perform the service which they have undertaken, the former shall receive one *lakh* [100,000 rupees] and the latter, 50,000 rupees, besides getting the present, and everything else they require." In return for these handsome incentives, the Kizzilbash chief and the Ghilzye chief were to use their influence to quiet the rebellion, unconvincingly described as a futile cause by Macnaghten. "Assure them that whatever bluster the rebels might make, they will be beaten in the end,"[7] he instructed Mohan Lal—who could only hope this was true.

Mohan Lal promised generous subsidies to certain leaders if they would betray their cause. He told Macnaghten that he could even work on Dost Mohammed's influential son, Akbar Khan, who had just arrived in Bamiyan en route to Kabul, where he would take command of the rebellion. Akbar had, in fact, let it be known that if given a subsidy he would surrender, but Macnaghten was shrewd enough to reason that this was a trick; he had no intention of abandoning the cause. It would soon become apparent that the insurrection had ballooned into an uncontrollable upheaval beyond manipulation; money alone could not stop it. The Afghans were intoxicated with hatred of the *ferangi* and exhilarated by their demonstrated ability to twist the lion's tail. Only evidence of British power could speak convincingly, and this was conspicuously lacking. The Kizzilbash was the one group that the British could hope would remain friendly. It had been this Persian community of the Shia Moslem sect on which Mohan Lal had relied to plead the British cause at the Afghan court ever since Burnes's mission to Dost Mohammed. But in the present atmosphere, poisoned by the sorry spectacle of British impotence, even Shirin Khan was reluctant to declare himself openly for the feeble *ferangi*. Macnaghten's hope that the Kizzilbash chief would perform "quick and good service" to the British bespoke more hope than expectation.

If money would not work and power was wanting, was there an alternative to surrender and retreat, so unthinkable to Macnaghten? The desperate envoy apparently thought so when he secretly instructed Mohan Lal to arrange for two of the rebel leaders to be assassinated. This dark episode in the Kabul crisis may have seemed justified to Macnaghten considering the dire circumstances in which the cantonment found itself, but it accomplished nothing and left a stain on British honor not easily forgotten by the Afghans.

The plot began on November 5, when Macnaghten urged Mohan Lal to press the Kizzilbash for help in quelling the Kabul uprising. Macnaghten's aide, Lieutenant John Conolly, was more explicit; he added a gruesome postscript to the message, giving Mohan Lal authority to promise "10,000 rupees for the head of each of the principal rebel chiefs." Macnaghten himself on November 11 wrote Mohan Lal that the archscoundrels Aminullah Khan, a landowner from the Logar Valley who had raised ten thousand tribesmen for the revolt, and Burnes's old nemesis,

Abdullah Khan, "should be executed if we could catch them." And on the same day Conolly got down to details, writing Mohan Lal: "There is a man called Haji Ali, who might be induced by a bribe to try and bring in the heads of one or two of the *mufsids* [rebels]. Endeavour to let him know that 10,000 rupees will be given for each head—or even 15,000 rupees."[8]

Mohan Lal did proceed with murder plans, and in a macabre letter to Macnaghten he wrote that the men now employed to do the deed promised to enter the houses of the intended victims, defined as Abdullah Khan and Mir Misjidi and described as "movers of the attack on Burnes's house," and "cut off their heads when they may be without attendants."[9]

By the end of November both of these rebel leaders were dead. Abdullah Khan died of his wounds in battle, but Mohan Lal's hired assassin, one Abdul Aziz, demanded the blood-money reward promised him, insisting that it was he who shot his victim from behind with a poisoned bullet. Mir Misjidi simply disappeared, never to be seen again. A second assassin, Mohammed Oolah, had strangled him in his bed and disposed of the body somewhere. Mohan Lal refused to pay either man the entire sum promised them on the technicality that the heads had not been produced.[10]

——— •-•-• ———

NOVEMBER 6 BROUGHT SOME LITTLE RESPITE FROM BAD NEWS. A STORMING party successfully took the Mohammed Sharif Fort with very few casualties. Poor Ensign Raban, flushed with the ecstacy of victory, was shot dead as he waved the Union Jack from the ramparts, but otherwise it had been an easy operation. It was discovered that the fort, contrary to Elphinstone's fears, had been lightly manned.

Another hopeful development occurred that day when after four days of foraging, Captains Johnson and Boyd discovered enough food in the nearby village of Beymaru for at least a few more days. This reprieve from imminent starvation did little, however, to lift Elphinstone's spirits or infuse him with any greater will to resist. In a melancholy note to Macnaghten on November 6, he now agonized over the ammunition situation. The general had somehow convinced himself that the armory was empty. Nothing could have been further from the truth, but this did not prevent him from writing: "Our next consideration is ammunition; a very serious and indeed awful one." Though, he added hastily, "Do not suppose from this I wish to recommend or am advocating humiliating terms." But, in fact, surrender was very much on his tired mind.

Shelton was no more optimistic than Elphinstone about British prospects, but his solution was more dynamic. He believed that they should fight their way to Jalalabad and join up with Sale rather than endure a siege in Kabul. Elphinstone and Shelton agreed on very few matters and their relationship was badly strained. Although given responsibility for the cantonment, Shelton soon found that Elphinstone continually interfered with his orders, creating a dangerously chaotic command situation. The general simply did not like or trust Shelton, whom he found "contumacious" and "actuated by an ill feeling." And, indeed, it must have been trying for Elphinstone to suffer his second-in-command's disrespect with Shelton curled up in a bedroll in the corner, snoozing through the staff meetings, as so often happened.

As the first week of the uprising ended, there was little room for optimism, but the paralysis of Elphinstone and the disagreeable pessimism of Shelton plunged the troops into even deeper depression. Lieutenant Eyre noted in his journal that Shelton's despondency "soon spread its baneful influence among the officers and was by them communicated to the soldiery . . . lugubrious looks and dismal prophecies being encountered everywhere."[11] Lady Sale considered Shelton's transfer to the cantonment from the Bala Hissar "as a dark cloud overshadowing us." It had shocked her when upon his arrival in Kabul, well before the uprising, he ordered provisions to be stored in case of retreat, and now he was even more obsessed with "getting back to Hindostan."[12]

Macnaghten did not agree with Shelton and still believed that the garrison should try to hold out, no matter what the risk. Lieutenant Eyre, a friend and defender of Elphinstone, recorded at the time: "This difference of opinion on a question of such vital importance . . . deprived the General in his hour of need, of the strength which unanimity imparts."[13] It also set the officers to bickering rather than applying themselves to constructive thinking as to how the army could save itself from disaster.

Shah Shuja too was infected with the virus of despair. The Bala Hissar had come under attack and he considered himself in dire jeopardy. Lady Sale noted that the king had "quite lost all his self possession" and had even "warned the females of his zenana [amounting to 860] that in the event of the cantonment falling into the hands of the rebels, he should administer poison to them all." But was Shah Shuja now beginning to hedge his bets? Lady Sale asked herself if such reports were "merely set afloat to blind us to his own share in the insurrection?"[14]

Some greater military success was needed to revive morale in the cantonment as well as to discourage a major attack. For all his talk of retreat, Shelton provided a welcome draught of victory, proving him a brave officer, if a gloomy one.

Chapter 22

DISINTEGRATION

O NE OF THE SEVERAL SMALL AFGHAN FORTS DOTTING THE LANDSCAPE around the cantonment was one called Rikabashi. Only three hundred yards from the northeast corner of the cantonment, it was particularly troublesome because of snipers. The long Afghan *jazail,* steadied in its forked-stick cradle, was deadly when used for long-range sniping, and several soldiers within the cantonment had been dropped in their tracks by the tribal sharpshooters. With some difficulty, Macnaghten convinced Elphinstone that Rikabashi must not be left in Afghan hands.

On November 10, Brigadier Shelton led a detachment, drawn from his own 44th Foot, the 37th Native Infantry and one of Shah Shuja's regiments—two thousand in all—to attack the fort. Unfortunately, the breach blown in the wall was too small to admit more than one man at a time. Only Lieutenant Colonel Mackrell, Lieutenant Bird and a few sepoys had wiggled their way through a small wicket before an Afghan cavalry charge scattered the others. Apparently some nervous sepoy had shouted, "Cavalry," creating panic among the exposed troops before they could form a defensive square, and they fled the field in confusion.

Shelton kept his composure and at great risk to himself rallied his men to mount a second attack, this one successful. Although casualties were high, the fort was seized. Lieutenant Colonel Mackrell, who had been trapped inside, was found badly hacked up and soon died of his wounds. His last words were: "This is not battle, it is murder!"[1] Of the others who had first penetrated the fort with Mackrell, only Lieutenant Bird and one sepoy, who had barricaded themselves in a room, survived. A pile of dead Afghans outside the room was testimony to the fierceness of the two men's defense.

Afghan casualties were also high, but the best prizes of all gained by Shelton's action were badly needed grain stored in the fort and a much-needed morale boost by their victory. The capture of Rikabashi, moreover, enabled the British to seize four other fortified compounds around the perimeter of the cantonment and convince the headman of nearby Behmaru village that he should sell them more grain.

Lady Sale's comment on the Rikabashi engagement exuded optimism: "The events of today must have astonished the enemy after our supineness, and shown them that, when we have a mind to do so, we can punish them." But this was the last victory for the British to savor. Nothing but bad news would henceforth cascade on the beleaguered cantonment and sap its will to resist.

For a moment hope soared when Colonel Dennie's dog and another mongrel belonging to Major Kershaw suddenly appeared in the cantonment. Were they the vanguard of Sale's force ordered back to help defend Kabul? If the dogs had made their way home, could Dennie and Kershaw with Sale be far behind? But this was a vain hope; whatever homing instincts had brought the dogs back—and one of the poor beasts was savagely rabid—their masters did not follow. Sale's brigade had begun its march from Gandamak in quite another direction toward Jalalabad on November 11.

It had been a particularly agonizing decision for Fighting Bob Sale not to comply with Macnaghten's repeated orders—in reality, pleas—to return to Kabul. The envoy had begged Sale: "If you have regard for our lives or for the honour of our country, you must return."* And, of course, Sale's

---

*Considering the hostile state of the country surrounding Kabul, it was remarkable that the British were able to maintain communications with the outlying garrisons. In fact, their native couriers, or *cossids*, deserved the credit. At tremendous risk to themselves they rode through enemy territory with their messages, often written in invisible ink made from lemon juice, secreted on their persons. In the event that they were intercepted, they had instructions to swallow their messages rather than give them up. Some *cossids* were caught, of course, and their fate was inevitably death, after torture and mutilation.

wife was among those trapped in Kabul, adding further urgency to his return. But the brigadier and his staff were in agreement that the brigade could not possibly make it through the passes controlled by the Ghilzyes, who lay in wait for just such an opportunity to annihilate them. Moreover, to attempt returning would mean abandoning some three hundred wounded. The only hope for the brigade's survival was to reach Jalalabad and hold out until relief could come from Peshawar.

Sale's brigade, somewhat battered, arrived in Jalalabad on November 13, 1841, only to find the fort in such a state of disrepair that it offered little protection, but the troops set about making a defensive bastion out of the crumbling mud walls.

Had only the Kabul garrison moved into the Bala Hissar and, like Sale, relied on a fortress defense instead of trying to survive in an exposed cantonment, events would probably have turned out much differently than they did. But Macnaghten still hoped that the cantonment could survive until Nott, at least, could send a relief column from Kandahar. General Nott, however, was no more able to respond quickly to Macnaghten's order than was Sale. Nott had not even received the envoy's order until November 14. When a detachment from his forces was massacred between Ghazni and Kabul, the general realized that it would not be an easy task to relieve Kabul, although he did order Brigadier Maclaren, then bound for India, to turn his brigade around and make the attempt despite deep snow in the passes.

In the meantime, the Kabul cantonment faced a new danger. The insurgents had mounted two guns on the Behmaru Heights west of the cantonment and were bombarding the British with telling effect. Macnaghten saw immediately that to let this threat go unchallenged would be an admission of weakness, undoing the good effect of capturing Rikabashi fort. Elphinstone was unenthusiastic about trying to knock the guns out by a risky action, and Shelton had a dozen flimsy reasons why such an attack could not succeed. Not until late afternoon on the thirteenth did the envoy convince the army leaders to move, and then only by taking full responsibility for the attack himself. Macnaghten, in fact, had to overrule Shelton, threatening that if he did not advance and seize the two guns by evening, he "must be prepared for any disgrace that may befall us."

As at Rikabashi, the British infantrymen at Behmaru were first scattered by a determined Afghan cavalry charge, creating terrible confusion in the ranks. Lady Sale, who watched the action from her rooftop, crouched behind a chimney, scribbled in her diary: "My very heart felt as if it leapt to my teeth when I saw the Afghans ride clean through them."[2] The British were able to regroup, however, and, led by their own cavalry charge, drove the Afghans back. One gun was taken, but when the British troops prematurely retreated rather than press the attack, the other was abandoned for the enemy to reclaim, provoking Lieutenant Eyre later to pass contemptuous judgment on the British soldiers: "They remained unmoveable, nor could the [native] sepoys be induced to lead the way where their European brothers so obstinately hung back."[3] Before darkness obliged the British to leave the field and return to the cantonment, Eyre singlehandedly managed to spike the abandoned gun even if he could not take it with him.

The engagement had perhaps been a limited success, but, in his account of events, Lieutenant Eyre wrote sadly in his memoir: "Henceforward it becomes my weary task to relate a catalogue of errors, disasters and difficulties, which following close upon each other, disgusted our officers, disheartened our soldiers and finally sunk us all with irretrievable ruin, as though Heaven, itself, by a combination of evil circumstances for its own inscrutable purposes, had planned our downfall."[4] It may not have been fair for Eyre to blame Heaven when mortals on earth were so obviously at fault, but his gloom was justified. Suddenly more bad news arrived.

On November 15, the cantonment learned the fate of the 4th Ghurkha Regiment stationed at Charekar, forty miles north of Kabul and unheard from for many days, when Major Eldred Pottinger and Lieutenant J. C. Haughten—missing one hand—stumbled into the cantonment to tell of the tragedy. The two officers, an Indian civilian clerk and one Gurkha sepoy who accompanied them were the only survivors of the regiment— 750 Gurkha combatants and 140 of their womenfolk and children—that had been wiped out by Kohistani tribesmen. Pottinger, hero of Herat, told a harrowing story of how the isolated garrison had met its end.

Since the Kabul uprising, the Gurkhas at Charekar had been menaced by the neighboring Kohistani tribesmen, according to Pottinger's testimony. Their anguish had been the more intense for having to watch the suffering of their wives and children, who for some misguided reason had been permitted to join them in this remote, dangerous station. The real trouble began, however, when some of the chiefs treacherously took advantage of a "friendly" meeting to murder Lieutenant Rattray. Ironically, the meeting had been called to fix new subsidies for the Kohistanis to ensure their loyalty in the face of the rising tide of rebellion.

Separated from the garrison, some two miles away, was a castle known as Lughmani, where Pottinger, as political officer, Rattray and the regimental physician, Dr. Grant, made their residence. Rattray's murder signaled an uprising in which at least three thousand tribesmen surrounded the castle, cutting it off from the Charekar garrison. Pottinger's meager escort of seventy-five Kohistani levies and a company of Gurkhas could not defend him against such odds, and anyway he could not expect to hold out very long with his food and water supplies rapidly dwindling. Already Pottinger could hear the telltale scraping noise of Afghan sappers mining the castle wall. Despairing of relief, he led his men out at night through a back gate, somehow managing to reach the garrison just before a major assault engulfed it on November 5.

The garrison defenders with their women and children, commanded by a few British officers, now found themselves besieged by twenty thousand tribesmen who had poured in from the hills. Pottinger pitched in to man the two six-pounders while a detachment under Haughten defended an exposed outpost to protect the vital water supply until they were driven back to the compound by enemy fire. Troop casualties were already running high and two British officers were killed before the day was over. The next day began ominously with the sounds of incessant drumming and intensified firing from the tribal lines. Afghan gunners now found their range and salvos of grapeshot began dropping within the fort.

Although prostrate with a ball in his leg, Pottinger received two chiefs under a flag of truce on November 8. Their mission was to offer terms: they promised to spare the garrison if, to a man, it would embrace Islam. On hearing this, Pottinger was furious and roused himself indignantly from his sickbed to reject such apostasy as unthinkable for any good Christian soldier. And to do so probably would still not save them from the treacherous Afghans. An outraged Pottinger reminded the tribal emissaries that the British had come to Afghanistan to help a Moslem sovereign regain his throne and therefore deserved the protection of Islam.

The situation was now hopeless. Forty-four more men were buried that day and the last drops of water were passed out in half-filled wineglasses. The ammunition was also nearly exhausted. In desperation the men dug spent lead from the mud walls and recast it into new bullets, or wrapped it in carpeting to serve as makeshift shot canisters for the remaining three guns.

For one glorious moment Haughten thought he saw the 5th Cavalry approaching to relieve them, but his hopes were dashed when the distant images proved to be only cattle distorted in a mirage. In fact, George Lawrence had volunteered to lead a relief cavalry column from Kabul after hastily written messages calling for help were delivered to the cantonment by a native runner. But this had been rejected by Elphinstone, who was hard pressed to defend the Kabul cantonment and could ill afford to risk any more men on such a hazardous mission.

Desertions were increasing as the situation became more hopeless. The artillerymen had already bolted. Now serving the enemy, they taunted the troops for fighting for the *ferangis*. One deserter whom Haughten had tried to capture slashed at him with his sword, severing his hand so badly that it had to be amputated and cutting some of his neck muscles. Dr. Grant sewed up the stump of the arm as best he could, but Haughten was badly weakened by the ordeal.

By now discipline had almost totally disintegrated in the garrison; the only alternative to death was escape. The garrison survivors, organized into two columns, slipped out of the barracks after nightfall. A brave bugler, too wounded to march, sacrificed his life by staying behind to blow reveille so that the tribesmen would not immediately realize that the barracks had been abandoned, thus giving the Gurkhas a little more time to make good their escape.

It was a sorry remnant of the 4th Gurkhas that Pottinger tried to lead on the long and hazardous march back to Kabul. He himself was crippled by the gunshot wound in his leg, and Haughten, the only other officer still alive, was barely able to sit on his horse. Haughten's encounter with the deserter had not only cost him his hand—a saber slash to the shoulder had severed a nerve, so he had to prop up his sagging head with a pillow tied around his neck. The two columns became separated in the dark and were unable to link up again. Others, occupied with their women and children, fell behind. Debilitated by thirst and hunger, the ever-dwindling number of survivors grew weaker by the hour, and various misadventures with tribal marauders along the way soon finished the doomed regiment.

Pottinger and Haughten pushed on, with the clerk and sepoy who trotted along after them on foot. Haughten was now so weak from his wounds that he repeatedly fell off his horse. Only because Pottinger refused to leave his side did he muster his last reserves of will to go on. Somehow the little party reached Kabul and stole through the hostile town in the dead of night without being detected. One drugged fakir, sucking on his pipe of opium, revived himself enough to mutter a blessing as they went by him; otherwise everyone was asleep. But as they neared the cantonment, they were spotted in the breaking daylight and had to make a dash for it through a hail of bullets to reach the gate. Lieutenant Eyre described the moving scene as the men arrived: "They were received by their brethren in arms as men risen from the dead."[5]

Pottinger and the badly wounded Haughten had come back to "safety" just in time to see thousands of tribesmen swarming over the nearby Behmaru Heights above the cantonment. Macnaghten realized the jeopardy of the British position; not only had the enemy taken a strategically vital position but Behmaru village was the cantonment's main source of grain. Yet only by strenuously insisting did Macnaghten rouse the befuddled Elphinstone to mount another attack on the vital hill. In fairness to the general, however, it was his staff that had influenced his judgment against the operation on the grounds that it would be too costly in terms of casualties, as the previous effort to seize the Afghan guns had proved, and the hills could not be held even if captured. Realizing the state of troop morale, if not its own incompetence, the staff sadly would prove to be right in arriving at this judgment.

A halfhearted effort to drive the Afghans from the hills was mounted on November 22. Major Swayne, with a small cavalry detachment, one mountain gun and one horse artillery piece, approached the village of Behmaru, but hesitated when he saw that a large body of Kohistani tribesmen had barricaded themselves within the town walls. Although Swayne was under orders to storm the village, he temporized. Uncertain what to do, he spent the better part of the day huddled with his men under cover of a low wall while the cavalry and the gunners, drawn up in an open plain, suffered greatly from Afghan sniping. Shelton tried to reinforce and reinvigorate the becalmed Swayne, but the whole operation, inadequately manned and foolishly conceived, was abandoned at the end of the day.

At this moment of failure it was disheartening to learn that while Swayne had been timidly approaching the Kohistani village of Behmaru, Akbar Khan, a conquering hero, was approaching Kabul from Bamiyan at the head of his six thousand Uzbeks from the north. As son of Dost Mohammed and a warrior of repute in his own right who had refused to surrender with his father, Akbar was the logical leader to assume command of the rebellion, although titular leadership had already been given to the respected Nawab Mohammed Zaman Khan (interestingly, Mohan Lal's friend and benefactor), who had been proclaimed king by the rebels. His crown was meant to be a temporary one, however, pending the eventual return of Dost Mohammed. Arriving in Kabul, Akbar Khan could savor the spectacle of the hated British, trapped in their flimsy cantonment, cowering under Kohistani guns trained on them from the Behmaru Heights.

That night the British command held a council of war to consider Swayne's failure and what moves to make next. Again Macnaghten's will prevailed. "The loss of the cantonment," he warned, "would be the result of their supineness today." The dispirited military reluctantly agreed to move out once again to attack the Behmaru Heights. It was agreed that Shelton with a large force would sally forth at 2:00 A.M. with units of the 44th Queen's Regiment, the 37th and 5th Native Infantry Regiments, two squadrons of cavalry, a hundred troopers of Anderson's Horse and some sappers—but only one artillery piece. This violated a long-standing Indian

Army policy of never going into battle with only one gun, and indeed it proved to be a bad mistake when the gun's overheated vents soon put it out of action.

By daybreak the British could see that they had taken the Afghans by surprise by striking back at night so quickly. Majors Swayne and Kershaw were ordered to storm the village, now unprepared to resist. But Swayne, with his usual genius for failure, lost his way and could not find the one village gate that was open. In the meantime, more tribesmen from the city were streaming to battle. Some ten thousand now crowded the summit, and by 7:00 A.M. enemy fire was so galling that the few skirmishers sent to the crown of the hill could only with difficulty hold their ground. Lieutenant Colonel Thomas Oliver could be seen trying to lead his discouraged men up the hill to reinforce them, but no one would follow him. Seconds before he was killed by a *jazail* bullet, the unfortunate man was heard to say: "Although my men desert me, I myself will do my duty."

At one critical moment, Shelton in despair offered a reward of one hundred rupees to any man who could seize the enemy flag planted some thirty yards forward of the British square. A few brave officers advanced, but nothing could induce their troops to charge. Refusing to retreat, Shelton continued to expose his tightly bunched squares to murderous fire from the Afghans long after it served no purpose.

When the cavalry refused an order to charge to break up an Afghan attack party, most of Shelton's infantry panicked and fled to the rear, leaving their one gun in Afghan hands. Unexpectedly the Afghans at that moment also fell back in some confusion just as they had victory within their grasp. Their leader, Abdullah Khan, it seems, had been wounded and would shortly die, not from combat but from a poisoned bullet fired from the rear by the assassin who had been hired by Mohan Lal. This was the same Abdullah Khan who, seeking vengeance, had organized the attack on Alexander Burnes's house.

Temporary disarray in the Afghan ranks permitted Shelton to rally his forces, retake the abandoned gun and advance to the brow of the hill. But he could not take full advantage of the situation because the cavalry still would not follow their officers and charge. Elphinstone was also at fault for not pouring in reinforcements from the cantonment at this critical time to exploit this unexpected opportunity to rout the enemy. Macnaghten pressed him to do so, but the old general only mumbled, "It is not possible, it's a wild scheme," and let the golden opportunity slip by. Rebel leaders later said that if the British had given chase to the retiring Afghan force, it would have broken the back of the rebellion, or at least spoiled the tribesmen's appetite for further combat with the British. But, instead, Shelton's miserable performance convinced them that they had nothing to fear from British guns.

Lieutenant Eyre was appalled by the performance of the British troops at this crucial moment. Because of cavalry cowardice and the demoralized state of the infantry, "the whole force of the enemy came on with renewed vigour and spirit, maintaining at the same time the fatal jazail fire which had already so grievously thinned our ranks. . . ." Adding to the peril of Shelton's force was a new wave of fresh tribesmen who poured forth from Kabul to join the fray. Lieutenant Eyre remembered that so many came, "the hill occupied by them scarcely afforded room for them to stand."[6]

By shortly after noon the front ranks of the advance British square had been decimated by Afghan fire. Shelton finally called for retreat, but not before the attacking tribesmen broke the square, causing the troops to flee in panic. Eyewitness Eyre, whose hand had been shattered in the action, later wrote of the debacle: "All order was at an end; the entreaties and commands of the officers endeavouring to rally the men were not even listened to, and an utter rout ensued down the hill in the direction of the cantonment, the enemy closely following, whose cavalry, in particular, made a fearful slaughter . . ."[7] Lady Sale, as usual following everything with hawk eyes from her rooftop vigil, more crisply referred to it as "a regular case of *sauve qui peut.*"[8]

British losses were heavy and many of the wounded had to be left lying in the field. British forces were spared total destruction only because the rebel vizier, Osman Khan, in the vanguard of the cavalry pursuit ordered his men to withhold fire for reasons then not evident. He himself circled British soldiers without cutting them down with his saber, as he could easily have done—almost like a sheepdog shepherding his flock.

Lieutenant Eyre attributed this disastrous defeat to six military errors: (1) only one gun had been deployed; (2) the village of Behmaru had not been taken under cover of darkness when it could have been; (3) no adequate stone breastworks had been thrown up by the sappers to provide some semblance of cover; (4) the vaunted British square formation, inappropriate in these circumstances, had only bunched the troops, making them even more vulnerable to the Afghan *jazails'* unerring fire; (5) the cavalry had been demoralized to the point of inaction by being exposed too long to Afghan fire; and (6) Shelton had delayed too long in falling back when it became obvious that the cause was lost. Eyre could have added that the British musket was no match for the longer-range Afghan *jazail.*

Eyre's analysis, that of a professional soldier who was there, was doubtless accurate, but more fundamentally, the battle had been lost because general despair and poor leadership at the top had sapped the will of the troops to fight. The Battle of Behmaru Heights destroyed what little morale and discipline had survived in the cantonment, and would fatally compromise future British moves. Sita Ram, who saw it all through the eyes of a native soldier in the forefront of the fighting, described it more simply: "This dispirited the sepoy army very much and, as the cold increased, we became helpless. . . . The whole English Army was in a miserable plight, since the men were worn out by continual fighting, guard duties and bad food."[9]

Elphinstone was plunged into depression by the whole miserable affair. As the defeated remnant of his force streamed into the cantonment, he thought vaguely of trying to rally them for one more try, but instead he turned to Shelton helplessly and complained: "Why Lord Sir, when I said to them 'eyes right,' they all looked the other way." This day had broken the spirit of the Kabul force and thus decided its fate.[10]

Chapter 23

---·•·---

TREACHERY

Their defeat at Behmaru left the British in a quandary. After this demonstration of ineptitude, no military solution to their predicament seemed feasible to Elphinstone or, for different reasons, to Macnaghten. And making matters worse, food supplies were again dangerously low. Akbar Khan realized that the easiest way to bring the British to heel was by starving them, and this he set about doing by intimidating villagers from whom the commissariat officers, Johnson and Boyd, were discreetly buying grain. Morale sank as supplies dwindled, and now the question was not how long, but if, the cantonment could hold out.

Elphinstone was eager to negotiate while Shelton still wanted them to fight their way to Jalalabad, although that option seemed fainter with every day that passed and ignored the problem of the camp followers who would be left stranded. Macnaghten favored sticking it out in Kabul a little longer, hoping "something would turn up."

Shah Shuja was understandably worried and urged Macnaghten to move the British garrison into the Bala Hissar; now he was quite ready to see his harem suffer a little inconvenience. But neither Elphinstone nor Shelton was willing to accommodate him. The old general feared that the troops could not make it to Shah Shuja's citadel, two and a half miles away, in the face of a concerted effort by the Afghans to block them. The rebels had already burned the Kabul River bridge, which the British would have to cross. Shelton saw no point in taking the risks implicit in moving from one Kabul garrison location to another at this time if they were going to leave Kabul anyway.

Mohan Lal, a somewhat more detached observer from his refuge with the Kizzilbash in town, contemptuously commented on the illogical reasoning of both officers: "A great many obstacles and danger were thrown [by Elphinstone] on the idea of the safety of our troops and camp followers in passing between our cantonment and the Bala Hissar, a distance of two and a half miles, while to travel eight to ten days to Jalalabad through the frozen passes . . . occupied by the ferocious and plundering Ghilzyes, was considered by our military superiors [i.e., Shelton] far from dangerous!!"[1]

Lieutenant Sturt, engineering officer who had from the outset recommended that the cantonment be located within the defensible Bala Hissar, now pressed again for moving all personnel to the great fortress. His mother-in-law, Lady Sale, was incensed to hear that his plan was rejected on the silly grounds that it would mean abandoning good buildings erected at great expense.

Mohan Lal concluded that Macnaghten had no alternative but to attempt to negotiate a withdrawal from Afghanistan, unless at least "a portion of the people or chiefs wished us to remain." This last statement was the essential rationale behind the political agent's secret intrigues whose object was to divide and rule. While Macnaghten negotiated with Akbar Khan and his camp, Mohan Lal hoped to build a secret constituency of tribes antagonistic to the Barakzai clan that would rise in defense of the British and Shah Shuja at the appropriate time.

Mohan Lal was a realist and understood with more clarity than most the predicament in which the British found themselves. He realized that his intrigues invited treachery, but under the circumstances he believed that the risk was worth taking. His principal Afghan agent, Naib Mohammed Sharif, was doing all he could do to "buy over the Ghilzyes." In fact, some of the Ghilzye chiefs had inscribed the flyleaf of a Koran with a solemn oath to support Shah Shuja, supply provisions to the British and even open the route to Jalalabad, in return for which they would expect to be handsomely paid. Mohan Lal knew, however, that these were probably empty promises, as cynically given as British money was cynically promised as a reward. In the end the tribes would do what they considered expedient, regardless of promises made. But Mohan Lal justified his efforts on the ground that there was no alternative; the army was not fit to fight, the troops were demoralized and the leadership was moribund. Moreover, Mohan Lal's intelligence revealed that Afghan spies within the cantonment were accurately reporting on Brigadier Shelton's defeatist croaking and interpreting it to mean that the British were now ready to give up. The Afghans also knew that British food supplies were nearly exhausted. On November 25, Vizier Osman Khan, who had spared the lives of many British soldiers as they fled the field at Behmaru, sent word to Macnaghten that the British must quietly and peacefully leave Afghanistan. His magnanimity on the battlefield had been based on the premise that the British Army must be allowed to survive with strength enough to make a peaceful, strategic retreat, in exchange for which Dost Mohammed would be allowed to return from exile in India. Had the British been massacred at Behmaru as they could have been, grounds for a deal would be gone and Calcutta would have no motive in permitting Dost Mohammed to return and reclaim his throne. The vizier, however, may also have been conscious of the value of keeping his own credit good with the British in the event that a twist of Afghan politics would force him to flee to Indian territory, or in the event that a British army of retribution reestablished control of Kabul.

On receipt of Osman Khan's request, Macnaghten began talks almost immediately, but the Afghans proved rude and unreasonable; they demanded unconditional surrender by the British and relinquishment of all arms. When the envoy refused to accept such humiliating terms, which would leave the British completely at the mercy of the Afghans, the chiefs stomped out of the conference promising ominously to meet next in battle. Macnaghten's rejoinder to this threat, more accurate than he knew, was: "We shall at all events meet at the day of judgment."

While the stormy session was taking place within the cantonment, a curious drama was occurring just outside. Afghan tribesmen, excited by rumors that the British were surrendering, and British soldiers, relieved that their ordeal might be over, openly fraternized. Lady Sale was flabbergasted with the spectacle of English soldiers of the 44th mingling unarmed with the Afghans. The half-starved troops gratefully accepted gifts of cabbages from their enemy. The adjutant soon put a stop to all this, fearing it was some kind of ruse "to throw us off our guard and surprise us"[2]; perhaps spirits were hidden in the cabbages, intended to intoxicate the English soldiers and leave the cantonment vulnerable to attack! In fact, it was simply the traditional hospitality of the Afghans, shown to strangers who were willing to stay in their house in peace. To the Afghans negotiations signified a British declaration of peace.

Rumors spread rapidly. On the following day, a crowd of unarmed Afghans again milled around outside the cantonment, curious about the *ferangi* army, which they believed was about to give up and go home. Even Lady Sale now depended on rumors. For once not privy to what was happening, she wrote in her diary on November 30: "The politicals are again very mysterious, and deny that negotiations are going on, but letters come in constantly; and we know they are treating with the Ghilzyes."[3] Within the cantonment, every day brought fresh rumors of attack. Everyone waited apprehensively for the blow to fall—everyone, that is, except Macnaghten, who at least kept up a pretense of optimism.

Although the cantonment was not attacked, the nearby Mohammed Sharif Fort was. On December 6, a small party of Afghans, so few that Lady Sale thought "A child with a stick might have repulsed them," rushed the fort, sending the British defenders fleeing in panic and abandoning their precious stock of ammunition.

"The 44th say that the 37th ran first," noted Lady Sale in her diary, but the commander of the fort said, "there was not a pin to choose—all cowards alike."[4] If the Afghans had any lingering doubts about British feebleness, the fall of the fort dispelled them. The main body of the 44th, the only queen's regiment with all-British troops, further disgraced itself that day. When they heard that their comrades had fled the fort, the regiment, fearing a general attack, almost ran from their placid guard posts within the cantonment bazaar. The 37th Native Infantry had to be sent in to relieve them. Lieutenant Eyre accused the 44th of having disintegrated because of bad leadership. "The regiment fell prey to a vital disease, which the Horse Guard alone could have remedied," he wrote, pointing his finger at the British Army Headquarters in London for having had the poor judgment to entrust the 44th to Brigadier Shelton in the first place.

Macnaghten still prayed that reinforcements from Kandahar would arrive. "We hear rumors of their approach," he told Elphinstone, trying to put off the terrible day when they must surrender unconditionally to the Afghans. The general, who now believed he needed the added weight of Shelton, Anquetil and Colonel Chambers of his staff to convince the envoy to negotiate, submitted a reply on December 8 bearing all their signatures. It read: "I beg to state that my opinion is that the present situation of the troops here is such that, from the want of provisions and the impracticality of procuring more, no time ought to be lost in entering into negotiations for a safe retreat." As for expecting help from a Kandahar relief column, Elphinstone reminded the envoy that they only had rumors of uncertain authenticity that he was trying to get through, certainly not enough "to risk the sacrifice of the troops . . ."⁵ There were even those who suspected that Nott was not that eager to pull Macnaghten's chestnuts out of the fire and perhaps was not making the effort he was capable of.

On December 10, rumors gave way to stark reality. Maclaren's brigade, sent by Nott, it was learned, had been stopped by the winter snows and would have to turn back. Macnaghten could hold out no longer; only enough food for a day or so remained. He knew he would have to try again to negotiate.

Macnaghten, with Captains Lawrence, Trevor and Mackenzie, on December 11 met the principal chieftains on the banks of the Kabul River, a mile from the cantonment. Akbar Khan was there, sounding a discordant note by rudely interrupting the envoy as the latter read out his proposals.

After two hours of arguing the chiefs finally agreed to accept the main provisions of Macnaghten's draft treaty: the British agreed to evacuate the cantonment within three days while the Afghans promised to provide them with food in the meantime. Captain Trevor was handed over to the Afghans and an Afghan chief, Musa Khan, was given to the British as hostages to guarantee the good faith of the signatories. A stray shot that rang out as the British party made its way back to the cantonment was perhaps an ominous sign, a tolling of the bell, but Macnaghten could only hope that the Afghans would keep their word.

It was later learned that Akbar Khan had wanted to seize Macnaghten then and there, but had been dissuaded by the other chiefs. Such impetuousness was typical of the Afghan leader; his emotional unpredictability made him dangerous and difficult to deal with, as Macnaghten was discovering to his dismay.

Macnaghten had surrendered to the Afghans. This he knew would ruin his career—the Bombay governorship would certainly not be given him— but the fate of the British cantonment was now the most pressing issue. This was a sad chapter in British history and he knew that he bore much of the responsibility for it. His only defense was that he had obtained the best terms he could, the only alternative being the destruction of the garrison of some forty-five hundred troops and its twelve thousand camp followers, which course "would little have benefited our country."⁶

However humiliating this all was, the British community was relieved to hear that arrangements had been made for what they hoped would be an orderly and safe evacuation from Afghanistan. But almost immediately it became apparent that the ordeal was by no means over. When the British detachment stationed in the Bala Hissar as added protection for

Shah Shuja was marched out to the cantonment in preparation for departure, some of Akbar Khan's tribesmen tried to force their way through the gate into the citadel. Shah Shuja's soldiers repelled them, inflicting heavy casualties as they struggled to slam the gates, but the incident was a harbinger of more trouble to come from the undisciplined Afghans, who cared little for agreements reached by their leaders.

The Afghans claimed that they had wanted to enter the Bala Hissar only to negotiate with Shah Shuja as to his own future. The chiefs did, in fact, offer to let Shah Shuja remain on his throne, provided he marry off his daughters to various Afghan sardars and appoint a vizier from the Barakzai clan. At first the shah had been tempted by this offer, but he concluded that he could not trust his treacherous countrymen and might be better off returning to India with the British. While the shah dithered about his decision, however, the British lost valuable time, and with every day's delay in departing their position became worse. Moreover, bad weather was rapidly closing in.

Promises made by the rebels to supply provisions were not kept. Forage for the animals on which the British relied for their exodus now became a critical issue. Starving horses, reduced to eating their own dung and chewing on tent pegs, were a pitiful sight. And Akbar Khan, who had been provided with money to buy camels for the British, had yet to produce any. When the British complained, the chiefs' standard reply was that they could not prevent their people from plundering the food and livestock intended for the cantonment. Captain Johnson, charged with building up supplies for the retreat, was at his wits' end. The Afghans, in his opinion, were "the most barefaced, impertinent scoundrels under the sun. . . . Armed with swords, daggers and matchlocks, they acknowledged no chief." Townfolk bringing precious grain were often plundered and beaten, he complained, yet "no measures are taken by our military authorities to check all this."[7] Lady Sale, now among the skeptics, wrote cynically in her diary: "Our allies, as they are now called, will be very magnanimous if they let us escape, now that they have fairly got us in their net."[8]

The three days stipulated by the treaty passed without the Afghans providing any of the promised supplies. When an exasperated Macnaghten met again with the Afghans to demand adherence to their agreement, the chiefs counterdemanded that the British first relinquish the forts held by them, which were essential to the cantonment's security, and provide more hostages as guarantors of their good faith. Outraged by this latest development, Macnaghten, like Shelton, was now all for making one last, heroic effort to march on the Kabul bazaar with all forces available, including the detachment just brought in from the Bala Hissar—an all-or-nothing effort. The alternative, in his opinion, was to remain supine while the Afghans dismembered them piecemeal. Elphinstone, however, could not be persuaded; the troops were not up to it—certainly he was not.

Macnaghten could only look on with sadness as the nearby forts were abandoned according to the agreement. Lawrence felt dismay as he witnessed "these strongholds, the last prop of our tottering power in Kabul, which had cost us so much blood to seize and defend, made over, one after the other, to our treacherous and exulting enemies."9

After relinquishing the forts and turning over four more hostages, Airey, Pottinger, Warburton and Conolly, the British were at the mercy of the Afghans. A new departure date, December 22, was agreed upon, but Macnaghten had no reason to believe that even with the benefit of a week's delay the Afghans would provide the necessary provisions and escort by this time. Mutual trust was lacking as they both intrigued behind the façade of agreement. Even nature seemed to conspire when on the eighteenth a heavy snow began to fall, inspiring historian Kaye's comment tinged with Victorian melodrama: "It was more and more painfully obvious, every day, that the curse of God was brooding over the agents of an unrighteous policy." Certainly the snow would make it more difficult for the British to get through the passes over which the Ghilzyes hovered in eager anticipation of their massacre of the infidels.

On the nineteenth Macnaghten heard the disheartening news that Maclaren's brigade had definitely given up its effort to reach Kabul and had returned to Kandahar. Deprived of this hope, faint as it had been, Macnaghten was consumed with despair. He and Elphinstone sent joint instructions to the three other British garrisons in Afghanistan—in Ghazni, Kandahar and Jalalabad—to return to India. If none of them could relieve Kabul, their retirement to India while they still could do so seemed to be the best course of action. Moreover, the Afghans demanded it as a condition of permitting the Kabul garrison to withdraw.

Macnaghten would not yet give up; he clung to the one remaining hope that he might still pit Afghan against Afghan to salvage something from the crumbling British position. After all, the Ghilzyes had never liked Barakzai rule under Dost Mohammed. Nor did the Persian Kizzilbash have any love for other Afghans. The threads of common cause against the *ferangis,* which bound the ever-feuding Afghans together at this time, were tenuous. On the basis of Mohan Lal's intelligence, Macnaghten could fairly reason that there was dissension beneath the surface, open to encouragement as the various factions already jockeyed for power. But his secret maneuvers to engineer some eleventh-hour reprieve from disaster, executed through Mohan Lal, lacked coherence; they were the thrashings of a drowning man.

Operating precariously from his sanctuary with the Kizzilbash chief,

Mohan Lal now assumed an even more important role in the unfolding drama. According to Macnaghten's strategy, it was now vital to convince certain Ghilzyes and the Kizzilbash to emerge from their secret relationship with him and side openly with the British against the Barakzais. The envoy sent word to Mohan Lal on December 20: "You can tell the Ghilzyes and Khan Shereen [Shirin Khan, chief of the Kizzilbash] that after they have declared for his Majesty [Shah Shuja] and sent in 100 *kurwars* of grain to the cantonment, I shall be glad to give them a bond for five lakhs."[10]

Macnaghten had an ornate rationale for his intrigues. He was probably justified in resorting to any means, however duplicitous, to save his sixteen thousand or so charges from destruction. But he seemed to feel a need to assuage his conscience, to put a better face on his secret offer to the Ghilzye and Kizzilbash leaders. He instructed Mohan Lal to tell them: "I am to stand by my engagement with the Barakzais [i.e., Akbar Khan] . . . but if any portion of the Afghans [i.e., the Ghilzyes or Kizzilbash] wish our troops to remain in the country, I shall think myself at liberty to break the engagement which I have made to go away, which engagement was made believing it to be in accordance with the wishes of the Afghan nation." Mohan Lal more explicitly added: "If the Ghilzyes and Kizzilbashes wish us to stay, let them declare so openly in the course of tomorrow and we will side with them." To signify their sincerity these groups were to deliver a large quantity of grain to the British.

While Mohan Lal was secretly talking with the Ghilzye and Kizzilbash leaders, the envoy himself was dickering, not too successfully, with Akbar Khan and other Barakzai chiefs, who kept increasing their demands. This was a dangerous double game, and Macnaghten began to lose his nerve as Mohan Lal was unable to get the Ghilzyes and Kizzilbashis to make their move. Now recognizing that he would have to abide by his Barakzai treaty, as hollow as it appeared, Macnaghten told Mohan Lal to refuse any further grain shipments from his friends. With more than a trace of panic, Macnaghten feared "The sending of grain to us just now . . . would lead the Burukzyes [Barakzais] to suppose that I am intriguing with a view of breaking my agreement,"[11] which, of course, he was.

Akbar Khan, who had learned of Macnaghten's game, now had an ace up his sleeve, and launched his own devious plot. The Barakzai chief had always thought that the treaty with the British was too lenient. Now he saw a way of repudiating it and enhancing his own position in preparation for the inevitable struggle for power following Shah Shuja's fall. Through intermediaries, Akbar Khan made a new proposition to Macnaghten on December 22, stipulating that Shah Shuja remain king, while he himself would become vizier and enjoy a generous subsidy from the British for the rest of his life. In return, Akbar Khan would seize his rival, Aminullah Khan, the old but still influential Barakzai landowner, and deliver his head to the British. With a regime thus favorable to them the British could remain until the good weather of spring before gracefully leaving. Akbar asked Macnaghten to keep the proposition secret so that it could not be discovered and foiled by Aminullah Khan. Macnaghten leaped at the offer—except for the part about Aminullah's murder, and certainly he did not want the old man's head as a trophy. Instead, it was agreed that the chief would be made prisoner and handed over to the British.

Mohan Lal learned from his sources at 10:00 A.M. on December 23 the reasons for Akbar Khan's generous-sounding offer: it was a trap and Aminullah was the bait. Akbar had no intention of abiding by his offer. In fact, he intended to exploit their discussions and accuse the envoy of deceit; on this basis he would repudiate the treaty. Macnaghten, in his desperation, had fallen into the trap—and sealed his own doom! Akbar planned to seize Macnaghten and either poison him or shoot him with the very pistols the envoy had presented to him the evening before as a gesture of goodwill.[12]

This was critical intelligence, and Mohan Lal sent a warning to Macnaghten by messenger just as the envoy was preparing to leave for his fatal meeting with Akbar Khan. When Macnaghten received the message, he blanched. It was not clear whether he was frustrated by the bad news or alarmed at its implications.[13]

Mohan Lal begged Macnaghten not to meet Akbar Khan outside the cantonment "as he is a man that nobody can trust." Macnaghten's wife, frantic with worry, wept as she implored her husband not to meet the Barakzai leader. On the morning of the twenty-third, the day of the meeting, several staff officers joined him for breakfast. When he explained the new agreement to them, Captain Mackenzie saw immediately that this was a plot and said so. Macnaghten, now committed to his course of action, testily replied: "A plot! Trust me for that!" Even Elphinstone, when he heard of the envoy's plan, roused himself to warn of treachery, but Macnaghten turned a deaf ear and ordered him to ready two regiments with which to recapture one of the adjacent forts. "Leave it all to me," he barked irritably. "I understand these things better than you do."[14]

To Elphinstone's credit, he tried to emphasize his protest with a more formal letter to the envoy, pointing out certain warnings: "I hope there is no fear of treachery. . . . The sending of two guns and two regiments away would divide our forces. . . . What guarantees have we for the truth of all that has been said?" Somehow, Macnaghten never received this letter—not that it would have dissuaded him from the step he was determined to take. The tension under which he had lived for the last six months had exhausted him. "Rather than live it all over again, I would risk a thousand deaths,"[15] he told Lawrence.

At noon Macnaghten, accompanied by Lawrence, Trevor and Mackenzie in their scarlet jackets and high black shakoes, rode forth to meet Akbar Khan with only a modest, ceremonial escort of ten mounted troopers. Suddenly Macnaghten, remembering that he intended to present Akbar Khan with a horse as further evidence of his goodwill, sent Mackenzie back for it. By the time Mackenzie caught up with the party, it had reached the Barakzai chief at the agreed-upon rendezvous on the banks of the Kabul River. Something seemed odd, however; there were more Afghans than they had expected. The ambiance was hardly what the British wanted for a secret negotiation.

After the usual exchange of salaams (Moslem greetings), Akbar thanked the envoy for the horse just given him and suggested they dismount to talk. Trevor and Mackenzie joined Macnaghten, who, parting the tails of his black frock coat, squatted on the horse blankets spread for him on the ground. Mackenzie later explained his feelings. "Men talk of presentiment," he wrote. "I suppose it was something of the kind that came over me, for I could scarcely prevail upon myself to quit my horse."[16] Lawrence hung back cautiously and knelt a few yards away, ready to spring into action at the slightest sign of treachery. When he protested to Akbar Khan that the onlookers were crowding them, the Barakzai chief made light of it: "We are all in the same boat," he said.

Suddenly Akbar Khan shouted, "Seize them, seize them!" At this signal one of the chiefs pinioned Lawrence while others captured Mackenzie and Trevor. All three were mounted on horses behind the saddles of their Afghan captors and hastily driven off. They had time only to watch Macnaghten being dragged down the hill, and saw him valiantly wrestling with Akbar Khan in an effort to break free. Lawrence's last view of the hapless envoy was a contorted posture in which "his head was where his heels had been"; there was a look of "consternation and horror depicted in his countenance." Akbar Khan then murdered Macnaghten.

None of the British officers saw Macnaghten killed, although Afghan witnesses later reported that his last words, "For God's sake!"[17] were uttered in anguish before Akbar Khan shot him with one of a brace of pistols the envoy had given him, just as Mohan Lal had predicted.

At the first sign of violence the mounted escort fled to the cantonment. Only one trooper, Jemendar Ram Singh, stayed behind to fight. His reward for bravery was to be killed almost immediately by the sword-brandishing Afghans.

Trevor fell off his horse and was butchered by an Afghan who called him a "dog," one of the worst possible epithets for an Afghan to utter. Lawrence and Mackenzie were rescued from a similar fate and taken to the fort of Mohammed Sharif to be held prisoner. Aminullah Khan, obviously aware that the British had conspired against him, visited the prisoners to vent his rage. "Death will be too good for you," he screamed. Then the two British officers, narrowly escaping assassination by a frenzied tribesman who fired at them in their cell, were treated to the sight of a severed human hand being made to wave at them through the window in a macabre gesture of farewell. It was Macnaghten's hand.

Lady Sale had the grim task of informing Lady Macnaghten and Mrs. Trevor of their husbands' deaths. "Over such scenes I draw a veil," she wrote in her diary. "It was a most painful meeting to us all." Why the bodies were not retrieved mystified Lady Sale, who felt the cavalry could easily have done so.

Even in death, Macnaghten was not accorded much respect by his countrymen. As Lady Sale noted, "A fallen man meets but little justice; and reports are rife that the Envoy was guilty of double-dealing."[18] The last anyone saw of Macnaghten was his head on a pikestaff as it was paraded through Kabul by the exultant Afghans while his limbs likewise were exhibited as trophies. Only his trunk remained, to be hung in the bazaar with Trevor's corpse, macabre symbols of a failed British policy.

Chapter 24

—————— •═•═• ——————

RETREAT

I WAS HAULED OUT OF MY SICK ROOM," COMPLAINED ELDRED POT-
tinger, "and obligated to negotiate for the safety of a parcel of fools who
were doing all they could to ensure their destruction."[1] Elphinstone had
asked him to replace Macnaghten as senior political officer and preside
over the British capitulation. Pottinger had rarely agreed with Macnaghten
on anything, much less treating with the treacherous Afghans; now he had
to pick up the shattered pieces left by the late envoy. Pottinger had a low
opinion of Elphinstone, whose infirmities prevented any semblance of
leadership, and who himself complained that he had been "degraded from
general to the Lord-lieutenant's head constable." Now, in the supreme
crisis of his command, old Elphie could think of nothing but capitulation.
This was an anathema to Pottinger, who was a lone voice of dissent in the
staff, crying out against acceptance of the treaty drafted by Macnaghten
before he was killed.

The new terms now demanded by the Afghans would strip the British of their treasury and all but six of their guns. What seemed cruelest of all, the Afghans wanted married officers, their wives and children left behind as hostages.

Elphinstone called a council of war on Christmas Eve to discuss the terms. There were predictable howls of anguish from the officers with dependents who did not want to be left behind and expose their families to the whims of the Afghans; one officer even threatened to shoot his wife rather than leave her at the mercy of the natives. Except for that provision, however, all members of the dispirited staff were reconciled to accepting Afghan terms—all, that is, except Eldred Pottinger, who argued strenuously with them. He also opposed the decision to order the other garrisons to leave Afghanistan as demanded by the Afghans. General Nott had already been designated commander in chief by Calcutta; that he had not been able to reach Kabul did not change this. Elphinstone, therefore, did not have the authority to command other garrisons, particularly since he would be acting under duress.

More fundamentally, Pottinger was against leaving Kabul at this time. Their best hope, he argued, was to defend themselves in the Bala Hissar, at least until spring, by which time a relief force might have arrived and the weather would be kinder. But if the staff insisted that evacuation take place now, he believed that the army must be prepared to fight unencumbered with baggage. As sensible as this seems, Shelton and the others could not bear to leave their goods behind. Logic had flown from men too depressed to face reality.

There was a glint of good news, a welcome Christmas present that arrived on December 26 to support Pottinger's position. Letters from both Jalalabad and Peshawar told of reinforcements on their way from India. Political officer Mackeson in Peshawar wrote of an advance contingent with ammunition that had arrived at the border town, and the 16th Lancers, accompanied by the 9th and 31st Regiments, were close behind. There were other hopeful developments: Mohan Lal's intelligence told of growing dissension among the various Afghan factions. Shah Shuja's support seemed to be increasing, perhaps because of the news that a British relief column was on the way. Osman Khan, who had all along hedged his bets, now sent a secret message offering to escort the British safely to Peshawar. Certainly, he was more trustworthy than Akbar Khan, although neither of them could necessarily control the Ghilzyes along the way who were eager for loot.

Mohan Lal had bad news as well that supported Pottinger's contention that the Afghan chiefs could not be relied upon. The British agent relayed critical intelligence given him by his protector, Shirin Khan, leader of the

Kizzilbash faction, that Akbar Khan had no intention of escorting the British. It was all a plot to get them out of the cantonment, where they could then be plundered and killed. Shirin Khan urgently advised the British to take refuge in the Bala Hissar as soon as possible rather than risk certain death in the passes.

Mohan Lal was not the only source of such ominous information. Even Mackenzie and Lawrence, prisoners of the Kabul chiefs, heard a drunken Ghilzye brag of how British troops would never reach Jalalabad alive. And Captain Johnson picked up a terrifying rumor that the British men were to be murdered while the wives and children would be held hostage for the safe return of Akbar Khan's wives and family. Lady Sale, who rarely missed anything, filled in the gory details of this story: "It is their intention to get all our women into their possession; and to kill every man except one, who is to have his hands and legs cut off and be placed with a letter *in terrorem* at the entrance to the Khyber Pass to deter all *ferangis* from entering the country again."[2]

Despite all this evidence that a plot was afoot, Pottinger could not move Elphinstone or his staff, argue as he might. Like lemmings they seemed to have an irresistible urge to march to their destruction. Shelton was the real problem. He was the whip who bullied Pottinger and kept the pack in line. His will prevailed and in surly tones he commanded Pottinger as political officer to accept all the Afghan terms except the clause requiring the women and children to be left behind with their husbands. (Elphinstone had roused himself to oppose leaving women and children behind; he would not go along with an arrangement that would disgrace him forever in England. A spark of chivalry remained in the old general even if most of his other faculties had atrophied.) Mackenzie later commented that Pottinger "signed the treaty in soldierly obedience, knowing full well that he would be held responsible for that which was the work of others. . . . The hero of Herat was obliged to do the thing that he abhorred."[3]

Pottinger did not have the power that Macnaghten had had as envoy. He was simply filling in as senior political officer, a hired hand, so to speak. He was powerless against Shelton, who resorted to ridicule and scorn to drown out his voice of dissent. Having appealed to logic and pleaded his case as forcefully as he knew how, Pottinger in the end had no choice but to carry out the decisions of the Council of War controlled by Shelton.

Unlike Burnes, who when faced with overpowering views which he could not change had accommodated himself to the prevailing policy, Pottinger made it clear that he was acting on orders with which he did not agree and which he carried out under pressure. The record would ultimately prove useful to him, but at the time he could conclude that his

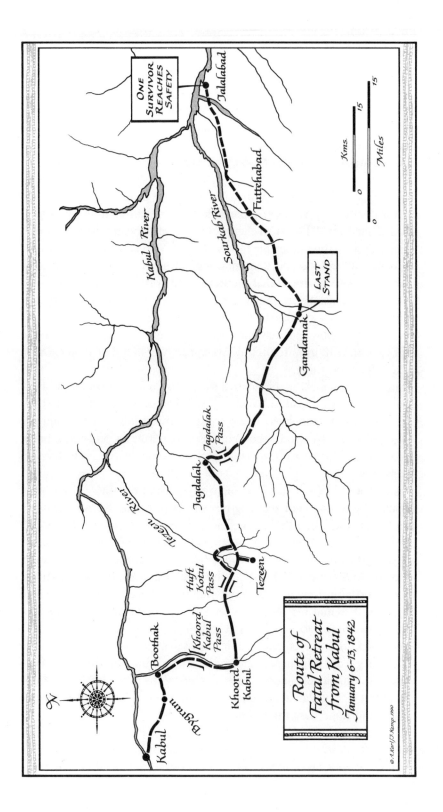

ONE SURVIVOR
REACHES
SAFETY

Jalalabad

Futtehabad

Sourkab River

Kabul River

LAST
STAND

Gandamak

Jagdalak Pass

Jagdalak

Tezeen River

Huft
Kotul
Pass

Tezeen

Khoord
Kabul Pass

Boothak

Khoord
Kabul

Bygram

Kabul

Kms.

Miles

15

15

0

0

Route of
Fatal Retreat
from Kabul
January 6-13, 1842

© A. Karl/J. Kemp 1990

stand would cost him his career—if he lived through the gathering storm.

As for Mohan Lal's warnings, the only response given him by the unbelieving military staff wedded to its suicidal course of action was a curt note saying: "The chiefs you name [as conspirators] have signed the treaty, and the most of them accompany us. As for others attacking us on the road, we are in the hands of God, and in him we trust—We hope to be off tomorrow."[4]

The Indian sepoys by now had a thoroughly jaundiced view of their British "betters." "Wisdom seemed to have departed from everyone," recalled Sita Ram. "The usual energy of the English officers had vanished." Indeed, despite the intolerable provocation of Macnaghten's and Trevor's murders, Elphinstone had done nothing. After the heinous act, the Afghans had been convinced that the stern hand of British retribution would be raised to punish them; they rushed to prepare defenses in the city. But while the Afghans, shocked by the enormity of the act committed by their chiefs, waited apprehensively for a British attack, the British cowered in their cantonment, misinterpreting Afghan activity in Kabul as preparation for an attack on them.

Sita Ram, more charitable toward the British officers than many of the English themselves, made allowances: "they had suffered such severe trials that their spirits had been depressed by misfortune."[5] This forgiving statement was a tribute to the long-suffering nature of Sita Ram, but it glossed over the abysmal leadership that had brought the misfortune on themselves.

But what of Shah Shuja? Was there any truth to the rumors that swept through the cantonment accusing him of betraying the British and going over to the rebels' side? In fact, he had good reason to feel that the British had betrayed him. Brigadier Anquetil, commander of his forces, was now preparing to join the British exodus, taking with him the shah's army, necessary to defend His Majesty in the Bala Hissar. Shah Shuja's pathetic appeal to Elphinstone not to forsake him in his hour of need fell on deaf ears. The shah and his enormous zenana were being abandoned to their fate. Shah Shuja had hoped that the British would move into the Bala Hissar with him, thereby defending themselves as well as the throne for which they were responsible until relief arrived. But the British decision to depart immediately under terms dictated by the rebels left him with no choice but to reach an accommodation with the chiefs permitting him to remain and hope they would honor it.

The matter of British hostages now arose. Captains Drummond, Walsh, Webb and Warburton, having been selected by the British to sacrifice themselves, were taken to the house of Nawab Mohammed Zaman Khan, temporary sovereign, where they were joined by Captains Conolly and Airey to await an uncertain fate as prisoners of the Afghans until Dost Mohammed and his family were safely returned to Kabul by the British. One of the hostages smuggled out a note to Lady Sale assuring her that their host, the nawab, was treating them well, although they were cooped up in a room only eighteen feet by ten feet and were harassed daily by crowds that gathered in the courtyard below their rooms to taunt them.

Captain Lawrence, needed to arrange the turnover of the British treasury to the Afghans according to the terms of the agreement, was released, as was Captain Mackenzie, also seized at the time of Macnaghten's murder. Lady Sale thought Lawrence looked haggard and ten years older for his ordeal. Both told how Akbar Khan had sworn to them that he had not been responsible for Macnaghten's death and wept copiously for two hours to prove his sadness at the envoy's demise. While neither man believed him, they did admit that he and other chiefs had been responsible for saving their lives from the inflamed tribesmen who assaulted the British negotiating party. Mackenzie was convinced that Akbar Khan had intended to seize Macnaghten as a prisoner, not kill him, but while struggling with him the hot-blooded chieftain's temper had erupted and he shot him in a fit of anger. This, however, did not square with Mohan Lal's intelligence that the murder had been premeditated.

Captain James Skinner was also sent back to the cantonment from the city, where he had been trapped during the uprising. He had lived a precarious existence, masquerading for a while as a veiled Afghan woman to avoid detection. When finally discovered and held captive by the rebel chiefs, he proved useful to them as a go-between with the cantonment during the early period of the negotiations. Now he was released to rejoin the British exodus, doubtless a relief to him—if only briefly.

The sick and wounded also had to be left behind, including Lieutenant Haughten, who had narrowly avoided death with the 4th Gurkhas at Charekar but still suffered from his wounds. Medical officers drew lots to see who would stay behind to care for them. Assistant Surgeon Primrose of the 44th and Campbell were the ones selected, although Dr. Berwick volunteered to change places with Primrose and remain in Kabul instead. This decision would cost Primrose his life.

Within the cantonment the pall of apprehension hung heavily. The biting chill of winter depressed spirits even more. Snow had been falling since December 18 and the passes through which the British had to travel were by now clogged with heavy drifts. The sepoys, not used to cold weather, were particularly miserable. Firewood was exhausted and they had to huddle together in an effort to keep warm. Several of them died of exposure. Officers, fortunate enough to have a few pieces of furniture, burned them for warmth. Lady Sale burned her favorite mahogany dining-room table, raising the temperature in her sitting room momentarily to eleven degrees.

As the latest date set for departure, January 5, approached, and the British relinquished most of their cannons, the Afghans became bolder. Captain Johnson noted in his journal that the tribes "infest our gates and insult us in every possible way—stop our supplies coming in from town and ill-treat those who bring them." Making it all the more humiliating was Elphinstone's refusal to permit the troops to rescue their supplies or defend themselves. The Afghans, complained Johnson, "attribute our forbearance to dastardly cowardice."[6] Some five hundred tribesmen intent on plunder attacked the rear gate on December 30, but were driven off by the threat of one of the few remaining guns trained on them.

Discipline within the cantonment diminished as the days dragged on, and spirits were depressed by new rumors that the Afghans intended to annihilate the British once they left the cantonment. On New Year's Day Afghan friends called on Sergeant Deane, who was closer to the natives than most because of his Afghan wife, and confided in him the horrifying news that some ten thousand Kohistanis planned to fall upon the British after they had cleared the Khoord Kabul Pass and reached Tezeen. Those not killed then would be massacred by the Ghilzyes at a village called Soorkhab.

Lady Sale noted calmly in her diary on January 4: "The Afghans still tell us we are doomed . . ." One Afghan friend warned her and her daughter, Mrs. Sturt, to "wear neemchees—common leather ones—and turbans [Afghan clothing], and ride mixed in with the suwars [Indian soldiers], not near the other ladies, as they are very likely to be attacked."[7] As confirmation, Captain Johnson claimed to have heard from an Afghan friend that Akbar Khan would seize the British ladies as hostages for the safe return of his own wives and family from British captivity.

Agents among the Kohistanis advised the British to postpone their departure so that the tribesmen could bring in more food supplies. And they passed on tempting promises: the Kohistanis would burn Kabul and escort reinforcements from Sale's brigade in Jalalabad if sent. But could the Kohistani agents be believed; was this but a trap to lure Sale and his garrison to their destruction? Certainly this did not square with Sergeant Deane's information. Shelton warned Sturt "to keep the matter quiet—it would only cause excitement."

Each day brought new maddening delays. Agreed-upon departure dates, the first having been December 14, had been slipped several times on the excuse that the escort force was not yet ready or that arrangements along the route had not been completed. This provoked nagging fears that the arrangements were not for their safety but for their annihilation. Captain Lawrence was particularly worried, as evidenced by a letter he wrote as he prepared to leave stating: "The troops march tomorrow [January 5], treachery is feared." And Lady Sale noted: "We are to depart without a guard, without money, without provisions, without wood." Lieutenant Sturt, no less gloomy, was convinced that if they had to fight, they would fight but once, "the result is in the hands of God." While rummaging through her son-in-law's books before jettisoning them to reduce luggage, Lady Sale came upon a poem by Campbell on the Battle of Hohenlinden. It sent a shiver of presentiment through her when she read:

> *Few, few shall part where many meet,*
> *The snow shall be their winding sheet;*
> *And every turf beneath their feet,*
> *shall be a soldier's sepulchre.* 8

Since no Afghan escort troop had arrived, the march was delayed still another day to January 6, 1842. Indicative of the British determination to march that day, escort or no escort, the engineers on the eve of departure cut a large opening in the cantonment walls to permit the troops to march out in better order than if they had to funnel through the narrow gate.

Pottinger made a last-minute effort to dissuade Elphinstone and the staff from proceeding without a reliable escort, urging them instead to make a dash for the Bala Hissar as they pretended to leave. No one would listen. The departure was set for 8:00 A.M. on January 6. The buglers roused the cantonment at daybreak to make ready. It was an ungainly procession that formed up that fateful morning to venture forth from the protection of the cantonment with the intention of walking ninety miles in subzero weather, hip-high in snowdrifts and surrounded by hostile tribes. No more likely recipe for disaster could be imagined.

Mohan Lal, intending to accompany the exodus, had made his way to the cantonment from town despite Shirin Khan's efforts to dissuade him from leaving. The Kizzilbash chief knew the fate awaiting the column; if the British would not heed his warnings, at least he would try to save his friend Mohan Lal. Mohan Lal, however, was ordered to remain with the Kizzilbash; he still had a vital job to perform in Kabul if he could survive in that caldron of intrigue and hostility. With his net of spies and runners, he would be Peshawar's only link with the hostages left behind, and he was needed there to salvage whatever tribal support he could as the various factions, no longer with a common enemy present to bind them together, fell to squabbling among themselves.

The force consisted of 700 British troops, 34 British women and children including Mrs. Macnaghten and Lady Sale, 2,000 men of the Bengal Native Infantry, 250 Bengal Cavalry, 1,150 Irregular Horse, 400 of Shah Shuja's levy and an estimated 12,000 camp followers. Brigadier Anquetil led the advance column out from the cantonment at 9:00 A.M., an hour later than planned. The main column followed under Brigadier Shelton. But Colonel Chambers and the rear guard ran into trouble as the Afghans rallied to harass the column.* The plan fell apart at the outset. The order of battle was perfectly reasonable, but any hope of maintaining discipline disappeared almost immediately as the terrified camp followers rushed ahead, inundating the ranks, creating intolerable congestion and confusion. For safety they mingled with the soldiers in the vanguard, inhibiting forward movement and confusing the command structure.

That morning Nawab Jubbar Khan, once the British friend in court and now sincerely anxious to save his old friends from destruction whatever their differences with him were, sent word that they should postpone any further advance until a proper escort could be made ready. But his warning came too late; the force had begun to move and could not be stopped without placing in jeopardy the now-unprotected troops if they tried to spend the night camped in the open so near the town. Nevertheless, Elphinstone in a fog of confusion ordered Shelton to halt. Fortunately, Mackenzie, charged with delivering the order, refused to pass on the inane message and the main body of the force lumbered on as best it could, leaving the rear guard to keep the hovering Afghans at bay. Even before the rear guard had completely extricated itself from the cantonment, tribesmen had rushed in to the northern part of the enclosure and in a frenzy began to plunder what had been left behind by the British.

The Kabul River, only 150 yards from the cantonment gate, unnecessarily slowed progress. The erection of a temporary bridge spanning the river fell behind schedule; not until after noon could the advance column and the main column, jammed up in the narrow space between the cantonment and the river, begin to cross. The camp followers, who could just as well have waded across the river, insisted on using the bridge, making a traffic jam of monumental proportions and seriously interfering with troop

*The advance guard consisted of the 44th Queen's Regiment, 4th Irregular Horse, Skinner's Horse, two Horse Artillery six-pounders, sappers and miners mountain train and the envoy's escort. In the main body there were the 5th and 7th Native Infantry, Anderson's Horse, Shah Shuja's 6th Regiment, and two Horse Artillery six-pounders. The rear guard consisted of the 54th Native Infantry, the 5th Cavalry and two six-pounders.

movements. For reasons best known to Elphinstone, Sturt's earlier advice that everyone ford the river at any one of several shallow places rather than waste time bridging it had been ignored. The delay that this caused would prove crucial.

Finally across the river, the advance and main columns could move through the Siah Sung Hills toward the Khoord Kabul Pass less than twenty miles from Kabul. The rear guard, however, which had not been able to get completely clear of the cantonment until dusk, became stalled at the river's edge and was forced to take up an exposed position to guard the baggage stacked up awaiting transport across the narrow bridge. By this time the Afghans, gorged with loot, had mounted the cantonment walls and were firing at them. Some fifty men were killed before the column could move on.

As darkness fell, the blaze of cantonment buildings, put to the torch by the Afghans, illuminated the miserable rear-guard troops as they struggled to extricate themselves from their predicament. As they fought their way out of the Kabul plain in an effort to rejoin the main column, Lawrence was shocked to see "A continuous line of poor wretches, men, women and children, dead or dying from the cold and wounds"—camp followers who had already fallen victim to Afghan marauders. Those still alive but unable to move pleaded that someone should kill them and put them out of their misery. Many children, too exhausted to keep up, collapsed in the snow while their mothers wailed in despair until too numb with cold to cry. With each mile more fell by the wayside to clutter the route with their bloody and frozen bodies in a wrenching scene of tragedy unfolding.

Not until two in the morning did the rear guard catch up with the first two columns, which had chaotically pitched camp for the night at Bygram, only five miles from Kabul. Arriving in disarray, the exhausted soldiers woke up the encampment with their shouts as they tried to find their units in the dark. Much of the baggage had been left behind as a result of Afghan harassment; without shelter, food or fire, everyone fared badly that night. By morning frostbite hobbled most of them.

The Afghans, distracted by looting the cantonment, were not ready to turn their full attention to the departing British until the second day. Had the British been able to clear the dangerous Khoord Kabul Pass, festooned with tribal marksmen, and reach Tezeen by the end of the first day before the full force of the Ghilzyes had assembled, they might have been spared the fate that awaited them. Progress had been painfully slow, and with a critical day lost their chances of getting through the pass were diminished.

As dawn broke on the seventh, a scene of indescribable chaos met the eye. Strewn about the ground were men who had frozen in their sleep during the night. Poor old Macgregor, an aging noncommissioned officer, could be seen rigidly holding his sword aloft, a macabre statue of resolute devotion as he lay dead in the snow. Most serious, all of Shah Shuja's 6th Regiment had decamped in the night—better to face slavery in Kabul than be frozen to death or slaughtered on the march.

Without rations and half-frozen, the troops straggled forth at 8:00 A.M. In Vincent Eyre's judgment, not more than half of the retreating force were fit for duty by this time. Most could not hold their rifles because of their frostbitten hands. Ahead of the column could be seen crowds of camp followers, now beyond regimentation, who had pushed on ahead in confusion during the night rather than endure their beds of snow any longer.

The rear guard, under Colonel Chambers, whose force still suffered from the attacks of the day before, now took the lead while Brigadier Anquetil, previously in the van, took his turn at the rear. The advance force only with difficulty forced themselves past the camp followers clogging the road, and regardless the going was slow through the snow. Clods of frozen snow lodged in the horses' hooves was another problem. Eyre recalled that it took chisel and hammer to break the ice and snow loose from their mounts. The soldiers fared no better. "The very air we breathed froze in its passage out of the mouth and nostrils, forming a coating of small icicles on our moustaches and beards," recalled Eyre.

It was no longer a real army that moved. Fatigue, fear and frostbite had turned it into a rabble in arms. Eyre called it "a mingled mob of soldiers, camp followers and baggage-cattle," totally devoid of "even the faintest semblance of that regularity and discipline on which depended our only chance of escape from the dangers which threatened us."9 Some of the sepoys stripped off their insignia and tried to blend in with the followers in what would prove a vain effort to escape Afghan sniping.

As the columns moved fitfully forward, Afghan horsemen could be seen around the fringes keeping pace. On one occasion they struck at the rear guard, now consisting of the all-British Queen's 44th, a squadron of Irregular Horse and a unit of mountain-train guns. Three precious guns were seized before the dispirited 44th could rally to defend them. Lieutenant Green, commander of artillery, managed to spike the guns in a daring raid with two other officers, but, failing general support from the 44th, the guns could not be retrieved. Now but two nine-pounders remained.

As the horrors of the second day began to unfold, Pottinger received a message from Nawab Mohammed Zaman Khan. Although titular head of state in the rebel government in Kabul, he was nonetheless one of the few Afghan leaders who had exhibited a sense of honor. He had been consistently fair to the British throughout their ordeal, and now he again urged them to halt until he could organize some kind of defense against the uncontrollable tribesmen who lay in wait in the rocks high above the Khoord Kabul Pass. Better the British had listened to him. The pass, some five miles long, was so narrow in places that the towering crags blotted out the sun's rays, even in midday. A fast-flowing mountain stream repeatedly crisscrossed the trail, making progress difficult in the best of times, but under these circumstances it would prove a serious impediment.

Upon receipt of Nawab Mohammed Zaman Khan's letter addressed to Pottinger as political officer, Elphinstone called a halt for the remainder of the day in the hope that the proferred supplies would arrive and to give time for the rear guard, still threatened, to close up before being cut off. This provoked an outraged Shelton to protest that valuable time was being lost. Moreover, to halt in snowdrifts without food or shelter, he believed, invited further disaster. Nonetheless, Elphinstone stopped the column at Boothak near the head of the pass. It was now 1:00 P.M. and the retreating column had advanced no farther than ten miles since leaving Kabul.

Suddenly, Akbar Khan approached at the head of several hundred Afghan horsemen. Captain Skinner, sent to remonstrate with him over broken Afghan promises, was met by only more demands. The British, Akbar Khan said, had only themselves to blame for their suffering since they had not waited for their escort. The Afghan chief promised to escort them to Jalalabad and provide food, forage and firewood, but only on the condition that they not proceed beyond Tezeen until General Sale evacuated the Jalalabad garrison. Moreover, Akbar Khan insisted that more British hostages be given up as guarantee of good faith.

By now Akbar Khan's word was scarcely to be believed, but there was nothing the British could do about it. As night fell on the frozen eight-thousand-foot plateau where the columns had paused, no decision was reached. Elphinstone had wanted to force the pass that night, but wiser counsel convinced him that it would be dangerous to attempt to get through the narrow defile in the snow and dark. The wretched remnant of an army settled in for a second night exposed to the elements. The British had little expectation that the dawn would make things seem any brighter.

Chapter 25

AN ARMY DIES

O N JANUARY 8 THE SUN ROSE ON ANOTHER SCENE OF HORROR. MORE corpses in macabre frozen postures profaned the bleak plateau. Vincent Eyre, grateful for having awakened to see another day, could not imagine a more agonizing death than one in which "frost tortures every sensitive limb until the tenacious spirit itself sinks under the exquisite extreme of human suffering."[1] Those who survived the subzero night roused themselves and shambled forward through the snow without waiting for orders. Panic suddenly seized thousands of camp followers and propelled them forward as they struggled to avoid the thicket of gunfire. Taking advantage of the confusion, the Ghilzyes massed for attack at the head of the pass, but in a spasm of resolve Major Thain rallied the 44th and charged. The tribesmen scattered rather than face a pitched battle, proving what could be done with determined leadership even at this stage of the army's disintegration. Swept up in the fleeting spirit of small triumph, the horse artillerymen got drunk on spirits of another kind raided from the stores, and would have dashed madly after the fleeing Afghans had they not been restrained by Sturt.

The fate of the British force was, in fact, being decided then in negotiations with the Afghans rather than by indecisive skirmishes that gave only momentary respite. Captain Skinner again served as negotiator with Akbar Khan—not that he had much bargaining power on his side. Akbar Khan insisted that Jalalabad be evacuated by Sale and demanded more hostages. He particularly wanted Shelton and Lawrence to be turned over to him. When Shelton flatly refused to leave his troops, Pottinger, whose wounds incapacitated him for combat anyway, volunteered to take his place. The hero of Herat later noted in his official report that by his action he had hoped to spare Shelton and Lawrence. Akbar Khan accepted Pottinger in place of Shelton but insisted on taking Lawrence as well. Captain Mackenzie, whose command by this time had been nearly wiped out, was also included in the new group of hostages.

The jumbled mass of soldiers and camp followers were ordered to move forward into the Khoord Kabul Pass and make for Tezeen. Here they would await word of Sale's departure from Jalalabad, the precondition for their being allowed to proceed farther. The sad picture of a broken remnant of an army preparing to face disaster—few believed they had any chance of getting through—made an indelible impression on Eyre. Most men were incapacitated by the two nights of exposure, and "even the cavalry, who suffered less than the rest, were obliged to be lifted on their horses." As one of the few survivors, Eyre looked back with terror on that morning: "The idea of threading the stupendous pass before us, in the face of an armed tribe of bloodthirsty barbarians, with such a dense, irregular multitude, was frightful, and the spectacle they presented by that waving sea of animated beings, the majority of whom within a few fleeting hours would transform into a line of lifeless carcasses to guide the future traveller on his way, can never be forgotten by those who witnessed it."[2]

The torrent of ice water that flowed through the pass was frozen solid along its banks, making the slippery paths perilous for animals and people alike. More serious were the Ghilzyes, who began to appear high on the rocks overhead flourishing their long *jazails*. Akbar Khan's orders to desist had clearly made no impression on them and a hail of bullets rained down on the column with devastating effect. Some officers swore that Akbar Khan was guilty of a cruel charade; he had been heard exhorting the tribesmen in Pashto to kill the English, while in Persian, a language better known to British officers, he dutifully shouted at them to cease firing.

Lady Sale remembered how "bullets kept whizzing by" as she and other ladies sat uneasily on their horses. Rather than wait helplessly to be slaughtered, several of the ladies at the head of the column spurred their mounts to a gallop and passed through unscathed, except for Lady Sale who took a bullet in her wrist. Others were less fortunate. Mrs. Boyd had her youngest boy snatched away by an Afghan horseman, and Mrs. Anderson's daughter Mary, age four, was also carried off. Mrs. Mainwaring, clutching her baby, was attacked by an Afghan who grabbed her heavy shawl, depriving them of their only protection against the cold, as she picked her way forward though the corpses in the snow. Horrified, Lady Sale jotted in her diary that Mrs. Bourne, little Seymour Stoker with his mother and Mrs. Cunningham were seized by tribesmen. In fact, Mrs. Bourne, a soldier's wife, was soon rescued by one of Akbar Khan's lieutenants, who providentially came upon her as a ferocious Ghilzye was about to sever her fingers in a rage because he could not get her rings off. Baby Stoker also survived, having been found alive in the arms of his murdered mother.

The rear guard, made up of Her Majesty's 44th and the 54th Native Infantry, took the heaviest fire. Lady Sale's keen eye for military matters caught the scene: ". . . the pass was completely choked up; and for a considerable time the 44th was stationary under heavy fire. . . . The 37th continued slowly, moving on without firing a shot, being paralyzed with cold to such a degree that no persuasion of their officers could induce them to make any effort to dislodge the enemy."[3] Unsupported, the men of the 44th suffered appalling casualties. By the end of that terrible day more than three thousand in all had lost their lives.

Lieutenant Sturt had almost cleared the gorge safely when he was struck in the groin by a Ghilzye bullet. Two fellow officers risked their lives to go back and rescue him, but he soon died of his wounds. Lady Sale was distraught but saw to it that her son-in-law was given a Christian burial—the only casualty known to be so blessed.

In the meantime, Pottinger in Akbar Khan's camp was trying to prevail upon Akbar Khan to do his duty as protecting escort and call off the Ghilzyes. It was obvious, however, that he could not control them—assuming he really wanted to—and he strenuously objected to the British proceeding farther, on the grounds that he could not protect them. Some of the British had already started out when Elphinstone, at Akbar Khan's insistence, recalled them to the town of Khoord Kabul at the far end of the pass. This provoked Shelton to howl in protest, predicting that any delay would doom the army.

Death and desertion had already done its grim work on the force. By now the Native Infantry regiments had no more than 60 men each, a negligible remnant of its original strength. The Irregular Horse, which could muster only 100 troopers, was virtually wiped out, while the 5th

Light Cavalry, no better off, was down to 70 combat-worthy men. The ranks of the core regiment, the Queen's 44th, had been reduced to less than 200 Englishmen, less than 10 percent of its usual complement. Among the sepoys, desertion had become a problem so serious that the troops were warned that anyone caught leaving his unit would be executed. One deserter was shot on the spot as an example.

Akbar Khan now made a startling suggestion: all widowed women, married couples and children should be sent to him for protection so that he could convey them safely to Peshawar. As distrustful of Akbar Khan as most officers were, on reflection there seemed to be no good alternative. To keep the women and children with them under the circumstances would be to sentence them to almost certain death by either violence or exposure. While their fate under Akbar Khan's "protection" was uncertain, the fact that his womenfolk and family, particularly his father, Dost Mohammed, whose return was important to the Barakzais, were hostages of the British could be seen as insurance for good treatment. And the fact that the British would give this evidence of trust in the Afghan chief might encourage him to take stronger measures to control the rapacious Ghilzyes. With much apprehension General Elphinstone agreed to the arrangement. It was a wrenching decision, one certain to cause protest in England when it became known, but there were few on the spot who doubted the wisdom of it.

The group escorted by Akbar Khan's men to his nearby fort included Lady Macnaghten, whose state of mind when she learned that she must remain with her husband's murderer can be imagined. Lady Sale, nursing her wrist wound, and her recently bereaved daughter, Mrs. Sturt, were also in the group, although Lady Sale for one mad moment had considered making a dash for Jalalabad on her horse. And there were Mrs. Boyd and her two children, Mrs. Mainwaring and one child, Mrs. Anderson and two children—including a ten-day-old infant born just before her departure from Kabul—Mrs. Eyre and one child, Mrs. Waller and one child, Mrs. Trevor with her brood of seven, Mrs. Ryley and two children, Mrs. Wade, Mrs. Smith and Mrs. Bourne. Among the wounded husbands accompanying them were Eyre and Waller. Two other officers, Lieutenant Mein and Captain Troup, neither any longer serviceable, also went along. A gracious welcome by Akbar Khan did little to relieve the apprehensions of the hostages, and it was a grim little group that bedded down for the night in their captor's fort after a meal of mutton-bone gruel and greasy rice.

On the morning of January 10, the march toward Jalalabad was resumed heedless of Akbar Khan's warning; by now few had any confidence in anything he said. It was the usual confused mass pushing and shoving to reach the front of the line (presumed safer than the rear) that set out that day with forebodings of further disaster. No more than a quarter of the 16,500 persons—troops and camp followers—who left Kabul four days before were by now still alive, and as the native ranks evaporated, only the few remaining British soldiers of the 44th and a handful of cavalrymen could be considered effective as combatants. As Eyre described it, "Hope seemed to have died in every breast. The wildness of terror was exhibited in every countenance."[4] The remains of rifled baggage were strewn along the route interspersed with the corpses of their onetime owners—the camp followers and deserters who in their frenzy had pushed too far ahead.

A narrow defile called Haft-Kotul, where Ghilzyes again could direct their fire from overhanging rocks, caused more casualties. Shelton and the remnant of the 44th Foot fought a valiant rear-guard action. Eyre credited Shelton's performance with preventing a massacre of everyone.

The indefatigable Captain Skinner, used by the British as emissary to Akbar Khan's camp, urged Akbar Khan to save the few survivors still left, but the Afghan chiefs now demanded as a condition for a cease-fire that the British lay down their arms. Having to choose between Akbar Khan's demonstrated treachery and keeping their guns, the British chose the latter. They were determined to try a forced night march in a last effort to reach Jagdalak.

Spiking their only remaining gun rather than burden themselves with it and slow their progress, the British began the march by moonlight. But the inevitable camp followers clung to them for protection, slowing them down. Renewed firing by the Ghilzyes caused the crowd to surge forward, then backward in terrified confusion, completely preventing the soldiers from properly forming up to resist. By daybreak on the eleventh the British were ten miles short of their night's objective.

While waiting for Shelton to bring up his rear guard, Elphinstone in an odd move ordered his officers to stand erect, shoulder by shoulder, and "show an imposing front." The imposing front was, if nothing else, a tempting target for the Ghilzyes. Poor Captain Grant was rewarded for his part in this act of senseless bravado with a bullet-shattered jaw.

The hard-pressed Shelton and his men finally joined the rest and together they fought desperately to reach shelter at Jagdalak behind the walls of an old ruin. But a massing of Ghilzyes, who held the high ground above them, made their position untenable. The pitiful group of survivors ate snow in a vain effort to quench their raging thirst while they were tormented by the sight of a bubbling stream only 150 feet away, unreachable without almost certain loss of life. A brave effort by the soldiers of the 44th to sally forth with fixed bayonets brought only brief relief from the deadly curtain of fire that fell upon them.

Akbar Khan, who tracked the British column in its agony, now insisted that General Elphinstone, wounded in the fusillade, join the ranks of hostages. Brigadier Shelton and Captain Johnson, who had both gone with Skinner to parley again with Akbar Khan, were also forcibly held. The Afghan chief genuinely wanted to save the officers' lives by keeping them under his protection, but not out of compassion; they would provide leverage in bargaining with the British for his father's release as well as ensure that Sale's brigade left Afghanistan. Dead officers could not be bartered.

Johnson was struck by the bitterness of the Afghan chiefs in their expressions of hate against the British. Despite apparent efforts by Akbar Khan to conciliate them, even with offers of large bribes, the chiefs "declared that nothing would satisfy them and their men but . . . extermination." Johnson, who could follow the side remarks made by the chiefs in Persian as Akbar Khan tried to reason with them, realized that they were more eager to cut the throats of the infidels than to capture loot.[5] They had wanted Dost Mohammed to kill Alexander Burnes during the latter's "commercial" mission, convinced that he was simply the vanguard of a British invasion and "would return with an army and take our country from us." Now, the tribesmen felt, Akbar had the "opportunity to kill the infidel dogs"[6] and should grasp it. All hope of saving the remaining survivors was gone; with every hour more tribesmen, howling for blood, flocked in for the kill. By the evening of the twelfth, word reached the British—what few were left—that the Ghilzyes had finally agreed to permit their onward march to Jalalabad without further molestation. But even Akbar Khan had little confidence in the word of the assembled chiefs and begged Captain Johnson to summon three or four of his "most intimate friends" so that they might be saved from certain death. Johnson would not countenance such favoritism and, on Elphinstone's instructions, smuggled off a message to Brigadier Anquetil, now in charge of the decimated column, ordering the remaining force to make a run for it by morning since treachery was suspected. The message never arrived, but Elphinstone had no need to warn his comrades since renewed Afghan firing made the point dramatically enough. Perhaps most galling of all, Captain Skinner in his peripatetic role as go-between was killed by a Ghilzye tribesman as he rode out from camp to meet a messenger from Akbar Khan. Thus ended the life of "Gentleman Jim," as he was fondly known by his fellow officers.

Brigadier Anquetil, with some 120 remaining infantrymen of the 44th and 25 artillerymen, pushed onward toward Jalalabad during the night of the twelfth without waiting for morning. They were obliged to abandon the sick and wounded to their fate so that they could maintain their mobility, but, again engulfed by the ubiquitous camp followers, the handful of soldiers were hard pressed to maintain an effective defense. Not only were they under constant fire from the Afghans, but the emboldened tribesmen darted in and out among the massed camp followers, slaying them with long knives. Then, at the mouth of Jagdalak Pass, another steep defile where the British would be powerless to defend themselves, they found a barrier made from prickly oak erected by the Ghilzyes to block their progress. "A terrible fire was now poured in from all quarters," wrote Eyre, and "Afghans rushing in furiously upon the pent-up crowd of troops and followers committed wholesale slaughter."

Here the once-grand Army of the Indus ceased to exist as its pitiful remnant was massacred. Brigadier Anquetil and twelve of his remaining officers perished as they struck out with their sabers in a futile effort to defend themselves. Sepoy Sita Ram, still alive, remembered, "The men fought like gods, not men."[7] At least those who died had a moment of glory after weeks of humiliation as they made their last brave stand. For years thereafter the Dum Dum headquarters of the Indian Army Horse Artillery near Calcutta commemorated the final defense by their men under Captain Nicholl at Jagdalak Pass in a yearly ceremony during which their heroic action was recounted.

It had been the few remaining infantrymen, many of whom gave their lives, who had breached the prickly oak barrier, tearing the thorned branches away with their bloody hands under furious fire. When the mounted officers and men galloped through to momentary safety, apparently heedless of the men they were leaving to die, it must be sadly recorded that some embittered soldiers fired on them as they passed.

The survivors who reached Gandamak, twenty officers and forty-five men, crouched together in the rocks of a hillside on February 13, vowing to expend their last two rounds of ammunition to good effect against the horde of tribesmen surrounding them before joining their comrades who died at Jagdalak. Their final moments, romantically immortalized by W. A. Wollen's famous painting "The Last Stand of the 44th Foot at Gandamak," has become a revered memory in British imperial history.

Captain Souter, who had wrapped the regimental colors around his waist to preserve them, was thought to be of special eminence worthy of great ransom because of his strange and colorful cummerbund, and was taken prisoner rather than killed. Only six British officers managed to escape the massacre and reach Futtehabad, some sixteen miles from Jalalabad, but there the villagers fell upon them, killing two. Three more were killed as they fled on their horses. Now but one was left free, a British surgeon seconded to Shah Shuja's army named Dr. William Brydon.

Brydon's own account of what then befell him as he struggled the last few miles toward Jalalabad is a story of determination—and luck. First he was attacked by marauding Afghans who viciously stoned him. "Taking the bridle in my teeth," he wrote, "I cut right and left with my sword as I went through them." He then met another group of hostile tribesmen who blocked his way. "Of this party one man on a mound over the road had a gun, which he fired close down upon me and broke my sword, leaving about six inches in the handle." Brydon survived this ordeal, faint with fatigue, but his pony was wounded in the loins. Next he met five hostile horsemen. "I tried to get away," he recalled, "but my pony could hardly move and they sent one of their party after me, who made a cut at me. . . . He passed me, but turned and rode at me again. This time, just as he was striking, I threw the handle of the [broken] sword at his head." This last act of desperation by Brydon caused his assailant to swerve and miss his target. "He only cut me over the back of the left hand,"[8] recalled Brydon.

By some miracle Brydon's attacker abruptly rode off without further attack. "Suddenly all energy seemed to forsake me," remembered Brydon. "I became nervous and frightened at shadows, and I really think I would have fallen from my saddle, but for the peak of it." In the distance he could now make out Jalalabad fort against its mountain backdrop; then he could see a party of horsemen riding toward him from the fort. Believed to be the only survivor of the retreating British Army to avoid death or capture, he had reached safety to tell of the catastrophe.[9] Colonel Dennie, whose grim prophecy seemed to have come true, announced mournfully: "Did I not say so? Here comes the messenger."

Chapter 26

CAPTIVITY

Ｎews traveled slowly and days passed before British official-dom in India learned of the disturbing events in Afghanistan. Frontier political officer George Clerk sent word of the November 2 uprising in Kabul and Burnes's murder to the governor general in mid-November. But he did not wait for a reply before taking precautionary action on his own initiative. Clerk ordered the 64th Bengal Native Infantry regiment stationed in Ferozepore and the 60th in Ludhiana to cross the Sutlej River and move up to Peshawar near the Afghan border. Soon afterward he sent the 53rd and 30th Regiments as well.

Upon receiving the disturbing news, Auckland forwarded his views to his commander in chief, General Sir Jasper Nicolls, then traveling in north India. The governor general believed that sending relief units was out of the question: "The safety of the force at Caubul can only come from itself." Even "if all should be lost at Caubul, we will not encounter new hazards for reconquest," he wrote.[1] Such opinions found ready acceptance by Sir Jasper, who had never favored the Afghan invasion anyway—and had predicted its consequences. As a practical strategist, he believed in protecting British provinces in India, not defending a vaguely defined British sphere of influence beyond effective reach. Shah Shuja was not worth the cost of defending him, in terms of either money or risk, nor would punitive action be useful.

The man on the spot saw things differently. George Clerk, conscious of his responsibility for the defense of the northwest frontier, had rushed reinforcements to Peshawar in preparation for relieving Sale in Jalalabad, if not saving the beleaguered Kabul garrison. While Auckland approved Clerk's troop movements to Peshawar after the fact, he was not yet ready to permit any further buildup on the frontier, much less send forces into Afghanistan. "We do not conceive it to be called for," he wrote, "and we think it inexpedient to despatch any greater number of troops than be absolutely necessary for our own provinces."[2]

Not only did Auckland lack decisiveness with regard to troop deployment, but he initially made a bad choice as to who should command the frontier forces. Over the objections of Sir Jasper Nicholls, he first chose Major General James Lumley, the tired and sick adjutant general of the Indian Army. But Lumley's health deteriorated further, making it necessary for Auckland to withdraw the appointment. Instead the governor general named General George Pollock, commander of the Agra garrison south of Delhi. Pollock enjoyed a good reputation; no better choice could have been made. Events were now facing the British with serious decisions and it was well that Pollock could move rapidly up to Peshawar to take command. The news from Afghanistan was bad and getting worse.

Clerk's "alarmist" attitude and his hasty reaction had annoyed Lord Auckland. Confident that the Kabul force could deal with the problems facing it, he could not see what good it would do to reinforce Peshawar. If Elphinstone and Macnaghten were in serious trouble, help could not reach them until at least April, when the winter's snow would relax its grip on the passes, by which time it would probably be too late. But as the situation in Kabul worsened, the governor general's concern mounted. Macnaghten's violent death at the hands of Akbar Khan on December 23 and the decision to evacuate Kabul shocked Auckland when he received news of these new disasters on January 20. Macnaghten's death was a terrible blow to the governor general since the late envoy had been a close friend of the family. Auckland's sister, Emily Eden, wrote: "We knew him so well and it has been such an atrocious act of treachery."[3]

Then the massacre of the entire Kabul force while retreating toward Peshawar struck Auckland another devastating blow when he received news of it from Jalalabad on January 30. Writing in evident agony to his friend Charles Greville, Lord Auckland expressed disbelief that nearly five thousand well-trained British and British-led troops with artillery had not been able to defend themselves against an estimated ten to twelve thousand Afghans armed only with matchlocks and spears, since it was a common assumption in India that Company troops could defeat any native force ten times their number. The conceit of Imperial Britain to assume that its forces were vastly superior to any other native army east of Suez would more than once prove disastrous, but this was the most egregious miscalculation of all. Self-confidence had its value in battle, foolhardiness did not. In Afghanistan the simple fact was that the natives usually commanded the heights where they were very much in their element and fought with homemade long-barreled rifles—*jazails*—which were more accurate and had longer range than British muskets. The British had the theoretical advantage in artillery, but rarely could the guns be brought into play in the narrow defiles where the Afghans chose to fight.

Macnaghten's murder and the British decision to capitulate and retreat from Kabul had jarred Auckland into ordering Nicolls to send another brigade to the frontier. But still the governor general did not favor any action beyond rescuing British troops in Jalalabad. George Clerk and Sir Jasper Nicolls had met near Karnal in the Punjab to review the situation in light of developments. Even now the two men could not agree. Despite, or perhaps because of, the catastrophe, Nicolls had seen little justification for sending reinforcements. With Kabul evacuated, he believed that Jalalabad need no longer be held and that Sale's brigade could make it back to Peshawar without help. Clerk, to the contrary, worried about Sale's increased vulnerability in the face of the general tribal uprising taking place, the fulcrum of which was shifting from Kabul to Jalalabad. And, just as important, he believed that the honor of the British had to be defended if in the longer run the frontier was to be held. Clerk was now convinced that the British should retake Kabul, then withdraw "with dignity and undiminished honor."[4]

Although shocked by events in Afghanistan, Auckland wrote the Court of Directors in London that he felt himself "obliged to look at things more calmly" than most of his advisers. This, of course, was a scarcely veiled criticism of Clerk. But the governor general's calmness was suddenly shattered on January 30 when he learned details of the disastrous retreat culminating in the total destruction of the Kabul army.

Auckland announced, with more assurance than he felt: "The most active measures have been adopted, and will be steadfastly prosecuted for expediting reinforcements to the Afghan frontier and for assisting such operations as may be required . . . for the maintenance of the honour and interests of the British Government."[5] But the governor general still directed his focus on relieving Sale in Jalalabad, not on marching on Kabul to exact revenge or restore "honor"—or rescue British captives.

Even relieving Jalalabad would not prove an easy operation, but it was made even more difficult when a premature, ill-conceived attempt ended in humiliating defeat. Without waiting for General Pollock and his main force to arrive and with only a few cannons in poor condition borrowed from the Sikhs, Brigadier Wild in an excess of zeal had plunged forward into the Khyber Pass on January 18 to begin the relief of Jalalabad. The first problem to face him was the mutiny of a Sikh battalion. Although Sikhs always feared the terrors of the Khyber, there was strong evidence that this battalion had been tampered with by the ambitious Dogra leader, Gulab Singh, who saw no advantage in helping the British, particularly since he considered them potential enemies in an inevitable struggle for the Punjab. Then, as Wild regrouped and tried again to breach the Khyber, his Indian sepoys, already demoralized by the Sikh mutiny, broke under the relentless marksmanship of the Afghans and fell back to Jamrud at the mouth of the pass to wait for Pollock.

Auckland's agonies would soon come to an end, however, and the terrible responsibilities burdening him would devolve upon his successor, Lord Ellenborough. Ellenborough, he knew, would sit in judgment of him, not a pleasant prospect, nor one to encourage Auckland to take dynamic action that might only make matters worse. The catastrophe in Afghanistan would mean the destruction of Lord Auckland's professional reputation just as he was to leave India for a much-needed rest and respite from official worries. In one of her letters home, Lady Eden hinted at the depth of his depression: "George is looking shockingly. . . . All this worry has made a difference of ten years at least in his look."[6]

In England too reputations would suffer. The unfolding Afghan fiasco provided Sir Robert Peel, who had become prime minister in September 1841, with further grounds on which to discredit his Whig predecessor, Lord Melbourne. Peel had also been eager to replace the bungling Lord Auckland with Lord Ellenborough, a good Tory stalwart, as governor general of India. But since Ellenborough would not arrive before late February 1842, Auckland had to cope as best he could with the catastrophe his policies now faced him with. The change of administration complicated his task and inhibited him from making decisions of lasting consequence.

Doubts as to the wisdom of his course had long nagged at Auckland. Despite Macnaghten's cheerful optimism and all the encouragement freely given him by his secretariat in Calcutta, the governor general had felt uneasy about Afghanistan ever since he realized that there seemed to be no way for the British to extricate themselves honorably from the burden of supporting an Afghan regime clearly unable to support itself. And he knew that the Company's Court of Directors in London, for some time nervous about the prospects of an indefinite British presence in Afghanistan, was upset that his initiatives beyond the Indus had already cost the Company some £15 million. But he had not expected such a dramatic denouement or such a total repudiation of his policies. For all his mistakes, Auckland had meant well. He had a conscience and now suffered the remorse of an honest man who had failed.

———————— •·•· ————————

WHILE CALCUTTA AND LONDON CONCERNED THEMSELVES WITH ISSUES OF high policy, the British prisoners taken by Akbar Khan worried about their own survival. A few British officers and other ranks, even fewer wives and children—in all, some 105 souls—and an undetermined number of native sepoys, either deserters or enslaved, were glad to be alive, but what would be their fates? They could only pray they would eventually be rescued.

Sita Ram was perhaps typical of the sepoys who survived the slaughter in the passes only to be captured and sold into slavery. His Afghan captors quieted his protests by threatening to circumcise him then and there and forcibly convert him to Islam if he did not behave. For a good Hindu this would be a fate worse than death. Although wounded, he was sold to a wealthy Afghan for 240 rupees, and warned that if he tried to escape he would instantly be transformed into a eunuch.

The British hostages, who had value as bargaining chips, fared better in Akbar Khan's custody, but had to endure acute worry, primitive conditions of Afghan life—the unpalatable food, vermin, dark rooms filled with smoke from cooking fires—and all the little miseries that derive from living at close quarters with one another.

The petty problems of the cantonment would be reproduced on a small scale as they settled into the routines of living. Now, however, life was anything but routine; they were tortured by the terrible sights that met their eyes as they traveled with Akbar Khan's camp in the wake of the retreating British. They saw scenes of unspeakable horror, the detritus of defeat. They often had to pick their way around British corpses as they traveled, some still recognizable as old friends and comrades. They cringed with fear and loathing as Ghilzyes rode by flourishing swords caked with the blood of their victims. And as a reminder that treachery, as well as hostility, had brought them to this state, they saw some four hundred men of Alexander's Irregular Horse who had deserted to the enemy and now bivouacked in relative comfort, enjoying the rewards of disloyalty.

The sights at Jagdalak were the worst of all. The hostages gazed horror-stricken at the walled enclosure where the pathetic British remnant had struggled in vain to defend itself. The place was now heaped high with bloody corpses, a grisly memorial to the destruction of an army. The hostages for the first time realized that they were probably the sole survivers, but would this terrible scene be their fate as well?

At Jagdalak, Elphinstone, Shelton and Johnson, just taken as hostages by Akbar Khan, joined the band of other British captives. The general, a broken man, and Shelton, even more sullen than usual, were no consolation to the other hostages.

BY NOW, AKBAR KHAN REALIZED THAT SALE HAD NO INTENTION OF GIVING up Jalalabad. Exasperated, he forced Major Pottinger, as ranking political officer in his custody, to order the brigadier to surrender. But in a secret letter to Macgregor, Sale's political officer, Pottinger warned that Akbar Khan's professions of reasonableness were "only a sham," and that he was in fact dedicated to treachery. Then, in a curious aside, suggesting the depth of his bitterness toward Macnaghten, Pottinger told Macgregor of the late envoy's own treachery in trying to play one tribal faction against another during the last days of his negotiations. "I regret that our own conduct in this country has put our government's faith on a par with themselves," he wrote.[7]

Akbar Khan left his hostages to attend to Sale. If the brigadier would not willingly do his bidding, he must force him to his knees. The story of Sale's defense of Jalalabad is the story of brave soldiers. Having found the Jalalabad fort in a state of disrepair, the brigade, under Broadfoot's energetic leadership, worked rapidly to make it defensible. But news of the Kabul army's destruction and then Wild's defeat in the Khyber gave them a sense of terrible vulnerability. Even nature did not seem to favor them; on February 19 a severe earthquake struck, leveling the defenses that Sale's men had so arduously erected. With Akbar Khan only seven miles away, the garrison braced for what they thought would be certain attack. Akbar Khan hesitated because of his fear of British artillery—and English witchcraft, which somehow permitted the garrison to survive the earthquake. He was, however, able to blockade the garrison and prevent British foraging parties from replenishing their food stocks.

Rather than be starved out, Sale after much urging by Broadfoot marched his five-thousand-man brigade out at daybreak on April 7 to engage Akbar Khan's army of six thousand. The British won the day and hundreds of Akbar Khan's men drowned as they tried to cross the swift-running Kabul River in their headlong retreat. Not only were the Afghans thoroughly routed but vitally needed arms and stores captured from them gave new life to the garrison.

Now feeling that it would be safer to retreat to Kabul, since Pollock's army, now ominously dubbed the "Army of Retribution," was preparing to relieve Jalalabad, Akbar Khan turned northward with his army, hostages in tow. Moreover, Akbar Khan treated his prisoners more civilly. Eyre went so far as to record: "We found the Afghan gentry most agreeable traveling companions." Akbar Khan suddenly played the perfect host, carrying Mrs. Waller, who was inopportunely pregnant, across the river on his horse, and feasting the senior officers when they stopped for the night. But the villagers they passed were anything but civil. They taunted the hostages unmercifully, often threatening them with death.

The hostages saw more sights of grief and tragedy as they marched northward to Kabul. Perhaps the most wretched of those who suffered in the tragic exodus of the British from Kabul were the camp followers. Lady Sale told of seeing some two or three hundred "miserable Hindustanis, who had escaped the massacre of the 12th," but now "were all naked and frost-bitten." Wounded and starving, "they huddled all together to impart warmth to each other." Lady Sale recoiled with horror to learn that "they had sustained life by feeding on their dead comrades."[8]

Forever imprinted on Eyre's memory was the sight of snow "dyed with streaks and patches of blood for whole miles." He was horrified at the sight of "the mangled bodies of British and Hindoostani soldiers and helpless camp followers lying side by side, victims of one treacherous, undistinguished fate."[9]

The hostages passed tantalizingly close to Jalalabad before climbing higher up the valley. Despite her prayers, Lady Sale realized: "all hopes of going to Jalalabad were annihilated."

The hostility of the tribesmen increased as they climbed into the hills. Even the womenfolk gathered by the roadside to revile the British ladies as "immoral" and taunt them for looking like "scarecrows." They spat even more disparaging epithets at the British men. Mercy and compassion were not qualities of the Afghan tribeswomen, who were infamous for the mutilations with which they often profaned their wounded enemies. The animus of the natives had become dangerous, and Akbar Khan hustled the hostages on their way to avoid their being massacred despite some two hundred soldiers escorting them.

At a place called Buddeabad the hostages were turned over to Mohammed Shah Khan, Akbar Khan's father-in-law, for safekeeping, and housed in six rooms of his large fort. The traditional chasm between officer and rankers was duly preserved even under these trying circumstances. The nine "ladies," their fourteen children and twenty "gentlemen" were billeted separately from the seventeen British soldiers and two rankers' wives.

It was here that the hostages learned that Dr. Brydon had been the only man to reach Jalalabad. Lady Sale must surely have reflected on the report she had heard in Kabul before leaving that Akbar Khan would annihilate the whole army except for one man, who would be permitted to reach Jalalabad to tell the grisly tale.

POLLOCK'S ARMY OF RETRIBUTION WAS BEHIND SCHEDULE. WILD'S DEFEAT in the Khyber had seriously damaged troop morale. Various native regiments even held secret nocturnal meetings to discuss mutiny if they were ordered to advance through the dreaded Khyber Pass. The Sikhs, particularly, could not be relied upon. All of February and March had been needed to rebuild the spirit of the men.

Pollock finally began his advance to Jalalabad on April 5. Shrewdly, he borrowed his tactics on mountain warfare from the tribesmen: advance parties climbed the towering rocks flanking the pass to position themselves above the unsuspecting Afghan riflemen below. Seeing British troops hovering above them, the Afridi fled, abandoning their perches in the rocks and leaving uncontested passage through the dreaded Khyber by the main body of Pollock's army. This was the first time in history that a foreign army had successfully fought its way through the Khyber Pass. Even Tamerlane had bought off the Afridis rather than risk combat with them. As Pollock's column came into view, Sale had his band strike up the old Scottish air "Oh, But Ye've Been a Lang O'Coming," but Fighting Bob was overjoyed to see help at last.

The other British garrisons, those along the southern route, had had their share of drama too. General Nott and his nine-thousand-man garrison at Kandahar had also managed to survive. Like Sale, he had not been able to return to Kabul when ordered to do so by Macnaghten, but had been faced with formidable attacks from the tribes. A horde of some twenty thousand Ghilzyes had besieged Kandahar on January 12, but in a strong counterattack Nott soundly defeated his much larger adversary.

Lieutenant Colonel T. Palmer, in command of the British outpost at Ghazni, closer to Kabul, was not as fortunate. Harassed by tribesmen from the surrounding areas and hostile townfolk, Palmer in November had had to withdraw his regiment to the citadel. Without artillery support and with supplies running low, Palmer made the fatal decision to surrender on the promise of "honorable treatment." On March 1, 1842, the British garrison peaceably marched out only to find itself under furious assault. The sepoys panicked and abandoned their formations in a misguided attempt to flee to Peshawar. Not having the slightest idea of the immense distance, impossible terrain, bad weather and hostile tribes that lay between them and their goal, they were soon either slaughtered or enslaved. Their British officers fared little better, being imprisoned and subjected to unconscionably bad treatment.

Palmer's surrender was criticized by some and he was unfavorably compared with Sale and Nott, who had managed to hold out. In the end, he was officially exonerated; the garrison's water had run out and, objectively viewed, it seemed doubtful that the beleaguered force without artillery could have broken out of the citadel, much less fought its way to safety.

KABUL, IN THE MEANTIME, WAS RENT BY AFGHAN INTRAMURAL POLITICAL infighting. Mohan Lal was an interested observer as clan intrigued against clan, tribe against tribe. He was also a player in this Byzantine process, operating as best he could from his cloistered sanctuary in the Kizzilbash chief's home to strengthen British supporters with promises and frighten their antagonists with threats. He took full advantage of the fact that many Afghans could not believe that the British had given up and thought it prudent to hedge their bets against the day a punitive army might arrive.

The Barakzais quareled among themselves, the Durranis quarreled with the Barakzais and, according to Mohan Lal, "a desperate thirst of all for snatching money from the King became a chief topic of concern of the day."[10] The Kabul chiefs were so busy with their plots and counterplots that they paid little attention to events at Jalalabad, and had no inclination to raise tribal reinforcements for Akbar Khan's army.

Abandoned by the British, Shah Shuja survived by playing an intricate game of balance. He had been reinstated as figurehead monarch with no power when the rebels' acting sovereign, Nawab Mohammed Zaman Khan, pledged his support to him in return for being made vizier. Mohan Lal's patron, Shirin Khan and his Kizzilbash community also backed the shah. In the haze of Afghan politics only one thing was clear: the Afghans had lapsed into their traditional feudal chaos once they had driven their common enemy, the British, from Kabul.

An announcement by Governor General Auckland promising that he would display "the stability and vigour of British Power," combined with news that additional troops were indeed marching toward Jalalabad to relieve Sale's brigade, caused consternation among the Afghans. Fearing punishment, many of the wealthy fled to the hills, and the politicians in Kabul scrambled to adjust to still another shift in the power equation should the British return to Kabul. Nawab Mohammed Zaman Khan even brought Mohan Lal out of his sanctuary to read aloud the governor general's statement to the assembled chiefs. Auckland's reference to "British power" meant one thing to them: a British army would again come to Kabul and overwhelm them.

Shah Shuja could now hope for British rescue, but he still had to play his charade as ceremonial patron of the Afghan cause. When the chiefs prevailed upon him to lead an army to Jalalabad against Sale, he dragged his heels; to leave the Bala Hissar would be dangerous for him, but to refuse to join the holy war, raising suspicions of disloyalty to the Afghan struggle against the British, would be equally dangerous. Either way he was doomed. When he finally emerged from his citadel on April 5, his own godson, the wayward son of the Nawab Mohammed Zaman Khan, shot and killed him in cold blood on the road near the Bala Hissar. As fate would have it, the assassination took place at the site of a crude and weathered tomb in memory of one John Hicks, an English mercenary who had fought for the Moghul Emperor Aurangzeb in 1666, the first Englishman ever to reach Kabul.

Shah Shuja's last act as he lay dying beside the road was to retrieve a pouch of his most precious jewels from inside his tunic, where he always hid them for safekeeping, and fling it into the field. A simple tribesman who found the pouch thought the contents were only pretty pieces of glass and sold them for a pittance. Eventually, however, the crown jewels were tracked down by the assassin, who extorted them from their owner by threats. On seeing the dazzling collection of gems, he congratulated himself for being well rewarded for his treachery.

LORD ELLENBOROUGH ARRIVED IN CALCUTTA ON FEBRUARY 28, 1842, TO take up his position as governor general. It was a time, he announced in high-flown rhetoric, when "men's hearts were failing them because of fear." What he found appalled him; Company administration had largely been left to the senior secretariat officers by Lord Auckland, a situation that he felt had contributed to the catastrophe in Afghanistan. Ellenborough resolved to take the reins himself and restore confidence in British power at the same time that he restored the Company's treasury, depleted by his predecessor's Afghan fiasco. He announced boldly his intention to reestablish British military reputation "by the infliction of some signal and decisive blow upon the Afghans. . . . India was won by the sword and must be maintained by the sword,"[11] he announced with more than a trace of bombast.

To be closer to the action, he set out from Calcutta for the northwest frontier on April 6, but by the time he reached Benares, less than halfway, his resolve was wavering. Bad news made him cautious. Sale's victory and Pollock's successful breaching of the Khyber to relieve Jalalabad on April 16 had been encouraging, but Ghazni's capitulation was disheartening. And now news reached the governor general that a column under Brigadier Richard England sent from Quetta, intended to reinforce Nott in Kandahar, had been decimated by the Afghans in the Bolan Pass and forced to fall back to Quetta before trying again.

Discouraged by the British Army's apparently infinite capacity for disaster at the hands of the primitive Afghans, Ellenborough suddenly and unexpectedly ordered Pollock and Sale in Jalalabad to withdraw to Peshawar, and Nott in Kandahar to retreat to Quetta, both moves preparatory to abandoning Afghanistan altogether—hostages and all. Pollock and Nott were shocked and dismayed by Ellenborough's orders and each found a different way to resist them.

Pollock stalled for time, claiming that he needed more transport before retracing his steps through the tribe-infested Khyber. From Jalalabad he wrote Calcutta an unvarnished appraisal of the consequences of withdrawal on May 13. The letter, which Ellenborough claimed not to have received, somehow vanished from the files for a while. That it presented a picture that could not help but display Ellenborough's decision in a bad light may have had something to do with its disappearance.

Pollock feared that a British withdrawal would deprive Mohan Lal of leverage in his political-action activities in Kabul aimed at bringing down Akbar Khan and the Barakzai clan. He also pointed out the problem of obtaining the release of the British hostages in the event that British forces withdrew from Afghanistan; "it would be supposed that a panic had seized us,"[12] eliminating any sense of urgency for action on the part of Akbar Khan. British withdrawal, in Pollock's opinion, would be construed as defeat, destroying Britain's reputation as a powerful nation in that part of the world.

Nott in Kandahar was no less appalled at the order to withdraw than Pollock was. On receiving Ellenborough's order on May 10, he ordered Major Rawlinson to protest. (He did not trust himself to write a temperate letter on this subject.) "The peremptory order to retire," wrote Nott's political officer, "has come upon us like a thunderclap. When our intended retirement is once known, we must expect to have the whole country up in arms."[13] This would make withdrawal more difficult. Moreover, Persian and Russian influence could be expected to fill the vacuum of power left by the British abandonment of Afghanistan.

Not only were the field commanders dismayed by Ellenborough's apparent change of policy but British public opinion was aroused to an extent not anticipated by the governor general. What of British honor? What of the fate of the British hostages, particularly the women and children? To walk away from Afghanistan now would be as dishonorable as Elphinstone's disorderly retreat from Kabul in the first place, and would only worsen the situation.

After three months of indecision, Ellenborough found a face-saving way to reverse field once again, and on July 4 he sent word to Nott that his orders to withdraw still stood, but if he were able to withdraw by way of Kabul rather than through the Bolan Pass, this would be understood— even welcomed! At the same time Ellenborough sent a copy of the letter to Pollock in Jalalabad, permitting him also to proceed to Kabul in support of Nott. The governor general had preserved consistency while appeasing British public opinion. He had also craftily drafted his instructions to the two generals in such a way as to give them discretion as to whether or not they marched on Kabul. If they chose to do so—which they surely would—but failed, they, not Ellenborough, would bear the responsibility. If they succeeded, Ellenborough could claim the credit. The British Army of Retribution could now proceed to restore honor and rescue the British hostages.

Chapter 27

———————— ✦ ————————

FINALE

The fate of the British hostages weighed heavily on General Pollock. And Brigadier Sale, of course, had particular reason to worry since his wife and daughter were among those held. It had been a cruel separation for Fighting Bob; he could only imagine what hardships Lady Sale had endured while held by Akbar Khan, and the tragedy of Lieutenant Sturt's death at Khoord Kabul, leaving his daughter a widow, surely added to Sale's burden of grief. So when Captain Colin Mackenzie suddenly appeared before the gates of Jalalabad on April 25, having just arrived from Akbar Khan's camp, Sale and Pollock eagerly welcomed him and pumped him for their first news of the hostages. Akbar Khan had released Mackenzie on parole as an emissary to carry a proposal for release of his prisoners.

Akbar Khan was still recovering from his defeat by Sale when news reached him that Pollock and his Army of Retribution had successfully breached the Khyber and reached Jalalabad. The danger he faced now loomed as a frightening reality. Lady Sale, shrewdly sizing up her captor, noted that he was convinced that, if captured, he would surely be hanged or blown from a cannon.

This was a time for Akbar Khan to mend fences and extract as much leverage as possible from the British hostages to save his own neck. When, on April 21, Mrs. Waller gave birth to a daughter, Akbar Khan with misplaced joviality commented that the more hostages he held, the better.*

Akbar Khan's proposal to Pollock called for either total evacuation of British forces from Afghan territory or, alternatively, the return of Dost Mohammed and his family to Kabul before the British hostages would be released. Pollock did not have the authority to negotiate such an arrangement even if he had wanted to, and he hoped that by the time he referred it to Calcutta and received a response he would be in Kabul.

Mackenzie returned to Akbar's camp with Pollock's negative reply— however tempting it must have been to break his bond and remain in Jalalabad. Then, once again, Akbar Khan dispatched Mackenzie to Jalalabad, this time with a somewhat modified proposal; again the British officer returned with Pollock's rejection. As Pollock and Sale prepared to march on Kabul, Akbar Khan hurried to remove his prisoners from the path of the British advance so as to prevent their liberation, and accelerated his retreat to Kabul.

Major Pottinger protested to Akbar Khan that it was inhumane to shunt them all from one place to another under such trying conditions; surely the sardar did not intend to "make war on women and children."[1] Indeed it was a grim journey; the sights along the way were sickening. It was a landscape of corpses that met their eyes. With evident revulsion Lady Sale noted in her diary: "The sight was dreadful; the smell of blood sickening; and the corpses lay so thick it was impossible to look from them as it required care to guide my horse so as not to tread upon their bodies."[2]

Fever and dysentery were the hostages' constant companions. Frequent earth tremors added to their uneasiness, since they feared a recurrence of the big one of February 19—the shock that had frightened both the hostages traveling with Akbar Khan and the troops of Sale's brigade at Jalalabad. On that occasion Lady Sale had fled the flat roof of her quarters, where she had been hanging her laundry only seconds before the building collapsed. Hostages Shelton and Mackenzie also had a close call, escaping from their building just before it crumbled. (Shelton chastised Mackenzie for fleeing the collapsing building ahead of himself—a flagrant breach of etiquette for a junior officer.)

*While in captivity, Mrs. Boyd, Mrs. Ryley and Mrs. Bourne also successfully delivered babies.

Intense heat alternating with torrential rains added to everyone's misery. It was no wonder that old General Elphinstone died. On April 23, the ailing man at last found relief for his tortured soul. Before he died, he had confessed to Lawrence that he blamed himself more than anyone else for what had occurred. Shelton, horrid even in adversity, could not resist telling anyone who would listen that he intended to file a report indicting Elphinstone for his incompetence. Lieutenant Eyre was more charitable to the dead general, and in his diary he wrote a gracious eulogy of a "fine man" who he believed "exhibited a measure of Christian benevolence, patience and high-souled fortitude, which gained for him the affectionate regard and admiring esteem of all who watched his prolonged sufferings and his dying struggles." Eyre, always an apologist for the general, maintained that Elphinstone had been a victim "less of his own faults than of the errors of others."[3]

Akbar Khan agreed to send Elphinstone's remains to Jalalabad, but even as a corpse the general was not spared humiliation. Near Jagdalak a band of Afghan marauders smashed open the crude coffin and pelted the body with stones. They also savaged the escort, Elphinstone's faithful servant, Trooper Miller, who barely escaped with his life. The general's remains, somewhat the worse for wear, finally reached Jalalabad and were buried by the garrison with full military honors.

On May 25, Akbar's prisoners, taken during the ill-fated retreat toward Jalalabad, reached Kabul to join the others who had been captured at Ghazni and those left behind as hostages when the garrison had been evacuated from Kabul. Mohan Lal, in his unique role as British agent, had survived and was still serving bravely and with considerable ingenuity to keep Pollock well informed about developments in the capital. Although confined to his room under the protection of the Kizzilbash chief, Shirin Khan, Mohan Lal was able to learn from his host details of the power struggle going on and smuggle out messages to Pollock, written on small thin pieces of paper secreted under the locks of the messengers' muskets. Shirin Khan knew what he was doing and tolerated it, but he made it clear that should any of his messages be intercepted, he would be severely dealt with by Akbar Khan and there would be nothing the Kizzilbash could do to defend him. Security was essential; only Pottinger and a very few other officers among the hostages knew the role he was playing.

There was much for Mohan Lal to report. Futteh Jung, Shah Shuja's feckless second son, had been declared king after his father's murder. The Kizzilbash community and the influential but troublesome Aminullah Khan supported him, although the latter was only interested in gaining access to the royal treasury. Akbar Khan's Barakzai clan refused to recognize the Saddozai pretender creating a virtual civil war, and when Akbar

Khan returned to Kabul, his own intricate maneuvering for power contributed to the confusion.

Mohan Lal's luck gave out when Akbar Khan, upon his arrival in Kabul, took custody of him. In an effort to extort some three thousand rupees still in the agent's possession, which he needed to finance his bid for supremacy among the quarreling factions, Akbar Khan tortured him. Mohan Lal managed to smuggle out a message to Pollock relating his trials, how his feet were wounded by bastinadoing and how red pepper was burned before his nose and eyes. He wrote of one occasion when he was placed under a couch on which his tormentors jumped up and down, and frequently he was beaten with sticks "in a very rude and unmerciful manner." He wrote that Akbar Khan had threatened to "pull out [his] eyes and burn [his] body with a hot iron."[4] Mohan Lal was so despairing of his life that he pleaded with Pollock to see that the British cared for his wife and two children if he died from his ill-treatment. Only when Pollock sent a stern letter to Akbar Khan, holding him responsible for Mohan Lal's bad health, did the abuse cease.

Mohan Lal was also grateful for the solace he received during this time of trial from fellow hostage John Conolly, who was among the prisoners kept in Kabul after the British evacuation. Conolly had become a pillar of strength for the British captives and sepoys who had been held in the capital. Somehow endearing himself to many of the more charitable Afghans, he had managed to raise money and collect old clothes to ease the lot of the unfortunate prisoners. But the stress and bad conditions of his captivity took their toll and Conolly died of a heart attack before he could be rescued. This saddened his fellow prisoners, particularly Mohan Lal, who had come to rely on him. Unexpectedly, he was mourned by many Afghans as well.

SHORTLY BEFORE JOHN CONOLLY DIED, NEWS HAD REACHED HIM THAT HIS brother, Captain Arthur Conolly, and Colonel Charles Stoddart had both been tortured, then murdered, by the emir of Bokhara earlier in the summer. Mohan Lal was convinced that this sad news had hastened John's death. Poignant passages from Arthur Conolly's journal chronicling his and Stoddart's ordeal in Bokhara, which surfaced mysteriously twenty years later,* told a story of bravery and endurance under the vilest of

*Conolly kept his journal in the margins of a little prayer book. After his death, the book appeared in a Bokhara bazaar, where it was bought as a curiosity by a Russian slave. He gave it to General Ignatieff, whose mission visited Bokhara in 1858. At Orenburg, Ignatieff gave the book to a Major Salatzki of his mission to pass on to the Royal Geographical Society in London, but since it was personal in nature, the Society in 1862—twenty years after

conditions. At the end of February 1842, Conolly noted that he and Stoddart had been in prison for seventy-one days. Their treatment varied with the emir's whims, but became worse when news reached Bokhara that the Afghans had risen in rebellion. This meant that Emir Nasrullah no longer needed to fear the British; he could do what he pleased with his two captives. Irritated that he had received no personal reply from a letter he had sent to Queen Victoria, his caprice, "not far from madness," was beyond control.

According to his journal, Arthur Conolly's health began to deteriorate in mid-March. He managed to send a message to his brother, John, in Kabul that he was dying. "This will probably be my last note," he wrote. "Send my best to [brother] Henry and to all our dear sisters."[5] Stoddart was in no better shape and Conolly was moved to write: "I looked upon Stoddart's half-naked and nail-lacerated body . . . and wept as I pleaded with one of their guards to tell the Emir he should direct his anger upon me and not further destroy my poor brother, Stoddart, who had suffered so much and so meekly here for three years."[6] The two men embraced each other and prayed. Recalling a saying of the tribal people when faced with a tyrant, they recited together: "Let him [the emir] do as he likes; he is a demon, but God is stronger than the Devil himself." This was not Conolly's last letter, however; he rallied from his fever and lived a little longer, but only to face a more hideous death soon thereafter.

A pessimistic letter dated May 28, 1842, was the last to be received from Conolly; his sense of futility was justified. Both men, sentenced to die, had first been exhibited in the public square of Bokhara, where a multitude had gathered to savor their deaths, on June 17. The doomed men were made to watch as their own graves were dug. Stoddart cried out against the tyranny of the emir as he knelt before his executioner. With one stroke of the sword, his head was severed.[7]

Witness to this horrible spectacle, Conolly was then offered his life if he would denounce Christianity and embrace Islam. His righteous response was: "Stoddart became a Mussulman, and yet you have killed him; I am prepared to die."[8] And die he did as the executioner once more lowered his sword. Stoddart at the end professed he would die a Christian, not a Moslem. Conolly's last words to his comrade were: "Stoddart, we shall see each other in paradise near Jesus."* Thus ended the lives of two

---

Conolly's death—delivered it to Conolly's sister, Mrs. Macnaghten, in Eaton Place, London.

*The eccentric British missionary Joseph Wolff had gone to Bokhara on a bizarre, self-inspired mission to plead for the two men's lives but he had arrived too late. He was the principal source for the details of how Stoddart and Conolly died. (*A Mission to Bokhara*, ed. Guy Wint. London: Routledge & Kegan Paul, 1969 (first published 1845), p. 142.

English prisoners in Bokhara who were no less victims of the Kabul uprising than Alexander Burnes and the others killed as a consequence of that
fateful day.

Not yet having heard that Stoddart and Conolly were already dead, Lord
Ellenborough on October 1 appealed to the emir of Bokhara to release
them. Curiously, the governor general denied they were "employed by
their government," and insisted they were "innocent travellers." This
transparent denial of what was obviously true must surely have infuriated—or perhaps amused—the emir. But whatever the emotions of
that capricious tyrant, Ellenborough's inept message by itself would not
likely have saved the two doomed men even if it had arrived in time.[9]

Mohan Lal was convinced that neither Conolly nor Stoddart would have
been killed by the emir of Bokhara had the British Army of Retribution
set out for Kabul earlier—at least by the end of the winter of 1841–42.
He believed that fearing the prospect of British revenge, the emir would
probably have released the two men.

———— ·•· ————

NOTT DID NOT BEGIN HIS MARCH TO KABUL UNTIL AUGUST 4. HE DIVIDED
his army,* sending the greater part back to Quetta en route to India under
Brigadier England's command. Nott himself began his march to Kabul
with two Queen's regiments, the 40th and 41st, and one Native Infantry
regiment to link up with Pollock's Army of Retribution. Pollock and Sale,
with a force of eight thousand men, set out from Jalalabad soon thereafter
on August 20. Akbar could now visualize his fate as the two British armies,
bent on revenge, tightened the noose around Kabul. One symptom of
Akbar Khan's concern was his sudden kindness toward Mohan Lal. On
several occasions Akbar Khan invited him to dine and, according to the
British agent, often asked his advice as to what he should do. "He said he
knows well that he cannot stand against our troops in the field," reported
Mohan Lal, and that "British money will in its influence, pursue and
oppose him wherever our arms cannot reach."[10] Akbar Khan asked if he
should "throw himself on the honour of the British Government as his
father did." But when Mohan Lal promised he would be well treated if
he surrendered to Pollock, he seemed skeptical: "After all, when Napoleon
threw himself on the mercy of English justice, they made him a prisoner
and sent him to a distant island to die."

Mohan Lal's role now became even more important. He played a critical
part in trying to negotiate with Akbar Khan for the release of the hostages

*At that time Nott had roughly fifteen thousand men under his command.

in advance of Pollock's and Nott's arrival in Kabul. Pottinger was given most of the credit for freeing the prisoners, but Mohan Lal's contribution, perhaps because he was Indian, not British, or perhaps because as an intelligence agent he was accustomed to working unsung in the shadows, tended to be passed over by many historians. In his book on Dost Mohammed, he wrote: "I do not presume to say that none but myself took a share in transmitting intelligence and negotiating the release of the prisoners—far from it,"[11] and, indeed, he gave much credit to Major Pottinger. But he was later resentful of his detractors, such as George Broadfoot with Sale's brigade, who belittled his accomplishments.

Obviously sensitive about this matter, Mohan Lal included in his published account of events numerous letters praising him. Lord Ellenborough himself credited the agent with keeping the government fully informed on events in Kabul and being the first to discover that Dost Mohammed in exile had found a way to correspond secretly with his son, Akbar Khan, in Afghanistan. While Ellenborough's indecision had been responsible for the delay in the march of the Army of Retribution, the governor general acknowledged that Mohan Lal had been right in urging the British Army to reach at least to Gandamak at an early date so as to accelerate the political demise of Akbar Khan and make easier a timely release of the hostages.[12] Pollock too was full of praise for Mohan Lal, pointing out that if any of his letters had fallen into the hands of their enemy, "his life would have been forfeit." Richmond Shakespear, with Sale's brigade, gave Mohan Lal the kind of accolade any intelligence agent likes to receive: "While at Jalalabad, we were entirely dependent on him for intelligence on the state of affairs and of parties at Kabul. . . . I do not remember a single instance of the information which he gave being incorrect."[13] Sale's political officer, Major Macgregor, who had asked Mohan Lal to remain behind in Kabul as agent in the first place, discreetly noted: "His services are too well known to render it necessary that I should here detail them."

Consolidating his strength in the maelstrom of political infighting in Kabul as Pollock and Nott drew nearer, Akbar Khan on June 20 maneuvered to place Shah Shuja's son, Prince Futteh Jung, on the throne despite opposition from his rivals, and to name himself vizier. Akbar Khan also moved his hostages—in effect, his life-insurance policy—to Bamiyan, northwest of Kabul. Liberation had seemed so near to the hapless prisoners before they were jammed once again into the camel panniers and marched toward the Hindu Kush, out of reach of rescue. Akbar, "with an expression of savage determination," threatened Captain Troup that if Pollock persisted in his advance, the hostages would be sold as slaves to the Turkomans. Alternatively, the hostages could imagine that, when pressed to the wall, Akbar Khan might murder them all in one of his unpredictable fits of rage. Eldred Pottinger one day had the unnerving experience of overhearing an argument between Akbar Khan and his lieutenants as to whether the hostages should be killed. Fortunately the majority of the Afghan leaders were opposed to any such mass murder and the hostages were spared.[14]

Adding a somewhat surrealistic touch to the pathetic caravan of captives, the escort now consisted of troopers of the native Irregular Horse regiment who had deserted the British at Bamiyan in October 1840; the fife-and-drum band played British regimental marching tunes to "cheer" their charges. But the escort commander, a rollicking mercenary who had defected from Shah Shuja's army, at least seemed friendly, probably because he realized that this was the time to switch sides again rather than find himself in the bad graces of the rapidly advancing British.

As the British hostages in Bamiyan settled into still other quarters, a brooding Shelton continued to set himself off from the others, abdicating altogether the command role his rank entitled him to. Lawrence, who had earlier assumed charge, now seemed exhausted, while Mackenzie was too sick to function effectively. Even the indomitable Lady Sale seemed dispirited. Rising to the occasion, Major Eldred Pottinger and Captain Johnson took the lead to determine their next move.

In the meantime, Pollock's army inexorably advanced toward Kabul. At Jagdalak the Ghilzyes again commanded the heights from which they had always been able to rain down fire on their passing enemies, but this time the general, using the same tactics as he had in the Khyber Pass, ordered his infantry to scale the rocks and rout them out. Akbar Khan fell back again to take his last stand at Tezeen. On September 13, he massed there the largest force ever to take the field against the British, but it proved no match for Pollock's force, which by now had its blood up and was determined to wreak revenge on the Afghans. Again seeking the advantage of height, Pollock ordered his men to mount the rocks and attack the Ghilzyes with bayonets. Broadfoot led the attack with his Gurkhas. At home in the mountains, the tough little soldiers scrambled up the steepest cliffs to rout out their enemy. Those Ghilzyes fortunate enough to survive fled in terror at the sight of the Gurkhas waving their *kukris,* or curved knives designed to sever an ox's—or a man's—neck in one blow. If there was ever an example of heart and good leadership winning a battle, this was it. Pollock's dispatch glowed with admiration: "Seldom have soldiers had a more arduous task to perform and never was an undertaking of this kind surpassed in execution."

As Pollock approached Kabul, he was met on the road by Mohan Lal, who was moved by the general's warm greetings. The general expressed his gratitude for Mohan Lal's services and passed on the warming message that his bravery had been also "appreciated by the Governor General."[15]

On September 15, Pollock entered Kabul triumphantly and camped on the Kabul racecourse. He placed the Union Jack conspicuously atop the Bala Hissar to wave mockingly before the Afghans. Two days later Nott's column, having fought and won a battle at Ghazni marked by excessive cruelty on the part of his soldiers and having gratuitously destroyed the great citadel, reached Kabul to join Pollock.

Nott brought with him the "Gates of the Temple of Somnath," a special symbolic act that Lord Ellenborough had ordered him to perform in Ghazni when he retook the city. The sandlewood gates, according to legend, had been stolen from the Hindu temple of Somnath eight hundred years earlier by the army of Sultan Mahmud of Ghazni and reerected at the entrance to the great Moslem ruler's tomb at Roza, just outside Ghazni. In fact, the gates dated from a much later period than the reign of Mahmud of Ghazni, but Ellenborough was convinced that a return of the sanctified gates to India would gain him merit in the eyes of the Indian Hindus—a politically useful purpose. It did nothing of the sort; the Hindus considered the gates polluted by the many years of Moslem possession. Nonetheless, in a ringing proclamation to Hindus on November 18 that inspired only ridicule, Ellenborough announced: "The insult of 800 years is at last avenged . . ." Because of the Hindu attitude, which ranged from resentment to apathy, the gates were, in fact, never restored to Somnath and were unceremoniously relegated to a warehouse in Agra.

Pollock wasted no time in sending a rescue party to Bamiyan to free the hostages. The general's military secretary, Richmond Shakespear, who it will be recalled had made a name for himself by rescuing the Russian slaves in Khiva, dashed off with an advance force made up of six hundred or so Kizzilbash irregular cavalry. As might be guessed, the fine hand of Mohan Lal was behind Shirin Khan's offer of his Kizzilbash fighters for this purpose. Pollock had meant Nott to follow with a more substantial column, but the irritable general objected to dividing his force and committing men already tired from their march from Kandahar and Ghazni to unknown danger in the Hindu Kush. Privately he grumbled, "Government had thrown the prisoners overboard, why then should I rescue them?"[16] Thoroughly disgusted by Nott's attitude, Pollock instead sent Brigadier Sale with the 3rd Dragoons and the 1st Light Cavalry. Eager to rescue his beloved wife and daughter, Fighting Bob was, of course, overjoyed to be given the task.

The prisoners at Bamiyan had in the meantime actually engineered their own escape. Captain Johnson deserved much of the credit; he had worked hard to ingratiate himself with their keeper, the mercenary Saleh Mohammed, by listening admiringly to his tall tales of adventure and valor. Johnson also hinted that generous subsidies would be his if he released his prisoners.

Johnson's cultivation soon bore fruit; on September 11, Saleh Mohammed assembled Johnson, Pottinger and Lawrence to show them two letters. One was an order from Akbar Khan to take the British farther north and deliver them to the Uzbeks to be enslaved. The other was a message from Mohan Lal promising him a generous allowance for life if he would free the hostages. On the word of the three officers present that the British offer was genuine, the Afghan agreed to ignore Akbar Khan's order and give the British their freedom.

Once free, the British immediately raised the Union Jack. Major Pottinger, who now assumed command, even had the audacity to summon the neighboring chieftains to demand their fealty and recruit from their people a local levy of guards to serve as escort on the hazardous march back to Kabul. Saleh Mohammed, entering into the spirit of things, proudly informed Captain Lawrence that he had been able to find a few muskets with which they could defend themselves. The flamboyant mercenary thought it would be more suitable to have a small advance guard of Englishmen as a "show" when they entered Kabul, rather than appear to be in the hands of their escort. "I blush to record," Lady Sale wrote in her diary, "that when Lawrence asked for volunteers, a dead silence ensued." Even when she announced disdainfully to Lawrence, "You better give *me* one [a gun], and *I* will lead the party," none of the men came forth to volunteer. Lady Sale thought it "sad to think the men were so lost to all right feeling . . ."[17]

The joy of liberation was marred by the discovery of little baby Stoker's body lying unattended and dying on the cold ground. After his mother's death on the terrible march from Kabul, he had been entrusted to Sergeant Wade's wife, a half-caste who secretly took the side of the Afghans, betraying her fellow hostages. Frequent beatings by this miserable woman had apparently been the cause of the little Stoker boy's death.

The liberated British, fearing attack by Afghan tribes approaching to attack them, were hurrying toward Kabul when they learned of the rescue column headed their way. On September 17 a cloud of dust in the distance heralded Shakespear and his Kizzilbash column. In his exuberance Shakespear rushed to embrace Lady Sale and give her greetings from her husband, who was soon to follow. This earned him a rebuke from the choleric Shelton, who was outraged that he had not given him the first salute as military protocol demanded before engaging in such emotional outbursts.

It was late in the afternoon of the twentieth when Fighting Bob Sale himself appeared. As he rode toward the British camp, Colin Mackenzie made an effort to congratulate him on being about to rejoin his wife. "The gallant old man turned . . . and tried to answer," recalled Mackenzie, "but his feelings were too strong; he made a hideous grimace, dug his spurs into his horse and galloped off as hard as he could." Filled with emotion, Sale found his wife, and silently embraced her. Lady Sale noted in her diary that her happiness "so long delayed as to be almost unexpected, was actually painful, and accompanied by a choking sensation which could not obtain the relief of tears."[18]

As the liberated hostages entered Kabul to a gun salute and the cheers of the British troops they passed, they saw the still-smoldering ruins of the great bazaar, which had been systematically destroyed on Pollock's orders. This was his way of carrying out Ellenborough's instructions specifying that the Army of Retribution must leave behind proof of its power without causing acts of inhumanity. Although an effort was made to prevent gratuitous cruelties, the troops got out of control, looting and burning indiscriminately. Revenge was theirs and Britain's will had been done— but at a price to friend as well as foe. Mohan Lal was particularly offended that the homes and shops of Afghans who had risked death to help him and be kind to the hostages now lost everything, while the real perpetrators of the atrocities, including Akbar Khan himself, escaped to the hills. Mohan Lal had also accompanied a column to Charekar to destroy the village where the 4th Gurkhas had been annihilated. The Indian agent confessed to having felt ill by it all. He did not approve of such indiscriminate punishment. He was also distressed that the chiefs who had remained friendly to him during his long and dangerous service in Kabul would be left to their fate under Akbar Khan's rule when the Army of Retribution withdrew from Kabul after making its grand gesture: "This was not honorable on our part."

Lord Ellenborough savored the thought of going down in history as the man who restored British honor. On November 16, he issued a manifesto repudiating Auckland's policies and in grandiloquent terms praising his own. The manifesto's style and substance, in fact, opened Ellenborough to ridicule; it was all a bit too much. And that he backdated the document to October 1, the anniversary of Lord Auckland's Simla Manifesto launching British policy on its catastrophic course, struck many as a tasteless gesture.

The grand finale of the tragic, misbegotten British adventure in Afghanistan occurred in Ferozepore, where the Army of the Indus had strutted so magnificently before marching off to Afghanistan in 1838. On December 9, Lord Ellenborough presided over an extravaganza in Ferozepore meant to dazzle the princes and potentates of the Punjab and dramatize the British retrieval of its honor. In his moment of glory, Ellenborough refused to let news that Prince Futteh Jung, left behind helplessly on the Kabul throne, had just been overthrown by Akbar Khan spoil his triumph.

Sir Robert Sale crossed the Sutlej River and entered Ferozepore to the strains of "Conquering Hero" at the head of his gallant defenders of Jalalabad as centerpiece of the gala. Riding by his side were Mohan Lal, thrilled to be so honored, Major Macgregor and Major Claude Wade. Sale's star was meant to outshine all others. Two days later Pollock arrived, followed on December 13 by Nott bearing the Gates of Somnath.

The celebrations struck a sour note with many of the troops, who wondered why one of the greatest debacles in British military history should be so grandly memorialized. It was said that even a phalanx of elephants, taught to kneel respectfully before the conquering heroes, refused to do so. The climax, a grand military display involving forty thousand British and Sikh forces and one hundred guns, was witnessed by the important Sikh notables from Lahore, whom the British meant to impress. In fact, it did not impress the Sikhs, nor did it erase the disgrace of the humiliating British evacuation from Kabul. Within three years the Sikh army, the Khalsa, remembering the British defeat and convinced of its own superiority, would attack British forces in the Punjab without warning, to begin the Sikh wars. But, now at least, Ellenborough found satisfaction in his great show, which provided him with an opportunity to bask in the victories of the Army of Retribution.

A humiliating and inauspicious episode in the Great Game had ended. Begun as an effort to halt Russian expansion in Central Asia, it accomplished just the opposite. The Afghan War was a demonstration that the British raj was not omnipotent and this would contribute to the growing unrest in India, culminating in the Great Mutiny fifteen years later, which brought the empire to the brink of destruction.

Dost Mohammed, as he bid Ellenborough farewell before returning to the throne in Kabul from which he had been ejected, said, more in puzzlement than in anger: "I have been struck with the magnitude of your resources, your ships, your arsenals; but what I cannot understand is why the rulers of an empire so vast and flourishing should have gone across the Indus to deprive me of my poor and barren country."[19]

Few others could understand either.

EPILOGUE

THE AFGHAN DEBACLE HAD TAKEN A HIDEOUS TOLL. EVEN BEFORE THE destruction of the 4,500-man British garrison in Kabul and its 12,000 camp followers along the bloody route of retreat, there had been 1,500 killed or wounded in battles with the Afghans. In fact, before the terrible denouement at Jagdalak there had been a total of thirty-four combat engagements, of which thirteen had resulted in the British being bested by the Afghans. The financial cost of the Afghan experience had also been enormous, and this had to be borne by the East India Company—meaning, ultimately, the people of India, not the British government.

As can be imagined, a catastrophe of this dimension could not pass without recrimination and awarding of blame. The Government of India in late 1842 issued a proclamation condemning the policies of Governor General Auckland. But for all the governor general's mistakes, ultimate blame should have been borne by a government in England that had not lived up to its obligation to intervene in a matter of such moment. Auckland's manifesto of October 1, 1838, had not only been flawed in its logic, but was conspicuously contrived to justify his actions. Yet Auckland's correspondence in August 1838 elicited from the India Office and the British government only tepid reservations as to the wisdom of the policy he intended to follow.

At the root of the problem had been the fear that Russia presented an immediate military threat to India, a fear widely felt in England as well as in India and one encouraged by no less a statesman than Foreign Secretary Palmerston. This could have been the only real justification for taking such excessive risks in the invasion and occupation of Afghanistan. But in the atmosphere of the times, the British government seemed incapable of realistically assessing the feasibility of a Russian military advance on Afghanistan—just as they misjudged their own chances of success in doing so.

Perhaps the greatest significance of the Afghan disaster was the revelation that the British were not invincible, even against primitive tribesmen armed only with their homemade *jazails*. And the irony is that while mesmerized by an exaggerated Russian threat, the British, by their inept efforts to contain it, set in train events that would more surely put its Indian empire at risk.

The end of what has come to be known as the First Afghan War was not the end of turmoil on the northwest frontier of Britain's Indian empire, nor did it resolve British-Russian rivalries in Central Asia. The Russians continued their inexorable advance on the khanates of Central Asia and would again provoke the British to ill-advised adventures in Afghanistan. More immediately, however, the British would become involved in a series of bloody engagements in the Indus Valley, the kinds of campaigns Kipling called "savage wars of peace." Justified as necessary for the defense of empire, they marked the last expansion of British India's frontier, and resulted in the demise of the family oligarchy of emirs that ruled Sind and the end of the Sikh dynasty that ruled the Punjab. Some of those who survived the Afghan disaster reappeared in these and other wars, many to lose their lives. Others faded from public view, content to watch from the sidelines as history passed them by. Whatever their fates, curiosity demands a last glimpse of these heroes, villains and fools of the Afghan debacle.

As Lord Auckland boarded the ship in Calcutta bound for home, his devoted sister Lady Eden saw tears in his eyes, "pricked on not by sentiment but by suffering." He manfully bore the intense criticism leveled at him in London upon his return without complaint. The Board of Control heaped blame on him, and the press, always eager to bay at public leaders who stumble, treated him to a barrage of attacks. For so terrible a disaster there had to be scapegoats and Auckland made a good one, although Foreign Secretary Palmerston, chronically obsessed by the Russian threat and a sometimes reckless advocate of a foreward-thrusting frontier policy, was probably more deserving of blame. Auckland was particularly dejected when his successor, Ellenborough, publicly disparaged him. The two men, while in different parties, had been good family friends; now Ellenborough referred to Auckland's administration in India as having been "corrupt." But the storm of criticism passed, and when Lord John Russell formed a new government in 1846, he made Auckland his First Lord of the Admiralty.

At age sixty-four Lord Auckland died of a stroke on New Year's Day, 1849. Friends raised a subscription of £2,000 for a bronze statue honoring him that was duly erected in Calcutta. He had been a good man, but, like those of many good men, his works had bred disaster. Auckland's devoted sister Emily, a talented woman whose letters from India were classics of insight and verve and whose sketches captured India so charmingly, followed him to the grave twenty years later after a long illness. So much had transpired since Lady Eden's portrait of Queen Victoria was presented to Ranjit Singh during the grand durbar at Ferozepore, celebrating with such high hopes the imminent invasion of Afghanistan.

There was, of course, a Court of Inquiry for officers. Even those simply held hostage had to be exposed to scrutiny lest they be found to have been guilty of desertion or misconduct rather than victims of capture. Major Pottinger, who had distinguished himself in the defense of Herat, narrowly escaped death at Charekar and had been the lone, shrill voice to cry out against the decision to evacuate Kabul, earned acquittal and high praise, but only after Brigadier Shelton, as principal witness against him, grudgingly admitted that Pottinger had signed the infamous document of surrender under protest and on his explicit orders. The Court of Inquiry concluded its deliberations by acknowledging the "painful position in which Major Pottinger was unexpectedly placed" and lauded the "energy and manly firmness that stamps his character as one worthy of high admiration."

Pottinger was most touched, however, when the other surviving hostages signed a letter praising him for his role at Bamiyan engineering their escape. "The cheerfulness and determination with which you entered on the difficult task imposed upon you must be ever gratefully remembered by us . . ." were words more precious than any official accolade could ever be. Only Shelton and Palmer (who surrendered Ghazni) refused to associate themselves with this gracious gesture, which fact speaks loudly of their meanness of spirit. Unfortunately, Pottinger's promising career was cut short when soon afterward he died of fever while returning home to England on furlough.

Shelton, who tried to place all blame on the late General Elphinstone, was himself tried by the Court of Inquiry. He was acquitted of all but one charge of wrongdoing: that was the charge of "entering into clandestine correspondence with Akbar [Khan] to obtain forage for his own horses while Macnaghten's negotiations were in progress." But if Shelton was spared more serious criticism by the Court of Inquiry, he was never forgiven by his own men of the 44th, who literally cheered when his death from a riding accident was announced on the parade ground in Dublin in 1845.

Of all the hostages, Lady Sale perhaps deserved as much credit as anyone. She had borne her trials with courage and grace. After being joyfully reunited with her husband, she was to lose him again, this time forever, when he was killed in the Battle of Mudki against the Sikhs on December 18, 1845. Fighting Bob had a reputation for emerging wounded from nearly every campaign in which he took part, but this time his wounds were mortal. If not a brilliant officer, he had been a brave one and died a hero remembered by a grateful nation for his defense of Jalalabad. The *Pictorial Times* was typical of all newspapers when it expressed his country's "sacred and affectionate sorrow" for his death.

Florentia Sale lived out most of the rest of her life in the Indian hill station of Simla on a special pension awarded her by the Company. Her daughter, who had been widowed by Sturt's death during the terrible retreat from Kabul, was murdered with her second husband, Major Holmes, during the Indian Sepoy Mutiny in July 1857. Lady Sale was spared the grief of this tragic episode by her own death four years earlier in Capetown, South Africa, on July 6, 1853. Her epitaph read simply: "Underneath this stone reposes all that could die of Lady Sale."

What of Dr. William Brydon? He had been miraculously spared in the slaughter of the death march from Kabul to fight again, this time in the defense of Lucknow in the Indian Mutiny. For his valor during the siege of Lucknow he was made a Companion of the Bath. Brydon, whose experience in reaching Jalalabad became a legend of British military history, died a peaceful death at a ripe old age in Scotland, land of his birth, in 1873.

Charles Masson, last noted as he returned to England in 1842 an embittered man, would have his say about the Afghan episode. While his book, *Narrative of Various Journeys in Baluchistan, Afghanistan and The Panjab,* was, as its title implies, a memoir of his life and explorations, it included some scathing remarks about British policy. Appearing just as the first news of the Kabul debacle became known, his views could not easily be gainsaid, but he and his book were nonetheless attacked from several quarters. The *Calcutta Review* accused him of spitefulness, and the British officials in India who knew his background generally felt that it was presumptuous and ill-mannered for a deserter who had been forgiven to turn on his benefactors. Sir Henry Lawrence was particularly outspoken on the subject of Masson, accusing him of being "the most matter of fact fabulist in the world."[1]

Masson died on November 5, 1853, at the age of fifty-three, carrying the secrets of his youth to the grave. He had sinned against the empire by deserting the Indian Army in his youth, but had redeemed himself by serving as an agent in Kabul under dangerous circumstances. In speaking out against British policy he had sinned again. However justified his criticism and accurate his predictions, Charles Masson could not be forgiven by a vested establishment whose members considered it presumptuous for an outsider with a clouded past to excoriate his "betters." Nevertheless, the East India Company found it in its heart to grant his widow a small sum when he died and took care of her orphaned children when she passed on. For all the disdain shown him by the likes of Lawrence, his political judgments on Afghanistan were sounder than most.

Generals Pollock and Nott had not been feted by Ellenborough at Ferozepore with the same enthusiasm as had been Brigadier Sale, but they were each given the Grand Cross of the Bath for their part in the punitive campaign in Afghanistan. Lord Ellenborough himself was rewarded with an earldom for his efforts to retrieve British honor, although his critics were loud in their condemnation of his administration, and he was finally recalled from India by the Company for his excessive zeal in seizing Sind and the princely state of Gwalior in north-central India.

The Afghan campaign's most neglected hero was Mohan Lal. General Pollock had been generous in his praise of the British agent, writing in a dispatch of September 23, 1842, that the release of the hostages "may be attributed in great measure to the negotiations of Mohan Lal . . ." but Mohan Lal was generally passed over when awards were handed out. Sent off to the Northwest Frontier Agency in January 1843, he found himself with little to do and in the bad graces of his superior, British agent George Broadfoot who had served so ably in Jalalabad.

While Mohan Lal's many achievements, duly chronicled in dispatches, gathered dust in intelligence archives, unwarranted accusations were leveled at him in the acrimonious aftermath of the Afghanistan disaster. Only because he had preserved certain key documents himself was he able to prove that the assassinations of the two rebel chiefs, Mir Misjidi and

Abdullah Khan, had been carried out on Macnaghten's orders and were not actions perpetrated on his own initiative. Mohan Lal was resentful that Company accountants questioned many of his expenditures in Kabul incurred under press of dangerous duty and for the urgent cause of saving the British hostages. Documents were finally discovered authorizing his expenditures, and the full record of his achievements, brought about by artfully dispensed bribes, was tucked away elsewhere in the files, but few had rushed to his defense—certainly not Broadfoot.

Not until 1852, after a special Investigative Commission found his transactions justified, could Mohan Lal hope for personal financial relief, but, astonishingly, James Andrew, Earl of Dalhousie, by then governor general, rejected the commission's findings and overturned its verdict. It also hurt Mohan Lal deeply that certain Afghan chiefs who had rendered him signal service and to whom he had made solemn promises in behalf of his government were ignored, ill-rewarded or even mistreated by the British in the aftermath of the Afghan fiasco.

Mohan Lal had for a while escaped the pettifoggery of an ungrateful Indian government by a trip to England in 1844. There, at least, he could find friends who had valued his services. Upon arriving in England, Mohan Lal was kindly received by Sir Claude Wade at the latter's home on the Isle of Wight and had the opportunity to meet the former political officer's charming new wife, still shy of twenty. In London Mohan Lal, of course, called on his old friend and patron Sir Charles Trevelyan, who then held a high position in the British Treasury. To Mohan Lal, Trevelyan had not only been the man who launched him on his career in the Political Department but had been like a father to him. Mohan Lal could feel proud that he had more than justified the confidence placed in him by so distinguished a civil servant.

Mohan Lal called on the East India Company's chairman. The Company was hospitable—far more than its administrators in India had seemed to be after the retreat from Kabul. The London directors impressed him; he was filled with wonder that "They rule India, collect the revenue, encourage trade, raise and discipline armies, preserve peace and administer the laws in the rich and extensive empire in the East"[2] from their Leadenhall Street offices in London.

Mohan Lal basked in the praises of Eldred Pottinger's uncle, Sir Henry Pottinger, Alexander Burnes's superior officer in Kutch, who wined and dined him at the Oriental Club in London. The Honorable Mountstuart Elphinstone, statesman emeritus of frontier affairs, whom Mohan Lal's father served during the Company's memorable first mission to Shah Shuja in 1808, also received Mohan Lal warmly.

In all, Mohan Lal's visit to London, a glorious reunion with the greats of the frontier, was a heady experience, but the high point was his audience with Queen Victoria. He was also favored with an invitation to a royal ball, which to him was "beyond anything of the kind in the world!" with its profusion of "beautiful women in rich dresses and jewels."[3]

Mohan Lal also visited Scotland, where he paid a visit to members of Alexander Burnes's family in Montrose and delivered to them Burnes's last journal, current to the night before his murder. It saddened Mohan Lal, always loyal to the memory of his late friend, to hear "false stories" spread against Burnes's private character in England and among his friends in Scotland.

The Company's Court of Directors was gracious enough to approve an annual pension of some £1,000 for Mohan Lal. Returning to India in 1846, he found the Company less charitable in Calcutta, and fell on hard times. Perhaps frustrated by not having enough to do, he went into debt and was arrested in Ludhiana on charges brought by irate creditors.

During the mutiny of 1857, Mohan Lal faced problems of a more serious kind, and only narrowly escaped death at the hands of the mutineers in Delhi. He survived this uprising as he had the Kabul uprising, however, and took service with the rajah of Kapurtala before dying in 1877. His remains still lie under an inconspicuous stone slab along the Delhi-Panipat road. Among the first Indian civil servants trained by the British, Mohan Lal had set a high standard of achievement and loyalty in the service of empire. At a critical moment he had been thrust into a dangerous role as political agent left behind when the British cantonment marched out to its doom. He acquitted himself with quiet distinction, enduring torture and daily risking his life for the Company as he worked to have the British hostages released.

Dost Mohammed, released by the British to reclaim his lost throne, reached Lahore on his way to Kabul on January 20, 1843. He was cordially greeted by the Sikhs, who now saw advantage in détente with the Afghans. A secret treaty of alliance was signed behind the backs of the British by Dost Mohammed and the Sikh maharajah of the moment, Sher Singh.

While interned in India Dost Mohammed had been well treated by the British and gave every evidence of being a model prisoner. But, as Mohan Lal discovered, the emir had found a secret means to keep in touch with Akbar Khan, and while professing good behavior in Ludhiana, he was, in fact, exhorting his son to further excesses against the British.

On his return to Kabul, Dost Mohammed was greeted by Akbar Khan at the Khyber Pass amid much rejoicing by an assemblage of chiefs. But success caused Dost Mohammed to lapse into his dissolute ways, which he had long ago foresworn upon becoming emir. He took to drink and debauchery and ruled with a tyranny untypical of him. Mohan Lal quoted him as saying: "While I was an enemy of wine, I was always involved in difficulties, and that since I drink, I am prosperous and have gained my liberty after being in an English prison."

Dost Mohammed could not resist meddling in the Sikh uprisings against the British following the Afghan War, but he refrained from giving aid and comfort to the Indians during the 1857 mutiny. Nor did the Russian-influenced Persians benefit from his reign, as the Company pundits had so direly predicted. For this the British were grateful.

Dost Mohammed died a natural death in 1863, a rarity for Afghan leaders. But his son, Akbar Khan, having been poisoned by his physician in Jalalabad, was not so fortunate. He died in 1847 before his time and well before his father.

If everything was reverting "to the old state of things" in Afghanistan following the war, as Major Rawlinson put it, this was not the case in Sind. Lord Ellenborough seemed to be obsessed with restoring British honor, and acquiring honor for himself while he was about it. Sind seemed to be a good place in which to do it. For all his peaceful protestations, he plunged India into a campaign against Sind, whose emirs had always been troublesome for the British but hardly enough to warrant an outright invasion. The real issue, of course, was control of the Indus River delta, ensuring British access to the great river as an avenue of commerce.

Few in London could see much sense in Ellenborough's new adventure, and it was roundly denounced by such luminaries as Gladstone, Peel and Wellington. Lord Mountstuart Elphinstone, the revered old pioneer of Afghanistan fame (not to be confused with his kin, General William Elphinstone, bungler of Kabul), grumbled: "Coming after Afghanistan, it puts one in mind of a bully who had been kicked in the street, and went home to beat his wife in revenge." But General Napier, who commanded the campaign, was nonetheless sent off with an army to do battle with the Sind chieftains, whose shouts of anger "rolled like peals of thunder" and whose warriors' "sharp swords, gleaming in the sun," attacked the invaders.

Napier triumphed in a short campaign in March and, according to *Punch* magazine, announced his victory with the single Latin verb *peccavi,* "I have sinned." Napier's bad pun, probably apocryphal, was almost as embarrassing as his description of Sind's annexation by the British as a "useful, humane piece of rascality."[4] Less cynically he described the Sind campaign as "the tail of the Afghan story."

Ellenborough's decision to invade Sind had made Prime Minister Peel uneasy, and there was no dearth of critics who felt that the action had been unnecessary, even immoral. The East India Court of Directors had registered its disagreement, but it came too late to stop Napier. Despite the opposition in London, Sind was annexed by British India on June 13, 1843. Ellenborough, however, paid for his expensive forward-thrusting propensities when the Court of Directors, despite vigorous opposition from Wellington and Peel, recalled him from India and replaced him with his brother-in-law, Sir Henry Hardinge.

The Afghan disaster, interestingly enough, reverberated in the United States, becoming something of a political issue in the 1842 elections. Josiah Harlan, after being ejected by the British when the Army of the Indus occupied Kabul, had slowly wended his way homeward, arriving in Philadelphia in August 1841, and his statements to the press did much to make Americans conscious of the Afghan drama—in which they were inclined to take the side of the natives.[5]

The westward movement in the United States bore at least a faint resemblance to Russia's eastward expansion. And, just as Russia's imperial momentum in Central Asia provoked the British misadventure in Afghanistan, the United States found itself viewing British enterprise in Oregon in 1842 with some suspicion. The existence of the British Hudson Bay Company in Oregon, with its several trading posts, was seen as a threat to the western destiny of the United States. The Webster-Ashburton Treaty of 1842 had amicably settled territorial disputes in the northeast part of the United States and the Great Lakes region, but what about the northwest? Did British aggression in Afghanistan presage a grab for Oregon?

Harlan's criticism of British policy and actions in Afghanistan was liberally quoted by the press. The *Illinois State Register* of April 7, 1843, for example, dwelt at length on the alleged slaughter of "tens of thousands of Afghans" by Pollock in Kabul. The venerable Duke of Wellington in a letter to Ellenborough decried American rejoicing over "our disasters and degradation," and exulted that the governor general would "teach them that their triumph is premature."[6]

The Russian attitude toward events in Afghanistan was of continuing concern to the British. Yet now the perceived threat from Russia seemed to have evaporated into thin air. Had it just been a mirage, a figment of the imagination of Palmerston and other hard-liners? Russia had in its own self-interest restrained Persia from taking advantage of British agonies in Afghanistan, perhaps invading Herat again, for example. A new Persian offensive, the Russians reasoned, would trigger a British invasion of Persia via the Gulf and a decision to hold Afghanistan at any cost. It was better to let events unfold naturally in Afghanistan, since there was every indication that the British would stumble without any need for the Russians to push them.

The atmospherics between Great Britain and Russia following the Afghan War were for the moment good. Czar Nicholas and Nesselrode even paid a goodwill visit to England in 1844. But the British annexation of Sind in 1843, matched by the signing of a Russian treaty with Khiva the following year, obtained under threat of a Russian invasion from Orenburg, and the establishment of a Russian garrison on the Aral Sea, were signals that neither power had abandoned its ambitions in Central Asia.

If the Russians had Khiva to absorb their attention now, the British had the Punjab to absorb theirs. For the moment Afghanistan was left to its own devices, spared foreign interference. By 1845 the kaleidoscopic series of political murders had left the Sikh nation in a state of utter chaos as a cast of characters worthy of the most improbable melodrama vied for political control in Lahore. Real power was held by the proud and jingoistic Sikh military brotherhood, the Khalsa, which after the Afghan fiasco no longer held the British Indian Army in awe, and plotted to retake that part of the Punjab held by the Company. One of Ranjit Singh's widows, a beautiful scheming nymphomaniac known as Rani Jindan, watched over her eight-year-old son, Dhulip Singh, who had by then inherited the unsteady Sikh throne, and played her own game of intrigue.

The fate of the Punjab would, however, be determined by Sikh rivalry with the British now that Ranjit Singh was gone. It was inevitable that the East India Company would collide with the Sikhs. Major George Broadfoot, whom we had last seen as one of Brigadier Sale's stalwart officers in Jalalabad, was now an aggressive British political agent in Ferozepore accredited to the Sikhs and personally dedicated to pushing Company borders to the Indus. He contemptuously reported on the events in Lahore, vilifying Sikh leadership at every turn. As for the queen regent— the Rani Jindan—he reported: "I sometimes feel as if I were a sort of parish constable at the door of a brothel rather than representative of one government to another." Her excesses, he believed, had seriously affected her mind: "Messalina picked big men, and Catherine [the Great] liked variety, but what do you think of four young fellows changed as they ceased to give satisfaction every night with the Rani?"

The British political agent warned of a Sikh military buildup. And, indeed, a Sikh army fifty-thousand strong plunged into war against the British when it crossed the Sutlej on December 12, 1845, violating the thirty-six-year treaty with the British signed by Ranjit Singh.

Suddenly at Ferozshah, in the midst of an attack by the Sikhs, we again see Sita Ram, last noted as a slave enduring harsh captivity in Kabul. The

Indian sepoy had had a hard time of it. Even hope of liberation was denied him when his master, fearing Pollock's approaching army, fled to the hills, dragging Sita Ram along with him. But somehow the tough little soldier managed to escape, disguised as a Pathan, and reach India. Sita Ram's joy at finally reaching the British garrison at Ferozepore in October 1843 was blighted when he discovered that his incredible story of escape was not believed. Even worse, the paymaster refused to pay his wages, which had so long been accumulating while he was held captive in Kabul. When he finally convinced his betters that his odyssey had been a genuine one he was allowed to rejoin his old regiment, but, adding to his woes, he found himself shunned by his peers, the other sepoys, because his service with a Moslem had, in their eyes, caused him to lose caste.

Now serving with the Company army at Ferozshah, the long-suffering sepoy faced death once again. As battle raged about him, "the fate of the British Empire seemed to be hanging on a thread."[7] In the final engagement of the First Sikh War a determined British attack finally dislodged the Sikhs, however, sending them fleeing across a pontoon bridge spanning the Sutlej. Some ten thousand Sikhs lost their lives that day, ending the first Sikh contest with the British.* The Second Sikh War, which followed close on the heels of the first, was won by the British in 1849 at the Battle of Gujerat, seventy miles north of Lahore, and the Company annexed the Punjab, which never again would exist as a sovereign kingdom.

Still to be accounted for is the fabulous Koh-i-noor diamond, a symbol, if not a player, in the Great Game. As victors, the British seized the fateful gem from the defeated Sikhs as a prize of war.

Lord Dalhousie, by then governor general, had written Henry Lawrence to take "proper precautions" and provide maximum security for the Koh-i-noor until it could be escorted to England. Henry's brother, John Lawrence, who served with him on a Council of Three charged with administering the conquered Punjab, was given custody of the gem. Somewhat casual about such things, John put the largest diamond in the world into his waistcoat pocket and promptly forgot about it. When he changed for dinner, his waistcoat was hung in the closet. Only when Queen Victoria wrote the governor general some six weeks later, impatiently asking about the Koh-i-noor, destined to grace the royal crown, did John Lawrence try to track down his priceless charge. He searched his wardrobe to no avail, but when he cautiously asked his bearer whether he might have found anything in his waistcoat pocket, the faithful old servant ambled

---

*The Rani Jindan was permitted by the British to remain queen regent for the young maharajah, Dhulip Singh, and to keep her lover, Lal Singh, by her side at court. But her request that she be provided with an English husband was ignored.

over to a tin box and withdrew a bundle of rags that he slowly unwound to reveal the great gem. "I found nothing, Sahib," said the bearer, except this "bit of glass."

Shah Shuja, when he had been forced to give up the Koh-i-noor to Maharajah Ranjit Singh, sadly commented: "Whoever possesses it has conquered their enemies." For all their ineptitude in Afghanistan, the British now had the great gem to attest to their victory over the Sikhs and were now masters of the Indus Valley. But they had not checked their Russian rivals. The specter of the bear beyond the Hindu Kush still haunted the British; the Great Game was by no means over.

NOTES AND REFERENCES

Chapter 1

1. John William Kaye, *Lives of Indian Officers*, Vol. II (London: J. J. Keliher, 1904), p. 16.
2. Ibid., p. 6.
3. Ibid., p. 11.
4. Ibid.
5. The Marquess of Anglesey, ed., *Sergeant Pearman's Memoirs* (London: Jonathan Cape Ltd., 1968), p. 128.
6. Sita Ram, *From Sepoy to Subedar*, ed. James Lunt (Delhi: Vikas Publications, 1970) (first published in England, 1873), p. 75.
7. James Alfred Norris, *The First Afghan War, 1838–1842* (Cambridge: Cambridge University Press, 1967), p. 30.
8. Metcalfe had married one of Ranjit Singh's relatives whom he had met at the Lahore court during his 1808 mission to the Punjab, and despite the hard bargaining that took place before agreement was reached, the two men personally respected each other and remained good friends thereafter.
9. Norris, *The First Afghan War*, p. 45.
10. Alexander Burnes, *Travels into Bokhara and a Voyage on the Indus*, Vol. III (Karachi: Oxford University Press, 1973) (first published by John Murray, London, 1834), pp. 4, 5.

Chapter 2

1. Khushwant Singh, *Ranjit Singh* (London: George Allen & Unwin, 1962), p. 40.
2. G. Carmichael Smyth, ed., *A History of the Reigning Family of Lahore* (Calcutta: W. Thacker & Co., 1847), pp. xvii. Much of the material in this rare book was obtained by Smyth from the notes of an American soldier of

fortune, Alexander Gardner, who served Ranjit Singh and was close to the Sikh court in Lahore, but also secretly worked for East India Company intelligence in the Punjab.

3. Ibid.
4. Victor Jacquemont and A. Soltykoff, *The Punjab a Hundred Years Ago,* Monograph #18, Language Department, Punjab Government Record Office (Punjab: 1971), p. 44.
5. Burnes, *Travels into Bokhara,* Vol. III, p. 162.

Chapter 3

1. Burnes, *Travels into Bokhara,* Vol. III, p. 184.
2. John William Kaye, *History of the War in Afghanistan,* Vol. I (London: Richard Bentley, 1851), pp. 96, 97; Khushwant Singh, *Ranjit Singh,* pp. 108, 109; Lieutenant Colonel William H. Sleeman, *Rambles and Recollections of an Indian Officer,* Vol. I (London: Hatchard, 1884), pp. 475, 476.
3. Khushwant Singh, *Ranjit Singh,* p. 111.
4. Burnes, *Travels into Bokhara,* Vol. III, p. 185.
5. *United States Gazette,* Philadelphia, January 20, 1842, p. 1.
6. C. Grey, *European Adventurers of Northern India,* ed. Herbert L. O. Garrett (Lahore: Falcon Books, 1982), p. 254.
7. Ibid.
8. Burnes, *Travels into Bokhara,* Vol. III, p. 185.
9. Norris, *The First Afghan War,* p. 35.

Chapter 4

1. Mohan Lal, *Travels in the Panjab, Afghanistan and Turkistan to Balk, Bokhara and Herat and a Visit to Great Britain and Germany* (Patiala: Language Department Punjab, 1971) (first published in 1846), pp. 11, 12.
2. Burnes, *Travels into Bokhara,* Vol. I, p. 31.
3. Ibid.
4. Ibid., p. 33.
5. Mohan Lal, *Life of the Amir Dost Mohammed Khan of Kabul,* Vol. I (Karachi: Oxford University Press, 1978) (first published by Longman, Brown, Green and Longmans, 1846), p. xi.

Chapter 5

1. Burnes, *Travels into Bokhara,* Vol. I, p. 91.
2. Ibid., p. 94.
3. Kaye, *Lives of Indian Officers,* Vol. II, p. 29.
4. Mohan Lal, *Travels in the Panjab, Afghanistan and Turkistan,* p. 70.
5. Ibid., p. 77.

6. Ibid.
7. Josiah Harlan, *A Memoir of India and Avghanistan* (Philadelphia: J. Dobson, 1842), pp. 126, 134.
8. Josiah Harlan, *Central Asia, Personal Narrative of General Josiah Harlan,* ed. Frank E. Ross (London: Luzac & Co., 1939), p. 14.
9. Mohan Lal, *Life of the Amir Dost Mohammed,* Vol. I, p. 108.
10. Harlan, *Central Asia,* pp. 14, 15.
11. Ibid. p. 14.
12. Burnes, *Travels into Bokhara,* Vol. I, p. 165.
13. Norris, *The First Afghan War,* p. 58.
14. Mohan Lal, *Travels in the Panjab, Afghanistan and Turkistan,* p. 77.

Chapter 6

1. Mohan Lal, *Travels in the Panjab, Afghanistan and Turkistan,* pp. 82, 83.
2. Considering the time Moorcroft spent away from his regular job as superintendent of the Stud, traveling in strategically important corners of Asia, and the fact that he not only had "official permission" but for some time continued to draw his salary while he traveled on this trip to Bokhara, suggests that he had links with the government of Bengal intelligence service. In his correspondence with friends he said as much. In one letter he referred to his mission as "promoting the public [more] than their private interests." William Moorcroft and George Trebeck, *Travels in Hindustan,* ed. Horace H. Wilson (New Delhi: Sagar Publications, 1971) (first published in 1837), Vol. I, p. xxxii. In another letter he specified that if he died, his notes should be given to Captain Murray of the Bengal Intelligence Department—which, in fact, they were.
3. The U.S. Army contemporaneously used the same technique to explore the West; intrepid officers who volunteered were given "fishing and hunting" leave to do so. If they got into trouble, as Zebulon Pike, explorer of what is now called Pikes Peak in Colorado, did when he was captured by the Spanish and jailed as a spy, the War Department simply disavowed them.
4. Moorcroft meant well. He saw Ladakh as a potentially valuable entrepôt where the Company could establish an advance market serving Central Asia. He admitted that he had sought to secure for his country "an influence over a state which, lying in the British frontier, offered a central mart for the extension of commerce to Turkestan and China, and a strong outwork against an enemy from the north . . . the autocrat of the Russians." Moorcroft, *Travels in Hindustan,* pp. 132, 136.
5. Burnes, *Travels into Bokhara,* Vol. I, pp. 273–77.
6. Ibid.

Chapter 7

1. Burnes, *Travels into Bokhara*, Vol. II, p. 93.
2. K. Waliszewsski, *Le Regne D'Alexandre I, 1818–1825* (Paris: 1925), pp. 256, 257.
3. There was no substance to his claim to be a descendant of Genghis Khan.
4. Sir Robert Ker Porter, *Travels in Georgia and Persia*, Vol. I (London: 1821), pp. 325, 326.
5. Sir John Malcolm, *The History of Persia*, Vol. II (London: John Murray, 1829), p. 454.
6. Burnes, *Travels into Bokhara*, Vol. II, p. 135.
7. John Rosselli, *The Making of a Liberal Imperialist, 1774–1839* (Berkeley: University of California Press, 1974), p. 233, Part II, Section 10, fn 27.
8. Mohan Lal, *Travels in the Panjab, Afghanistan and Turkistan*, pp. 225–227.

Chapter 8

1. Kaye, *Lives of Indian Officers*, Vol. II, p. 37.
2. Norris, *The First Afghan War*, pp. 65, 66.
3. Charles Masson's three-volume memoir chronicles his life as he wanted it to be known: *Narrative of Various Journeys in Baluchistan, Afghanistan and the Panjab* (Karachi: Oxford University Press, 1974) (first published by Richard Bentley, London, 1842).
4. "Gentlemen Rankers," from *Barrackroom Ballads*, 1892, 1893. (Parodied and set to music in Yale University's "Whiffenpoof" song.)
5. Gordon Whitteridge, *Charles Masson of Afghanistan* (Warminster, England: Aris and Phillips Ltd, 1986), p. 2. (From Bengal Secret Consultations, Volume 380, June 19, 1834, Wade to Macnaghton, April 9, 1834.)
6. Potter's life as a mercenary with Ranjit Singh's army, his service with the Sikhs in the First Sikh War against the British until taken prisoner by the British during the Battle of Aliwal, and his pathetic later years after having gone blind are described in C. Grey's *European Adventurers of Northern India* (Lahore: Falcon Books, 1982) (first published in 1893), pp. 220–24.
7. Seyyid Keramat Ali's secret role as agent in Kabul for Wade had earlier been discovered by Dost Mohammed because of the interception of one of the British agent's messages. Thanks to the intervention of of Nawab Jubbar Khan, consistently a partisan of the British cause, Keramat Ali was released from prison on the promise that he would confine his espionage activities to Persians hostile to Dost Mohammed, Sikhs and Persian movements that were menacing western Afghanistan. Enjoying the protection of Nawab Jubbar Khan, Keramat Ali ignored this restriction and delved even more deeply into Afghan politics.
8. Grey, *European Adventurers of Northern India*, ed. Herbert L. O. Garrett (from Punjab Records Book No. 139, letter no. 6), pp. 188, 189.
9. Whitteridge, *Charles Masson of Afghanistan*, p. 102.

Chapter 9

1. Kaye, *History of The War in Afghanistan*, Vol. I, p. 130.
2. H. Pearse, ed., *Memoirs of Alexander Gardner* (Edinburgh: 1898), p. 185.
3. Masson, *Narrative of Various Journeys in Baluchistan, Afghanistan and the Panjab*, Vol. III, p. 337.
4. Harlan, *Central Asia*, p. 58.
5. Kaye, *History of The War in Afghanistan*, Vol. I, p. 132.
6. *United States Gazette*, Philadelphia, August 1842, p. 1.
7. John Martin Honigberger, *Thirty-five Years in the East* (London: H. Bailliere, 1852), pp. 55, 56.
8. Grey, *European Adventurers of Northern India*, pp. 206, 207 (from Punjab Records Book No. 142, letter no. 78).
9. *United States Gazette*, Philadelphia, January 20, 1842, p. 1.

Chapter 10

1. Norris, *The First Afghan War*, p. 71, fn 53.
2. Ibid., p. 74.
3. Ibid., p. 75.
4. Kaye, *History of The War in Afghanistan*, Vol. I, p. 162.
5. Norris, *The First Afghan War*, p. 83.
6. Ibid., p. 84.
7. A. Lobanov-Rostovsky, *Russia and Asia* (Ann Arbor, Mich.: The George Wahr Publishing Company, 1965) (first published in 1933), p. 119.
8. Norris, *The First Afghan War*, p. 90.
9. Ibid., p. 92. (Letter from Dost Mohammed to Auckland dated May 31, 1836, p. 1839, Indian Papers 5.)
10. Ibid., p. 93.
11. Alexander Burnes, *Cabool* (Graz, Austria: Akademische Druck u. Verlagsanstalt, 1973) (first published London: John Murray, 1842), p. 1.

Chapter 11

1. Norris, *The First Afghan War*, p. 109.
2. A veteran of Napoleon's army in the Kingdom of Naples, Avitabile had served the shah of Persia for six years before joining Ranjit Singh's service in 1826.
3. Masson, *Narrative of Various Journeys in Baluchistan, Afghanistan and the Panjab*, Vol. III, p. 445.
4. Harlan, *A Memoir of India and Avghanistan*, pp. 138, 139.
5. Calvin to Burnes, January 21, 1838, Auckland 37692, FOS 91.

Chapter 12

1. Kaye, *History of The War in Afghanistan*, Vol. I, p. 187 fn.
2. Burnes, *Cabool*, p. 162.

3. Norris, *The First Afghan War*, p. 141.
4. Harlan, *A Memoir of India and Avghanistan,* pp. 170–72.
5. Ibid. p. 193.
6. Masson, *Narrative of Various Journeys in Baluchistan, Afghanistan and the Panjab,* Vol. III, p. 245.
7. Ibid. p. 463.
8. Harlan, *A Memoir of India and Avghanistan,* pp. 19, 20.
9. Kaye, *History of The War in Afghanistan,* pp. 194, 195.
10. Ibid. p. 194.
11. W. G. Osborne, *The Court and Camp of Runjeet Sing* (Karachi: Oxford University Press, 1973) (first published by Henry Colburn, London, 1840), p. 139.
12. Harlan, *A Memoir of India and Avghanistan,* p. 140.
13. Ibid.
14. Central Asia Collectanea, No. 4, Washington, D.C.: 1960, "Ivan Viktorovich Vitkevich, 1806–39," by Melvin M. Kessler, from *Atky Sobranie Kavkazkoiu Archeografich—Eskoiu Kommissieiu,* ed. A. P. Berzhe (Tiflis: 1888), Vol. 8, entry no. 874, pp. 944, 945.
14. Mohan Lal, *Life of the Amir Dost Mohammed Khan of Kabul,* Vol. I, p. 333.
16. Masson, *Narrative of Various Journeys in Baluchistan, Afghanistan and the Panjab,* Vol. III, p. 481.
17. Ibid.
18. Kaye's source, according to Sir Henry Rawlinson, was Russian Prince Soltikov. Rawlinson, *England and Russia in the East* (London: John Murray, 1875), p. 148 fn.
19. Kaye, *History of The War in Afghanistan,* Vol. I, p. 200 fn.
20. Count Vasili Alexseevich Perovski, *A Narrative of the Russian Military Expedition to Khiva Under General Perovskij in 1839,* St. Petersburg. Trans. by the Foreign Department of the Government of India (Calcutta: Office of Superintendent Government Printing, 1867), p. 75.
21. Kessler, *Ivan Viktorovich Vitkevich 1806–1839, A Tsarist Agent in Central Asia,* pp. 16, 17, from Pol'ferov, "Predatel" ("The Traitor"), *Istoricheski Vestnik* (St. Petersburg: 1905), Vol. 100, p. 503.
22. George Buist, *Outline of the Operations of the British Troops in Scinde and Afghanistan* (Bombay: Bombay Times, 1853), p. 23.

Chapter 13

1. Kaye, *Lives of Indian Officers,* Vol. II (from Eldred Pottinger's journal).
2. Ibid. p. 237.
3. Norris, *The First Afghan War*, p. 117.

Chapter 14

1. Masson, *Narrative of Various Journeys in Baluchistan, Afghanistan and the Panjab,* Vol. III, p. 495.
2. Kaye, *History of The War in Afghanistan,* Vol. I, p. 340.
3. Osborne, *The Court and Camp of Runjeet Singh.*
4. Norris, *The First Afghan War,* p. 209 (from correspondence from Palmerston to Hobhouse, August 25, 1838, Broughton papers 46915, FOS 105, 106).
5. Masson, *Narrative of Various Journeys in Baluchistan, Afghanistan and the Panjab,* Vol. III, p. 490.
6. Pottinger, *The Afghan Connection,* Appendix I, p. 207.
7. Norris, *The First Afghan War,* p. 244.
8. Ibid., p. 228.
9. Patrick A. Macrory, *The Fierce Pawns* (Philadelphia: J. B. Lippincott Company, 1966), p. 95.
10. Kaye, *History of The War in Afghanistan,* Vol. II, pp. 54–56.
11. James Lunt, *Bokhara Burnes* (London: Faber and Faber, 1969), p. 192.

Chapter 15

1. Unnoticed by Auckland was an event occurring shortly before the grand durbar that was destined to have important consequences for the British in the Punjab some years hence. Ranjit Singh's youngest and exceptionally beautiful wife, Jindan Kaur, gave birth to a son whom he named Dhulip Singh. This fourth acknowledged son of Ranjit Singh had, in fact, not been sired by the maharajah though duly claimed by him. Moreover, Dhulip was born under the sign of Pisces, considered inauspicious by the Sikhs. And inauspicious it turned out to be when a little more than a decade later the boy was forced to relinquish his throne and give up the Punjab to the British.
2. Emily Eden, *Up the Country* (London: Curzon Press, 1978) (first published by Oxford University Press, 1930), p. 284.
3. Ibid. p. 207.
4. Ibid. p. 209.
5. Sita Ram, *From Sepoy to Subedar,* pp. 85, 86.
6. Sita Ram Pande seems to have been persuaded to write his memoirs after serving forty-eight years in the Indian Army, from 1812 to 1860, by Lieutenant Colonel James Norgate, his commanding officer in the 12th Punjab Infantry during the Great Indian Rebellion of 1857. The memoir was first published in an Indian magazine in 1861 or 1862. The first English edition, translated by Lieutenant Colonel Norgate, was published in 1873. Most recently it was published under the title *From Sepoy to Subedar* (Delhi: Vikas Publications, 1970) and edited by British Major General James Lunt, a veteran of Indian military service himself.
7. Sita Ram, *From Sepoy to Subedar,* p. 86.

8. Ibid., p. 87.
9. Kaye, *History of The War in Afghanistan,* Vol. I, p. 387.
10. Mohan Lal, *Life of the Amir Dost Mohammed,* Vol. I, p. 466.
11. Sita Ram, *From Sepoy to Subedar,* p. 88.
12. Kaye, *History of The War in Afghanistan,* Vol. I, p. 409.
13. Mohan Lal, *Life of the Amir Dost Mohammed,* Vol. II, p. 192.
14. Sita Ram, *From Sepoy to Subedar,* p. 90.
15. Ibid.
16. Ibid., p. 99.
17. Kaye, *History of The War in Afghanistan,* Vol. I., p. 453 fn.
18. Harlan, *Central Asia,* pp. 17–19.
19. Grey, *European Adventurers of Northern India,* p. 252.

Chapter 16

1. Captain George F. Atkinson, *Curry & Rice (on forty plates) or The Ingredients of Social Life at "Our" Station in India* (London: Day and Son, 1859), pages unnumbered.
2. Ibid. Chapter entitled "Our Pack of Hounds," pages unnumbered.
3. Sita Ram, *From Sepoy to Subedar,* p. 103.
4. Atkinson, *Curry & Rice,* chapter entitled "Our Theatricals," pages unnumbered.

Chapter 17

1. Pottinger, *The Afghan Connection,* Appendix I, p. 207.
2. Sir Henry Rawlinson, *England and Russia in the East* (New York: Praeger reprint, 1970) (first published by John Murray, London, 1875), p. 155 fn (from *A Narrative of the Russian Military Expedition to Khiva Under General Perofski,* trans. J. Michell, Calcutta: Government of India, 1867).
3. Ibid., p. 150.
4. Norris, *The First Afghan War,* p. 309 (taken from Palmerston to Hobhouse, February 14, 1840, Broughton 46915, FOS 196–199).
5. Kaye, *Lives of Indian Officers,* p. 50.
6. Kaye, *History of The War in Afghanistan,* Vol. I, p. 512.
7. Masson, *Narrative of Various Journeys in Baluchistan, Afghanistan and the Panjab,* Vol. IV, p. 67.
8. Ibid., p. 110.

Chapter 18

1. Sir Henry Lawrence, destined to become one of the most accomplished British governors of the Punjab, tried to capture the atmosphere of these chaotic times in a novel called *The Adventures of an Officer in the Service of*

Runjit Singh (Karachi: Oxford University Press, 1975 edition. First published in London in 1845). But no novel could be more fanciful than the facts. In Lawrence's romance the fictional hero, named Colonel Bellasis, a mercenary in the Sikh army, was modeled in part on the American artilleryman Alexander Gardner. Gardner's own memoir (*Memoirs of Alexander Gardner*, ed. H. Pearse, London, 1898), written before he died at an advanced age in Kashmir, chronicles the strange and horrible events attendant to succession. The American claimed to have been intimately involved in what occurred. While some historians dismissed Gardner as a Baron von Münchhausen, others who knew him, including the respected Henry Lawrence, accepted his version of events as accurate. And, indeed, as a secret British agent within the turbulent Sikh court in Lahore, Gardner provided much of the information that made its way into the official British records during this period of Punjab history. (See Major G. Carmichael Smyth, ed., *A History of the Reigning Family of Lahore*, Calcutta: W. Thacker & Co.; London: Blackwood, 1847, p. xvii.)

2. Emily Eden, *Letters from India*, Vol. 2 (London: 1872), p. 207.

3. Alexander Gardner, who was sent away just before the accident occurred, felt that his absense during the accident had been purposely arranged on a pretense and thus he suspected foul play. In his memoir, he wrote: "When first struck, the Maharajah's wound seemed slight, yet when the room was opened, blood in great quantities was found around the head of the cloth on which the body lay." It also seemed significant that all but one of the men who first carried the unconscious Nao Nihal Singh to the palace and thus could bear witness that his injuries were but minor abrasions were killed or suddenly fled, never to be seen again.

4. Kaye, *History of The War in Afghanistan*, Vol. I, p. 515.

5. Smyth, ed., *A History of the Reigning Family of Lahore*, p. xvii.

6. Pearse, ed. *Memoirs of Alexander Gardner*, p. 235.

7. Ibid., p. 237.

8. Kaye, *History of The War in Afghanistan*, Vol. I, p. 526.

9. Kaye, *Lives of Indian Officers* Vol. II, p. 75.

10. Ibid., p. 81.

11. Ibid., p. 40.

12. Ibid., p. 72.

13. Ibid., p. 98.

14. Ibid., p. 101.

15. Ibid., p. 94.

16. Ibid., p. 112.

Chapter 19

1. Kaye, *Lives of Indian Officers*, Vol. II, p. 64.

2. Ibid., p. 65.

3. Ibid., p. 66.
4. Both the governor general and Macnaghten were critical of Eldred Pottinger for his constant quareling with the Herat leaders. Pottinger had reason to dislike them. "Kamran is an imbecile," he wrote, "and the Minister [Vizier] Yar Mohammed is a bold but doubtful man." Not only was the vizier continuing to flirt with the Persians and the Russians, but he was protecting a flourishing revival of slaving activities. It had also irked Pottinger that there had been an attempt on his life and, as a threat, one of his servants had had a hand chopped off. George Pottinger, *The Afghan Connection* (Edinburgh: Scottish Academic Press, 1983), p. 79.
5. Kaye, *Lives of Indian Officers,* Vol. II, p. 68.
6. Ibid., p. 85.
7. Kaye, *History of The War in Afghanistan,* Vol. I, p. 549.
8. Ibid., p. 532 fn.
9. Ibid., pp. 554, 555.
10. Norris, *The First Afghan War,* p. 341.
11. Ibid.
12. Ibid., p. 344.
13. James Morris, *Heaven's Command, An Imperial Progress* (New York: Harcourt Brace Jovanovich, 1973), p. 101.
14. Buist, *Outline of the Operations of the British Troops in Scinde and Afghanistan,* p. 296.
15. Ibid.
16. Ibid.

Chapter 20

1. Kaye, *History of The War in Afghanistan,* Vol. I, pp. 535, 536.
2. Lady Sale, *The First Afghan War,* ed. Patrick Macrory (London: Longmans, Green and Co., 1969), p. 8.
3. Ibid., p. 12.
4. Kaye, *History of The War in Afghanistan,* Vol. II, p. 8.
5. Buist, *Outline of the Operations of the British Troops in Scinde and Afghanistan,* p. xi.
6. Lunt, *Bokhara Burnes,* pp. 204, 205 (from Captain Johnson's journal).
7. Mohan Lal, *Life of the Amir Dost Mohammed Khan,* Vol. II, p. 400.
8. Lady Sale, *The First Afghan War,* p. 13.
9. Sir George Lawrence, *Forty-three Years in India* (London: 1874).
10. Kaye, *History of The War in Afghanistan,* Vol. II, p. 3 (from unpublished papers of Sir W. V. Macnaghten).

Chapter 21

1. George Bruce, *Retreat from Kabul* (London: Mayflower-Dell, 1967), p. 129.
2. Lieutenant Vincent Eyre, *Journal of an Afghanistan Prisoner*, ed. James Lunt (London: Routledge & Kegan Paul, 1976) (first published in 1843), p. 33.
3. Lady Sale, *The First Afghan War*, p. 20.
4. Ibid.
5. Eyre, *Journal of an Afghanistan Prisoner*, p. 39.
6. Bruce, *Retreat from Kabul*, p. 137.
7. Kaye, *History of The War in Afghanistan*, Vol. II, p. 40.
8. Ibid., pp. 55–58.
9. Ibid., p. 57 (from correspondence of Mohan Lal quoted in the *Calcutta Review*).
10. Perhaps typical of a well-ordered bureaucracy, it was Government of India accounting records that shed the most accurate light on this incident. Obscure references in the Punjab Records of September 15, 1843, noted that Mohan Lal had claimed to have paid one agent only half the sum promised for Mir Misjidi's murder because the victim's head had not been produced. The killer of Abdullah Khan Achakzai was likewise given only half the promised fee because he could not prove that it had been his bullet that killed the victim in the field of battle.

     To clear himself of accusations burdening him with full responsibility for these acts once they were uncovered and decried by the Indian government, Mohan Lal in September 1843 produced correspondence proving that Macnaghten and Conolly had authorized the operations—indeed ordered it. (Punjab Records, Lahore, Book 87, September 15, 1843, p. 332.)
11. Eyre, *Journal of an Afghanistan Prisoner*, p. 54.
12. Lady Sale, *The First Afghan War*, p. 37
13. Eyre, *Journal of an Afghanistan Prisoner*, p. 55.
14. Lady Sale, *The First Afghan War*, p. 38.

Chapter 22

1. Lady Sale, *The First Afghan War*, p. 39.
2. Ibid., p. 43.
3. Eyre, *Journal of an Afghanistan Prisoner*, p. 64.
4. Ibid., p. 67.
5. Ibid., p. 88.
6. Ibid., p. 109.
7. Ibid., p. 110.
8. Lady Sale, *The First Afghan War*, p. 55.
9. Sita Ram, *From Sepoy to Subedar*, p. 111.
10. Lady Sale, *The First Afghan War*, p. 56.

Chapter 23

1. Mohan Lal, *Life of the Amir Dost Mohammed Khan of Kabul*, Vol. II, p. 419.
2. Lady Sale, *The First Afghan War*, p. 59.
3. Ibid., p. 62.
4. Ibid., p. 65.
5. Kaye, *History of The War in Afghanistan*, Vol. II, p. 119.
6. Ibid., p. 126 (from unfinished report of Macnaghten's MS records).
7. Ibid., p. 139.
8. Lady Sale, *The First Afghan War*, p. 75.
9. Bruce, *Retreat from Kabul*, pp. 159, 160.
10. Kaye, *History of The War in Afghanistan*, Vol. II, p. 143.
11. Ibid., p. 145.
12. Mohan Lal, *Life of the Amir Dost Mohammed Khan of Kabul*, Vol. II, p. 421.
13. Ibid., p. 422.
14. Kaye, *History of The War in Afghanistan*, Vol. II, p. 147.
15. Ibid., p. 152.
16. Eyre, *Journal of an Afghanistan Prisoner*, p. 165.
17. Kaye, *History of The War in Afghanistan*, Vol. II, p. 154.
18. Lady Sale, *The First Afghan War*, p. 82.

Chapter 24

1. Pottinger Papers, Public Record Office of Northern Ireland, PRO/NI D 1584, June 1, 1842.
2. Pottinger, *The Afghan Connection*, p. 157 (from Mackenzie, *Storms and Sunshine of a Soldier's Life*).
3. Ibid., p. 157.
4. Mohan Lal, *Life of the Amir Dost Mohammed Khan*, p. 429.
5. Sita Ram, *From Sepoy to Subedar*, p. 113.
6. Kaye, *History of The War in Afghanistan*, Vol. II, pp. 185, 186.
7. Lady Sale, *The First Afghan War*, pp. 91–93.
8. Ibid., p. 98.
9. Eyre, *Journal of an Afghanistan Prisoner*, pp. 201, 202.

Chapter 25

1. Eyre, *Journal of an Afghanistan Prisoner*, p. 2.
2. Ibid., p. 207.
3. Lady Sale, *The First Afghan War*, p. 106.
4. Eyre, *Journal of an Afghanistan Prisoner*, p. 217.
5. Kaye, *History of The War in Afghanistan*, Vol. II, p. 241 fn (from Captain Johnson's journal).
6. Ibid., pp. 242, 243 fn (from Captain Johnson's journal).

7. Sita Ram, *From Sepoy to Subedar*, p. 115.
8. Lady Sale, *The First Afghan War*, Appendix 1, p. 167.
9. According to an article in the *Victorian Military Society Newsletter* (England) No. 17 of May 1989, based on a letter to the editor of the London *Sunday Telegraph* of February 27, 1989, submitted by Pamela Magrath, Miss Magrath's great-grandfather, Captain Doctor Beauchamp Magrath, also survived the retreat from Kabul to reach India.

In Dr. Brydon's own account of his escape he mentions Dr. Magrath as among eight officers discovered by him in Tezeen to have been killed or missing. (Lady Sale, *The First Afghan War*, Appendix 1, p. 163.) In Lady Sale's journal entry of April 21, she describes Dr. Magrath as one of the prisoners held with her by Akbar Khan. (Lady Sale, *The First Afghan War*, p. 141.) Vincent Eyre also recorded being with him on that date. And, in another trace, Dr. Magrath was described by one of the prisoners as having been taken captive by tribesmen, then handed over to Akbar Khan on January 13 to be held prisoner with the group of British in his custody then housed in a fort near Jagdalak. (Pottinger, *The Afghan Connection*, p. 171.) It would thus appear that Dr. Magrath survived and was taken prisoner with the group ultimately rescued by the British Army of Retribution. Dr. Brydon's luck was to have been the only one of those who took part in the retreat from Kabul to have reached Jalalabad without having been killed or taken prisoner. (Copies of some of Dr. Magrath's letters as provided by Miss Pamela Magrath are among the archives collected by the late Afghan scholar, Dr. Louis Dupree, which are now held at Duke University.)

Chapter 26

1. Kaye, *History of The War in Afghanistan*, Vol. II, pp. 262, 263.
2. Ibid., p. 267.
3. Marian Fowler, *Below the Peacock Fan* (New York: Viking, 1987), p. 83 (from Miss Eden's "Letters From India," p. 300).
4. Kaye, *History of The War in Afghanistan*, Vol. II, p. 275.
5. Ibid., p. 280 fn.
6. Fowler, *Below the Peacock Fan*, p. 84 (from Miss Eden's "Letters from India," pp. 292, 293).
7. Pottinger, *The Afghan Connection*, p. 174.
8. Lady Sale, *The First Afghan War*, p. 128.
9. Eyre, *Journal of an Afghanistan Prisoner*, p. 244.
10. Mohan Lal, *Life of the Amir Dost Mohammed Khan*, Vol. II, p. 437.
11. *Cassel's Illustrated History of India*, Vol. II (London: Cassell, Petter and Galpin, 1882), p. 124.
12. Kaye, *History of The War in Afghanistan*, Vol. II, pp. 465, 466.
13. Ibid., pp. 465, 468.

Chapter 27

1. Lady Sale, *The First Afghan War*, pp. 141, 142.
2. Ibid., p. 482.
3. Eyre, *Journal of an Afghanistan Prisoner*, p. 287.
4. Mohan Lal, *Life of the Amir Dost Mohammed Khan*, Vol. II, p. xxiv.
5. Kaye, *Lives of Indian Officers*, p. 117.
6. Ibid.
7. Ibid., p. 137.
8. Ibid.
9. Kaye, *History of The War in Afghanistan*, Vol. II, p. 527.
10. Mohan Lal, *Life of the Amir Dost Mohammed Khan*, Vol. II, pp. 455, 456.
11. Ibid., p. 460.
12. Ibid., p. 465.
13. Ibid.
14. R. Bosworth Smith, *Life of Lord Lawrence*, Vol. I (London: Smith Elder and Co., 1883), p. 165.
15. Mohan Lal, *Travels in the Panjab, Afghanistan and Turkistan*, p. 473.
16. Kaye, *History of The War in Afghanistan*, Vol. II, p. 618.
17. Lady Sale, *The First Afghan War*, p. 156.
18. Ibid., p. 157.
19. Grant, *Cassell's Illustrated History of India*, Vol. II.

Epilogue

1. *Calcutta Review*, Vol. XI, No. XXI (1849), pp. 220–230.
2. Mohan Lal, *Travels in the Panjab, Afghanistan and Turkistan*, p. 496.
3. Ibid., p. 514.
4. Grant, *Cassell's Illustrated History of India*, Vol. II, p. 141.
5. Brief obituaries of Harlan appeared in *The Press* of Philadelphia on November 4, 1871, and *The Philadelphia Sunday Dispatch* of November 12, although they could not convey the real drama that had marked the life of this curious American freebooter who had made his own way in an untamed Afghanistan.

A last glimpse of Harlan's curious career after Afghanistan reveals a restless man who continued to dabble in various enterprises. Clinging to his Afghan rank of general, Harlan tried to settle down near Cochranville in Chester County, Pennsylvania, where he built a manorial estate befitting a nabob and married a local lady named Elizabeth Baker. In 1856 Harlan became involved as a consultant in an ill-starred project to import camels as beasts of burden in the United States' arid southwest. Then, when the Civil War broke out, Harlan raised a regiment called Harlan's Light Cavalry that saw action with the Union's Army of the Potomac. But the aging general's thoughts frequently returned to Afghanistan. Convinced that he would be hospitably received by his old friend Dost Mohammed, he made an official proposal to

Congress that he head an expedition to Afghanistan to collect native fruits suitable for cultivation in the United States. He found no takers for this exotic scheme, so after the Civil War he moved to California, where in his declining years he once again turned to practicing medicine. The old soldier died in October 1871, leaving a widow and a daughter named Sarah Victoria.

6. Norris, *The First Afghan War*, pp. 396–98 (from Ellenborough Papers, Duke of Wellington to Lord Ellenborough, March 31, 1842).

7. Sita Ram, *From Sepoy to Subedar*, p. 138.

BIBLIOGRAPHY

The following comprehensive bibliographies proved useful in doing research for this book:

Donald N. Wilber. *Annotated Bibliography of Afghanistan.* New Haven: Human Relations Area File, 1956.

Leslie Hall. *A Brief Guide for the Study of Afghanistan in the India Office Records.* London: India Office Library and Records, 1981. Appendix I is a "Summary List of Principal India Office Records regarding Afghanistan"; Appendix II lists "Archival Materials in Other Repositories."

Noel Mathews and M. Doreen Wainwright, compilers; J. D. Pearson, ed. *A Guide to Manuscripts in the British Isles Relating to the Middle East and North Africa.* Oxford: Oxford University Press, 1980.

Aitchison, C. U., ed. *A Collection of Treaties, Engagements and Sanads Relating to India and Neighboring Countries.* Calcutta: Superintendent Government Printing, 1909.

Alexander, Michael, and Sushila Anand. *Queen Victoria's Maharajah, Dhuleep Singh, 1838–1898.* New York: Taplinger Publishing Co., 1980.

Atkinson, James. *The Expedition into Afghanistan.* London: W. H. Allen & Co., 1842.

Barthorp, Michael. *The Northwest Frontier, British India and Afghanistan, 1839–1947.* Poole, England: New Orchards Editions, 1982.

Blanch, Lesley. *The Sabres of Paradise.* New York: Viking Press, 1960.

Broadfoot, W. *The Career of Major George Broadfoot.* London: 1880.

Bruce, George. *Retreat from Kabul.* London: Mayflower-Dell, 1967.

Burnes, Alexander, *Cabool.* Graz, Austria; Facsimile Edition, Akademische Druck u. Verlagsanstalt, 1973 (first published London: John Murray, 1842).

———. *Travels into Bokhara and a Voyage on the Indus,* 3 vols. Karachi: Oxford University Press, 1973 (first published London: John Murray, 1934, under the title: *Travels into Bokhara: being the account of a journey from India to Cabul, Tartary and Persia performed under the orders of the Supreme Government of India in the years 1831, 1832 and 1833*).

Campbell, George Douglas, First Duke of Argyll. *The Afghan Question from 1841 to 1878*. London: Strahan & Co., Ltd., 1879.

Caroe, Olaf. *Soviet Empire*. London: Macmillan, 1953.

———. *The Pathans*. London: Macmillan, 1932.

Conolly, Lieutenant Arthur. *Journey to the North of India Overland from England Through Russia, Persia and Afghanistan*. London: 1834.

Correspondence Relating to Persia and Afghanistan (British Foreign Office correspondence). London: J. Harrison & Son, 1839.

Davis, H.W.C., British Academy. *The Great Game in Asia (1800–1844)*. Humphrey Milford, London: Oxford University Press, 1927.

Disalkar, D. "Some Letters About the First Afghan War." *Journal of Indian History*, Vol. XII (II) (1933), pp. 251–86, Vol. XIII (III) (1933), pp. 405–22.

Dodwell, H. H. *The Cambridge History of India*. Delhi: S. Chand & Co., 1968.

Dunbar, Janet. *Golden Interlude, the Edens in India, 1836–1842*. Gloucester, England: Alan Sutton, 1955.

Durand, Sir Henry Marion. *The First Afghan War and Its Causes*. London: Longmans, Green & Co., 1879.

Dupree, Louis. *Afghanistan*. Princeton: Princeton University Press, 1973.

Eden, Emily. *Up the Country, Letters from India*. London: Curzon Press, 1978 (first published 1930).

Edwardes, Michael. *A History of India*. London: Thames & Hudson, 1961.

Elphinstone, Mountstuart. *An Account of the Kingdom of Caubul*, 2 vols. London: Oxford University Press, 1972 edition.

Eyre, Vincent. *Journal of an Afghanistan Prisoner*. London: Routlege & Kegan Paul, 1976 (first published under the title *The Military Operations at Kabul which ended in the retreat and destruction of the British Army, January 1842*. London: 1843).

Forster, George. *A Journey from Bengal to England, Kashmire, Afghanistan and Persia, and into Russia by the Caspian Sea*, 2 vols. London: 1808.

Fowler, Marian. *Below the Peacock Fan*. New York: Viking Penguin Books, 1987.

Frazer, James Baillie. *Military Memoirs of Lieutenant Colonel James Skinner*, 2 vols. London: 1851.

Frazer-Tytler. *Afghanistan*. London: Oxford, 2nd. ed., 1953.

Fredericks, Pierce G. *The Sepoy and the Cossack*. London: W. H. Allen, 1971.

Grant, James. *Cassell's Illustrated History of India*, 2 vols., London: Cassell, Peter and Galpin, undated, circa 1880.

Grey, C., *European Adventurers of Northern India—1785–1849*, ed. H.L.O. Garrett. Lahore: Falcon Books, 1982 (first published 1893).

Griffiths, John C. *Afghanistan, Key to a Continent*. Boulder: Westview Press.

Habberton, William. "Anglo-Russian Relations Concerning Afghanistan, 1837–1901," *Illinois Studies in the Social Studies*, Vol. 21, No. 4. Urbana: University of Illinois Press, 1933.

Hall, Leslie. *A Brief Guide to Sources for the Study of Afghanistan in the India Office Records*. London: India Office Library and Records, 1981.

Harlan, Josiah. *A Memoir of India and Avghanistan*. Philadelphia: J. Dobson, 1842.

――――. *Central Asia, Personal Narrative of General Josiah Harlan, 1823–1841*, ed. Frank E. Ross. London: Luzac & Co., 1939.

Haughten, J. *Char-ee-Kar and Service There with the 4th Gurkha Regiment in 1841: An Episode of the 1st Afghan War*. London: 1879.

Havelock, Henry. *Narrative of the War in Afghanistan, 1838–1839*, 2 vols. London: Henry Colburn, 1840.

Holdich, Sir Thomas. *The Gates of India*. London: Macmillan & Co., 1910.

Honigberger, John Martin. *Thirty-five Years in the East*, 2 vols. London: H. Bailliere, 1852.

Hough, William. *A History of British Military Exploits and Political Events in India, Afghanistan, and China*. London: Wm. H. Allen, 1853.

――――. *Narrative of the March and Operations of the Army of the Indus in Afghanistan in the Years 1838, 1839, Comprising Also the History of the Doorani Empire from Its Foundations to the Present*. London: W. H. Allen, 1841.

Howarth, Stephen, *The Koh-i-noor Diamond: The History and the Legend*. London: Quartet Books, 1980.

Ingram, Edward. *Commitment to Empire: Prophecies of the Great Game in Asia*. Oxford: Clarendon Press, 1979.

――――. *In Defence of British India, Great Britain in the Middle East, 1775–1842*. London: Frank Cass, 1984.

――――. *The Beginning of the Great Game in Asia*. Oxford: Clarendon Press, 1979.

Jacquemont, Victor, and A. Soltykoff. *The Punjab a Hundred Years Ago*, ed. H.L.O. Garrett. Lahore: Punjab Record Office, Monograph Number 18, Language Department, Punjab, 1971.

Kaye, John William. *History of The War in Afghanistan*, 2 vols. London: Richard Bentley, 1851.

――――. *Lives of Indian Officers*. London: J. J. Keliher, 1904.

――――. *Selections from the Papers of Lord Metcalfe*. London: Smith, Elder & Co., 1855.

――――. *The Life and Correspondence of Charles, Lord Metcalfe*, 2 vols. London: Richard Bentley, 1854.

Kessler, Melvin M. *Ivan Viktorovich Vitkevich, 1806–1839, A Tsarist Agent in Central Asia*. Washington, D.C.; Central Asian Collectanea #4, 1960.

Klass, Rosanne, ed. *Afghanistan, The Great Game Revisited*. New York: Freedom House, 1987.

Lal, Mohan. *Journal of a tour through the Panjab, Afghanistan, and part of Persia in company with Lieutenant Burnes and Dr. Gerard*. Calcutta: 1834.

――――. *Life of the Amir Dost Mohammed, Khan of Kabul*, 2 vols. Karachi: Oxford University Press, 1978 (first published 1846).

————. *Travels in the Panjab, Afghanistan and Turkestan to Balk, Bokhara and Herat*. Patiala: Language Department Punjab, 1971 (first published 1846).

Lissant, Sergeant Major. "The Retreat From Kabul." *Army Quarterly* (1928), pp. 143–50.

Lobanov-Rostovsky, Prince A. *Russia and India*. Ann Arbor, Mich.: The George Wahr Publishing Co., 1965 (first published 1951).

Lunt, Major General James. *Bokhara Burnes*. London: Faber and Faber, 1969.

Lawrence, Major H.M.L. *Adventures of an Officer in the Service of Runjeet Singh*. Karachi: Oxford University Press, 1975 (first published London: Henry Colburn, 1845).

Maclean, Fitzroy. *A Person from England*. London: Century Publishing Co., 1958.

Macrory, Patrick. *The Fierce Pawns*. Philadelphia: J. B. Lippincott, 1966.

Malcolm, Sir John. *Sketch of the Sikhs; a singular nation, who inhabit the Province of the Penjab situated between the Rivers Jumna and Indus*. London: Murray, 1812.

————. *The History of Persia*, 2 vols. London: John Murray, 1829.

Malleson, Colonel G. B. *The Decisive Battles of India, 1746–1849*. London: Reeves and Turner, 1914 edition.

Marshall, Dr. Lynn. "American Public Opinion and The First Afghan War." *Pakistan Journal of American Studies* (Islamabad: Area Study Center for Africa, North and South America, Quaid-i-Azam University), Vol. 2, No. 1 (March 1984), pp. 1–11.

Masson, Charles. *Narrative of Various Journeys in Baluchistan, Afghanistan and the Panjab*, 3 vols. Karachi: Oxford University Press, 1974.

————. The Masson Papers, unpublished. London: India Office Library, European Manuscripts, Vol. II, Part II.

M'Gregor, W. L. *The History of the Sikhs; containing the lives of the Gooroos; the history of the independent sirdars, or missuls, and the life of the great founder of the Sikh monarchy, Maharajah Runeet Singh*, 2 vols. London: James Madden, 1846.

Miller, Charles. *Khyber, British India's Northwest Frontier*. New York: Macmillan, 1977.

Moorcroft, William, and George Trebeck. *Travels in the Himalayan Provinces of Hindustan and the Punjab, in Ladakh and Kashdmir; in Peshawar, Kabul, Kunduz, and Bokhara by Mr. William Moorcroft and Mr. George Trebeck from 1819 to 1825*, ed. Horace Hayman Wilson. 2 vols. New Delhi: Sagar Publications, 1971 (first published London: 1841).

Napier, Major General W.F.P. *The Conquest of Scinde*, 2 vols. London: T. & W. Boone, 1845.

National Gazette, Philadelphia: August 25, 1841 (article regarding Josiah Harlan).

Norris, James Alfred. *The First Afghan War*. Cambridge: Cambridge University Press, 1967.

Osborne, W. G. *The Court and Camp of Runjeet Singh*. Karachi: Oxford University Press, 1973 (first published 1840).

Pearse, H., ed. *Memoirs of Alexander Gardner*. London: Blackwood, 1898.

Perovski, Vasilij Alexseevich. *A Narrative of the Russian Military Expedition to Khiva Under General Perovski, 1839*. Calcutta: Office of Superintendant of Government Printing, 1867, Foreign Department, Government of India.

Pottinger, George. *The Afghan Connection*. Edinburgh: Scottish Academic Press, 1983.

Pottinger, Lieutenant Henry. *Travels in Beloochistan and Sinde*. London: Longman, Hurst, Orme and Brown, 1816.

Ram, Subedar Sita. *From Sepoy to Subedar*, ed. James Lunt. Delhi: Vikas, 1970 (first published 1873).

Rawlinson, Sir Henry. *England and Russia in the East*. New York: Praeger reprint, 1970 (first published London, 1877).

Rochester Daily Advertiser: August 12, 1842 (article regarding Josiah Harlan).

Rodenbough, T. *Afghanistan and the Anglo-Russian Dispute*. New York: G. P. Putnam, 1885.

Roseberry, J. Royal, III. *Imperial Rule in The Punjab, 1818–1881*. Riverdale, Md.: The Riverdale Company, 1987.

Ross, Frank, ed. *Central Asia, Personal Narrative of General Josiah Harlan*. London: Luzac and Co., 1939.

Rosselli, John. *Lord William Bentinck, The Making of a Liberal Imperialist*. Berkeley: University of California Press, 1974.

Sale, Lady Florentia. *The First Afghan War*, ed. Patrick Macrory. London: Longmans, Green, 1969.

Shakespear, Captain Sir R. "From Herat to Orenbourg." *Blackwood's Magazine* (June 1842).

Shand, Alexander Innes. *General John Jacob*. London: Seely & Co., 1901.

Singh, Khushwant. *Ranjit Singh, Maharajah of The Punjab*. London: George Allen & Unwin, 1962.

———. *The Fall of the Kingdom of The Punjab*. Bombay: Orient Longman, 1962.

Singhal, D. P. *India and Afghanistan, A Study in Diplomatic Relations, 1876–1907*. Melbourne: University of Queensland Press, 1963.

Smith, Sir Harry. *The Autobiography of Lieutenant General Sir Harry Smith*, 2 vols., ed. G. C. Moore Smith. London: John Murray, 1902.

Smyth, Major G. Carmichael. *A History of the Reigning Family of Lahore*. Calcutta: W. Thacker & Co., 1847.

Spain, James. *The Pathan Borderland*. The Hague: 1963.

———. *The Way of the Pathans*. London: 1962.

Spear, Percival. *A History of India*, 2 vols. Baltimore: Penguin Books, 1965.

Suri, Sohan Lal. *Umdat-ut-Tawarikh*, 5 vols., trans. U. S. Suri. Lahore: 1889; New Delhi: S. Chand & Co.,

Sykes, Sir Percy. *A History of Afghanistan*, 2 vols. London: Macmillan, 1940.

————. *A History of Persia,* 2 vols. London: Macmillan, 1951 (first published 1915).

Thornburn, S. S. *The Punjab in Peace and War.* New Delhi: Usha Publications, 1987 (first published 1904).

Trotter, Lionel J. *The Life of John Nicholson, Soldier and Administrator.* London: John Murray, 1898.

United States Gazette, Philadelphia: January 20, 1842 (article regarding Josiah Harlan).

Vigne, Godfrey Thomas. *A Personal Narrative of a Visit to Ghuzni, Kabul and Afghanistan, and a Residence at the Court of Dost Mohammed.* London: Wittaker, 1840.

Whitteridge, Gordon. *Charles Masson of Afghanistan.* Warminster, England: Aris and Philips, Ltd., 1986.

Wilber, Donald. *Annotated Bibliography of Afghanistan.* New Haven, Conn.: Human Relations Area File, 1956.

Wolff, Joseph. *A Mission to Bokhara,* ed. Guy Wint. London: Routledge & Kegan Paul, 1969 (first published in 1845).

Woodruff, Philip. *The Men Who Ruled India,* 2 vols. (Vol. 1, *The Founders*). London: Jonathan Cape, 1953.

Wright, Denis. *The Persians Among the English.* London: I. B. Tauris & Co., 1985.

INDEX

ABOUT THE AUTHOR

JOHN H. WALLER, a graduate of the University of Michigan, served in the U.S. Foreign Service and the Office of Strategic Services in the Middle East during World War II. His interest in the Central Asian cockpit of British-Russian rivalry—the Great Game—of the nineteenth century began when he opened the first U.S. consulate in Meshed, Iran, near the Soviet border a few years after the end of the war, and traveled throughout Iran and Afghanistan, sometimes living with the nomadic tribes. He also served six years in India where he came to know the Punjab and travel through the Khyber Pass into Afghanistan.

In 1976 Mr. Waller was appointed inspector general of the Central Intelligence Agency, where he served until 1980. Since then he has devoted his time to writing and lecturing on historical subjects.